THAT 90's VIBE

Stories Behind The Songs From
The Last Great Decade Of R&B

A.J. TAVARES

All rights reserved. No part of this publication may
be reproduced, stored in a retrieval system, or transmitted,
in any form or by any means---electronic, mechanical,
Photocopying, recording, or otherwise—without prior
written permission of the author.

ISMB 979-8-9882271-0-6

Manufactured in the United States of America

First Printing 2023

to
the woman
who helped me reach my level,

she knows who she is.

Table of Contents

12
13
14
14
15
16
27
32
42
54
61
62
64
72
86
92
100
104
105

Introduction

    The Charts Explained

    Writing Credits Explained

    Key

    Sales Explained

Love Makes Things Happen: R&B Enters the 90's | 1990 - 1992

    Artist Profile: New Edition

Rumpshaker: The New Jack Era | 1986 - 1992

Can We Talk: New Kids on the Block | 1991 - 1994

    Interlude: Boys II Men vs. Jodeci

    Interlude: The Rise and Fall of Swing Mob

    Interlude: What About Tony! Toni! Tone!

Boombastic: The Dancehall Influence | 1992 - 1995

Unforgettable: They Still Got It

Where My Girls At: Females Take Over R&B | 1992 - 1996

    Interlude: Jermaine Dupri Gets So So Def

    Interlude: Janet Jackson Dominates the Charts

    Interlude: Prince of Petty—The Emancipation of Jimmy Jam and Terry Lewis

    Artist Profile: Mariah Carey

Table of Contents

112
114
128
130
140
142
150
168
176
184
193

208
216
254
256

Interlude: Mary J Blige vs. Mariah Carey

This Is How We Do It: The Hip-Hop Hybrid Era | 1994 - Present

    Artist Profile: R. Kelly

Soul Searchin': The Dawn of Neo-Soul 1996 - Present

    Artist Profile: Me'shell Ndegeocello

The One-Hit Wonders

The Remakes

I'll Be Missing You: The Tribute Songs

In Case You Missed It

Happily Ever After: The Decade Closes 1996 - 1999

    Artist Profile: The Staying Power of Keith Sweat & Gerald LeVert

Debatable

Charts & Numbers

Song Index

Artist Index

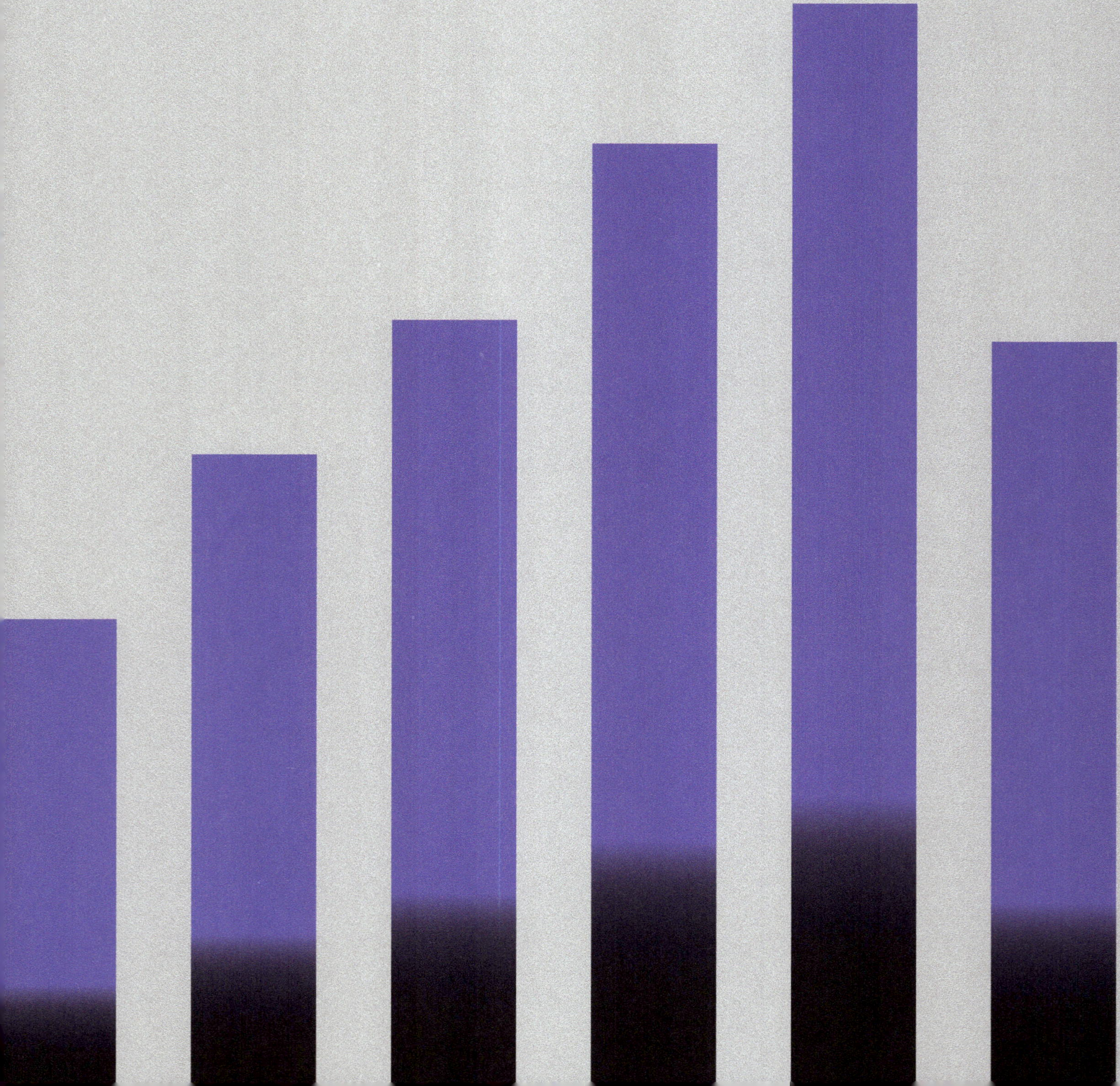

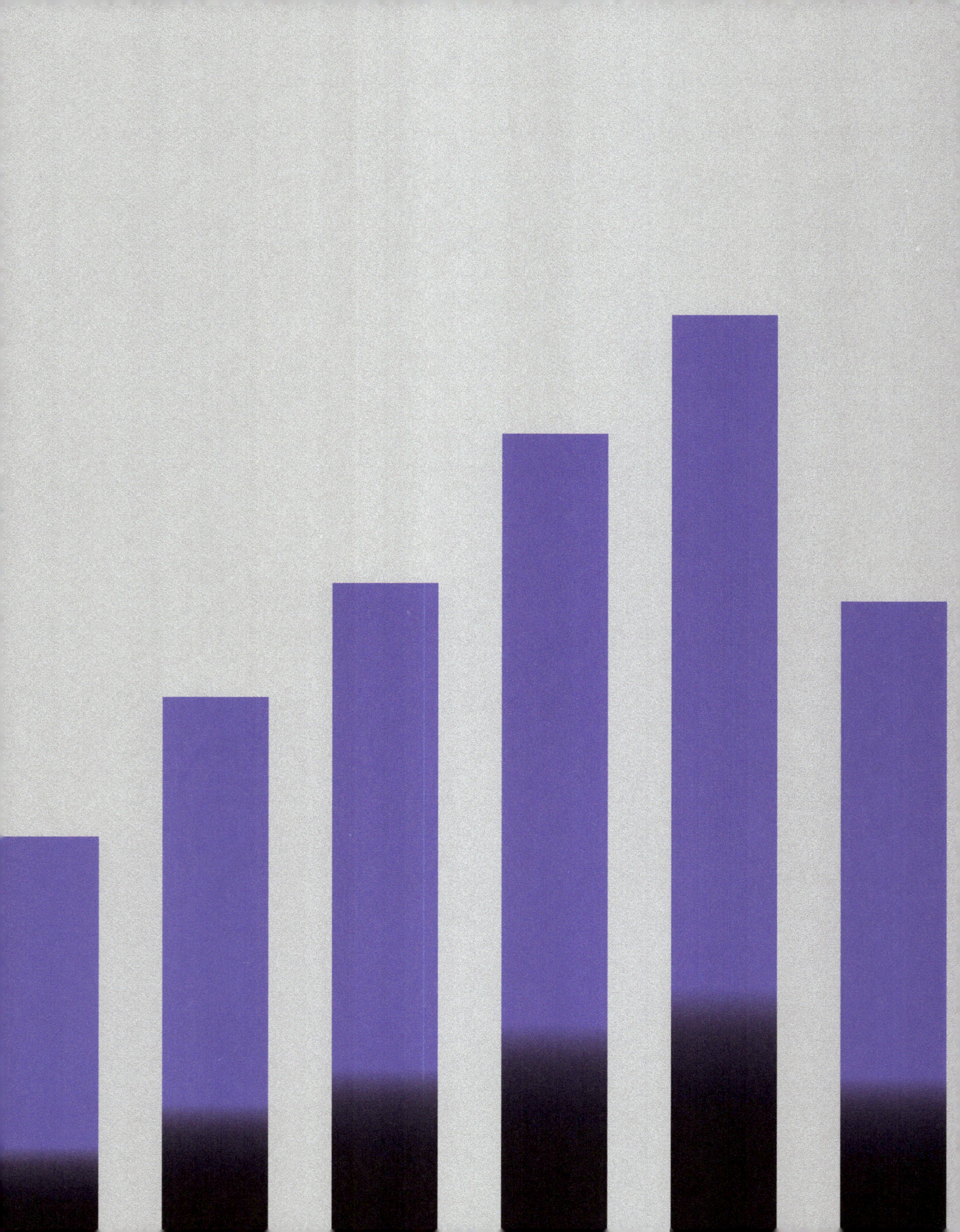

Introduction

The Charts Explained
Writing Credits Explained
Key
Sales Explained

Introduction

This book celebrates the artists, songwriters, and producers that made the 1990s the last great decade of R&B music, before record labels abandoned talent and artistry in favor of overproduction in search of crossover appeal. Here we trace R&B's evolution throughout the decade, from the new jack era to the rise of neo-soul and beyond, highlighting some of the lesser-known stories and relationships behind the songwriting, performance, and production excellence that led us to fall in love with the genre.

The Charts Explained

When it comes to U.S. chart success, *Billboard* is the standard for all genres of music. Historically, music deemed to be black music—that is, music either made by black artists or predominantly intended for black audiences—was often segregated on the *Billboard* charts. Now, this phenomenon is not unique to *Billboard*, as critics, music historians, and award-governing bodies also struggle with the question of what genre to put "black" music into. An early example of this involved the rap group Untouchable Force Organization (UTFO), the group behind hip-hop classics such as "Roxanne, Roxanne" (1984) and "Ya Cold Wanna Be With Me" (1987). UTFO's 1985 song "Fairytale Lover" was a full-on R&B ballad, without a rap verse in it, yet the song was then, and is still today, classified as a rap/hip-hop song. Perhaps the most notable recent example of this dilemma took place in 2016 when the artist Drake won Grammys for best Best Rap Song and Best Rap/Sung Collaboration for his number song "Hotline Bling," which like "Fairytale Lover" does not have a single rap verse yet was and is still classified as a rap/hip-hop song. The mis-categorization did not go unnoticed by Drake, who in response to winning the award stated, "I'm a black artist, I'm apparently a rapper, even though 'Hotline Bling' is not a rap song. . . . The only category that they can manage to fit me in is in a rap category, maybe because I've rapped in the past or because I'm black."

Drake echoed the frustrations that had been felt by many black artists for decades. As it relates to '90s R&B, the discussion is, well....still complex. During this decade the popularity of rap music skyrocketed among demographics that were traditionally R&B and/or pop fans, and by the end of the decade rap would become the best-selling genre of music represented on the charts. But somewhere in the middle, the world of '90s R&B would see rap songs top the R&B charts. To see how this happened, let's go to the beginning of the previous decade. In 1980, black music was ranked on *Billboard*'s Hot Soul Singles chart. That year saw Sugar Hill Gang's "Rapper's Delight" reach number 4 on the chart, the first rap song to do so. Despite this chart success, rap was still fairly regionalized and in the infant stages of emerging as a stand-alone genre.

By 1982, *Billboard*, in recognizing the diversity of the black music space as the popularity of rap music began to grow, renamed its Hot Soul Singles chart the Hot Black Singles chart. That year saw Grandmaster Flash & the Furious Five's classic "The Message" reach number 4 on that chart. In the eight years that the chart existed, only two rap songs would occupy the number 1 spot, LL Cool J's "I Need Love" (1987) and De La Soul's "Me Myself and I" (1989), the latter of which largely sampled Parliament-Funkadelic's number 1 R&B hit "(Not Just) Knee Deep" (1979). The chart's name and criteria would largely remain unchanged until October 1990 when *Billboard* again changed its name, this time from the Hot Black Singles chart to Hot R&B Singles. While the name of the chart changed, the standards were largely the same with both rappers and singers vying for the same number 1 spot. The 1990 *Billboard* change came one year after the Recording Academy formally recognized rap as a genre of its own by instituting the Grammy Award category for Best Rap Performance in 1989, which DJ Jazzy Jeff & the Fresh Prince won for their song "Parents Just Don't Understand." The song was also a number 10 R&B hit.

It wasn't until 1991, that technology would define the relationship between hip-hop, R&B, and pop music for the rest of the decade. SoundScan technology enabled *Billboard* to gather accurate retail music sales. The availability of this information and the increasing popularity of black music elevated hip-hop and R&B to a level that rivaled pop music on the Hot 100 charts, mainly because *Billboard* considered hip-hop and R&B to be one and the same, which is how you get rap artists and rap songs like Dr. Dre's "Nuthin' but a 'G' Thang" (1992), the Notorious B.I.G.'s "One More Chance/Stay with Me" (1995), and Bone Thugs-n-Harmony's "Crossroads" (1996) spending several weeks at number 1 on the R&B charts. We account for this phenomenon in this book and do our best to not classify rap songs as R&B songs in the discussions.

In December 2002, *Billboard* got a step closer to distinguishing the two genres and changed the Hot R&B Singles chart to the Hot R&B/Hip-Hop Singles & Tracks chart, and the R&B Albums chart became the R&B/Hip-Hop Albums chart. Lastly, you will notice that a few popular songs did not chart at all. This is because *Billboard* rules during parts of the 1990's deemed songs that were not released as commercial singles as ineligible for the charts, regardless of their popularity. This is why popular songs like The Fugees' 3× platinum Pop/R&B hit "Killing Me Softly," which dominated the airwaves in 1996 and is considered by *Rolling Stone* magazine to be one of the 500 Greatest Songs of All Time, was excluded from the charts. Songs that fall into this category are noted in the headings as "Song did not chart."

Writing Credits Explained

The issue of songwriting credit is long and complicated. Elvis Presley, "the King of Rock and Roll," who reaped millions from publishing royalties once famously remarked, "I've never written a song in my life." Peter Guralnick's biography *Last Train to Memphis: The Rise of Elvis Presley* detailed how Presley's management team arranged for him to receive a portion of the songwriting royalties for each song he released, no matter who wrote it. Here, you will notice we simply report who is listed as a credited writer on the songs and do not delve too deeply into whether they are deserving of the credit.

Due to the heavy reliance of music sampling in the 1990s, interpolations, and the borrowing of vocal elements from previous hits, you will notice that writing credits include some familiar names in surprising places. For example, Adina Howard's 1995 hit "Freak Like Me" lists William "Bootsy" Collins as a writer. While Bootsy did not actively write "Freak Like Me," he did write and record the 1976 hit "I'd Rather Be With You," which "Freak Like Me" samples, thus Collins is credited as a songwriter. Conversely, Faith Evans' 1995 hit "Soon as I Get Home," which was an extremely personal song written about Evans' relationship with her famous husband the Notorious B.I.G., was almost entirely written by Evans and co-writer Chucky Thompson. However as Evans recalled, "Diddy [Sean Combs] probably changed one or two words" and was also given writing credit, holding true to the industry saying, "Change a word, take a third." These instances are provided as examples of the complex nature of writing credits, as credit and compensation for writing each song is unique and influenced largely by the relationships and agreements between the artists and writers.

Key

One or two numerals in parenthesis following a song or album title (e.g., 2, 14) indicates the song or album's highest R&B chart position.

Four numerals in parenthesis following a song or album title (e.g., 1993) indicates the year the song or album was released.

Sales Explained

Diamond

Sales
Over 10,000,000 copies sold

Albums
Over 10,000,000 copies sold

Multiplatinum

Sales
Over 2,000,000 copies sold

Albums
Over 2,000,000 copies sold

Platinum

Sales
1,000,000 copies sold

Albums
1,000,000 copies sold

Gold

Sales
500,000 copies sold

Albums
500,000 copies sold

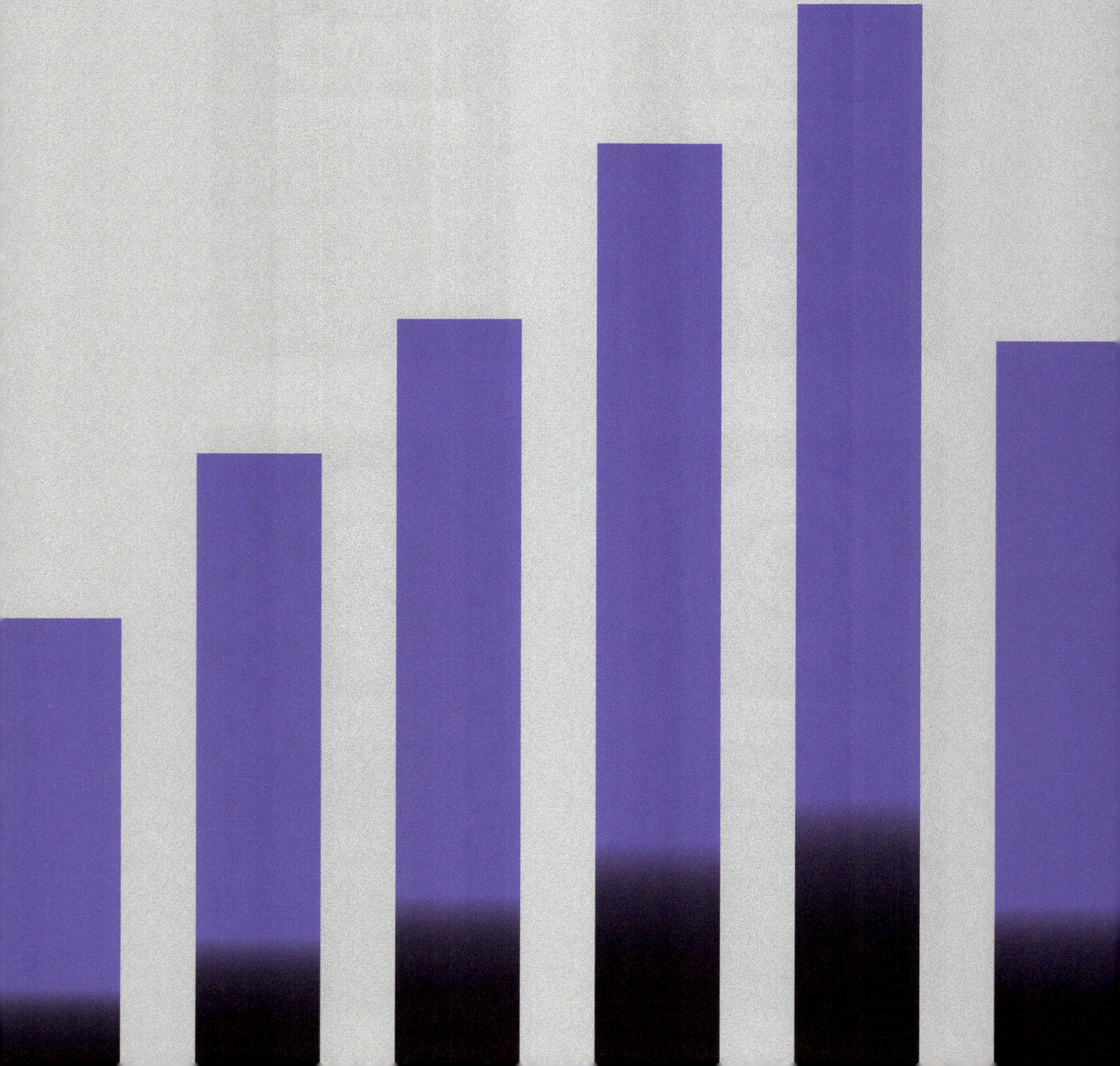

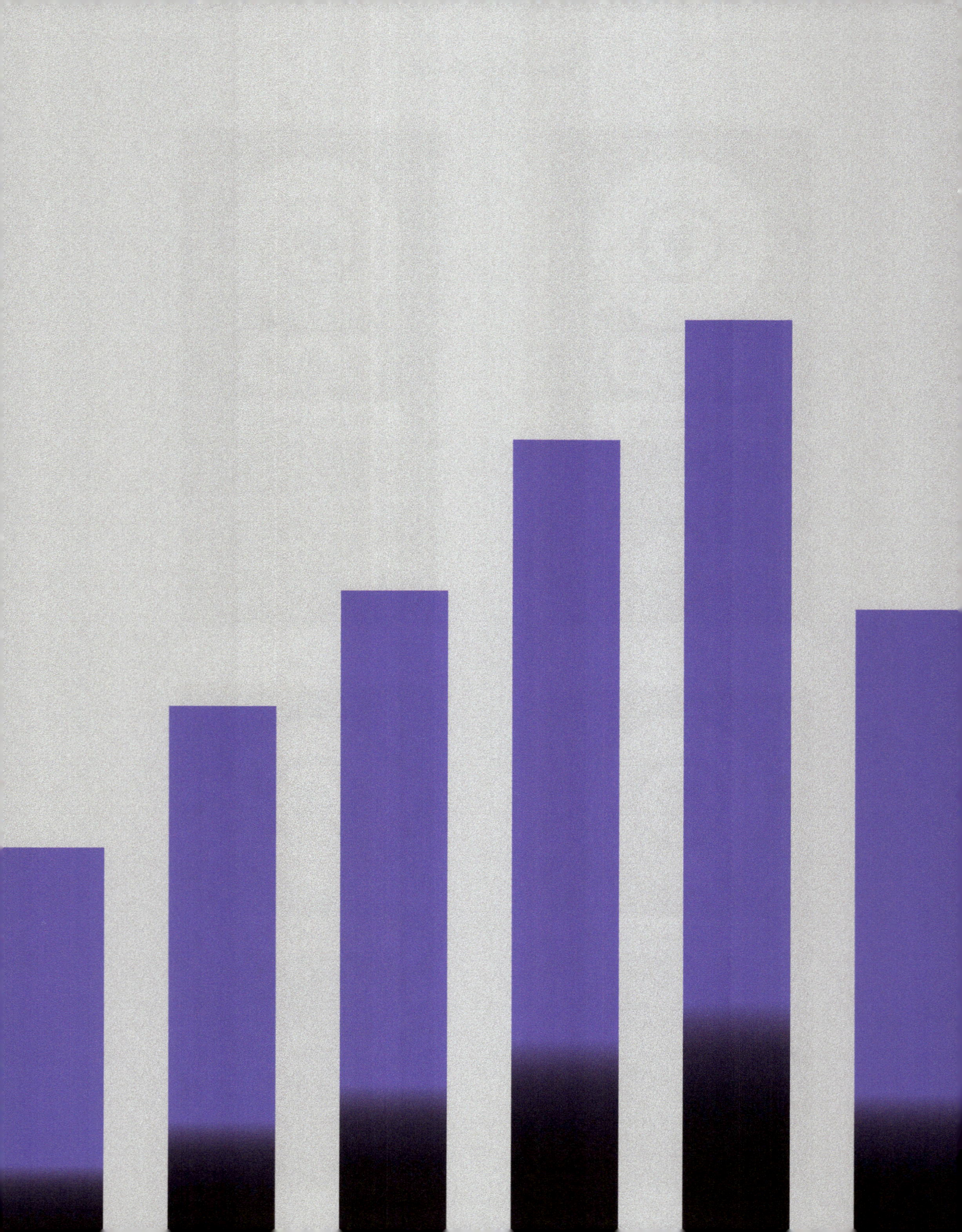

Love Makes Things Happen: R&B Enters the 90's
1990 -1992

Love Makes Things Happen
Tender Kisses
With You
Kissing You
It Ain't Over Til It's Over
Rush Rush
I Love Your Smile
Games
Artist Profile: New Edition
My, My, My
Poison
Sensitivity

Love Makes Things Happen: R&B Enters the 90's | 1990 - 1992

Early '90s R&B was on the cusp of change. The genre was balancing the old-school ballads where singing and vocal range were critical to success with the emerging new jack swing that relied heavily on hip-hop production, including the overt use of sampling, interpolations, and studio mixing to create hits. This section showcases a diverse group of songs that became top 20 R&B hits in the face of the emerging new jack revolution.

Love Makes Things Happen

Artist: Pebbles
Album: Always
Year: 1990
Writers: Kenneth "Babyface" Edmonds, Antonio "L.A." Reid
Producers: Kenneth "Babyface" Edmonds, Antonio "L.A." Reid
Highest R&B Chart Position: 1
Highest Hot 100 Chart Position: 13

Oakland native Perri Arlette Reid (born Perri Arlette McKissack) began her music career as a backup singer for the likes of artists Paula Abdul on hits like "Forever Your Girl" and the R&B group Con Funk Shun, where she also wrote for the band.

However, it was while working in a real estate office that Pebbles and her then husband bankrolled a demo tape and video for her song "Mercedes Boy." It was unheard of at the time for an unknown artist to bank on themselves that way, but it was the "Mercedes Boy" demo/video that scored Pebbles a record deal with MCA Records.
In a 1988 *The Los Angeles Times* interview, the former background singer proclaimed, "Nobody ever got anywhere by hiding in the background. I've always tried to make my presence felt. I've always gone after what I wanted."
In fact, going after what she wanted was how she secured her first hit single, "Girlfriend." After getting signed to MCA, the record company had the production team of L.A. Reid and Kenneth "Babyface" Edmonds meet with her to discuss songs for her new album. When Reid and Babyface heard her work, they asked her to try singing their song "Girlfriend," which they had written for beauty queen turned singer-actress Vanessa L. Williams. This song was to play a big part in Williams's re-branding herself after being stripped of the Miss America pageant title following *Penthouse* magazine's publishing of nude photos of her, which were distributed without her permission.
After hearing the song, Pebbles wanted it for herself. There was just one problem: Williams had already paid Babyface and Reid $12,000 for the song. Sensing it would be a hit and not wanting to be outbid, Pebbles offered $18,000 and two cars to Babyface and Reid for the chance to record it. Babyface and Reid then sold the song to Pebbles, who took the track to number 1 in 1988. A jilted Vanessa Williams never spoke to Reid again. "Girlfriend" was Pebbles second number one single from her platinum selling debut album *Pebbles*. The aforementioned "Mercedes Boy" reached number 1 in 1987.

Sparks flew between Reid and Pebbles when they were working together on "Girlfriend" and in July 1989, Pebbles, (who had already divorced her previous husband) married Reid, who was then co-president of LaFace Records. A successful artist but a businesswoman at heart, Pebbles formed the Pebbitone production company and Savvy Records in 1989, which became her vehicle to find and cultivate talent. She would go on to develop the Atlanta-based girl group TLC and turn them into diamond-selling artists.

In 1990, Pebbles released her second album, *Always*. The album included the title song, which featured singer Johnny Gill, and an intro by Pebbles' cousin and fellow R&B singer Cherrelle, whose R&B hits included 1984's "I Didn't Mean to Turn You On" (8) and 1985's "Saturday Love" (2). The first single off of the *Always* album, "Giving You the Benefit," spent three weeks at number 1 on the R&B charts. The track "Backyard," which featured rap group Salt-N-Pepa, peaked at number 4. The song's cringe-worthy 1990 video introduced the world to T-Boz and Left Eye of TLC (Chili hadn't joined the group yet), who appeared in the background of various scenes.
Most notably, the album also included "Love Makes Things Happen," which was written by Babyface. Babyface also provided vocals to the track. The song spent two weeks at number 1 on the R&B chart and peaked at number 13 on the Hot 100 chart.

"Love Makes Things Happen" was not only one of Pebbles' biggest R&B hits, it was also her last. The remainder of the 1990s would prove challenging for her personally and professionally. In 1995 she released her third album, *Straight from My Heart*, which despite having heavy-hitting producers Sean "Puffy" Combs, Chucky Thompson, and the Organized Noize team (Rico Wade, Ray Murray, and Sleepy Brown) did not produce any hits.

Also in 1995, TLC filed for bankruptcy and accused LaFace and Pebbitone of mismanagement of funds in the court filings. In 1996, Pebbles' marriage to L.A. Reid ended. It appears the TLC issue was a "big factor in it," Pebbles told DJ Frank Ski of Washington, D.C.'s WHUR radio station. "What happened there," she said, "in my opinion, was horrific because you [referencing TLC] tore my family up with this. This tore my family up. Now my G-code kept me quiet, but it was a whole bunch of dirtiness." L.A. Reid agreed—in an interview with *New York Magazine* he described TLC as "one of the breaking points in my marriage."

Following the 1996 divorce, Pebbitone Inc. filed a $10 million lawsuit against LaFace Records and its distributor Arista Records, charging that the companies tried to entice TLC away from Pebbitone. The matter has since been settled. Things would turn around, though, in 1997 after, as Pebbles says, "the hand of God touched [her] life." That year she became a minister and gospel artist now known as Sister Perri, and she founded the Women of God Changing Lives (WOGCL) Ministries.

In 2008, Pebbles released her fourth album and debut gospel album, *Prophetic Flows Vol I & II*, which peaked at number 12 on the *Billboard* Gospel Album chart.

Tender Kisses

Artist: Tracie Spencer
Album: Make the Difference
Year: 1990
Writers: Matt Sherrod, Paul Sherrod, Tracie Spencer, Sir Spence
Producers: Matt Sherrod, Paul Sherrod
Highest R&B Chart Position: 1
Highest Hot 100 Chart Position: 42

Tracie Monique Spencer was born to sing. The Waterloo, Iowa, native started singing at age three, competed in beauty pageants at age five, and won the TV show *Star Search's* Junior Vocalist competition by age eleven, where she wowed the audience by singing renditions of songs recorded by Whitney Houston. Spencer's talents were so astounding that Capitol Records signed her to a record deal that same year, which made her the youngest female artist ever to sign with the label.

The record that followed, 1988's *Tracie Spencer*, produced three top 40 R&B hits: "Symptoms of True Love," which peaked at number 11; "Hide and Seek," which peaked at number 32; and a soulful rendition of the 1971 John Lennon hit "Imagine," which peaked at number 31. To this day, listening to Spencer's version of "Imagine" still leaves listeners in disbelief that the singer was only eleven years old when she recorded it.

It was Spencer's second album, 1990's *Make the Difference*, that, well, made the difference in her status as an R&B hit-maker. The album yielded four top 10 R&B hits and one number 1 hit. The first single, "Save Your Love," was Spencer's first to reach the top 10 on the R&B charts, at number 7. Her second single, "This House," also peaked at number 7. The single "Love Me" barely missed number 1 chart status, peaking at number 2, while the single "Tender Kisses," which Spencer co-wrote, hit number 1 on the Hot R&B/Hip-Hop chart in August 1991. Her efforts in writing the song helped her to become the youngest female artist to receive the American Society of Composers, Authors, and Publishers (ASCAP) Songwriter of the Year award (1992). While these are memorable accomplishments for someone at any age, keep in mind that Spencer was barely a teenager at the time. In comparison, most kids who were Spencer's age in 1993 remember her and "Tender Kisses" best for the time she sang it in the form of a duet with the character Eddie Winslow (Darius McCrary) on the "Tender Kisses" episode of the sitcom F*amily Matters*, which aired in February 1993.

Following the success of *Make the Difference*, fans were excited to see what this star's future would be, but we would have to wait. Spencer inexplicably walked away from recording at the height of her success. She explained why years later in a 2019 interview with *UrbanBridgez.com*, stating, "I decided to take time out to finish school in Iowa, where I became involved with sports and began to have a life that was a little more normal! I wasn't even a teenager when I started out, and having a normal kind of childhood is difficult if you're in this business. I wanted some time to experience life as a teenager."

Spencer did just that…sort of. During her hiatus she was signed to the NEXT modeling agency, where she appeared in numerous magazines. She also worked as a fashion model for the likes of designers Chanel and Tommy Hilfiger. She eventually followed up *Make the Difference* in 1999 with the release of her third album, *Tracie*. The album produced two top 40 R&B hits, "Still in My Heart" (36), and the top 10 hit, "It's All About You (Not About Me)," which peaked at number 6.

With You

Artist: Tony Terry
Album: Tony Terry
Year: 1991
Writer: Raymond Reeder
Producer: Ted Currier
Highest R&B Chart Position: 6
Highest Hot 100 Chart Position: 14

Tony Terry began his professional singing career in the 1980s as a backup singer for the R&B/pop group Sweet Sensation and the hip-hop group the Boogie Boys. He was signed to Epic/CBS Records in 1987, where he released his debut album, *Forever Yours*. The successful debut included the three top 40 R&B hit singles "She's Fly" (10), "Forever Yours" (16), and his highest charting song to date, the upbeat "Lovey Dovey" (4).

Terry's 1991 self-titled sophomore album would best his debut in the number of top 40 R&B hits with the singles "That Kind of Guy" (38), "Head Over Heels" (13), "With You" (6), and "Everlasting Love" (6). While none of these songs would chart higher than "Lovey Dovey," Terry's second single, "With You," would become his only crossover hit, reaching number 14 on the Hot 100 chart, and would compete with "Everlasting Love" (which reached 81 on the Hot 100) for status as his most enduring song.

But Terry's record label did not think "With You" was a hit and attempted to bury the song. We all would have missed out on this hit if not for divine intervention and Anita Baker. As Terry told *RightOnDigital.com* in a 2020 interview when he described fighting his label to release the song, saying "There was something that would not let me back down. In other words, when it was time to choose the next single from the album, I felt passionate about it. I wasn't interested in choosing another song. They [the label] tried to convince me that it wasn't a good idea. It was serviced to radio stations with a blank label with no information on it . . . It stood out and it started to grow. And one day I got a call from Anita. She called our office; the receptionist wasn't at her desk, so I answered the phone. It was Anita Baker and she was looking for me . . . She said, 'I was in my bed and I heard one of the most beautiful songs I had ever heard in my life.' [Baker heard the song on Nia Peeples' TV series, *The Party Machine*.] She said she thought the song was amazing and wondered why she hadn't seen a video for it? I explained to her that people didn't think the song was a hit and that there would not be a video for it. She said she was going to send me a check so that I could shoot a video. Sure enough, a certified check for $50,000 showed up at my manager's office. So we shot the video; Blair

Underwood directed it and made a cameo appearance in it. So, if people have ever seen the video, it was shot with Anita Baker's blessing." Terry added, "Years later, she was on Mo'Nique's show. I found out she was going to be there and I got tickets. She saw me and she explained to Mo'Nique why she did it. She said she was 'being obedient to the spirit.' . . . It was God; it had nothing to do with me."

"Everlasting Love," the final single from the *Tony Terry* album, would be Terry's last top 10 song.

Kissing You

Artist: Keith Washington
Album: Make Time for Love
Year: 1991
Writers: Marsha Jenkins, Rodney Shelton, Keith Washington
Producers: Terry Coffey, Jon Nettlesbey, Trey Stone, Keith Washington
Highest R&B Chart Position: 1
Highest Hot 100 Chart Position: 40

Anita Baker figures prominently in this profile as well. Songwriter and singer Keith Washington is best known for this hit, which he recorded in 1991 for his *Make Time for Love* album. However, as Washington explained to KG Smooth of Majic 102.1 in Houston, Texas, "'Kissing You' was originally written with the intent to give it to fellow Detroiter Anita Baker. Washington said "I know her from Detroit, and she used to sing in a group called Chapter 8. I always wanted to write something for her. I felt her voice could perform it." While Washington wrote the first verse, it was musician Rodney Shelton and Washington's wife, Marsha Jenkins, who wrote the rest of the song, Jenkins adding a female perspective.

However, Washington would never get the chance to get the song to Baker. He used a demo that included "Kissing You" to help him to land a record deal with producer Quincy Jones' Qwest record label. But Washington explicitly did not want "Kissing You" on his album. He said, "When people would come by and hear stuff I've written, I would skip over that song." Thankfully, while going over some tracks with Qwest executive Richard Aaron, Washington accidentally played "Kissing You." It was Aaron who simply told him, "In my opinion this is your hit, this is your song." Fortunately, Washington heeded Aaron's advice and put the song on his *Make Time for Love* album. "Kissing You" ended up being a smash hit, peaking at number 1 in May of 1991. The song was also used as background music for the ABC television soap opera *General Hospital*, and "Kissing You" also landed Washington on an episode of the popular TV show *Martin* in 1993 where he played himself. The show was set in Detroit. "Kissing You" was also nominated for a Grammy Award for Best R&B Vocal Performance Male and won a 1992 Soul Train Music Award for Best R&B/Soul Single—Male.

Although Washington would later have some chart success with hits like 1991's "Candlelight and You," a duet with singer Chanté Moore which was on the *House Party 2* movie soundtrack and not released as a commercial single, and 1998's "Bring It On" (22), none of his follow-up songs would reach the heights of "Kissing You."

As for Anita Baker, Washington stated, "She was not even aware I was writing or knew I was writing something for her . . . The first time she heard the song was on the radio! She loved the song."

It Ain't Over 'Til It's Over

Artist: Lenny Kravitz
Album: Mama Said
Year: 1991
Writer: Lenny Kravitz
Producer: Lenny Kravitz
Highest R&B Chart Position: 10
Highest Hot 100 Chart Position: 2

In 1991, most people were more familiar with the women in Lenny Kravitz' life than they were with him. Although he was a successful underground writer-musician, he had largely evaded the bright lights of the mainstream consciousness, unlike his actress wife, Lisa Bonet, who was a character on the immensely popular *The Cosby Show*, and his actress mother, Roxie Roker, who played Helen Willis on the sitcom *The Jeffersons*.

However, "It Ain't Over 'Til It's Over" would change that and would become Kravitz's first big hit, although it would come to him in a dark time in his life. As his marriage to Bonet was coming to an end, Kravitz wrote the song about the demise of their relationship. He described his thinking then as "not just a depression, but a fog," stating "I didn't know which way was up."

Kravitz and Bonet first met at a New Edition concert in 1986, were married in 1987, and had one child together (Zoë Kravitz). However, by 1991 the two were experiencing marital problems. Kravitz told *Rolling Stone* in 2018, "I wrote that to my ex-wife. We were going through our break-off, which led to a divorce. We had our child and a great life together. We were sort of mirror images of each other; she was the female version of me, and I was the male version of her and we blended together. So, it was a very difficult time. . . . I remember being in a hotel room in L.A. and I had a Fender Rhodes [keyboard] that I'd brought up to the room. I sat in the dark, 'cause it was a very dark time for me, and played with the chords. All of a sudden I came up with the chord structure and the song came out. It was my belief that it ain't over 'til it's over. There's always a chance we can pull this together and make this happen. It didn't go that way, but that was the song."

Enjoying his non-A-list status and sensing this song would be a hit, Kravitz did not want to include "It Ain't Over 'Til It's Over" on his debut mainstream album. He was content being an underground artist. He told *The Guardian*, "I'm not putting that song on 'cos it's a hit. I wanted to stay underground and give it to Smokey Robinson." Kravitz's label, Virgin Records, disagreed and urged him to keep the song for himself. His soul was in this one—not only did he write the song from a deeply personal place, but he produced it himself, sung it, and played all of the instruments on the track except the strings and horns. The horns were performed by the Phenix Horns from Earth, Wind & Fire. This was Kravitz's biggest hit at the time, and it did ruin his underground status and all the privacy that came with it. Kravitz found out just how big the song was when he walked around the streets of New York City and heard it playing out of cars. Once the video started its rotation, he had to quit taking the subway because people started to recognize him. As he put it, "It f**ked up my commute." Seems like a small price to pay for a top 10 crossover hit.

Rush Rush

Artist: Paula Abdul
Album: Spellbound
Year: 1991
Writer: Peter Lord
Producers: Peter Lord, Vernon Jeffrey Smith
Highest R&B Chart Position: 20
Highest Hot 100 Chart Position: 1

This song was a number 20 R&B, number 1 pop hit. However, the lyrics and the composition are deliberately rooted in R&B. It turns out that the song was inspired by R&B mega-hitmaker Kenneth "Babyface" Edmonds and his writing style. "Rush Rush" writer, Peter Lord of the group The Family Stand, told *Songfacts.com* how the song came out of a conversation with his band-mate Sandra St. Victor, saying, "Babyface was one of the top songwriters-producers at that time, and I told her I could write one of his type of hit ballads in my sleep—no disrespect." He added: "I knew what his thing was. It's a pocket to a song. Every songwriter has his pocket, so when you figure out what his pocket is the rest is easy".

See if you agree: Does this sound like a Babyface-penned tune? The opening lines go:

You're the whisper of a summer breeze /
You're the kiss that puts my soul at ease /
What I'm saying is I'm into you /
Here's my story and the story goes . . .

The song also contains some suggestive language that is pervasive in past and present R&B hits, including these lines, which conjure thoughts of Minnie Ripperton's 1977 hit "Inside My Love."

I don't know just how or why /
But no one else has touched me / So deep, so deep, so deep inside /
Rush, rush / I can feel it, I can feel you all through me /
Rush, rush / Ooh, what you do to me.

As for the artist herself, Abdul was discovered by the Jacksons at a Los Angeles Lakers basketball game when she was a cheerleader-choreographer for the team. From there she became a choreographer for music videos, most notably Janet Jackson's "Nasty" (1). In 1987, Abdul used her savings to make a singing demo. Soon thereafter, she was signed to the newly formed Virgin Records America by Jeff Ayeroff, who had worked in marketing at A&M Records with Janet Jackson. Ayeroff recalled signing Abdul to a recording contract, stating, "Here's someone with a personality and she's gorgeous, and she can dance. If she can sing, she could be a star. So she went into the studio and cut a demo record and she could sing."

Her debut studio album, *Forever Your Girl* (1988), which consisted largely of up-tempo tracks, became one of the most successful debut albums of all time, selling 7 million copies in the U.S. and setting a record for the most number 1 singles from a debut album on the *Billboard* Hot 100 chart with four: "Straight Up," "Forever Your Girl," "Cold Hearted," and "Opposites Attract."

On her second album, *Spellbound,* Abdul was looking to make an artistic statement and she didn't work with any of the songwriters and producers who'd been her collaborators on *Forever Your Girl*.

"Rush Rush" was released in April 1991 as the first single from *Spellbound*. This was Abdul's first ballad, and it still stands as her biggest hit. Powered by a memorable video starring a young Keanu Reeves (who would later go on to play Neo in *The Matrix* movie franchise and John Wick in the *John Wick* movie franchise) as her love interest, "Rush Rush" not only made the R&B top 20, but it also topped both the Hot 100 and the Adult Contemporary charts.

I Love Your Smile

Artist: Shanice
Album: Inner Child
Year: 1991
Writers: Jarvis Baker, Sylvester Jackson, Shanice, Narada Michael Walden
Producer: Narada Michael Walden
Notable Sample: Arabesque No. 1, Claude Debussy (1926)
Highest R&B Chart Position: 1
Highest Hot 100 Chart Position: 2

By eleven years old, Shanice Wilson was already well on her way to stardom. She was a cast member on the TV show *Kids Incorporated*, and as with Tracie Spencer, she had won *Star Search* in the Junior Vocalist category, which led to her first record deal. By fourteen, Shanice had already released her first album, *Discovery*, which produced two top 10 R&B hits, 1987's "(Baby Tell Me) Can You Dance" and "No 1/2 Steppin'." Both peaked at number 6.

Despite the success of her first album, Wilson left her record label and signed with Motown for her next project. At Motown she was paired with über writer-producer-composer Narada Michael Walden, who had produced hits for Whitney Houston ("So Emotional," 1987) and Mariah Carey ("Vision of Love," 1990). Shanice and Walden were major creative forces behind the singer's second album, *Inner Child*, each writing or co-writing eight of the twelve tracks on the album, including "I Love Your Smile." The song would peak at number 1 in December 1991 and hold that spot for 4 weeks on its way to platinum sales.

But those platinum sales did not translate into riches for Shanice. In the years following the release of *Inner Child*, she was very vocal about her displeasure with how Motown profited more from her work than she did. However, as reported by *Medium.com* in 2016, "Though she may have been underpaid when 'I Love Your Smile' first came out, there is a silver lining to this story. Her songwriting credits continue to bring in revenue 25 years after the release of *Inner Child*." Shanice told the website, "I wrote many of my songs and that is where most of my money came from." She added, "Everyone got paid before me, but my song writing brought me royalty checks up to this day!"

Games

Artist: Chuckii Booker
Album: Niice 'n Wiild
Year: 1992
Writers: C. J. Anthony, Chuckii Booker, Gerald LeVert
Producer: Chuckii Booker
Notable Sample: Nasty (live in Japan), Janet Jackson (1990)
Highest R&B Chart Position: 1
Highest Top 100 Chart Position: 68

Eugene Allen Booker Jr., a.k.a. Chuckii Booker, has done it all in music. He is a successful singer, producer, songwriter, multi-instrumentalist (mainly keyboard and bass), and bandleader. Booker is a music titan, having produced for everyone from Stevie Wonder to Rihanna.

He got his big break in the music business when his godfather, musician Barry White, would bring the ten-year-old Booker into the studio with him. There Booker would watch "the Maestro" work on the production side of music. Booker cites this as being a pivotal time in his life where he learned the art of making music.
White later signed Booker to his production company in 1984. By 1986, Booker was featured as a keyboardist for the band Tease and contributed to their 1986 debut album. Booker favored the production side of music and never wanted to be an artist. He received his recording contract in spite of this when he gave his demo tape to saxophonist Gerald Albright's manager to showcase his skills as a musician, but Booker had forgotten about the songs on the other side of the tape that contained original works he recorded with his vocals. As a result of the B side of his demo, Booker was offered a recording contract with Atlantic Records.

Not turning away this blessing, Booker released his debut album, *Chuckii,* in 1989. The album was a complete showcase of his skills. Booker played most of the instruments and sang all vocals. The album included the number 1 hit single "Turned Away."

Even with his success as a vocalist, Booker doubled down on his desire to work behind the mic. In a 1990 interview with DJ and TV Personality Donnie Simpson for the Black Entertainment Television (BET) show *Video Soul*, he stated, "I wanted to concentrate on just producing and writing . . . after that I became an artist which I didn't want to do . . . I just pretty much wanted to be behind the scenes producing and writing."

Again, in spite of this desire, Booker found success as an artist when his second album, 1992's *Niice 'n Wiild,* gave him his second number 1 hit, "Games." This song was written by Booker, C. J. Anthony, and Gerald LeVert. Although writing was a team effort, the song was produced solely by Booker, and his influence is evident. From the infectious melody, which has been sampled on hits like 1995's "Playa Hata" by Luniz and 1996's "Return of the Mack" by Mark Morrison, to its genius simplicity, (the song managed to become a groove despite only having two chords). And if that voice repeating "Chuckii, Chuckii" in the background sounds familiar, it should, because you've heard it before. It's none other than Janet Jackson. The sample was lifted from the live version of her song "Nasty." Booker was the musical director, producer, and keyboardist for Jackson's Rhythm Nation World Tour as well as the opening act. As with any hit, there was a little good fortune involved with "Games." Booker was adamant that he hit his often imitated, rarely duplicated high note at the end of the song by pure luck.

Artist Profile
New Edition

The pre-teen group New Edition which consisted of members Ricky Bell, Michael Bivins, Bobby Brown, Ronnie DeVoe and Ralph Tresvant was formed in Boston Massachusetts in the late 1970's. The group was discovered by singer-producer and Manager Maurice Starr after finishing second in a talent competition. Starr then brought the group to his studio to record their debut album, *Candy Girl*. The album included the R&B hit songs "Is This the End" (8), "Popcorn Love" (25), and the title track "Candy Girl" (1). Despite the group's major success in the early 1980s, due to unfavorable contracts with Starr who was their manager, they had little money to show for it. In fact, all the group members and their families were still living in the Boston-area projects where they had started. Due to this and frequent "disagreements," Bobby Brown was voted out of the group in 1986 for what was termed "personality differences."
The sixteen-year-old Brown signed a solo deal with MCA Records, where he would release his first album, *King of the Stage*, that same year. This album yielded Brown his first solo number 1 R&B hit with the song "Girlfriend." However, the album barely went gold. With Brown no longer in the mix and lead singer Ralph Tresvant eyeing a solo project as well, the group would add singer Johnny Gill in 1987 to allegedly fill Bobby and Ralph's spot should Ralph leave for a solo career. With Gill, New Edition also signed a deal with MCA Records. They released their fifth album, *Heart Break*, in June of 1988. The Jimmy Jam, Terry Lewis, and Jellybean Johnson–produced album would sell over 2 million copies, peak at number 2 on the R&B Albums chart, and include the song "Boys to Men," which was written and produced by Jam and Lewis specifically for the album. The song described the lessons learned as the group transitioned from teenage pop stars to grown men. The album also included the classics "If It Isn't Love" (2), "N.E. Heart Break" (13), and "Can You Stand the Rain" (1).

Despite Brown being voted out of the group, the members remained on good terms, and Brown served as an opening act on New Edition's N.E. Heartbreak Tour.

In a clever maneuver by MCA to rule R&B in the summer of 1988, like *Heart Break*, Brown's sophomore album, *Don't Be Cruel*, was also released that June. The album—which was produced in part by Babyface, L.A. Reid, and Teddy Riley—launched Bobby Brown into mega stardom. It was the best-selling album in the U.S. in 1989. It was number 1 on the *Billboard* 200, included five top 10 Hot 100 hits, spent eleven weeks atop the *Billboard* R&B Albums chart, and yielded three number 1 R&B singles with "Every Little Step," "Don't Be Cruel," and "My Prerogative" and two top 5 singles, "Roni" (2) and "Rock Wit'cha" (3). The album has since been certified 7× platinum.

At the end of the N.E. Heartbreak Tour in 1989, it was obvious that despite the success of the *Heart Break* album, the lure of being a solo artist, which was instigated by Bobby Brown's mega solo success, led lead vocalists Ralph Tresvant and Johnny Gill to pursue solo deals of their own. Background vocalists Ricky Bell, Michael Bivins, and Ronnie DeVoe would also go on to form a group of their own.

As for Maurice Starr, the producer who discovered New Edition and signed them to their first management deal that left them broke, well, he made out fairly well. After parting ways with the group in 1986, he replicated the success of New Edition with another Boston-area boy group, New Kids on the Block (NKOTB). Starr intended New Kids on the Block to be a white version of New Edition. He stated, "I honestly believe that if they'd [New Edition] been white, they would have been twenty times as big." Starr may have been right: NKOTB would go on to sell over 70 million records worldwide, sell out arenas across North America, generate millions in revenue from merchandise (Starr held the rights to merchandise revenue) and have ten top 20 Hot 100 hits, including three number 1 hits between 1988 and 1990, one of which was 1989's "I'll be Loving You Forever" which was also a number 12 R&B hit.

My, My, My

Title: My, My, My
Artist: Johnny Gill
Album: Johnny Gill
Year: 1990
Writers: Kenneth "Babyface" Edmonds, Daryl Simmons
Producers: Kenneth "Babyface" Edmonds, Antonio "L.A." Reid
Highest R&B Chart Position: 1
Highest Hot 100 Chart Position: 10

The duo of Kenneth "Babyface" Edmonds and Antonio "L.A." Reid dominated '90s R&B. One of their first hits of the decade was the Babyface-penned "My, My, My," which he wrote with songwriter-producer Daryl Simmons. Babyface wrote the song for himself and originally performed it himself, but as he would later tell *Billboard* magazine, "I did an ok version of it, but Johnny [referring to Johnny Gill] turned it into his song." Indeed Gill did. Despite Gill's stellar career—which includes being a member of New Edition and having such other R&B number 1 hits as "My Body" while a member of the R&B group LSG and "Rub You the Right Way," which was the first single from his 1990 album *Johnny Gill* and immediately preceded "My, My, My" on the charts—it is the latter that became the Washington, D.C., native's signature song.

Following the breakup of New Edition in 1990, Gill inked a solo deal with Motown. With his talents being evident and a major label behind him, he had some of the industry's top names at his disposal. But being surrounded by that level of talent led to Gill doubting the song. As he told *Billboard*, "When I first heard 'My, My, My,' I played it for Jimmy [Jam] and Terry [Lewis] . . . and I said, 'I don't really know about this song.' It was a point where I was really close to the project and nothing was 'good enough' . . . When you're working with producers like Jam and Lewis and L.A. and Babyface, you're always looking for them to give you something that sounds like something they've done before. If you don't hear something that sounds like something they've done before, you think, 'Damn, I don't think they gave me their best stuff.' And what they've been so successful at doing is creating and giving everybody their own style and their own sound, and I didn't realize that was the process."

With respect to Babyface and Reid, Gill may have been right. The song is a bit of an outlier, as the title is repeated several times throughout—at least twenty-five times (not counting Gill speaking "my, my, my" in the beginning of the song or his falsetto singing the words near the song's end). Why so much praise for the love interest in the song? Babyface was looking for something to show the narrator's reaction to how "fine" his lover is. As Babyface put it, "Something that was like the ultimate compliment, but in a more ethnic way." Babyface borrowed the phrase "my, my" from a Marvin Winans track, saying, "Because when Marvin starts to sing, he sings, 'my, my, my, my, my.' I loved the way it sounded, so I started singing 'my, my' when I would sing something, and it turned into a song."

After Gill recorded the song, Edmonds added the finishing touches by enlisting his brothers Melvin and Kevon Edmonds of the group After 7 to provide background vocals (After 7 would go on to top the charts in 1990 as well with their songs "Can't Stop" (1) and "Ready or Not" (1)). Lastly, the saxophone played throughout the song was laid down by none other than Kenny G, who by 1990 had already had five top 25 R&B hits.

The result, "My, My, My," was released in April 1990 and became a number 1 R&B single, spending two weeks on top of the charts. The song also reached number 10 on the Hot 100.

Poison

Title: Poison
Artist: Bell Biv DeVoe
Album: Poison
Year: 1990
Writer: Dr. Freeze
Producers: Dr. Freeze
Notable Sample: Poison, Kool G. Rap & DJ Polo (1988)
Highest R&B Chart Position: 1
Highest Top 100 Chart Position: 3

This song set the tone for the new jack era in '90s R&B. Following the disbanding of New Edition, and with the immense success that the former group's front men, Johnny Gill and Bobby Brown, were having in their solo endeavors, each having multiple top 10 hits from their debut projects, group members Ricky Bell, Michael Bivins, and Ronnie DeVoe, who had largely sang background for the group, were in danger of being relegated to the boy band afterlife. Although still young by normal standards—Bell and DeVoe were twenty-three, Bivins was twenty-two—they were elderly in the world of boy band stardom. It was the New Edition *Heart Break* album producer Jimmy Jam (who was also already working on Gill's and Ralph Tresvant's solo projects) who proposed that the trio form a group and came up with their name. According to Alton Stewart of *Red Bull Music Academy*, "They were nervous as hell because Ralph [Tresvant] and Johnny [Gill] had been singing the leads on New Edition records. Mike, Ricky, and Ronnie were in the background. . . . They were in the embryonic stage. They heard the people laughing and joking. They already knew what the world was saying. They didn't know if they were going to make it or break it. I told Mike and Ronnie that they were going to sing. They said, 'We don't sing. That's what Ralph and Johnny do.' I told them, 'You have to get that out of your minds. Don't worry about them.'" The trio inked a deal with MCA, thus Bell Biv DeVoe (BBD) was officially formed. The group then began working on their debut album.

"Poison" was written and produced by Elliot Straite, a.k.a. Dr. Freeze, who would also write the Color Me Badd hit "I Wanna Sex You Up." According to Straite, "Poison" was not a song at first, and he didn't think it would do well. "I didn't think that record was going to be that big," he said, "because it was a personal love letter to my ex-girlfriend at the time. It wasn't a song at first. It was a letter. When I wrote it as a song, I let a lot of my friends hear it, and they said it was weird. After that, I put the music together. I was thinking it wasn't going to be on the album because such heavyweights were already on it. I ended up having two songs on the album: 'Poison' and 'She's Dope! (9)'" Straite added that he intended to use the song on his album but "when the guys [Bell, Biv, DeVoe] heard it, they went nuts." The guys may have gone nuts, but some of the group's contemporaries weren't impressed with the demo versions of the song. As polka-dot-clad rapper Kwamé told *HipHopWired.com*, "I was hanging out with Mike Bivins. It was me, Mike Bivins, and Dana Dane, we were going to a club, somewhere. And [Bivins] put in a tape of the demo of 'Poison.' No disrespect, I love the record now, but when I heard the demo I swore it was the worst thing I ever heard in my life . . . I was like, 'Y'all gonna put this out?' He was like, 'Yeah, man, me, Ronnie, and Rick, we going to do a group called BBD.' [I'm like], 'Who wanna see y'all three? I wanna see New Edition! All this breaking up, Bobby solo, Ralph doing his thing, now y'all . . . what happened to New Edition?!'" In an effort to help Bivins out, Kwamé started to write a rap verse on a napkin. By the time the three had reached the club, the verse ending with the line "me and the crew used to do her" was complete, and it ended up making the song and being performed by Ronnie DeVoe. Production was handled as a collaborative effort. According to producer Hank Shocklee, "It had to be collaborative. I think it's one of the reasons why people look back on this era of music and say it was f**king incredible. The reason it was dope is because there were no egos involved. Specifically with regard to 'Poison' I wanted to make sure that the hip-hop element was strong . . . When it came to me, the record was very mellow and laid back. I thought it was a little too laid back. I had to take it and give it a boost and pump it up. Besides changing kicks and snares, I wanted to make sure it had some power and punch. The drums had to be loud. When you hear the intro to the song, that's what set the whole song off. I wanted it to be loud and big." The result was a 4× platinum single that gave us one of the most memorable R&B/hip-hop lines ever, in the form of a valuable life lesson: "Never trust a big butt and smile." Despite being released in February 1990, this song continues to get decent radio airplay and heavy media usage.

Sensitivity

Title: Sensitivity
Artist: Ralph Tresvant
Album: Ralph Tresvant
Year: 1990
Writers: Jimmy Jam, Terry Lewis
Producers: Jimmy Jam, Terry Lewis
Highest R&B Chart Position: 1
Highest Hot 100 Chart Position: 4

By the time "Sensitivity" was released, Ralph Tresvant, the former New Edition lead singer and, with all respect to Bobby Brown, the primary voice behind most of the group's early hits, was the only former New Edition member without a solo hit. The Tresvant solo album was probably the most anticipated album out of all the New Edition spin-offs. Although he had previously started a solo project when tracks were recorded for the singer's *Living in a Dream* album in 1987, that album was never released.

After New Edition's *Heart Break*, album Bobby Brown, BBD, and Johnny Gill all found success. This caused Tresvant some anxiety. He would later say, "Everybody dropped before me . . . Bobby pretty much took the full campaign I was gonna come with as far as an artist. That was my whole look. I wasn't the bad boy, which is what he flipped it into . . . But the music was that. That same bad boy swing that he was on at the time. The concept with the dancers hadn't been done yet. It was all new. Everything that I was going to do back then had already been done with Bobby on *Don't Be Cruel*."

For his campaign, Tresvant felt there was much more on the line. He told *USA Today*, "My stomach was twisting up . . . I was scared. I didn't want to be the only one to put out something that didn't work. . . . There was a lot of pressure on me." Tresvant told *The Atlanta Journal-Constitution*, "I used to think I'd be compared to them [BBD, Bobby Brown, and Johnny Gill] and that really worried me." The producers were writing songs to cater to who they thought Ralph was in 1990. "That's where songs like 'Sensitivity' came from. That's what they read into me because that's the only side I was showing folks at the time."

"Sensitivity," was written and produced by Jimmy Jam (who also played most of the instruments on the track) and Terry Lewis with Tresvant in mind. Lewis said, "'Sensitivity' was born out of the way we saw Ralph." Jimmy Jam added, "I like tracks that have some depth to them and that take you someplace, and that's what we tried to do with 'Sensitivity,' make a bed for his voice to sleep on. It's a very soothing song but also a very funky song. It's very unorthodox in a way." The Ralph Tresvant album did not disappoint, yielding three top 10 hits: "Do What I Gotta Do" (2), "Stone Cold Gentleman" (3), and "Sensitivity," which was Tresvant's first solo number 1 R&B hit.

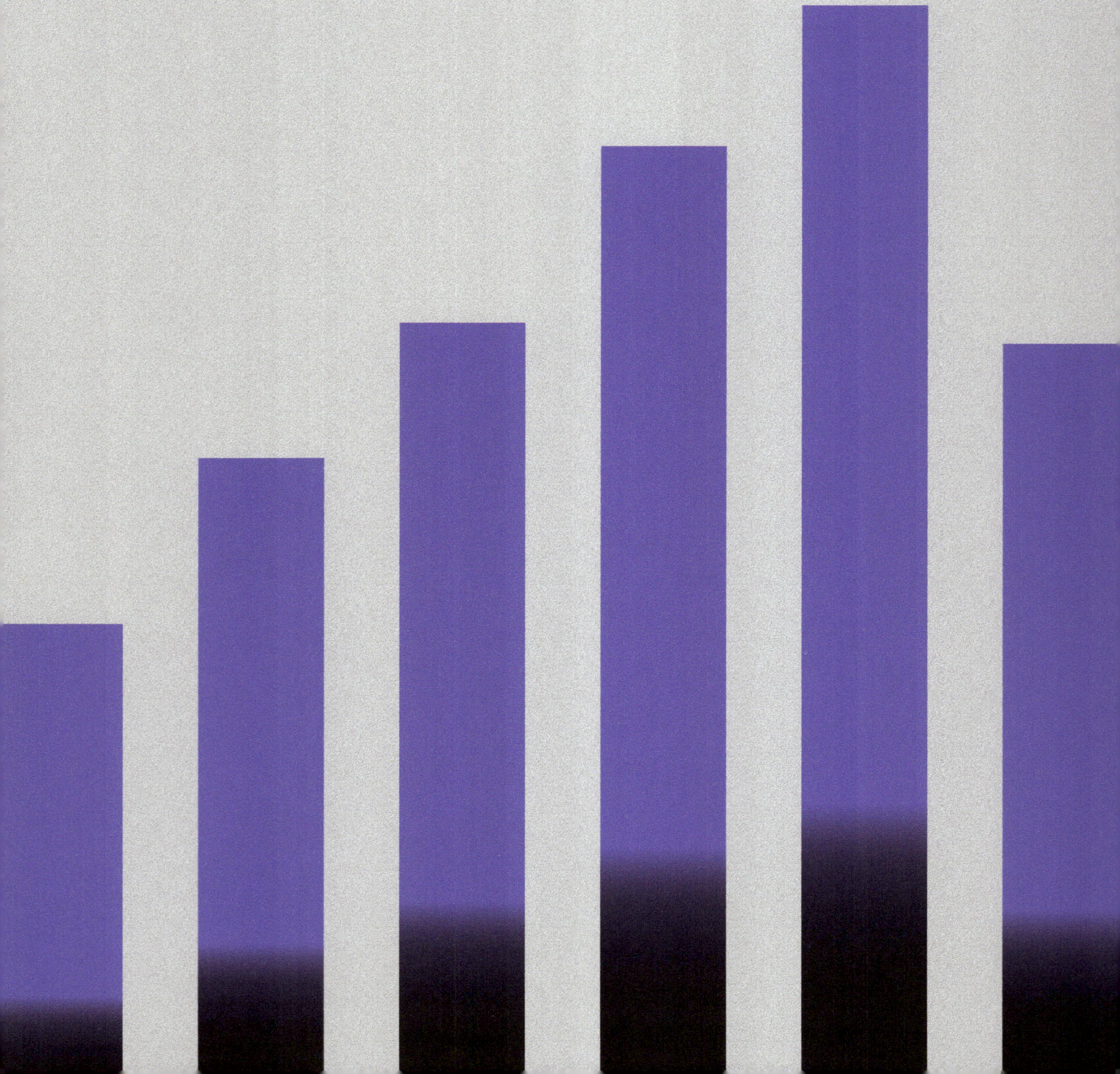

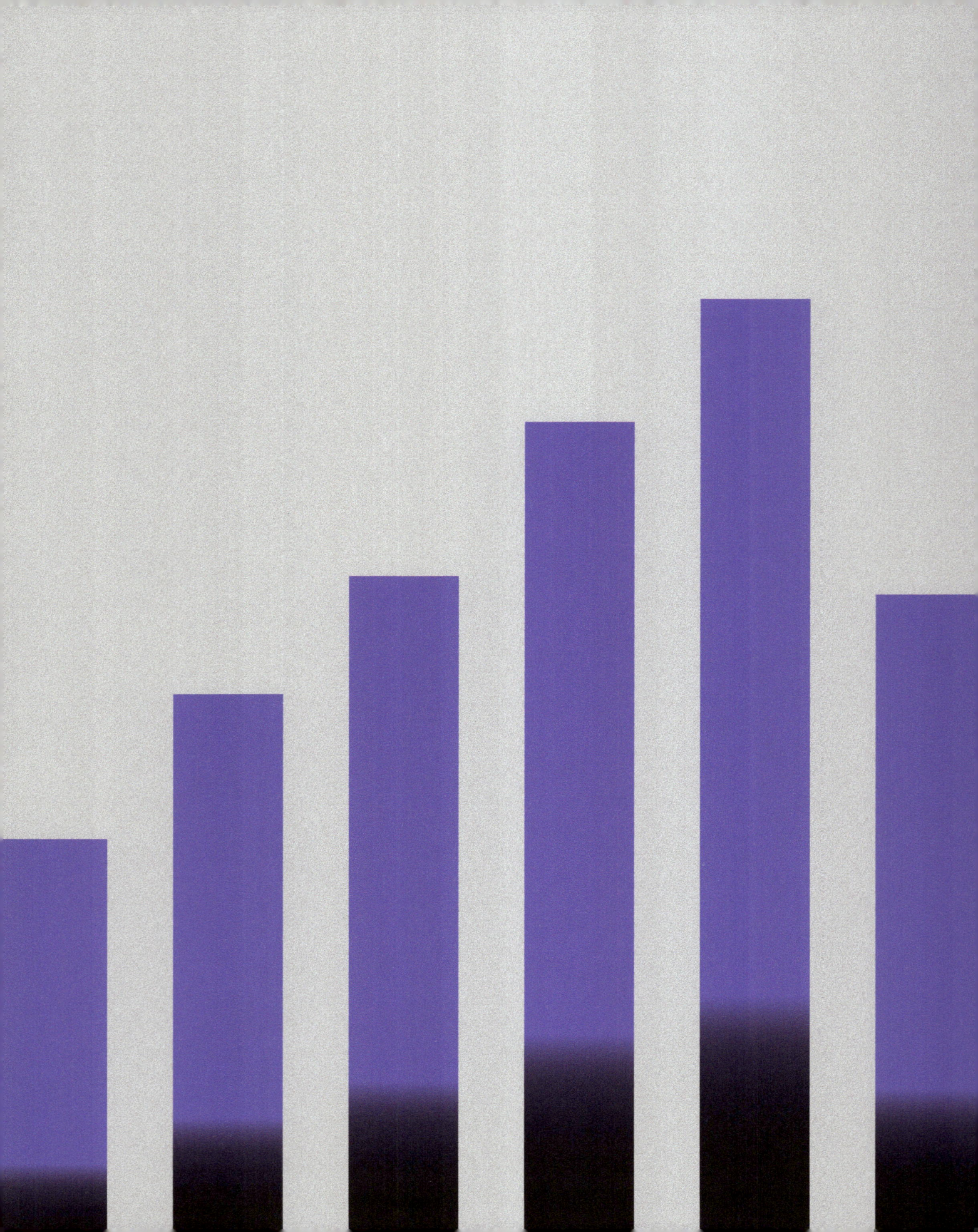

Rumpshaker: The New Jack Era
1986 - 1992

Iesha
Let's Chill
I Wanna Sex You Up
Motownphilly
Rump Shaker
Sexy MF

Rumpshaker: The New Jack Era | 1986 - 1992

The sub-genre of new jack swing fused elements of traditional R&B with hip-hop production techniques, including classic funk and soul samples, rapping, and the infamous Roland TR-808 drum machine. This sound, which dominated early '90s R&B, was driven by pioneers Bernard Belle, Teddy Riley, DJ Eddie F, Jimmy Jam, and Terry Lewis and had everyone from upstarts like Boyz II Men to living legends like Michael Jackson trying to capture that sound.

Iesha

Title: Iesha
Artist: Another Bad Creation
Album: Coolin' at the Playground Ya Know!
Year: 1990
Writers: Dallas Austin, Michael Bivins
Producer: Dallas Austin
Notable Samples: Total Kaos, EPMD (1989)
Rebel Without a Pause, Public Enemy (1988)
Christmas Rappin', Kurtis Blow (1979)
Cool It Now, New Edition (1984)
Highest R&B Chart Position: 6
Highest Top 100 Chart Position: 9

While Michael Bivins of New Edition/Bell Biv DeVoe fame received a lot of credit for discovering Another Bad Creation, (ABC) it should be noted that the group was already formed by the time Bivins came into the picture. The boys—Romell "RoRo" Chapman, Chris Sellers, David Shelton, and brothers Demetrius ("Red") and Marliss ("Mark") Pugh, as well as Adrian "G.A.." (General Austin) Witcher, all went to elementary school together and lived in the same Atlanta, Georgia neighborhood. Chapman explained how the group came together in a 1991 *New York Times* interview, stating, "One day, in the summer of 1988, we were sitting on the curb with nothing to do and just thought of it. Then, we got a little radio and would dance on the side of the street, so people would put money in our cans." Within a few weeks they caught the eye of local beauty shop owner Andrea Wales, who became a regular supporter of the group, having them sing in and around her salon. But it was her brother, Kevin Wales, who realized how talented the boys were. At the time Wales was a maintenance worker for Delta Airlines and a part-time singer in local clubs. He saw the group's potential and thought crowds would love to see these youngsters dance if he could teach them to sing. One of the biggest hurdles Wales faced as a manager was getting the approval of the kids' parents for the boys to be in the group. Wales recalled, "They saw me talking about getting the kids into show business . . . They didn't trust me—which I expected. We lived in a rough neighborhood where guys my age were into drugs and crime and whatever. I could have been somebody with something evil in mind."

Under Wales's tutelage, the boys, became known as Another Bad Creation and were winning Atlanta-area talent shows. With the parents on board and a talented group in the making, Wales then sought to parlay the group's connections into a record deal. Group member Dave Shelton was the nephew of singer Ralph Tresvant, who then was launching his solo career after being the lead singer for New Edition. Tresvant invited ABC to Los Angeles to meet him. It was in Tresvant's LA home studio that the group recorded their demo tape. Although they failed to land a record deal, an encounter with Tresvant's former band-mate Michael Bivins changed things.

While ABC was hanging out in an LA park, Bivins saw the boys walking together and asked them to sing for him. Bivins recalled, "They just looked like a group—a blind man could see the potential." He added, "and this was before I found out they could sing and dance." The group sang the song "Kind of Girls We Like," a New Edition staple. Long story short, Bivins loved the impromptu audition and the demo so much so that he signed ABC to his management company Biv Entertainment and introduced ABC to Motown Records president Jheryl Busby. A record deal with Motown soon followed, and ABC began work on their first album, *Coolin' at the Playground Ya Know!*

The album would be written and produced by Bivins, up-and-coming producer Dallas Austin, and Kevin Wales. At only nineteen years old, it was Austin who served as the album's primary writer and producer. He would later comment, "I knew this was my big shot, and I didn't want to blow it." Austin's previous credits as a producer to that point consisted of tracks on albums by the groups The Boys, Troop, and another Bivins-managed group, Boyz II Men. But "Iesha" would become Austin's first big hit in 1990. The songwriting Hall of Famer would later tell *Songwriter Universe*, "I told Michael Bivins, 'You know what? I'm going to try to make Another Bad Creation a small version of BBD, and I'm gonna write them a song like [their hit] "Poison," but for kids.' So I did 'Iesha.'"

Before recording the song, Austin invited the boys to his house, where he decided on an impromptu competition to decide who would sing what. "Red and Chris turned out to be the leads, and Romell was the rapper," Austin said. "In the studio we tried to keep things equal, so all the kids would feel like they were a part of things." He added, "It was all spur-of-the-moment composing . . . I'd record a musical track, and whoever was there sang on it."

The album was released in February 1991. "Iesha" was the first single, followed by "Playground (4)." Both reached the top 10 on the R&B and pop charts, and the album eventually went platinum.

With two singles in the top 10, the group's celebrity was in full swing. Mark and Dave appeared among other children (including Macaulay Culkin) in a scene of Michael Jackson's 1991 music video "Black or White." The group appeared in the Robert Townsend film *The Meteor Man*, and in March 1991, ABC appeared on the popular sketch comedy show *In Living Color*.

With so much publicity in a crowded new jack landscape, rivalries were inevitable. Naturally, one developed with their label-mates, the group The Boys. However, it was a rivalry with another Atlanta-based act on the So So Def recording label that apparently irked the members of ABC for years. In a 2020 interview, ABC member Red talked about the group's little-known rivalry with the rap group Kris Kross, saying, "When 'Jump' [Kriss Kross'] debut single] came out we wanted to fight." It turns out that ABC took the opening line of the song, "Don't try to compare us to another bad little fad," personally—"another bad little fad" being a play on ABC's name Another Bad Creation.
The song contained another jab that was aimed at ABC's habit of wearing their clothes inside out (Kris Kross wore their clothes backward) with the line, "And everything is to the back with a little slack / 'Cause inside out is wiggida, wiggida, wiggida wack!" Thankfully this rivalry did not reach Bad Boy vs. Death Row levels, but it does make one consider the Kris Kross verses differently.

Despite the platinum success of *Coolin' at the Playground Ya Know!* powered by "Iesha" and "Playground," ABC's second album, *It Ain't What U Wear, It's How U Play It*, which was released in September 1993, did not contain any charting singles. ABC would never recover from the sophomore slump and would have no more charting songs.

Let's Chill

Title: Let's Chill
Artist: Guy
Album: The Future
Year: 1991
Writers: Bernard Belle, Teddy Riley
Producer: Teddy Riley
Highest R&B Chart Position: 3
Highest Hot 100 Chart Position: 41

Two of the three original members of Guy, Teddy Riley and Timmy Gatling (Aaron Hall was the third member), were friends since childhood and were both part of the earlier New Edition–inspired teen group Kids at Work. Kids at Work was signed to CBS Records and released one LP before being dropped from the label after their manager, Gene Griffin, was jailed on drug charges.

Following the dissolution of Kids at Work, Riley jumped into the production side of music, earning credits on classic hip-hop and R&B tracks like Doug E. Fresh's "The Show" (1985), Keith Sweat's R&B number 1 "I Want Her" (1987), and Sweat's classic duet with singer Jacci McGhee, "Make It Last Forever" (1988), which became a number 2 hit. Despite the success of the Keith Sweat songs, Riley, who was instrumental in creating the hits, was paid only $1,500. Gatling took a day job at the Brooklyn department store Abraham & Straus, where he met aspiring gospel singer Aaron Hall. Hall and Gatling gelled around their love of music, with Gatling as the writer and Hall as the lead singer. Both eventually quit their jobs to focus on music full-time. Needing a producer, Gatling approached his old friend Riley to ask for help. Impressed with the duo's talent, Riley joined the group and Guy was created (the name comes from a local clothing store named Guy LTD), with Gatling as the songwriter, Hall as the lead singer, and Riley as the producer. By this time, Gene Griffin had completed his two-year sentence. Riley, still reeling from his experience producing hits for Keith Sweat and only earning $1,500, wanted to ensure that no one would take advantage of him again, and he reached out to Griffin, who had the street credibility and reputation as a tough guy, to manage the group. Riley recalled, "I need Gene Griffin, who's gonna make sure nobody's taking from me."

Under Griffin's management, the group was signed to Uptown Records in 1988. However, it soon became evident that Griffin's protection came at a cost as he demanded control and credit. According to *Pitchfork.com*, Griffin named himself a writer and producer on every track of the *Guy* debut album, though he'd had little to no hand in the music, and when he presented the group with management contracts, Gatling, the true author of nearly every song on the album, refused to sign. Griffin then kicked Gatling out of the group, replacing him with Aaron Hall's younger brother, Damion Hall. However, it was too late to remove Gatling's vocals or replace his photos on the album cover. Gatling would eventually go on to write and produce R&B hits such as "Promises, Promises" (7) for Christopher Williams and "When Will I See You Smile Again?" (3) for Bell Biv DeVoe.

Guy's first single was the modest hit "'Round and 'Round (Merry Go 'Round of Love)," which peaked at number 24. Their second single, the up-tempo new jack song "Groove Me," was the first of four top 20 singles from the album, not including the number 1 song "My Fantasy" from the *Do the Right Thing* soundtrack.

Teddy Riley told *Vibe* magazine about the group's creative process, saying "Guy recorded our first single 'Groove Me' in the bathroom," he said. "Aaron Hall stayed over my house because we didn't have the money to make the record at a professional studio. And Aaron did all his vocals in the bathroom. We put towels over the shower curtains so we didn't have too much of an echo. That was a special time for Guy. Aaron would always sleep on my couch. I would get up out of the bed, come to the living room, and he would still be there writing lyrics."

Riley continued, "In the beginning, it was me, Aaron, and Timmy Gatling. This was before Timmy left the group and Aaron's brother Damion Hall joined. Aaron is so underrated as a vocalist. There was some great singing on that first *Guy* album. 'Groove Me' took a year for people to really get *Guy*. The first show we did—a show we performed with Johnny Kemp—we got booed. And we only got booed because the crowd didn't know what we looked like. All they knew is that the 'Groove Me' song was playing on 98.7 Kiss and KTU. People were requesting that song every day, but when Kemp introduced us after he just performed 'Just Got Paid'—a huge song I produced that was supposed to be on Keith Sweat's first album—people were like, 'Get them off the stage!' Next thing you know our record came on, 'Groove me . . . baby . . . tonight!' Everybody went 'Oh, my God . . . that's them!' . . . Looking back, that first Guy album took a year and a half later to go platinum. I was just thinking, 'Dag, it takes this long to get famous?' But that's how God works. It's never on your time . . . it's on his time. God made us a successful group."

A year after the Guy album's release, the group encountered a number of challenges. They fired Gene Griffin, claiming he had appropriated funds from the group. While on tour with New Edition, one of New Edition's production managers shot and killed Anthony Bee, a member of Guy's security detail, and Riley's brother, Wreckx-n-Effect member Brandon "B-Doggs" Mitchell, was also killed the same year and the group was broke. Aaron Hall revealed, "There came a time where I just did not want to sing a single note. To be honest, it was the money. It just became too depressing. We were the biggest group in the world and we were flat broke. It took its toll."

As a result, Teddy Riley assumed the duties of lead vocals for Guy's second album, *The Future*. Riley recalled, "There was a lot of pressure doing that *Future* album. I was singing lead again on 'Wanna Get With U.' We thought that we had to start taking responsibility for ourselves and stop depending on people. We didn't want anything taken from us, and we didn't want our talents to be taken for granted. We knew we wanted to still do our love songs, but now we wanted to tell the truth about our lives. That's when we did songs like 'Let's Chill,' 'D-O-G Me Out,' and 'Long Gone,' which was about me losing my younger brother Brandon to violence. I also lost my best friend to violence . . . There were issues in the group."

For "Let's Chill," Riley collaborated with fellow new jack pioneer Bernard Belle and reconnected with Keith Sweat. Bell and Riley began working together in 1986 and produced the number 3 hit for the Winans, 1990's "It's Time," and the number 1 Hi-Five hit "I Like the Way (The Kissing Game)."

"Let's Chill" was released as the second single from *The Future* in February 1991 and became an instant classic. In fact in 2008, nearly thirty years after Guy's first breakup, hip-hop legend Snoop Dogg asked Guy to sing "Let's Chill" as part of his and his wife Shante Broadus' vow renewal ceremony. Two-thirds of Guy obliged (Teddy Riley and Damion Hall, with Charlie Wilson filling in for Aaron Hall), bringing the Doggfather to tears and leading him to explain to *MTV News*, "That record means a lot to me and my wife, my relationship . . . Just all the stuff me and my wife been through. . . . That one record right there, 'Let's Chill,' makes me feel good."

But even having released a classic song on *The Future* in 1991, the real-world future as a group for Guy would not be bright. By early 1992, each member would leave the group and embark on separate endeavors, with Aaron and Damion Hall releasing solo albums and Riley departing to produce for the likes of Michael Jackson and eventually starting the group Blackstreet. Riley told *Vibe* magazine, "I can only remember doing our last show at Madison Square Garden announcing my leave of Guy. We did 'Groove Me' like it was our last day on earth. People in the audience was crying. I ran off the stage and got out of there really quick . . . We couldn't even be in the same dressing room. I no longer wanted to be a part of Guy."

In 1999, Guy reunited and released the album *Guy III*, which became the number 5 album in the country and gave them their highest charting pop hit, "Dancin'" (19), but it was the album's only single and the group disbanded again soon after *Guy III's* release.

I Wanna Sex You Up

Title: I Wanna Sex You Up
Artist: Color Me Badd
Album: C.M.B.
Year: 1991
Writers: Color Me Badd, Elliot Straite
Producers: Dr. Freeze, Hitman Howie Tee, Spyderman
Notable Samples: Tonight Is the Night, Betty Wright (1974)
    La Di Da Di, Doug E. Fresh and Slick Rick (1985)
    Joanna, Kool and the Gang (1983)
    Change the Beat, Beside (1982)
Highest R&B Chart Position: 1
Highest Top 100 Chart Position: 2

"I Wanna Sex You Up" was the debut single for both Color Me Badd and their record label, Giant Records. Bryan Abrams, Kevin Thornton, Mark Calderon, and Sam Watters came together as Color Me Badd (originally called Take One) at Northwestern High School in Oklahoma City, Oklahoma. The group relocated to New York City in search of a record contract but ran into issues getting signed as a group. Calderon told *Richmond Magazine,* "The record labels, when they saw we were a multiracial group, they really didn't have anything to do with us . . . At that time, there just [weren't] multiracial groups . . . It was Giant Records who decided to take a chance on us."

Specifically, it was Giant Records executive Cassandra Mills who took the chance. She signed Color Me Badd and intended to use the *New Jack City* movie soundtrack and "I Wanna Sex You Up" as the group's introduction to the world. The song was written for the 1991 movie. Mills was looking for a modern new jack swing sound to accompany the film. To get it, she reached out to producer-songwriter Elliot Straite (a.k.a. Dr. Freeze), who had written the Bell Biv DeVoe (BBD) smash "Poison" that went to number 1 in May of 1990. But for *New Jack City* she was looking for a track closer to the BBD hit "Do Me" (4).

To give him inspiration for the song, Mills asked Dr. Freeze to watch the film and "pay close attention to the strip scene," where the character Uniqua does a striptease for the character Nino Brown. Dr. Freeze composed the song and wrote his part of "I Wanna Sex You Up" specifically for this scene.

This song samples the bass line and lyrics "I know you're not gonna sing that song" from Betty Wright's 1974 song "Tonight Is the Night" (11), which chronicles a young woman's very first "intimate encounter," and Slick Rick's "to the tik tok ya don't stop" from his 1985 song "La Di Da Di." When Color Me Badd first heard the instrumental, they knew it was a perfect match for their style. "It blew our minds because it was exactly who we were, that old-school sound," group member Mark Calderon told *Entertainment Weekly* in a 2016 interview.

While Color Me Badd was enamored by the instrumental, other bigger acts weren't so impressed. Calderon told *The*

Oklahoma Gazette, "We had heard so many other acts like Bell Biv DeVoe and Christopher Williams, and I think Keith Sweat had all turned down that track . . . We were able to jump on it."

Even the label had its doubts, according to Calderon. "The song wasn't meant to be a single at first," he said, "but radio stations started playing it nonstop once the *New Jack City* soundtrack dropped." The label took immediate notice and urged Color Me Badd to finalize their album. Calderon recalls, "When the record company saw everything that was happening with that song, I remember them calling us up and saying, 'Hey, we need that album, like, in a week.'" "I Wanna Sex You Up" was issued on the *New Jack City* soundtrack as well as Color Me Badd's debut album *C.M.B.* Their follow-on single, "I Adore Mi Amor," also reached number 1 on the R&B and Hot 100 charts. *C.M.B.* spent 77 weeks on the *Billboard* charts, selling 3 million units. Although Color Me Badd never again matched the success of "I Wanna Sex You Up," they continue to make a living through touring and royalties from the massive hit.

Motownphilly

Title: Motownphilly
Artist: Boyz II Men
Album: Cooleyhighharmony
Year: 1991
Writers: Dallas Austin, Michael Bivins, Nathan Morris, Shawn Stockman
Producer: Dallas Austin
Notable Samples: Treat 'Em Right, Chubb Rock (1991)
　　　　　　　　　Kool Is Back, Funk, Inc. (1971)
　　　　　　　　　Think (About It), Lyn Collins (1972)
Highest R&B Chart Position: 4
Highest Top 100 Chart Position: 3

Although Boyz II Men, the quartet composed of Nathan Morris, Wanyá Morris, Shawn Stockman, and Michael McCary (McCary left the group in 2003 due to health issues), are best known for emotional ballads and a cappella harmonies, their first single, "Motownphilly," was an up-tempo Dallas Austin–produced new jack track. It seems silly now, but at the time the song was confusing to a lot of radio DJ's because some thought it was called "Boyz II Men" and the group was named Motownphilly, since the words "Boyz II Men" are in the lyrics and the chorus states, "Motownphilly back again." There is, however, no confusing the message.

This song is essentially the Boyz II Men origin story. It tells how they dreamed of making it and made their dreams a reality set to a new jack beat. It includes a couple of Michael Bivins raps and an interlude that rivals En Vogues interlude on their song "My Lovin (You're Never Gonna Get it)" (1) as one of the most memorable interludes in R&B history.

Doom doom doom da da, doom doom doom da da /
Da di da di da di, da da, daa daa oh /
Doom doom doom da da, doom doom doom da da /
Da di da di da da, da da, daa daa oh oh oh

Although "Motownphilly" never reached higher than number 4, it set the stage for Boyz II Men to go on to international success, four Grammys, several multi-platinum albums, and status as one of the biggest groups of the 1990s in any genre.

Rump Shaker

Title: Rump Shaker
Artist: Wreckx-n-Effect
Album: Hard or Smooth
Year: 1992
Writers: Aqil Davidson, Ty Fyffe, Anton Hollins, Markell Riley, Teddy Riley, Pharrell Williams, David Wynn
Producers: Aqil Davidson, Ty Fyffe, Markell Riley, Teddy Riley, David Wynn
Notable Samples: Darkest Light, Lafayette Afro Rock Band (1972)
Midnight Theme, Manzel (1979)
Godfather Runnin' the Joint, James Brown (1988)
Blues & Pants, James Brown (1971)
I Like It, DeBarge (1982)
Highest R&B Chart Position: 3
Highest Hot 100 Chart Position: 2

Virginia Beach, Virginia, was not known for producing music talent before Teddy Riley's arrival in 1990. However, Riley and his Future Recording Studios laid the groundwork for some of the biggest names in R&B and hip-hop, such as Timbaland, Missy Elliott, and the Neptunes.

The New York City native's journey to a residency in Virginia began in 1983, long before he was a member of the group Guy, when he was looking for a place to build his music empire. As he told *Red Bull Music Academy* in 2015, "I was losing many of my best friends. They were all getting killed. I went to Virginia on a trip with . . . all my friends and street big brothers from Harlem. . . . They were there for the girls, but I had a vision of coming there to start my own music business . . . It was the place where God wanted me to be. Even though I knew it would be a challenge going there and trying to build a music scene when there wasn't one." Riley moved to Virginia Beach permanently at the end of 1990 to run Future Recording Studios. By this time he was already a certified R&B star, having produced mega-hits for Keith Sweat, Al B. Sure!, and Bobby Brown.

For their part, Wreckx-n-Effect (originally Wrecks-n-Effect) was founded in 1988 by Markell Riley (Teddy's brother), Aqil Davidson, and Brandon "B-Doggs" Mitchell and included Keith "K.C." Harris. They released their debut album *Wrecks-n-Effect* on Motown, which included the Markell Riley–produced track and *Billboard* Hot Rap Songs number 1 (R&B 14) "New Jack Swing" in 1989.

By 1992 the group had lost member Brandon "B-Doggs" Mitchell to gun violence and, like Teddy Riley, they were seeking a change of scenery. Markell and the remaining group members joined older brother Teddy in Virginia, where they produced and recorded their second album *Hard or Smooth*, which included the song "Rump Shaker."

It is the quintessential new jack song, consisting of multiple samples and elements of R&B with over-the-top hip-hop production and rap interludes, one of which was written by a teenage Pharrell Williams, who was given writing credit for his work.

The group met when Williams when he competed in a talent show that Riley hosted. "We had a talent show at his school, and [Pharrell] was a part of it, performing with his crew, the Neptunes," Teddy recalled to *HipHopDX.com*. "I took a liking to them all: Chad, Pharrell, Mike Etheridge, Shay [Haley], and the rest of the crew. I overrode the judges in the contest and said, 'This is what I'm looking for,' and wound up signing them." Riley went on to describe how he gave Williams the opportunity to write the rap, stating, "I produced the song, and there were so many versions of it and I didn't like the way my rap was . . . This was my chance to give Pharrell the opportunity to write it. He said, 'I can come up with something.' I said, 'Well, let's do it.' He came up with the rap. I studied it. I rapped it on my song, and that was his contribution to the song, writing my rap."

"Rump Shaker" was released as the lead single from *Hard or Smooth* in 1992. The song peaked at number 2 on both the Hot R&B/Hip-Hop and Hot 100 charts, with only the Whitney Houston smash "I Will Always Love You" keeping it from the number 1 spot. "Rump Shaker" did reach number 1 on the Hot Rap Singles chart. "Rumpshaker" was Wreckx-n-Effect's last R&B hit. Their single "Knock-N-Boots" peaked at number 71 in 1993.

Sexy MF

Title: Sexy MF
Artist: Prince and the New Power Generation
Album: Love Symbol
Year: 1992
Writers: Prince, Tony M., Levi Seacer Jr.
Producer: Prince
Highest R&B Chart Position: 76
Highest Top 100 Chart Position: 66

"Sexy MF" was the product of Prince and his then new backing group the New Power Generation (NPG) playing around in between studio sessions. As keyboardist Tommy Barbarella told *Rolling Stone* in 2016, band-mate "Levi [Seacer] was always joking around with some phrase he thought was funny. He'd start doing some simple little riff, stop and say the phrase 'sexy motherf***er.'" During one of the sessions the group turned the joke into a hit and 'Sexy Motherf***r' was recorded in about twenty minutes, half an hour."

The new jack swing vibe shows the influence that hip-hop had on Prince at the time. This influence is evident throughout the song, including its rap verse performed by band member Tony M.. As Prince told Spike Lee in a 1997 interview, "The music I make a lot of the time is reflective of the life I am leading, and 'Sexy MF' came during the period I had the Glam Slam disco, and I was hanging out a lot. There was a dance troupe there and the sexier the dancers, the bigger the revenues and the nosier the crowd. It's funny but you have to remember that was during the time when the biggest club song was 'Bitch Betta Have My Money' [AMG version, 1991]. When you hear something constantly, you can get swayed by the current. I was swayed by hip-hop at the time." Hence the constant "Sexy MF" refrain.
And NPG was the perfect complement to bring Prince's hip-hop-inspired vision to life. According to Barbarella, the "different kind of musicians in this band could actualize absolutely anything he [Prince] envisioned. If it was in his head, we could make it happen. I think he loved that for a while."

While the title and Prince's reputation may lend listeners to believe the song is overtly sexual, Prince contended that it was not. He told *The Observer*, "People hear the sex in my songs much more than I ever write it. If you listen to the words in 'Sexy MF,' you'll see they're about monogamy rather than promiscuous sex."

Although powered by Prince, who was already a megastar, and the provocative and catchy title, the song barely made the R&B top 20, peaking at number 19.

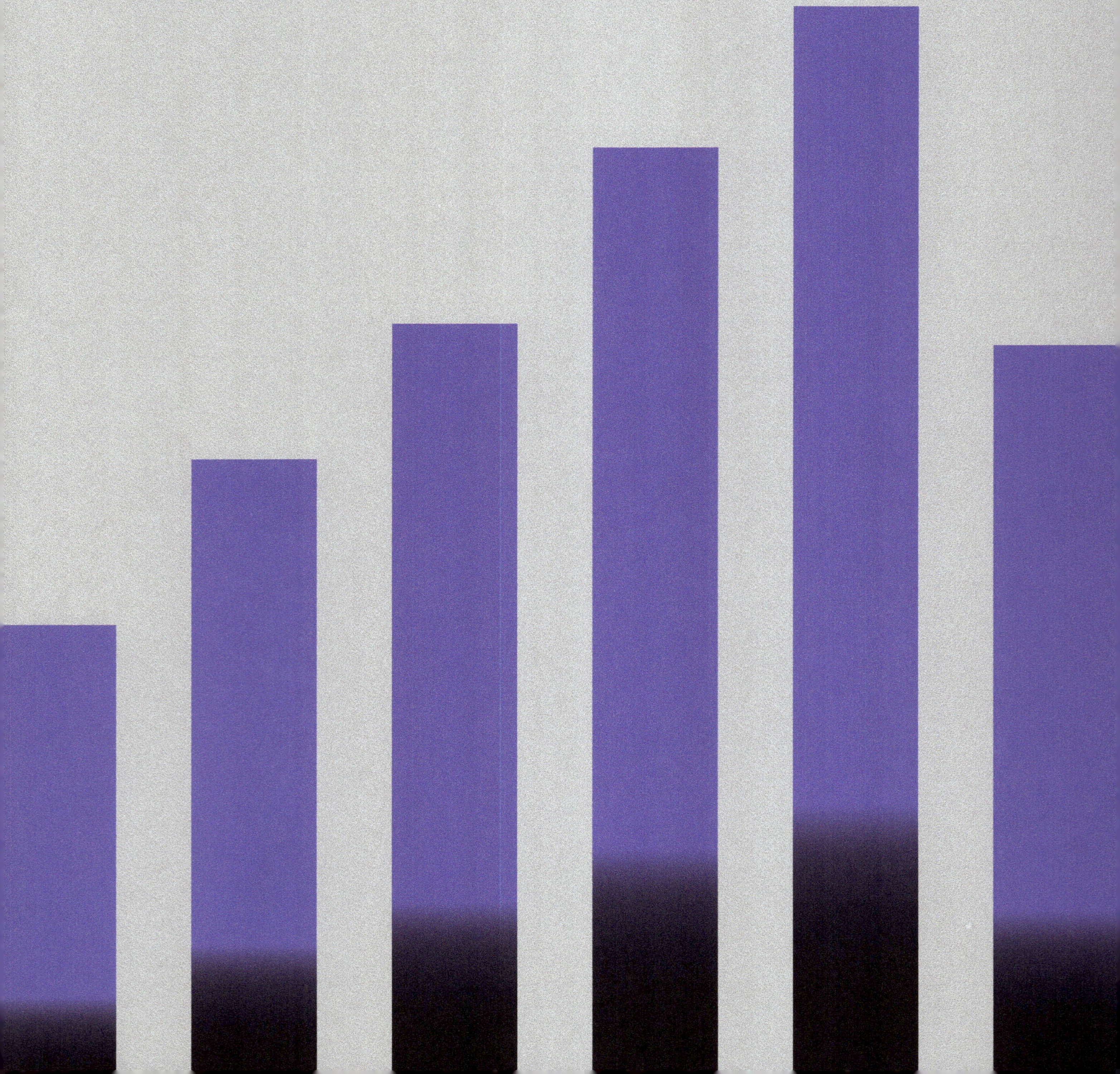

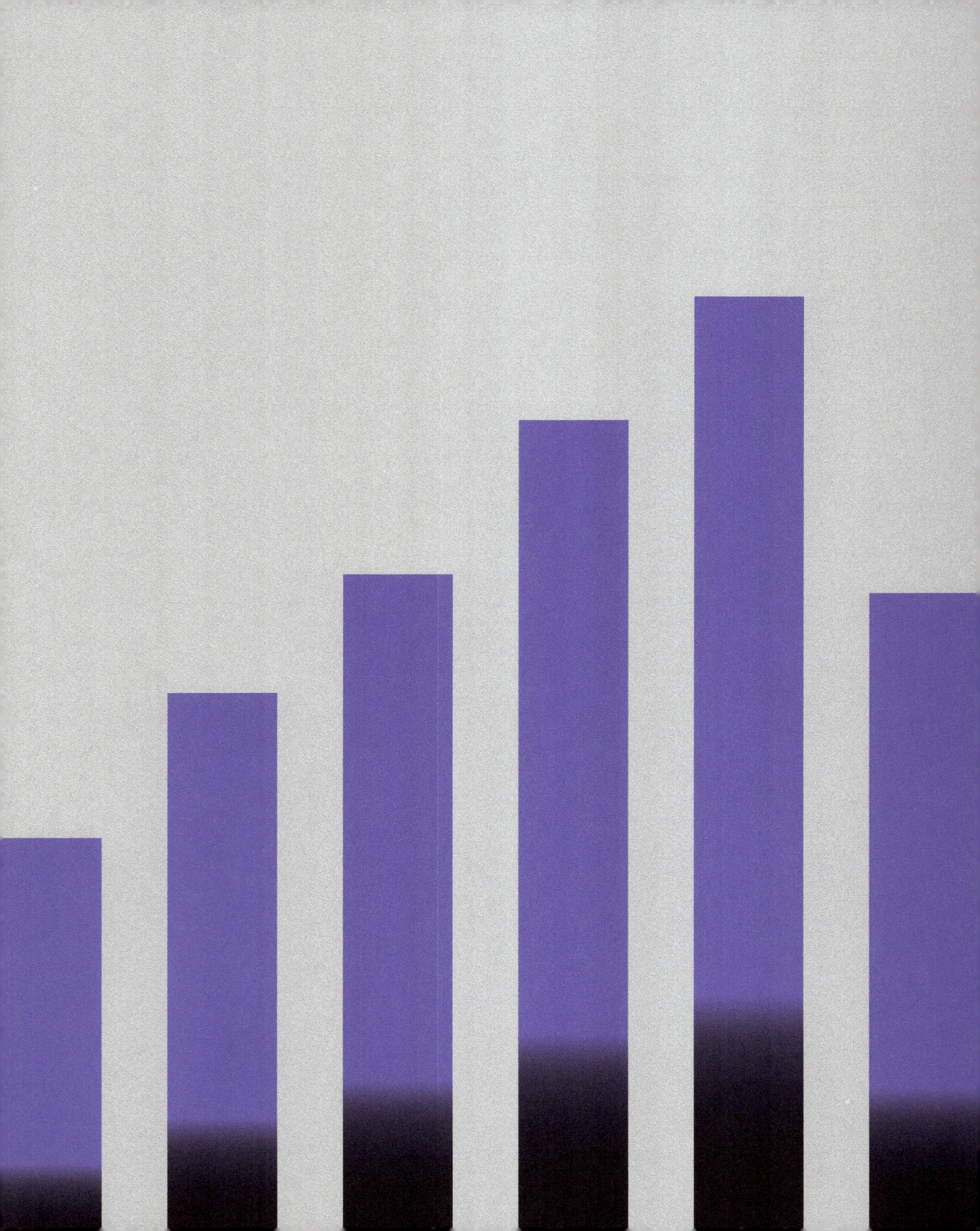

Can We Talk: New Kids On The Block
1991 - 1994

I Like the Way (The Kissing Game)
Breakin' My Heart (Pretty Brown Eyes)
If I Ever Fall in Love
Love Should'a Brought You Home
Hey Mr. D.J.
Knockin' da Boots
Shhh
Can U Get Wit It
Candy Rain
Interlude: Boyz II Men vs. Jodeci
Boyz II Men Backstory
End of the Road
On Bended Knee
4 Seasons of Loneliness
Jodeci Backstory
Forever My Lady
Cry For You
Love You 4 Life
Interlude: The Rise and Fall of Swing Mob
Interlude: What about Tony! Toni! Toné!?

Can We Talk: New Kids On The Block | 1991 - 1994

The 1990s introduced us to some artists that were just beginning their journeys to legend status and others whose names we would soon forget. However, both groups of artists endowed us with unforgettable classics. We analyze a selection of some of the best below.

I Like The Way (The Kissing Game)

Title: I Like the Way (The Kissing Game)
Artist: Hi-Five
Album: Hi-Five
Year: 1991
Writers: Bernard Belle, Teddy Riley, Dave Way
Producers: Bernard Belle, Teddy Riley,
Highest R&B Chart Position: 1
Highest Hot 100 Chart Position: 1

The teen group Hi-Five, which hailed from Waco, Texas, consisted of childhood friends Tony Thompson, Roderick "Pooh" Clark, Marcus Sanders, Russell Neal, and Toriano Easley.

Thompson was a prodigy, enamoring congregations while singing gospel music in and around Waco churches. He caught the attention of talent manager Vincent Bell, who was looking for a child singer to manage. Thompson impressed Bell during the audition, and his skills prompted Bell to build a New Edition–styled group around Thompson's talent. At the request of Bell, Thompson reached out to his friends, and they became "The Playmates." Bell signed the group to his entertainment company and later to Jive Records, which renamed the group Hi-Five in 1989. It was Jive that connected the group with super-producer Teddy Riley for production of their first album, *Hi-Five*.

However, prior to the release of the album, group member Toriano Easley, was jailed for manslaughter for the shooting death of a teenager in Oklahoma. Easley would serve six and a half years in prison for the crime. Surprisingly, Jive did not drop Hi-Five but instead sought a replacement for Easley and discovered New York City–area gospel singer Treston Irby, who soon after formally became a part of the group.

The album's second single, "I Like the Way (The Kissing Game)," became the group's first big hit and a Hot 100 and R&B number 1. The album went platinum powered by the success of "I Like the Way (The Kissing Game)" and sustained by the follow-up singles "I Just Can't Handle It" (10) and "I Can't Wait Another Minute" (1). Hi-Five's second album, *Keep It Goin' On,* produced the group's final top 5 R&B hits, "She's Playing Hard to Get" (2) and the R. Kelly written and produced "Quality Time" (3). In total, four of Hi-Five's first five singles hit the top 5 on the R&B singles chart.

Shortly after the release of *Keep It Goin' On*, during a promotional tour of the east coast the group was involved in a vehicular accident that left group member Roderick "Pooh" Clark paralyzed from the chest down.

Hi-Five continued as a quartet, and their third album, *Faithful*, was the last of their three-record deal with Jive. Prior to the release of *Faithful*, Russell Neal left the group over compensation issues (he was replaced by Shannon Gill and Terrence Murphy), and Hi-Five left Jive and signed with Giant Records.

In 1993, Hi-Five released *Faithful*, which featured the songs "Unconditional Love" (21) and "Never Should've Let You Go" (10). However, since Hi- Five had signed with Giant Records prior to the album's release, Jive, which had the rights to the album, did not do much to promote it. As a result the album failed to break into the top 20.

Once fully on board with Giant Records, the new label sought to produce a Tony Thompson solo record, followed by a Hi-Five record. This fractured the group. Adding to matters, it was revealed that Thompson had a drug addiction issue. Hi-Five would never record an album for Giant, and the group officially broke up in 1994. The group members, minus Thompson, would unsuccessfully attempt to sign with multiple labels between 1994 and 1999. Thompson would record a solo album for Giant Records, *Sexsational,* which was released in 1995. The album failed to break the top 40. Thompson eventually formed his own record label after a brief uneventful stint with Bad Boy Records from 1997 to 2000.

Thompson, Terrence Murphy, and three new members would release a Hi-Five album, *The Return*, in 2005. However, the other former band-mates successfully sued Thompson for improper use of the Hi-Five name. The members eventually reconciled but plans for a 2007 reunion were dashed when Thompson died unexpectedly in June of that year.

Breakin' My Heart (Pretty Brown Eyes)

Title: Breakin' My Heart (Pretty Brown Eyes)
Artist: Mint Condition
Album: Meant to Be Mint
Year: 1991
Writers: Jeffrey Allen, Lawrence Waddell, Stokley Williams
Producers: Mint Condition, Jellybean Johnson
Highest R&B Chart Position: 3
Highest Hot 100 Chart Position: 6

While the band Mint Condition consisting of Jeffrey Allen, Ricky Kinchen, Homer O'Dell, Larry Waddell, Stokley Williams, and Keri Lewis was formed in the early 1980s, their big break did not come until they were discovered by producers Jimmy Jam and Terry Lewis in Minneapolis in 1989, and their breakthrough song would not be released until November 1991.

Between their formation and being discovered by Jam and Lewis, Mint Condition built a large following in the Midwest mainly due to their highly diverse musical style and their energetic live shows.
Once signed by Jam and Lewis to Perspective Records, Mint Condition recorded their first album, *Meant to Be Mint*. The first single from the album was the upbeat new jack song "Are You Free." The song was a flop, only reaching number 55 on the R&B charts. Their second single was the ballad "Breakin' My Heart (Pretty Brown Eyes)," which would serve as the first of the band's many hits during the decade and beyond.

But after "Are You Free" failed on the charts the group's parent label did not believe the *Meant to Be Mint* album had any hits. It was then that Jam and Lewis decided to put Mint Condition on a black college tour to publicize their album. At the time, "Breakin' My Heart (Pretty Brown Eyes)" had already been released but had failed to make an impact in sales or on the charts. That was until Washington, D.C., radio station WHUR of Howard University put the song into heavy rotation, and it caught fire.

The song was a breath of fresh air for traditional R&B fans. Rashod Ollison of *The Baltimore Sun* recalled the era in a 2005 article about the band's impact, writing, "The days of Earth, Wind & Fire, Rufus and Chaka Khan, the Bar-Kays and Slave were long gone. Producer-driven new jack swing—with its busy, jittery, sample-heavy concoctions—ruled urban airwaves at the time, blurring the lines between rap and R&B. But in blew Mint Condition: a sextet from Minneapolis with a sleek, inviting sound, playing real instruments and writing heart-felt joints about 'pretty brown eyes.' In an era when Sir Mix-a-lot topped the charts with 'Baby Got Back,' a crude ode to fat backsides, Mint Condition's music kept things sharp and classy."

"Breakin' My Heart (Pretty Brown Eyes)" spent thirty-four weeks total and twenty weeks in the top 40 on the Hot R&B Singles chart. Mint Condition would consistently break the top 10 in the 1990s with tracks like 1991's "Forever in Your Eyes" (7), 1993's "U Send Me Swingin'" (2), 1996's "What Kind of Man Would I Be" (2), 1997's "You Don't Have to Hurt No More" (10), and 1999's "If You Love Me" (5).

If I Ever Fall in Love

Title: If I Ever Fall in Love
Artist: Shai
Album: . . . If I Ever Fall in Love
Year: 1992
Writer: Carl "Groove" Martin
Producer: Carl "Groove" Martin
Highest R&B Chart Position: 1
Highest Hot 100 Chart Position: 2

Originally called Beta, the group Shai (Swahili for "personification of destiny") formed while members Darnell Van Rensalier, Garfield A. Bright, Carl Martin, and Marc Gay were students at Howard University in Washington, D.C. The group originally formed for a talent show ten months before "If I Ever Fall in Love" was released, and according to *Songfacts.com*, group member Carl "Groove" Martin "came up with "If I Ever Fall in Love" when he was driving back to campus from his home in Louisiana after Christmas break while listening to the same songs on the radio over and over. He thought the airwaves needed something new and different, so he came up with the song in his head. He claims it all came to him in about fifteen minutes. Martin knew the song was meant to be because he didn't forget it when he arrived on campus. He taught it to his band-mates, and at the talent show they sang part of "If I Ever Fall in Love" along with some Boyz II Men songs. They eventually worked out the harmonies and performed the whole song at an open-mic night, getting a great reaction from the crowd.

The reaction prompted the college students to scrape up the $400 to record a demo, but the Howard University radio station, WHUR—the same station that launched Mint Condition's song "Breakin' My Heart (Pretty Brown Eyes)"—refused to play it. Undeterred, Martin slid the demo to WHUR's competitor station WPGC, and soon after the song dominated both stations' request lines. Although Martin admitted to *The Washington Post* in December 1992 that Shai themselves made a lot of the initial requests for the song to be played.

Martin recalled, "It's kind of funny. I just knew I liked ["If I Ever Fall in Love"], so I thought it would be a hit. I knew if we put it on the radio, people would respond. Within a few weeks it got to number 1 in rotation in D.C., so I assumed the same thing would happen again."

Martin's assumptions were correct. "If I Ever Fall in Love" became a huge hit nationwide, spending eight weeks at number 2 behind Whitney Houston's "I Will Always Love You" from *The Bodyguard* movie soundtrack. Shai signed a record deal with the Gasoline Alley record label and released the song and their debut album *If I Ever Fall in Love* in 1992. Although Shai followed up with the hits "Comforter" and "Baby I'm Yours," both of which went to number 10, "If I Ever Fall in Love" remains their biggest hit to date.

When the group's second album, 1995's *Blackface,* did poorer than expected, Shai began to fall apart. Member Darnell Van Rensalier recalled to writer Emiene Wright, "The whole thing happened faster than we were able to get a team together. We kind of self-imploded."

Van Rensalier prefers not to name names but says, "One dude thought he would be the man. He allowed the industry to come between us. . . . Those people don't really have the talent, that's why they do that. It's almost like a manual; it's the same story. Every group has one guy who's that."

Blackface would be Shai's last recording with all four original members.

Love Should'a Brought You Home

Artist: Toni Braxton
Album: Toni Braxton
Year: 1992
Writers: Kenneth "Babyface" Edmonds, Daryl Simmons, Bo Watson
Producers: Kenneth "Babyface" Edmonds, Antonio "L.A." Reid, Daryl Simmons
Highest R&B Chart Position: 4
Highest Hot 100 Chart Position: 33

When Eddie Murphy asked the production team of Babyface and L.A. Reid to provide music for the soundtrack to his 1992 film Boomerang, the duo turned to the film for inspiration.

Babyface recalled to EURweb.com, "We got to watch it as it was being made, we were able to see scenes of it as well. So as we were writing music for it, the whole thing was new for us because we hadn't written for a film at that point. There were particular songs that we wrote for the film, watching the dailies and going on and then watching the whole part of when Halle [Barry] said to Eddie Murphy . . . I forget the character's name at that particular point, but she was very emotional and then he said, 'I love you,' and she came with the famous line, and she said 'Love? Love should have brought your ass home last night.' So, it was like, 'Ding!'"

The duo wrote "Love Should'a Brought You Home" for the album with "the Songstress" herself, Anita Baker, in mind, but Baker passed on the song. When she passed, it was offered to the then unknown singer Toni Braxton, who had sung the demo. According to Songfacts.com "Babyface first met Braxton when she and her sisters auditioned for him and his producing partner L.A. Reid at their Atlanta-based label LaFace Records. The duo knew she had the chops to be a solo artist apart from her singing sisters and had her record the demo for "Love Should'a Brought You Home." The songs principal writer Daryl Simmons told Songwriters Universe, "We were trying to put this soundtrack together. So we started working on these songs for Anita Baker. But everytime we'd send a song to Anita Baker, she called back and said she didn't like it, for whatever reason. We sent her four songs, including "Give U My Heart," "Love Should'a Brought You Home" and "Another Sad Love Song." In the meantime, Toni and I were in the studio demoing these songs for Anita, with Toni putting the vocal down.

So we got Anita on the phone, and we're standing around hearing her on the speakerphone, and L.A. says, "What about this one?" And she says, "Well you know, I don't really…the beat on that one really scares me." Then she says, "What about the girl you got singing on the demo? Why don't you let her sing it?" And we all looked at each other, and L.A. says (to Anita), "Okay, thank you." (the phone clicks). He then said, "Toni, you got four songs for your album." And Toni was so ecstatic!

Babyface added, "At that particular point, it was like, 'All right, this is Toni's calling,' and that obviously became a very important song for that whole album. That's what you called a meant-to-be moment."

In 1993, speaking on her time before her successful rise from demo singer to superstar, Braxton told *The Los Angeles Times*, "I was trying to stay positive, but I wasn't sure what was going to happen—if I would ever make it."

"Love Should'a Brought You Home" was a crossover hit, and that "meant-to-be moment" launched Braxton's career, which to date has led to seven Grammys, eleven top 10 R&B hits, and 19 million records sold, including her sophomore album *Secrets*, which is one of the top 10 best-selling R&B albums of the decade.

"Love Should'a Brought You Home" was later included on Braxton's 8× platinum-selling self-titled debut album, which also featured the songs "You Mean the World to Me" (3) and "Another Sad Love Song" (2), both of which were written for Anita Baker. Babyface would later go on to write even more of Braxton's biggest hits, including "Seven Whole Days" (1) and "You're Makin' Me High" (1).

Hey Mr. D.J.

Title: Hey Mr. D.J.
Artist: Zhané
Album: Pronounced Jah-Nay
Year: 1994
Writers: Abdullah Bahr, KayGee, Zane Grey, Renée Neufville, Jean Norris, Leon Ware
Producers: Naughty By Nature, 118th Street Productions
Notable Samples: Looking Up to You, Michael Wycoff (1982)
Step to the Rear, Brand Nubian (1990)
Highest R&B Chart Position: 3
Highest Hot 100 Chart Position: 6

Zhané members Jean Norris and Renée Neufville met while both were freshman at Temple University in Philadelphia, Pennsylvania. After recognizing each other's talent, the duo sang together at local talent shows and other events, and in 1991 they got their first break when they met Philadelphia native DJ Jazzy Jeff. It was DJ Jazzy Jeff who produced their first professional recording on the song "Ring My Bell," which was a track from DJ Jazzy Jeff & the Fresh Prince's 1991 album, *Homebase,* the same album that included the perennial favorite "Summertime."

Although it was Zhané's first break, Neufville would later remark, "It was fun, but it didn't really lead to anything." However, it would be a meeting with KayGee of the rap group Naughty By Nature in 1993 that would "lead to" something. It was KayGee who brought the group, then known as Jhane (which is a combination of the group members' first names, Jean + Renée), into the studio to record their song "Hey Mr. D.J." for an Epic/Flavor Unit compilation album titled *Roll Wit Tha Flava.* The album also included tracks by Queen Latifah, D-Nice, and Naughty By Nature. But it was "Hey Mr. D.J." that would become the breakaway hit, prompting the label to release the song as a single and leading to Zhané (according to Norris, "We added a 'Z' for a little flavor, and we came up with Zhané") landing a record deal with Motown in 1994. Then Motown president Jheryl Busby said of the signing, "They're excellent songwriters and singers, and they're in the tradition of the great Motown acts."

The song was an international success, charting on several continents in addition to peaking at number 2 on the *Billboard* Dance Club Songs chart, which is appropriate as "Hey Mr. D.J." is a classic dance track. However, Zhané's music transcended the dance genre. Their debut album, *Pronounced Ja-Nay*, which contained thirteen tracks produced by Naughty By Nature, had two more hits: "Groove Thang" (2) and "Sending My Love" (5). Being larger than dance is also a point the duo made clear, As Norris stated "We're not dance-music artists . . . There's a variety of material on it—R&B, jazz, and some hip-hop . . . Also, we write our own material, we can really sing, and we're schooled in music. [Norris majored in music in college.] For us, dance music is a stepping stone to something bigger." She added, "Everybody wants to be taken seriously . . . Everybody wants respect and nobody wants to be pigeonholed or regarded as limited—certainly not with your first hit. We're well-rounded artists. Some of the dance artists are here today and gone tomorrow. That's not us."

Pronounced Jah-Nay achieved platinum status in 1996. The group also had success with the number 12 hit "Shame" recorded for the *A Low Down Dirty Shame* movie soundtrack. While Zhané's follow-up album, 1997's *Saturday Night* (which was also the group's final album of the 1990's) included the songs "Request Line," which became a hit peaking at number 9, and "Crush," which peaked at number 24, the album failed to produce any other significant hits and failed to break into the top 40 albums chart.

Knockin' da Boots

Title: Knockin' da Boots
Artist: H-Town
Album: Fever for da Flavor
Year: 1993
Writers: H-Town
Producers: Bishop Burrell, H-Town, Pierre Ushay
Notable Sample: Be Alright, Zapp (1980)
Highest R&B Chart Position: 1
Highest Hot 100 Chart Position: 3

H-Town (Keven "Dino" Conner, Solomon "Shazam" Conner, and Darryl Jackson) started out as the group The Gents while in high school in Houston, Texas. The teenage group wrote their own material, as they would continue to do for most of their career. They recorded their demo album *It's No Dream* and released it locally in 1990. The demo did little in Houston, but it made its way to Miami, Florida–based rapper Luther "Luke" Campbell of 2 Live Crew fame. At the time Campbell was known for sexually explicit lyrics and stage shows and eventually won a Supreme Court case over free speech in music. Luke signed the group to Luke Records and transformed The Gents from a traditional R&B group to the raunchier H-Town. Group member Shazam recalled that Luke "envisioned they were the going to be the R&B version of him." H-Town's debut single, "Knockin' da Boots" from their debut album *Fever for da Flavor,* showcased their transformation and their talents. The overtly sexual song, which would eventually become the number 1 song in the country for four weeks, was written and produced by H-Town, who were still in high school at the time. The album also included the modest hit "Lick U Up," which reached number 21.

Following the success of *Fever for da Flavor,* H-Town appeared on 1994's *Above the Rim* soundtrack with their single "Part Time Lover," which was produced by DeVanté Swing of Jodeci. The song peaked at number 9.

Also in 1994, the single "Emotions" released from H-Town's second album, *Beggin' After Dark*, reached number 11. By the end of 1996, however, H-Town had gone nearly three years without a top 20 hit before a cover version of the Persuaders' 1971 song "A Thin Line Between Love and Hate" from the Martin Lawrence–directed film of the same name reached number 6.

In 1999, H-Town cut ties with Luther Campbell and Luke Records and shed their sexually charged image on their third and final album with original members, *Ladies Edition, Woman's World*. The album was a respectful celebration of women and included titles like "Woman's World," "A Natural Woman," and "Ways to Treat a Woman." The more conscious album went gold despite only producing one single, "They Like It Slow." The song was H-Town's last entry on R&B charts, peaking at number 12 in 1997.

Shhh

Title: Shhh
Artist: Tevin Campbell
Album: I'm Ready
Year: 1993
Writer: Prince
Producer: Prince
Highest R&B Chart Position: Song did not chart
Highest Hot 100 Chart Position: Song did not chart

"I'd rather wait 'til everyone's fast asleep, then do it in the kitchen on the tabletop . . . Oh!" This line, which was written by Prince and sung by seventeen-year-old Tevin Campbell on "Shhh" from his 1993 album *I'm Ready,* was just one of the lines from this song that you didn't sing in front of your parents.

Campbell was discovered by Benny Medina, then the head of Black Music at Warner Bros. Records, in 1988. Medina introduced Campbell to Quincy Jones, who chose Campbell to perform the lead vocals for the song "Tomorrow (A Better You, Better Me)" on Jones's 1989 *Back on the Block* album. The song reached number 1 on the R&B chart in June 1990, and *Back on the Block* won the 1991 Grammy for Album of the Year.

From there Campbell got the opportunity to work with Prince on Prince's *Graffiti Bridge*, where he sang lead on the 1990 hit "Round and Round" (3).

In 1991, at just fifteen years old Campbell released his platinum-selling debut album *T.E.V.I.N.* with songs produced by Quincy Jones, Al B. Sure!, and Narada Michael Walden, among others. The album included the number 1 single "Tell Me What You Want Me to Do" and the song "Alone With You," which included background vocals by future superstars K-Ci & JoJo from the group Jodeci.

Campbell's ability in holding his own with K-Ci & JoJo left an impression on the future superstars. So much so that according to AL. B. Sure!, following the recording session, the duo (who are brothers) went to the payphone and called their mom in disbelief that the 15 year old Campbell could reproduce every one of their runs [A run or riff is a series of at least three notes close in pitch, sung consecutively, and very fast. Think of someone running down steps, where the person running is the voice, and each step is each note or pitch that they hit while singing downward.]

Riding a string of successes, including multiple number 1 songs and a platinum album, Campbell was already a bankable R&B star by 1993 when *I'm Ready* was released. The album became a double-platinum seller and contained three top 10 hits: the title track "I'm Ready" (5), "Always in My Heart" (3), and the Babyface-penned number 1 "Can We Talk," which Babyface was rumored to have originally written for Usher Raymond's debut. In a 2017 interview, Usher told the *Questlove Supreme* podcast, "When I first signed to LaFace Records, I wanted to do an album with Babyface and L.A. Reid, right? I signed specifically for that reason. So, L.A. Reid wanted Babyface to work on me and they were going through, you know, a lot of drama at the time. They were kinda severing their ties . . . he [Babyface] got mad.. . and he built an entire album for me, and he gave the whole album to somebody else . . . Tevin Campbell! 'Can We Talk' . . . was my song."

Babyface disagrees—he contends that the song was already given to Campbell in a deal with Quincy Jones prior to Usher coming into the picture. As Babyface told the *Questlove Supreme* podcast later that year, "L.A. had heard the record, I think, and he wanted it for Usher, but I had already given it to Tevin . . . and so the song was never really for Usher." He added, "Usher is not wrong in terms of how the song came to him [Campbell], but he don't know the full story behind it."

Despite the success of "Can We Talk," which is the most successful and most memorable song on the album, "Shhh" is perhaps the most intriguing cut. For *I'm Ready*, Campbell was looking to shed his boyish image. He told *Billboard*, "I wanted to make a more mature-sounding album to reflect my current state of mind . . . *I'm Ready* says a lot about who I am as a person because of the things I've been through during the last four years or so. I hope people will see that I'm not the same young kid that I was on my first album."

With this in mind, Campbell's friend and mentor Prince came on board and wrote four tracks for the project: "Shhh," "The Halls of Desire," "Uncle Sam," and "Paris 1798430." It would be "Shhh" that showcased Campbell's growth to the widest audience. The song is overtly sexual, and lines like "I'd rather do you after school like some homework" and "Drippin' all over like a ball of wax" would make you forget all about Campbell's carefully crafted boyish image up to that point, which included playing Ashley Bank's wholesome preteen crush on the "Just Infatuation" episode of *The Fresh Prince of Bel-Air* (1991).

Reportedly to achieve the sensual tone of the song, Campbell and Prince reached an agreement in which Campbell recorded it only if everyone was kicked out of the studio, the lights were shut off, and the curtains were drawn. The inspiration for the song was never disclosed, as Prince never spoke publicly about its conception, and the *I'm Ready* project was the last time Tevin and Prince worked together, possibly because of Prince's feelings about Campbell's label, Warner Bros.

"Shhh" was not eligible for the *Billboard* charts because it was a promotional single with no commercial release. The song reached number 45 on the *Billboard* Pop Airplay chart and number 8 on the R&B Airplay chart.

Campbell released two more albums during the 1990s, *Back to the World* (1996) and *Tevin Campbell* (1999). While both had charting singles, neither reached the success of either his debut or sophomore albums. To date, Campbell has certified sales of 5 million records in the U.S.

Can U Get Wit It

Title: Can U Get Wit It
Artist: Usher
Album: Usher
Year: 1994
Writer: DeVanté Swing
Producer: DeVanté Swing
Highest R&B Chart Position: 13
Highest Hot 100 Chart Position: 59

While Usher may or may not have missed out on a big hit with "Can We Talk," we think he made out quite well as an artist in spite of it. His career accolades include multiple number 1 songs and albums, multiple Grammys, and sales of more than 23 million albums in the U.S. alone (over 65 million albums worldwide). "Can U Get Wit It" was his first top 20 hit.

Usher became a recording artist before becoming a teenager while with the short-lived teen group Nubeginnings on their album *Nubeginnings*. The album was only released regionally.

After leaving the group due to not receiving enough exposure, Usher then performed at talent shows and was ultimately discovered by Bobby Brown's bodyguard A. J. Alexander in Atlanta. Usher recalled, "A. J. Alexander, that's the dude who discovered me, man, out of all the people who could claim and say I found him, I saw him first. That was the dude who really recognized my talent and was like, 'You, work with me.'"

With Alexander in his corner, Usher continued to compete in talent shows and auditioned in the parking lot of Atlanta's Club 112 for the likes of Keith Sweat, Jermaine Dupri, and Dallas Austin. Usher was also a contestant on the television show *Star Search* where, like others on the esteemed list of *Star Search* losers who would go on to superstardom—Aaliyah, Girl's Tyme (Destiny's Child), Justin Timberlake, etc.—his performance on the competition show got him exposure. Alexander parlayed that exposure into an audition for Usher to showcase his talent for LaFace Records president L.A. Reid, who signed him on the spot. In 1993, Usher recorded the song "Call Me a Mack" for the *Poetic Justice* soundtrack. The song only managed to peak at 56 on the R&B charts.

Barely a year later in early 1994, L.A. Reid is said to have become worried about whether Usher could be a star. Compounding things, Usher lost his voice for an extended period and Reid considered dropping him from the label. But he instead opted to ship him to New York and have Bad Boy CEO Sean Combs mentor the budding star in what Usher called "Flavor Camp." Although Usher described this as a hard time, stating to *Rolling Stone*, "I had to knuckle up, figure s**t out in New York," it did help him to become a star. He says of the time, "That became my normal . . . That culture was my normal, so naturally I progressed to be who I became." Combs ultimately convinced Reid to keep the teenage Usher. As Reid recalled, "I wanted to drop him. I wanted to be out of business with him. I broke his heart. I broke his mother's heart. It was a very tough period in both our lives. Then someone [Combs] said to me, 'Don't be a fool. Don't sell your stock in Usher. He's still going to be a star. He's everything you thought he was the day you signed him.'"

Combs would go on to produce Usher's first album, *Usher*, along with Chucky Thompson, DeVanté Swing, Al B. Sure!, and others. The album was a modest success, peaking at number 25. The highest charting single was "Think of You," which was written by Usher, Donell Jones, and Faith Evans. The song, driven by the Bad Boy machine, peaked at number 8, but it was the number 13, DeVanté Swing written and produced song "Can U Get Wit It" that became the more enduring hit.

Proving how hot Combs and Bad Boy were at the time, while most producers would kill for a top 25 album, Combs passed on producing Usher's follow-up album due in part to Usher's debut "underperforming." Usher recalled, "I'm not saying Puff was wrong. That first album wasn't my most successful, but it launched the career I've enjoyed for eighteen years since."

If Usher's first album launched his career, his sophomore effort *My Way*, which was produced in part by Manuel Seal and Jermaine Dupri, would carry the singer's career into the stratosphere. *My Way* would become a 6× platinum seller and place Usher among music's biggest superstars.

Candy Rain

Title: Candy Rain
Artist: Soul for Real
Album: Candy Rain
Year: 1994
Writers: Phife Dawg, Ali Shaheed Muhammad, Dwight Myers, Owen McIntyre, Trackmasters, Terri Robinson, Hamish Stuart
Producers: Heavy D., Trackmasters
Notable Samples: Check the Rhime, A Tribe Called Quest (1991)
   Ain't No Sunshine, Bill Withers (1971)
Highest R&B Chart Position: 1
Highest Hot 100 Chart Position: 2

Soul for Real is comprised of Trinidadian American brothers Christopher Sherman "Choc" Dalyrimple, Andre "Dre" Lamont Dalyrimple, Brian "Bri" Augustus Dalyrimple, and Jason "Jase" Oliver Dalyrimple from Wyandanch, New York.

The older members of the group were self-described "nickel-and-dime crack dealers," while doing music on the side. Desiring to get out of the drug game, the group began showing up at record labels in hopes of getting a deal.
It was while they were at Geffen Records that rapper Heavy D.'s brother's girlfriend heard them warming up and told them that they should enter the Mount Vernon Day Talent Show. She gave them an address to go to for an audition. It was there that the group met Heavy D. and his brother. After a successful audition, Heavy D. became the group's mentor and introduced them to Uptown Records CEO Andre Harrell, who signed them to a two-record deal. Heavy D.'s brother became their manager.

In 1995 the group released their debut album, *Candy Rain,* and single of the same name. The song was a crossover hit, topping the R&B chart and peaking at number 2 on the Hot 100 chart en route to going gold. The album also contained the second single, "Every Little Thing I Do," which made it to number 11, and a third single, "If You Want It," which reached number 53. The *Candy Rain* album went platinum.

"Candy Rain" was by far the standout song on the album. It and most of the other songs featured group member Jase as the lead singer, which was a departure from what the group was used to, as Christopher "Choc" Dalyrimple was also considered as a lead singer and was vocal about wanting to showcase his talent on the album. Soul for Real told *The Breakfast Club* that this caused tension between the group and Heavy D., culminating with Soul for Real being disowned by Heavy D. (whose brother was still managing the group) and blackballed by Uptown.

To make matters worse, "Candy Rain" was chiefly written by Choc but was credited to Soul for Real, Trackmasters (Poke and Tone), and Terri Robinson. According to the group, however, they received no publishing residuals.

While working on their second album, 1996's *For Life,* there was a shakeup at Uptown. Andre Harrell left to become CEO of Motown, and Heavy D. would eventually replace Harrell at Geffen. Soul for Real believes that their disagreements with Heavy D. led to them being an afterthought at the label, and their second album receiving little promotion. The group left Uptown after their second album, which was produced by Sean Combs, failed to break the top 20. They then signed with the independent label Chrome Dome Records and released their third album, *Heat.* Unfortunately, the album failed to chart.

In the 2000s, the group would release a fourth album and multiple singles, none of which charted.

Interlude
Boyz II Men vs. Jodeci

The perceived rivalry between these groups was largely fan created. Boyz II Men member Nathan Morris explained on the *Questlove Supreme* podcast, "It was not created by us, because we are all really good friends. It's yin and yang—there would be no Jodeci without Boyz II Men and vice versa . . . the audience made it more of the competition."

These two groups are forever linked as the pillars of '90s R&B but based on their upbringings their roles defy the reality. The members of Jodeci were raised in deeply religious homes with pastor fathers and gospel roots, while the members of Boyz II Men came from urban Philadelphia, Pennsylvania. However, it was Jodeci that was seen as the bad boys, creators of raunchy sexually themed songs that the urban audiences couldn't get enough of, while Boyz II Men represented the good guys, trained as singers in a prestigious performing arts school, dressed in prep attire in their videos, and curators of classic love songs that achieved crossover success with hits that dominated both the R&B and pop charts.

Morris spoke of the group's preppy image and Boyz II Men's envy of Jodeci's freedom, stating, "I used to have a problem having to do that because that wasn't me, that wasn't even close to me, so to watch them [Jodeci] get out there and have a chance to be regular ol' ni**as, I had a problem with that, I just wanted to be me and I couldn't because I had to protect the entity." Holding true to the good guy non-offensive perception, Boyz II Men laps Jodeci in crossover hits, sales numbers and awards, but to this day the culture loves Jodeci.

Boyz II Men Backstory

The group, originally known as Unique Attraction, was formed at the Philadelphia High School for the Creative and Performing Arts by Nathan Morris, Marc Nelson, George Baldi, Jon Shoats, and Marguerite Walker in 1985. Wanyá Morris joined the group in 1987. In 1988, Baldi, Shoats, and Walker graduated and left the group. The remaining members then recruited Shawn Stockman after seeing him perform a solo in the school's choir. One day, while Nate, Marc, Wanyá, and Shawn were practicing harmonies in a school bathroom, Michael McCary started singing along with them and eventually became the group's bass singer.

Unique Attraction studied New Edition and renamed themselves after the New Edition song "Boys to Men." In 1989, the group members snuck into a concert at the Philadelphia Civic Center for the Philadelphia Powerhouse music event in an effort to find Philly native Will Smith and perform for him. Local personality Charles Alston, a.k.a. "Charlie Mack", had arranged for the group to sing for Smith backstage at the venue. After the group waited outside the venue with no tickets and no way to get in, they bumped into Teddy Pendergrass' daughter, LaDonna Pendergrass, who helped them sneak backstage. They never found Smith, but did bump into Michael Bivins, Ricky Bell, and Ronnie DeVoe. (This was before the release of the BBD album.) Seizing the opportunity, the group sang New Edition's "Can You Stand the Rain." Nathan Morris recalled, "We just rocked into 'Can You Stand the Rain' and everybody was just standing around watching and by the time we finished Charlie showed up." Shawn Stockman added, "And when we finished Keith Sweat was there, Paula Abdul, Cherelle. As soon as we finished singing, Will [Smith] came in with Charlie." An impressed Bivins gave the group his number and told them to give him a call. Prior to getting signed, founding member Marc Nelson would leave the group. At the time it was reported that Nelson left to pursue a solo project. However, in a 2020 interview with *Youknowigotsoul.com* Nelson explained the reason for his departure from the group stating. "A lot of times, you'll hear people say I left the group. Clearly that wasn't the case…the biggest problem I was facing was me and the guys were signed to local management. I was signed to that management at 18 years old, I was considered an adult. The others were considered minors, 17 and under. The manager wasn't trying to let me go. That began the discrepancy of me not being able to join my guys with Boyz II Men." Although Nelson would have success and a number one single as a member of the group AZ-Yet with their 1996 hit "Last Night" from *The Nutty Professor Movie Soundtrack*, a Marc Nelson-less, Boyz II Men would sign with Michael Bivins and go on to sell millions of records and achieve R&B legend status.

End of The Road

Title: End of the Road
Artist: Boyz II Men
Album: Boomerang Movie Soundtrack
Year: 1992
Writers: Kenneth "Babyface" Edmonds, Antonio "L.A." Reid, Daryl Simmons
Producers: Kenneth "Babyface" Edmonds, Antonio "L.A." Reid, Daryl Simmons
Notable Sample: Love Don't Love Nobody, The Spinners (1974)
Highest R&B Chart Position: 1
Highest Hot 100 Chart Position: 1

"End of the Road" established Boyz II Men as a mega force in R&B and pop music. Recorded for the soundtrack to the 1993 Eddie Murphy movie *Boomerang*, it was released as a single in June 1992 and became one of Boyz II Men's biggest hits. It remained at the number 1 position on the Hot 100 for thirteen weeks and won Grammys for Best R&B Performance by a Duo or Group with Vocals and Best R&B Song.

In 1999, the song's writer, Daryl Simmons, detailed its backstory in an interview with *Songwriters Universe*, saying "We needed a song for Boyz II Men. They agreed to do the soundtrack. Kenny [Babyface] had bought a house in Buckhead [in Atlanta], just for us to work on music. So, we drive down there. I'll never forget it, it was a rainy, awful day.

Kenny's there—we knew we had to come up with this song. So he starts going through some ideas. . . . At the time, Kenny had been through a divorce, and I was going through a divorce. So here we go with this concept, thinking about [how things were at] the end of the road. That's how the concept came along. So, we know this is sad . . . we know it's just a sad story. So, we hit on it . . . Damn, I think we got something. . . . So, we work on it all day. Then L.A. comes in from the LaFace office with his suit on. He says, 'ok, you say you all got something—let me hear it.' I can still see him sitting on the couch, throwing his arms on the couch. Kenny plays it, and we sing it, and he goes, 'That's just a smash!'

"Then we jump on a plane to Philadelphia, because the next night, Boyz II Men are leaving for a tour. We arrive at the studio. I think Shawn [Stockman] comes in and says 'We've got a problem.' We ask, 'What's that?' 'Wanyá [Morris] has no voice. He's been singing so hard for this tour; he has no voice.' We say, 'ok, we'll give him a night's rest . . . we'll come back tomorrow.' Shawn says, 'No, we leave in the morning [for the tour].' So, Wanyá says, 'I can probably sing it, but I've gotta stand way back in the corner of the room and just sing it as loud as I can.' L.A. says, 'ok, stand back there.' So, Wanyá goes to the back of the room, puts a warm towel around his neck. And I tell people, when you listen to the fade of the record, when he sings 'Oh my God, help me out a little, baby'—that made the hair stand up on our arms. We felt so bad by taking him through this, but it was so much pain in what he said. I said, 'L.A., we've gotta put this on the record.' And L.A. said, 'Absolutely.' Wanyá must have sang the song twice, and then L.A. said, 'We've got enough.' We then jumped on a plane back to Atlanta, and we mixed it. That's how 'End of the Road' was created." Although the song was initially recorded for the soundtrack to *Boomerang* and was not originally featured on the *Cooleyhighharmony* album, "End of the Road" was such a smash that it was later added to a version of *Cooleyhighharmony* and reissued in 1993 as a special bonus track, which increased album sales. Nathan Morris remembered, "After *Cooleyhighharmony* was already out . . . that original album might have got to four and a half, five million records. The reissue with 'End of the Road' bumped the sales of *Cooleyhighharmony* to twelve million."

On Bended Knee

Title: On Bended Knee
Artist: Boyz II Men
Album: II
Year: 1994
Writers: Jimmy Jam, Terry Lewis
Producers: Jimmy Jam, Terry Lewis
Highest R&B Chart Position: 2
Highest Hot 100 Chart Position: 1

"On Bended Knee" was the second single from Boyz II Men's 1994 album *II*. The song, which was written and produced by mega-producers Jimmy Jam and Terry Lewis, showcased the group's massive talents.

Boyz II Men had long been admirers of Jam and Lewis. As you may recall, in their audition for BBD, they sang New Edition's 1988 single "Can You Stand the Rain," which Jam and Lewis had written and produced. As reported by *Stereogum.com*, "In 1994, Boyz II Men met Jam and Lewis at a music-industry dinner. They recounted the story of their audition, sang 'Can You Stand the Rain' once again, and told Jam and Lewis that they needed a song like that." A few weeks later, Boyz II Men, in Minneapolis for the NBA All-Star Game, dropped by Jam and Lewis's Flyte Tyme studio and played them the in-progress version of *II*, asking the duo what they thought the album needed. That's when Jam and Lewis decided on taking a nod from Boyz II Men contemporary Keith Sweat and writing the group what they called a "begging song" à la Sweat's 1987 song "I Want Her."

In a *Songfacts.com* interview, Jimmy Jam detailed how the song was made saying, "'On Bended Knee' came up because we didn't work on their first album, we got to know them on their second album. And our thought was that they sing what we'd like to call 'begging' songs really, really well. And when they played us their album and said, 'We want you guys to add something to this,' we didn't sense that there were any begging songs on there. And so that's how we came up with 'On Bended Knee.'"

Boys II Men reaped the rewards of their begging. Following the album's release, "On Bended Knee" replaced its first single, the Kenneth "Babyface" Edmonds –produced track, "I'll Make Love to You," at number 1 on the Hot 100. (It was the first time that an act had replaced itself at number 1 since the Beatles.) "On Bended Knee" would occupy the number 1 spot on the Hot 100 for six weeks but would peak at number 2 on the R&B chart.

4 Seasons of Loneliness

Title: 4 Seasons of Loneliness
Artist: Boyz II Men
Album: Evolution
Year: 1997
Writers: Jimmy Jam, Terry Lewis
Producers: Jimmy Jam, Terry Lewis
Highest R&B Chart Position: 2
Highest Hot 100 Chart Position: 1

This song is perhaps the least impressive of Boyz II Men's number 1 hits. It was also their last number 1 of the 1990s, and it would be Motown's last number 1 before being bought out by Universal.

As reported by *Stereogum.com*, "This time three years after 'On Bended Knee,' the All-Star Game was in Cleveland Ohio and Boyz II Men once again ran across Jam and Lewis. Boyz II Men were beginning the daunting task of following up their insanely successful album *II*, and they wanted to know when they could return to Minneapolis and get to work with Jam and Lewis again. Jam and Lewis had just come up with an idea for a song about a heartbreak that keeps repeating throughout the year, and they presented it to the group."

The concept of "4 Seasons of Loneliness" is simple, and it's also more than a little bit gimmicky. Here's how Jimmy Jam explained the idea in Fred Bronson's *The Billboard Book of Number 1 Hits*: "'Every time the season changed, the things that had to do with the season would remind you of this girl—like in the winter when the snow fell, or in the spring when the flowers bloomed.' The duo went back and forth on how to construct the song: Should they split the seasons up between choruses, or should they cram all four seasons into one chorus? They decided to cram."

Boyz II Men delivering their usual impressive performance, powered the song to the number 1 spot for one week in 1997.

Jodeci Backstory

Jodeci is composed of two sets of brothers: K-Ci & JoJo Hailey, and Donald "DeVanté Swing" DeGrate Jr. and Dalvin "Mr. Dalvin" DeGrate. Both sets of brothers were raised in religious families and developed their musical talents in church bands.

The DeGrate brothers began playing at their father's church in Charlotte, North Carolina, in the late 1970s. Reverend Donald DeGrate Sr. was a minor celebrity in his own right, having built a televangelist ministry as well as being a Christian recording artist. After their father scored a gospel hit with "I Wanna Be Ready," DeVanté and Mr. Dalvin began traveling around the country performing with him. By the time they were teenagers, they were already accomplished musicians and performers.

As for K-Ci & JoJo Hailey, they began singing in their family's church in Pageland, South Carolina, before relocating to Baltimore, where they began performing gospel music as Little Cedric and the Hailey Singers. The group scored a gospel hit with their song "Jesus Saves" in 1984. A year later, they released a successful album, *God's Blessing*. The family eventually moved to Monroe, North Carolina, where the Hailey brothers became acquainted with the DeGrate brothers.

The first time K-CI & JoJo met DeVanté and Dalvin was in the mid-'80s as Mr. Dalvin told writer Chris Williams of *OkayPlayer.com,* "We're all from Charlotte, North Carolina. Little Cedric and the Hailey Singers were K-Ci & JoJo's gospel group, then there was this girl gospel group called Unity, and then the Don DeGrate Delegation which DeVanté and I played in. So, we met some of the girls from Unity. Their names were Barbara Jean and Poo-Poo. These were some country girls as you can see from their names. Well, Poo-Poo was dating K-Ci before we even met. Barbara Jean would always tell us that we needed to meet K-Ci & JoJo. We heard about them before, but we hadn't met them yet. We were all between the ages of fourteen and sixteen. Barbara Jean and Poo-Poo took us to meet them. They had a little gospel studio joint, and next thing I knew K-Ci pulled a gun out on me. He thought I was messing around with Poo-Poo. I told him, 'Man, are you serious?' My brother was actually dating her sister, Barbara Jean. I told my brother these dudes are crazy and that I was leaving. I left and DeVanté stayed there with them. He would keep on telling me that they were writing songs, and he wanted me to come back to start working with them. I ended up coming back and a couple of months later we formed the group."

The switch to R&B came about via DeVanté's high school girlfriend Monica. Degrate continued: "My brother D [DeVanté] was dating this girl named Monica, and he wrote all of those songs for her. She ended up going into the Army, and she never came back. We used to do strictly gospel music back then. We never wrote any R&B songs until D wrote these songs for her. He let me hear the songs one day, and I told him they were dope." Those songs included the hits "Come & Talk to Me" and "I'm Still Waiting." Jodeci (the name comes from a mashing of the group members' names) would include both songs on their demo tape and debut album.

Jodeci caught a break when in 1989 they met and sang for singer/producer Al B. Sure! while Sure! was on tour in Charlotte, North Carolina. An impressed Al B. Sure! told the group that they should come to Uptown records in New York City. Heeding Al B. Sure's! advice, in 1989, with demo in hand, Jodeci headed to New York City seeking a record deal. They would detail this decision to go to New York and the journey to land a record deal on the track "Success" from their second album, *Diary of a Mad Band*. Jodeci made their way to Uptown Records, as Degrate recalls: "One day we drove to New York, and within that same day, we got our record deal. We went to Uptown Records. When we walked into the building, we didn't know anyone. We walked over to the receptionist, and we asked her if we could speak with an Artists and Repertoire [A&R]. She told us that if we didn't have an appointment, we couldn't speak to anyone. But after a while, she finally let us through the door. We met this guy by the name of Kurt Woodley. We were in there playing him our music and this dude fell asleep on us. So, we woke him up and he told us that we had to do better with our sound. We began singing to him live in the office and G-Whiz from Heavy D. and the Boyz knocked on the door and asked, 'Who is that singing?' He went to go get Heavy D. After Heavy D. heard us sing, he went and got Andre Harrell. We sung 'Come & Talk to Me' and "I'm Still Waiting" to him live. The next thing we knew, he was taking us out to dinner. He signed us to a deal that same day."

Forever My Lady

Title: Forever My Lady
Artist: Jodeci
Album: Forever My Lady
Year: 1991
Writers: Al B. Sure!, DeVanté Swing
Producers: Al B. Sure!, DeVanté Swing
Highest R&B Chart Position: 1
Highest Hot 100 Chart Position: 25

Forever my Lady introduced Jodeci to the world. The album was produced by Jodeci member Devante Swing and the groups mentor Al B. Sure!. It was a smash and to this day Al B. Sure! calls it his *Thriller*, referring to *Forever My Lady's* production as his masterpiece. Al B. Sure's! influence on the album is evident throughout, from the infectious groove "Stay" which Al B. Sure! describes as a slow version of his 1988 R&B number 1 (Hot 100 number 7) hit "Nite and Day", to the album's title track "Forever My Lady" which was released as the albums second single in 1991. "Forever My Lady" would be the first of five number 1 R&B hits for the group, spending two weeks at number 1 on the R&B chart and also peaking at number 25 on the Hot 100. The song was principally written by Al B. Sure! and was inspired by and dedicated to his then girlfriend Kim Porter, who was pregnant at the time with their son Quincy, hence the opening line, "So you're having my baby / and it means so much to me." Al B. Sure! was an early mentor of Jodeci and he guided them in perfecting their signature sound and style through their early days in the industry.

Cry for You

Title: Cry for You
Artist: Jodeci
Album: Diary of a Mad Band
Year: 1993
Writer: DeVanté Swing
Producer: DeVanté Swing
Highest R&B Chart Position: 1
Highest Hot 100 Chart Position: 15

An early DeVanté Swing gem, this song was the engine driving 1993's *Diary of a Mad Band* album. That year Jodeci was in a dispute with Uptown Records and threatened to leave the label for the immensely popular Death Row Records. Uptown responded by limiting promotion for the album, but that did little to hamper its success. *Diary of a Mad Band* would reach number 1 on the R&B Albums chart, where it stayed for two weeks. It spawned only one number 1 R&B hit, "Cry for You." In spite of Uptown, the album also had two number 2 hits, "Feenin'" and "What About Us." *Diary of a Mad Band* eventually went double platinum.

Love You 4 Life

Artist: Jodeci
Album: The Show, the After-Party, the Hotel
Year: 1995
Writer: DeVanté Swing
Producer: DeVanté Swing
Highest R&B Chart Position: 8
Highest Hot 100 Chart Position: 31

According to *ClassicRockHistory.com*, Jodeci was seeking a "raunchier style" for *The Show, the After-Party, the Hotel*. However, this track was not it. Instead it balances the other nastier vibes emanating from the album's tracks like "Freek'n You," "Let's Do It All," and "Pump It Back." This versatile song can fit at a wedding as well as in the bedroom." This straddling of the line between lust and love carried over into the video, which features T-Boz of TLC as the love interest/bride. T-Boz of course sang lead on the TLC smashes "Creep" (1) and "Red Light Special" (3), both anthems of females owning their sexuality.

Interlude
The Rise and Fall of Swing Mob

Al B. Sure! once described DeVanté Swing as the second coming of Teddy Riley. Swing was the creative force behind Jodeci's R&B takeover of the early1990s. As one-fourth of the quartet, he undertook more than his fair share of the work by playing a major role in writing and producing each of the group's three platinum-selling albums.

Lesser known is his role in the development of the artists, producers, and songwriters signed to his Swing Mob label. To build his label, Swing recruited talent later known as the Swing Mob Collective to work at his studio "Da Basement" in Teaneck, New Jersey, and later in Rochester, New York. It was in this collaborative environment that Swing Mob alums like Static Major, Ginuwine, Stevie J, Timbaland, and Missy Elliott perfected their craft and orchestrated the creation of game-changing hits that swung the sound of R&B in a new direction.

DeVanté and the Swing Mob's production was instrumental in Jodeci's second album, 1993's *Diary of a Mad Band*, going double platinum. However, everything shifted in July of 1993 as reported by the magazine *Da Shelter* in a 1994 article, which states, "Whatever happened that night literally changed Devanté's life forever and he clearly was never the same person. Intruders broke into Devanté's home in New Jersey and robbed him at gunpoint for $20,000 [dollars] worth of jewelry along with pistol whipping and assaulting him. Rumors even went so far as to claim he was even 'sodomized' during this attack. It's clear that something occurred during this event because it traumatized him, and his erratic behavior since the incident would show signs of that."

The robbery was cited as the point where things started to spiral downward for Swing, as he would have numerous run-ins with the law following the robbery, including his pleading guilty to gun charges later in 1993.
In an interview with *Vibe* magazine, DeVanté described his state of mind after the robbery: "They had a gun in my mouth and one to the back of my head, talkin' about 'Kill 'im.' I sleep lighter now. S**t made me want to f**k up a ni**a. I'm in trouble for guns, but you won't catch me not packing."

This change was also noted by those in Da Basement, and Swing Mob members would later describe how DeVanté would sometimes shout and intimidate the members of the collective. In a 2017 interview with *Drink Champs*, Stevie J. recounted an episode where DeVanté's behavior led him (Stevie J.) to come to blows with DeVanté's security.
One day Stevie J., Missy Elliot, Timbaland, and Ginuwine were in the studio and DeVanté walked in with his cousin and bodyguards. According to Stevie J., DeVanté "started smacking everybody. Ginuwine [smack!], Timbaland [smack!], Missy [smack!]," with DeVanté's cousin coming behind him and smacking them again while they stood there and did nothing.

Stevie J. said DeVanté knew not to try that with him, but DeVanté's cousin started to smack Stevie J., and Stevie and the cousin started arguing, and at some point DeVanté's bodyguard jumped in, which led to them all trading blows. This culminated in Stevie J. getting hit in the head with a bottle, causing a scar over his eye, which he still has today. When the fight ended, Stevie J. left the label for good, but not until after telling future stars Ginuwine, Missy Elliott, and Timbaland that they were "stupid if they stayed with the Swing Mob label."

Swing Mob officially disbanded in 1995 as members moved on to pursue record deals as songwriters, solo artists, and producers elsewhere. That year's *The Show, the After-Party, the Hotel* album would be Jodeci's last album of the 1990s, but the legacy of Swing's influence persisted with the success of Aaliyah's One in a Million (1996) and Ginuwine's The Bachelor (1996), both of which were built around beats that were developed in Da Basement.

Interlude
What About Tony! Toni! Toné!?

Tony! Toni! Toné! consisted of half-brothers D'wayne Wiggins and Raphael Saadiq and their cousin Timothy Riley. Each were musicians in their own right with Wiggins a guitar player, Saadiq a bass player, and Riley a drummer-keyboardist. In a 2019 interview with *The Breakfast Club*, Saadiq described how the group got their name from D'wayne Wiggins putting a relaxer in his hair and his teacher calling him "Tony" as a reference to the character Pretty Tony from the film *The Mack*. The name became a running joke that evolved when people would say he looked Italian and called him "Tony! Tony! Tony!" in an Italian accent. The name stuck after the group played a wedding reception and when the announcer asked them their name for the introduction and they didn't have one, they replied, "Tony! Toni! Toné!" As Saadiq put it, "Whatever that is sounded right," and the've been known as Tony! Toni! Toné! ever since. The group honed their skills in church bands and the Oakland, CA music scene and by listening to groups like Earth, Wind & Fire, the Delfonics, and the Stylistics.

Sure, the Oakland trio never had the cult following of Jodeci and lacked the crossover success of Boys II Men, but their catalog was just as popular as their contemporaries'. For example, if we take into account Tony! Toni! Toné's! debut album, 1988's *Who?*, which was produced in part by Denzil Foster and Thomas McElroy (the duo who would later develop and produce the vocal quartet En Vogue), then Tony! Toni! Toné! has just as many number 1 hits as Jodeci and Boyz II Men, with each having five. In terms of top 10 hits, Tony! Toni! Toné! leads both groups with eight, Boyz II Men and Jodeci having six and five respectively.

And then there are the other songs that maybe weren't quite chart hits but are songs we all can recite most of the lyrics to by memory to this day, like "Me and You" from the *Boyz n the Hood* soundtrack, which was all over radio in the summer of 1991, or the 1994 track "(Lay Your Head on My) Pillow" from the group's double-platinum *Sons of Soul* album. This album also included the catchy "My Ex-Girlfriend." (Notably this list does not include Raphael Saadiq's solo hit "Ask of You" from the *Higher Learning* soundtrack, which not only was a top 20 Hot 100 hit and an R&B number 2 hit, but it also inspired a generation of girls named Deja.) While admittedly Tony! Toni! Toné's sales numbers don't quite reach the level of Boyz II Men (few groups do regardless of genre), they are on par with Jodeci's, thus solidifying the group's claim to the throne of 1990s R&B royalty.

Boyz II Men	Jodeci	Tony! Toni! Toné!
Number 1 Songs		
Uhh Ahh	Forever My Lady	Blues
It's So Hard to Say Goodbye	Stay	Feels Good
End of the Road	Come and Talk to Me	It Never Rains
I'll Make Love to You	Lately	Whatever You Want
A Song for Mama	Cry for You	Little Walter
Top 10 Songs		
4 Seasons of Loneliness #2	Forever My Lady #2	Anniversary #2
On Bended Knee #2	Freakin You #3	Born Not to Know #4
Motownphilly #4	Get on Up #4	(Lay Your Head on My) Pillow #4
Water Runs Dry #4	Love U for Life #8	Baby Doll #5
In the Still of the Night #4	I'm Still Waitin #10	For the Love of You #6
Please Don't Go #8		Let's Get Down #5
		Thinking of You #5
		If I Had no Loot #8

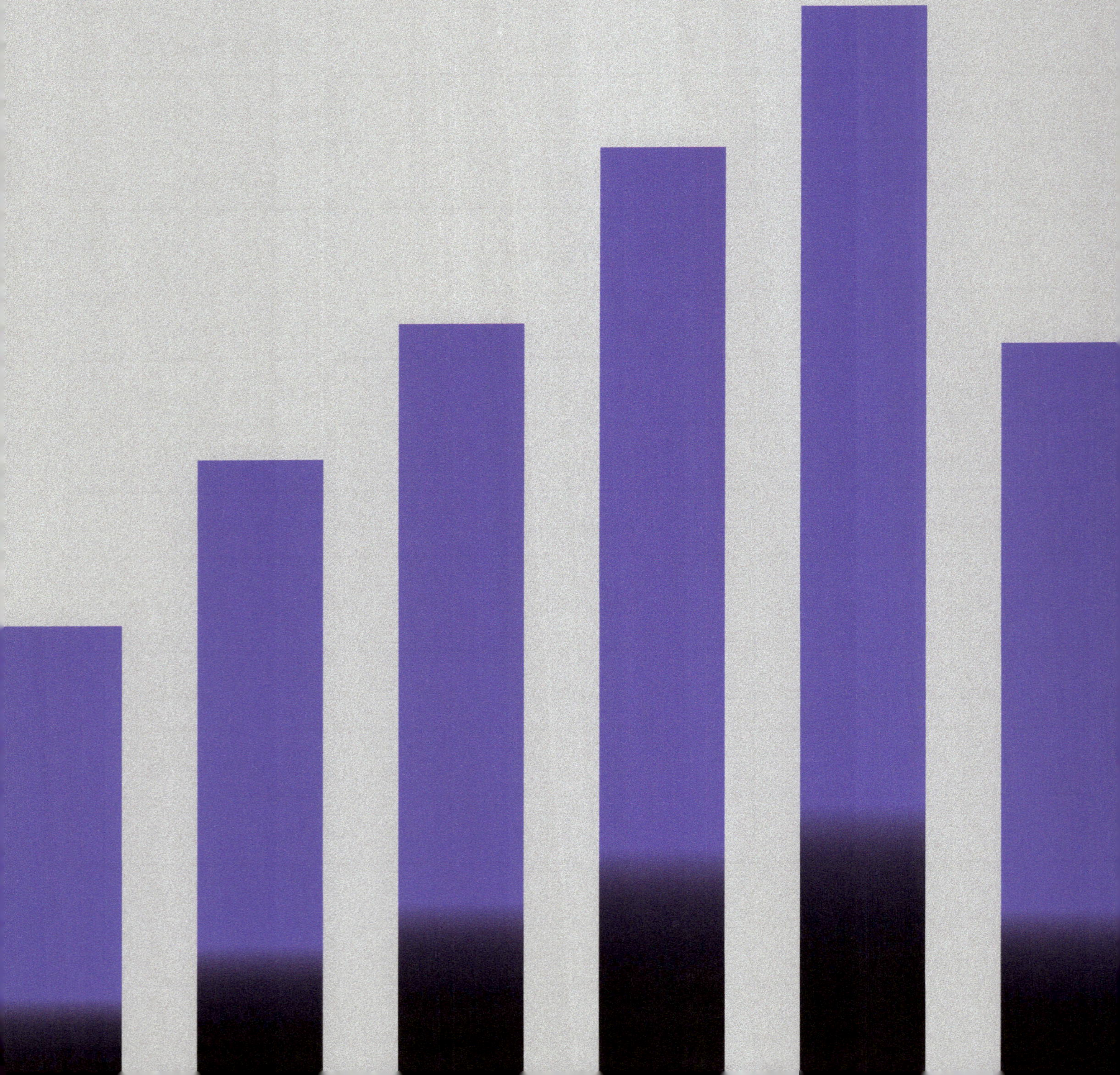

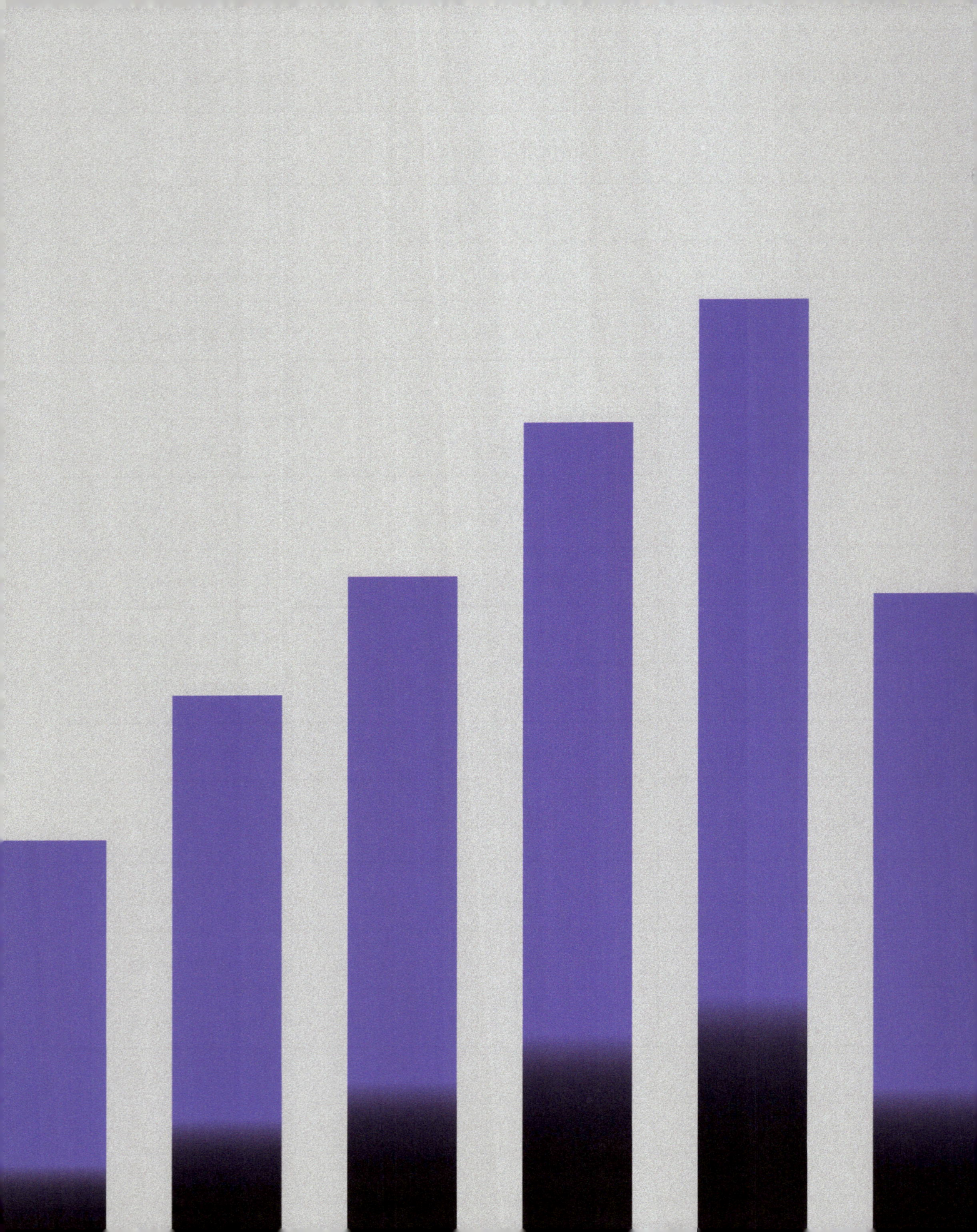

Boombastic: The Dancehall Influence
1992 - 1995

Mr. Loverman
Flex
Murder She Wrote
Dolly My Baby (Bad Boy extended remix)
Worker Man
Boombastic (Sting/Shaggy Mix)

Boombastic: The Dancehall Influence | 1992 - 1995

The '90s saw a growing appreciation for Dancehall music by R&B artists and hip-hop/R&B fans. As hip-hop was growing into an international art form, many artists saw similarities in the two musical styles, which meant that cross-pollination was inevitable. This section highlights some popular Dancehall songs that became R&B hits.

Mr. Loverman

Title: Mr. Loverman
Artist: Shabba Ranks, featuring Chevelle Franklyn
Album: X-tra Naked
Year: 1992
Writers: Mikey Bennett, Hopeton Lindo, Shabba Ranks
Producers: Mikey Bennett, Clifton Dillon
Notable Samples: Impeach the President, the Honey Drippers (1973)
Housecall, Shabba Ranks (1991)
Highest R&B Chart Position: 2
Highest Hot 100 Chart Position: 40

The Jamaican-born dancehall artist Shabba Ranks was signed to Epic Records in 1989. Within two years he would become one of the most popular reggae artists in the world. After scoring a hit with Maxi Priest on the track "Housecall" (4) in 1991, Ranks was a certified star. He would capitalize on that popularity by following up with "Mr. Loverman." According to *Songfacts.com*, "The hook and melody of Mr. Loverman are based on the 1988 song 'Champion Lover' by the British singer Deborahe Glasgow." Ranks shares the writing credit on "Mr. Loverman" with Mikey Bennett and Hopeton Lindo, the composers of "Champion Lover." Ranks' version replaced Glasgow singing the female vocals with Jamaican singer Chevelle Franklyn. This is the version that became most popular in the U.S.

The "Shabba!" vocal in "Mr. Loverman" comes from "Housecall," where Maxi Priest shouts the singer's name. This made "Shabba!" an instant catchphrase that was used in everything from adding emphasis in normal conversation to being a way to disparage someone's looks, as many considered Ranks to be unattractive. In fact a 1992 episode of the television show *In Living Color* included a parody of "Mr. Loverman" in a skit entitled "Mr. Ugly Man" which included comedian Marlon Wayans dressed like Shabba Ranks, rapping about how ugly he is to the beat of "Mr. Loverman." Shabba's dancehall style of reggae caught on in the early '90s, and his albums *As Raw As Ever* (1991) and *X-tra Naked* won the Grammy Awards for Best Reggae Album in 1992 and 1993 respectively.

Flex

Title: Flex
Artist: Mad Cobra
Album: Hard to Wet, Easy to Dry
Year: 1992
Writers: Mad Cobra, Clifton Dillon, Brian Thompson
Producer: Clifton Dillon
Highest R&B Chart Position: 8
Highest Hot 100 Chart Position: 13
Highest Hot Rap Songs Chart Position: 1

According to Mad Cobra, "'Flex' was like a trial song. It was not like a planned song." He wrote the lyrics on the back side of an airplane sickness bag while on a flight from New York to Jamaica. He recalled, "I was watching the television on the plane, and there was this woman doing this Soloflex exercise. She was on this Soloflex machine. So me say, 'How this lady flex like she want to have sex?' and me just jot it down. So me have the lyrics on the spit bag."

The success of the song took Mad Cobra and his label by surprise. "Flex" didn't initially get prime billing on Cobra's album "but instead was released on the album as a late entry. When reps from the music label, Columbia, heard the track, they were blown away. However, it was too late to be the title track on the album because the artwork was already completed." Cobra said. Otherwise, the set [album] would have been named "Flex", but, as it was, "Flex", the single, hit the streets."

Cobra continued, "Coming back to Jamaica now, I connected in New York. . . . me know the song hit, hit, really hit, and start the regular rotation on the mainstream stations."

The first time Mad Cobra performed "Flex" was in 1992 at Reggae Sunsplash, a popular Jamaican reggae music festival, where the song got three encores.

Murder She Wrote

Title: Murder She Wrote
Artist: Chaka Demus & Pliers
Album: Tease Me
Year: 1992
Writers: Chaka Demus, Sly Dunbar, Everton Bonner, Lloyd Willis
Producers: Sly and Robbie, Lloyd Willis
Notable Sample: Murder She Wrote, Pliers (1987)
Highest R&B Chart Position: 39
Highest Hot 100 Chart Position: 57

Chaka Demus & Pliers are a Jamaican reggae duo made up of DJ Chaka Demus (born John Taylor) and singer Pliers (born Everton Bonner). In the U.S. the pair are most known for their hits "Tease Me" and "Murder She Wrote." While both Chaka Demus and Pliers each found success as solo acts, as a duo they enjoyed more commercial success with mainstream pop fans after their collaboration began in the early 1990s. The partnership reached international success with a string of hit singles and a number 1 album in the U.K.. However, it was 1992's "Murder She Wrote" that caught the attention of the hip-hop and R&B communities in the U.S. Earlier that year, Chaka Demus & Pliers signed to Mango Records (a subsidiary distributed by Island Records). The following year, the pair released the album *Tease Me* (known as *All She Wrote* in the U.S.), which included the single "Murder She Wrote."

The song introduced a new song structure. Similar to rap/R&B collaborations, the juxtaposition of Demus's rugged "toasting" (lyrical chanting in the vein of rapping) and Pliers's vocals on the hook helped the song resonate with listeners. This fusion sparked a dancehall trend that paired rap-style verses with R&B-style hooks.

"Murder She Wrote" reached number 5 on the Rap Songs chart and number 39 on the R&B chart.

The song has since been sampled or interpolated over fifty times by other artists. Notable highlights include French Montana (2013's "Freaks"), Omarion (2014's "Post to Be"), Pitbull (2016's "El Taxi"), Daddy Yankee (2019's "Que Tire Pa Lante"), Jason Derulo (2019's "Too Hot"), IDK (2019's "December"), and HoodCelebrityy (2020's "Run Di Road"). The hit even caused *Murder, She Wrote* actress Angela Lansbury, who starred as Jessica Fletcher on the CBS series of the same name from 1984 to 1996, to weigh in. When Lansbury first heard the song, the actress remarked, "Oh, reggae! Oh, I'm thrilled to be part of reggae. Of course."

Dolly My Baby (Bad Boy Extended Remix)

Artist: Super Cat and Mary J. Blige (featuring 3rd Eye and the Notorious B.I.G.)
Album: Don Dada
Year: 1992
Writers: 3rd Eye, Diddy, Herbie Hancock, the Notorious B.I.G., Super Cat, Trevor Sparks
Producers: 3rd Eye, Diddy
Notable Samples: Ring a Ring O' Roses, Traditional Folk (1881)
                         Maddy Maddy Cry, Papa San (1991)
                         Papa Was Too, Joe Tex (1966)
                         Long Red, Mountain (1972)
                         Blues & Pants, James Brown (1971)
Highest R&B Chart Position: 64
Highest Hot 100 Chart Position: song did not chart

Super Cat is still considered one of the greatest DJs in the history of Jamaican dancehall. Early in his career he began appearing as a DJ under the name Cat-A-Rock but soon switched to the name Super Cat. He also appeared as Wild Apache, the name given to him by his mentor, fellow DJ and dancehall legend Early B.

Super Cat received a lot of buzz in the early to mid-'80s and had numerous dancehall hits by the end of the decade. In 1991, he moved to the United States and signed a contract with Columbia Records, releasing one of the first dancehall albums on a major label, *Don Dada* (1992). The following year, Sony Music issued the album *The Good, the Bad, the Ugly, & the Crazy*, teaming Super Cat with reggae artists Nicodemus, Junior Demus, and Junior Cat. Super Cat had a number of reggae hit singles in the early 1990s, including two that reached the R&B charts, "Ghetto Red Hot" (89) and "Dem No Worry We" (87), the latter song featured rapper Heavy D. In 1992, he was featured on the remix of the song "Jump" with Kris Kross, and he also collaborated with the group a second time in 1993 for their song "Alright" (8). These hits, and Super Cat's crossover appeal, helped him to be voted *The Source* magazine's Dancehall Artist of the Year in 1993.

The song "Dolly My Baby" was a dancehall success in its own right, but it was a then little-known record label that would carry the tune to R&B hit status.

As Super Cat explains, it was the Columbia label executives that wanted to market reggae with hip-hop, which he admits he "didn't have full insight of." He explained, "So they run through a whole lot of meeting . . . So they asked us how we feel about this. We said we don't have any problem. We see these people coming out of broken homes like some of us coming out the ghetto. They call their thing projects here, the same thing we call housing scheme in Jamaica. So, we didn't have any problem rubbing shoulder together, bringing the wheel forward and it happened there . . . They were remixing reggae with hip-hop. They said it was a marketing strategy and we were at a major label. They end up so excited about the record...so I just say 'let it roll.'"

Enter entrepreneur, record executive, rapper, and producer Sean Combs, a.k.a. Puff Daddy, and his Bad Boy record label to do, what else, but the Bad Boy remix. It would feature then equally unknown future superstars Mary J. Blige, The Notorious B.I.G., and rapper-producer Jesse Williams, a.k.a. 3rd Eye.

Although we may not have thought much of it at the time, the song would give us a preview of the next thirty years of what the label would offer with Mary J. Blige singing throughout, Puff Daddy's tight production, and one of the greatest rappers providing one of the most popular lines in rap history as his introduction. The "I love it when you call me big poppa" line that the Notorious B.I.G. uses to open his verse was the first time many of us ever heard his voice. B.I.G., who is of Jamaican descent, also played homage to dancehall at the end of his verse with the line, "Yes, it's Bad Boy, hard to the core / Lawwwwwddddd! Me cyan tek it no more," referencing Papa San's line from the hook of "Maddy Maddy Cry," one of the most "entertaining" songs in reggae and dancehall history.

Despite all this talent, the remix was all but buried by Columbia. It was the fourth of six remixes, and it was placed on the B side of "Dolly My Baby." However, the force of Bad Boy was undeniable. DJs discovered the track and gave it major airplay. A video followed, and it was put into heavy rotation by *BET*. The result, as Super Cat put it, "was one of the biggest song that they ever see to the fullest time with reggae and across hip-hop.

Worker Man

Title: Worker Man
Artist: Patra
Album: Queen of the Pack
Year: 1994
Writers: Patra, Tony Kelly
Producers: Clifton Dillon, Tony Kelly, Vivian Scott
Highest R&B Chart Position: 20
Highest Hot 100 Chart Position: 53

Patra was born Dorothy Smith in Kingston, Jamaica, and raised in Westmoreland Parish. In a 1994 essay, she described herself as "a country girl," saying, "I grew up in the church, which instilled morals and values in me." She began singing in her church choir and later tried her hand at deejaying. At age fifteen, she began to realize that music really could be her life. She would later say, "I always enjoyed music, but up until then I didn't really think about my goals." Patra explains, "In addition to many Jamaican artists, I listened to Tina Turner, Patti LaBelle, Sade, Alexander O'Neal, and Michael Jackson, of course—he really taught me how to dance!" (Although we doubt she learned her signature dance the Butterfly from watching MJ.)

In her beginnings as a female dancehall DJ in the late 1980s, Patra used the stage name Lady Patra. She soon entered neighborhood singing/deejaying competitions while in high school, where early supporters encouraged her to try recording in the studios. Following successful recording sessions with producer Gussie Clarke, Patra was in high demand as a singer. By the time her deal with the Epic record label was struck, her singing voice had taken precedence over her deejaying skills.

In 1993, Patra released her debut album, *Queen of the Pack*. It was led by the single "Think (About It)," which peaked at number 21 on the Rap Singles chart and number 89 on the R&B chart. But it was her follow-up single "Worker Man" that became a bigger hit, reaching number 53 on the Hot 100, the top 20 on the R&B chart, and number 1 on the U.S. Dance chart.

By July 1994, Patra's *Queen of the Pack* had spent thirteen consecutive weeks at number 1 on the Top Reggae Albums chart—the longest run at number 1 in the history of the chart. The following December, the album was certified gold. In addition to her own album, Patra embarked on successful collaborations with the acts C+C Music Factory and rapper Guru as well as joining in the all-female superstar recording of "Freedom" for the soundtrack of Melvin Van Peebles 1995 film *Panther*.

Eventually, the Butterfly gave way to the Tootsie Roll, and Patra took some time away from the music industry. During this hiatus she became more spiritually connected to God and earned degrees in history and political science.

Boombastic (Sting/Shaggy Mix)

Artist: Shaggy
Album: Boombastic
Year: 1995
Writers: King Floyd, Robert Livingston, Shaggy
Producers: Robert Livingston, Sting International
Notable Sample: Let's Get It On, Marvin Gaye (1973)
Highest R&B Chart Position: 1
Highest Hot 100 Chart Position: 3

In 2020, Jamaican-born Orville Richard Burrell, a.k.a. Shaggy, told the *Daily Mail Australia* how he got his stage name saying "I got the name Shaggy in high school. My hair was all over the place, and so they called me Shaggy, like a shaggy dog. I didn't like it." He continued, "Then I went to England. I was in a cab, and the guy driving the taxi said, 'Oh my God—I can't believe they're playing a song from a bloke with a name Shaggy!' I was like, 'What's wrong with Shaggy?' Then he explained what 'shag' meant. In England, the term 'shag' is colloquially used to describe sexual relations. I thought it was the coolest name after that!"

While he thought the name Shaggy was cool, he has also taken on other names such as Mr. Lover, a clear homage to Shabba Ranks' "Mr. Loverman," Mr. Boombastic after his smash 1995 song and Private Burrell from his time in the U.S. Marine Corps which is where Shaggy got his start making hits. During his stint with the U.S. Marine Corps Shaggy recorded his first major song "Oh Carolina," while literally wearing his Marine uniform. While stationed in North Carolina he would routinely drive to New York, City in his uniform (He says the uniform helped him to avoid speeding tickets from military friendly State Troopers) then speed back to North Carolina to resume duty. On these frequent New York excursions Shaggy would hook up with Brooklyn DJ, Sting International to record.

The success of "Oh Carolina" is evidence that this arrangement worked. The song was an international hit reaching number 3 in the U.K.. However major success in the U.S. eluded Shaggy for the next two years. Even the original version of "Boombastic" which was a smash in several other countries, was just a modest hit in the U.S. until Shaggy and Sting International created the "Boombastic, Sting/Shaggy Mix" which combined reggae elements with popular American music, i.e., the sample of Marvin Gaye's 1973 number 1 "Let's Get It On" as part of the hook. The 'Boombastic,' Sting/Shaggy Mix proved that big payoffs were possible for musicians who blend the Caribbean sound with an R&B groove.

The *Boombastic* album, which reached platinum status in the U.S. and sold more than 1 million copies overseas, won the 1996 Grammy for Best Reggae Album. The Sting/Shaggy Mix of its title track was a big hit on R&B and Pop radio, topping *Billboard* magazine's reggae, R&B, and rap charts. It also hit number 3 on the Hot 100 chart. Shaggy would have further success with this formula on the songs "Angel" (2000)—a pop hit number 1 hit, which features samples from Evie Sands' "Angel of the Morning" and "The Joker" by the Steve Miller Band—and with his 2000 international smash, R&B number 3 "It Wasn't Me," which sampled the War track "Smile Happy."

Unforgettable: They Still Got It

The Secret Garden (Sweet Seduction Suite)
If I Were a Bell
Unforgettable
Remember the Time
Do It to Me
No Ordinary Love
Somebody Love You Baby (You Know Who It Is)
Believe in Love
Practice What You Preach
Body and Soul
Eye Hate U
A Rose Is Still A Rose

Unforgettable: They Still Got It

The 1990s would see legendary acts like Maze featuring Frankie Beverly and Earth, Wind & Fire making their final appearance in the top 20 with new material. Both groups had hits in 1993, Maze with "The Morning After" (19) and Earth, Wind & Fire with "Sunday Morning" (20). However, as R&B was going through its natural evolution and musical Darwinism was driving some once standard acts into extinction, Maze and Earth, Wind & Fire would not be the only ones that adapted and produced memorable new material that showcased their mastery of the genre. Some of the other acts are profiled here.

The Secret Garden (Sweet Seduction Suite)

Artist: El DeBarge, James Ingram, Quincy Jones, Al B. Sure!, Barry White
Album: Back on the Block
Year: 1990
Writers: El DeBarge, Siedah Garrett, Quincy Jones, Rod Temperton
Producer: Quincy Jones
Highest R&B Chart Position: 1
Highest Hot 100 Chart Position: 31

Quincy Jones's *Back on the Block* album was another in a long line of successes for Jones, who by 1990 was already a music legend.

That year the album, (Which was released near the end of 1989) achieved platinum sales, was the number 1 R&B and jazz album in the country and won the 1991 Grammy for Album of the Year. Its songs perfectly balanced hip-hop, blues, jazz, and R&B tracks from the biggest names in music (George Duke, Ray Charles, Big Daddy Kane, Miles Davis, etc.).

"The Secret Garden" was no exception. The song—which was written by Jones and fellow legends El DeBarge, Siedah Garrett, and Rod Temperton and was performed by superstars El DeBarge, James Ingram, Al B. Sure!, and Barry White—became one of the highest charting tracks on the album.

According to El DeBarge, when he went to the studio to work on the song, the music was already written just enough to write words and a melody. Jones, DeBarge, and Garrett pulled several all-nighters to come up with the lyrics. DeBarge recalled when the lyrics were complete and he tried to leave to go to sleep, Jones, who was on a deadline objected and wanted him to go to the studio to record. DeBarge, worried about how he would sound after pulling back to back all-nighters, reluctantly went into the booth to warm up. He sang the newly written lyrics, then returned to the control room and to his surprise Jones sent him home. DeBarge though Jones sent him home because his recording sounded horrible. It was some time later that DeBarge discovered that Jones had used his warm-up on the final version of the song. DeBarge remembered, "I had anxiety for months until the track was released."

Jones apparently knew a thing or two about music and production, as the blending of Al B. Sure!, DeBarge, White, and Ingram's vocals created a masterpiece and breathed new life into the careers of the latter three artists, each of whom had previous number 1 songs in their careers but none within the five years prior to the release of "The Secret Garden." White's last R&B number 1 came in 1977 with "It's Ecstasy When You Lay Down Next to Me." DeBarge's last number 1 before "The Secret Garden" was the Hot 100 number 1, 1986's "Who's Johnny" from the *Short Circuit* movie soundtrack, and Ingram's last number 1 prior to "The Secret Garden" was his 1982, Hot 100 number 1 duet with singer Patti Austin on the song "Baby Come to Me."

As for Al B. Sure!, he was peaking in the late 1980's and early 1990's, with two R&B number 1's in 1988 ("Nite and Day" and "Off on Your Own (Girl)") and one in 1990 with "Misunderstanding." But according to Sure!, he was brought on to record the song as a backup after Jones's friend and longtime collaborator Michael Jackson had to drop out because of scheduling conflicts. Jones had produced each of Jackson's smash solo albums to that point (*Off the Wall* in 1979, *Thriller* in 1982, and *Bad* in 1987), and "The Secret Garden" co-writers Siedah Garrett and Rod Temperton each also had relationships with Jackson. Garrett co-wrote Jackson's number 1 song "Man In the Mirror" (1987) and sang opposite Jackson on his number 1 "I Just Can't Stop Loving You" (1987), and Temperton co-wrote the Jackson hits "Rock With You" (1) and "Thriller" (3), among others.

In 2018, Al B. Sure! told *HipHollywood.com*, "For a very long time people thought the very first verse was Michael Jackson and that's only because I Michaeled out. . . . It was really an appreciation because he was actually supposed to be a part of the song . . . We are very happy with the result, but it went through a metamorphosis. . . . There were a number of artists that were considered for the song, and I just think it was a complete blessing that I was, so I wanted to bridge the gap by almost doing a tribute to Michael." It should also be noted that Luther Vandross was also considered as a replacement for Jackson, but Ingram, White, DeBarge, and Al B. Sure! (channeling Michael Jackson) proved to be the perfect recipe for the chart-topping song.

Perhaps the writer Butta of *SoulBounce.com* summed the song up best: "Each singer brought their own unique sound to the track and made it work. Not only did they sound good together, but the song itself was a grown and sexy affair before we started referring to things as 'grown and sexy.' 'The Secret Garden' bridged the gap between musical generations and featured something for everyone. Al B Sure! and El appealed to the younger set while James and Barry held it down for the more mature folks. Under Quincy's watchful eye and thanks to his golden ear, these artists were brought together to create one of the most passionate songs to ever hit the Quiet Storm."

If I Were a Bell

Artist: Teena Marie
Album: Ivory
Year: 1990
Writer: Teena Marie
Producer: Teena Marie
Highest R&B Chart Position: 8
Highest Hot 100 Chart Position: song did not chart

Born Mary Christine Brockert, Teena Marie (a.k.a. Lady T, a.k.a. Shorty, a.k.a. Little Bit, a.k.a. Vanilla Child) was the R&B version of Eminem, gaining respect and acceptance for her abilities in a genre dominated by African American artists and producers. This fact was echoed by Writer Ta-Nehisi Coates in his essay "The Indomitable Blackness of Teena Marie," written for *The Atlantic* where he writes, "I'm sure some of the old-heads here can come up with a corollary, but I'm having trouble thinking of a white artist whose relationship to black music mirrored Teena Marie's. More specifically, I can't think of a white artist who was more beloved by such a large swath of black people than Teena Marie." But her whiteness was just one thing that set her apart in the genre, as she was a pioneer for more than just her skin color. During her career she was one of the first artists, black or white, to incorporate a rap verse into an R&B song as she did on 1981's "Square Biz" (3). And her countersuit of Motown resulted in a law known as the "Brockert Initiative," which made it illegal for a record company to keep an artist under contract without releasing new material for that artist. This action would enable artists such as Luther Vandross and the Mary Jane Girls to sign and release music with different labels instead of being held hostage by uncooperative labels. Lastly, Teena Marie is the only R&B artist to appear on the television show *The Beverly Hillbillies*, as she did at the age of eight in a 1964 episode.

In 1976, Motown head Berry Gordy signed Teena Marie as a solo act. It was there that she was noticed by label-mate Rick James, who would produce her first album, *Wild and Peaceful* (1979). The album included the hit "I'm a Sucker for Your Love" (8). In a crafty move by Motown not to prejudice fans or radio stations, neither the album nor its packaging had Teena Marie's picture on it. Many believed she was black until she performed the song with James on Soul Train in 1979.

Marie's second and third albums, *Lady T* and *Irons in the Fire*, were both released in 1980 and she handled most of the writing and production for both projects. The single "I Need Your Lovin'" from *Irons in the Fire* brought Marie her first top 40 hit (9). It was also the year that she appeared on James's album *Street Songs*, with the classic duet "Fire and Desire." The song would surely have charted and would have likely given Marie her first number 1 hit, but Motown did not release it as a commercially available single (a chart requirement at the time), so it never made any of *Billboard*'s singles charts.

Teena Marie continued her success with Motown in 1981 with the release of *It Must Be Magic*, which became her first gold record and included the hits "Square Biz" (3), "It Must be Magic" (30), and "Portuguese Love" (54).

In 1982 Marie would leave Motown and sign with Epic, where she established her own publishing company, Midnight Magnet, and released the album *Robbery*, which featured the songs "Fix It," a number 21 R&B hit, and "Casanova Brown," which was said to be written about Marie's romance with Rick James.

In 1984, Marie continued her success with the release of the album *Starchild*, which included her hit "Lovergirl" (9) and the R&B classic "Out on a Limb" (56). In 1986, she experimented with a rock-influenced concept album *Emerald City* before returning to her R&B roots with 1988's *Naked to the World*, which included the R&B number 1 hit "Ooo La La La."

Marie's next album, *Ivory*, was released in the fall of 1990. The album produced two R&B hits, "Here's Looking at You" (11) and "If I Were a Bell" (8).

Marie wrote, produced, and arranged all the songs for the thirteen-track album. Additionally, she played and/or programmed many of the instruments. The result on "If I Were a Bell" was timeless. As explained by *SoulBounce.com*, "This song is a beauty in a class of its own. In the poetic form you came to expect with Teena's lyrics, the song is not only a romantic masterpiece, but is executed in breathtaking brilliance. It was incredible how she managed to deftly dip from very high and back again with not so much than a quick breath in between." Marie doubled down and performed the song live flawlessly on BET's *Video Soul* in 1991 with only a piano accompanying her, cementing herself and the song as true classics.

"If I Were a Bell" would be Marie's last top 10 song. She would later sign with Cash Money Records in 2002 and reach number 23 with the Mannie Fresh–produced track "Still in Love" in 2004.

Unforgettable

Artist: Natalie Cole
Album: Unforgettable . . . with Love
Year: 1991
Writer: Irving Gordon
Producer: David Foster
Notable Sample: Unforgettable, Nat King Cole (1951)
Highest R&B Chart Position: 10
Highest Hot 100 Chart Position: 14

The original song "Unforgettable" was written by Irving Gordon in 1951, a year later, Natalie Cole's father, legendary singer Nat King Cole, recorded it for his 1952 album *Unforgettable*. Nat King Cole was the biggest seller for Capitol Records in the early 1950s, and Natalie would become a star in her own right nearly two decades later. She got her start performing as a child, most notably when she appeared with her father on his 1960 Christmas album *The Magic of Christmas*. Nat King Cole passed away in 1965.

By the mid-1970s, Natalie Cole began a meteoric rise to stardom, amassing a string of number 1 songs, platinum albums, and Grammy Awards. It started in 1975 with her first album, *Inseparable,* which included the number 1's "This Will Be (An Everlasting Love)" and the title track "Inseparable." Cole won the Grammy Award that year for Best New Artist, and "This Will Be" won the Grammy for Best Female R&B Vocal Performance.

After her second album, 1976's *Natalie*, produced another number 1 in "Sophisticated Lady (She's a Different Lady)," which won her a second Grammy for Best Female R&B Vocal Performance, Cole released her third album, 1977's *Unpredictable,* which became her first platinum seller on the strength of the number 1 R&B hit "I've Got Love on My Mind." The song won her a third Grammy for Best Female R&B Vocal Performance in as many years.

Also in 1977, Cole's fourth album, *Thankful*—which included another signature hit, "Our Love" (1)—resulted in her second platinum album in a year. And, you guessed it, the song also won Cole a Grammy for Best Female R&B Vocal Performance.

Cole's final album releases of the 1970s, *I Love You So* (1979) and *We're the Best of Friends* (1979), would both go gold. Between 1980 and 1985, Cole would release four underperforming albums. At the time it was revealed that she had been battling drug addiction on and off for several years.

Toward the end of the 1980s, Cole had begun her climb to sobriety and return to musical relevancy. In 1987 she released the album *Everlasting*, which included the number 2 song "Jump Start (My Heart)" and the number 4 ballad "I Live for Your Love." In 1989, she released the album *Good to Be Back*, which produced the number 7 hit "Miss You Like Crazy." Both albums won Grammys for Best Female R&B Vocal Performance. In 1991 Cole achieved her biggest success with the immensely successful album *Unforgettable . . . with Love* and the massive hit song "Unforgettable", which she recorded with her father in an innovative virtual duet.

Natalie Cole's version was a gigantic hit that cemented her comeback. The album sold more than 7 million copies in the U.S. and earned her three more Grammy Awards at the 1992 ceremony, including the Grammies for Song and Record of the Year.

The award for Song of the Year is remarkable, as "Unoforgettable's" writer, Irving Gordon, who had also written material performed by Billie Holiday and Bing Crosby, won the award forty years after having first published the song. Nat King Cole's original recording was inducted into the Grammy Hall of Fame in 2000.

Cole would release ten more studio albums after *Unforgettable . . . with Love*, but none would break the R&B top 40.

Remember the Time

Artist: Michael Jackson
Album: Dangerous
Year: 1992
Writers: Bernard Belle, Michael Jackson, Teddy Riley
Producers: Michael Jackson, Teddy Riley
Highest R&B Chart Position: 1
Highest Hot 100 Chart Position: 3

"Remember the Time" was released as the second single from Michael Jackson's eighth studio album, *Dangerous*, in 1992. Jackson was already a legend at this point and had created two of the top-selling albums of all time, *Thriller* (70 million) and *Bad* (35 million). *Dangerous* was another great success for Jackson, as it would go on to sell 32 million copies worldwide.

Teddy Riley always admired and wanted to work with Michael Jackson. Jackson reached out to him when Riley was still a member of the R&B group Guy, which is where Riley perfected his trademark new jack sound that was taking over the industry in the early '90s. Jackson wanted in on the new jack revolution and propositioned Riley to come to California to produce Jackson's next album, and Riley agreed. This all came at a time when internal conflicts were causing Guy to disintegrate, even though they still had sold-out shows with fans and promoters clamoring for more show dates. Riley would decline the additional shows and could not give a reason due to having signed a nondisclosure agreement with Jackson. This added even more turmoil to Guy's separation, and the group officially broke up in 1991. Riley then moved to Jackson's home at Neverland Ranch in California and immersed himself in Jackson's artistry. While there, he played hide-and-seek with Jackson, visited his zoo, and did other innocuous activities with the star that did not involve making music, which prompted him to ask Jackson, "When we gonna get to the music?" Riley recounted it was then that he realized that "he [Jackson] was learning me, as he wanted me to learn him." He recalled, "If you don't know what the artist likes outside of music, you won't really know the artist." Jackson built Riley a studio at Neverland Ranch, and the team eventually got to work on Dangerous.

The time spent getting to know one another was worth it. Riley told *MusicRadar* that "[Jackson] really blew me away. . . . I came to the project with this track. That was the sound I was thinking of for this album. Basically, it was the sound I wanted on *Dangerous* and he loved it—loved it from the beginning." And over Riley's production, Michael did Michael on "Remember the Time," including riffs and ad-libs that only he could get away with. The single became another in a long line of platinum sellers for Jackson.

Although the song would remain a popular track for generations thanks to being widely sampled and interpolated well into the 2010s, there is some mystery behind its inspiration. Upon its release, Jackson dedicated the song "To Diana Ross with Love," but in a 1996 interview, Riley told *The Los Angeles Times* that the song was inspired by Jackson's description of falling in love with Debbie Rowe, whom Jackson would later marry (1996–1999) and who would go on to bear two of his three children: Michael Joseph Jackson Jr. and Paris Katherine Jackson. (Jackson's third child, Prince Michael Jackson II, was carried and birthed by an unnamed surrogate.) In the years since, Riley has said the song was inspired by his friend, actress Sally Richardson.

Other than being known as Jackson's first new jack hit, the song is also remembered for the nine-minute ancient Egyptian–themed video/short film that was directed by *Boyz n the Hood* director John Singleton. Singleton told *Rolling*

Stone magazine, "When I first met him [Michael Jackson] . . . he asked me, 'What songs do you like?' and if I wanted to do a video. And I said, 'ok, well, can we put black people in the video?' [Laughs] I was challenging him. And he said, 'Whatever you want.' He was cool with me because I was straightforward with him, and I felt that everybody was always goose-stepping around him and never telling him the real deal." True to his word, the video featured a host of A-list black personalities, including actor-comedian Eddie Murphy, supermodel Iman, and basketball legend Magic Johnson. The "Remember the Time" video has over 500 million views on YouTube alone.

Do It to Me

Artist: Lionel Richie
Album: Back to Front
Year: 1992
Writer: Lionel Richie
Producers: Stewart Levine, Lionel Richie
Notable Sample: Sneakin' in the Back, Tom Scott and the L.A. Express (1974)
Highest R&B Chart Position: 1
Highest Hot 100 Chart Position: 21

Throughout his career as a solo artist, Lionel Richie has had five R&B number 1 singles and thirteen R&B top 10 singles. If we include his career with the Commodores, those accomplishments jump to six number 1 singles and nineteen top 10 songs. These stats don't include the 1984 song "We Are the World," which Richie wrote with Michael Jackson. That song raised $149 million for famine relief with star power like Richie and Jackson performing alongside legends Stevie Wonder, Kenny Rogers, Tina Turner, Paul Simon, and just about every other star artist at the time. "We Are the World" is still the eighth best-selling single of all time.

If that wasn't enough, the singer had six top 10 R&B albums, including two number 1 albums. *Can't Slow Down* (1984) was one of those albums. It won the Album of the Year Grammy that year (a year after Michael Jackson's *Thriller* took home the award), and it beat out some of the top-selling albums of the decade, including Bruce Springsteen's *Born in the U.S.A.*, Tina Turner's *Private Dancer*, Cyndi Lauper's *She's So Unusual*, and Prince's *Purple Rain*.

Surprisingly, by 1990 Richie hadn't had a top 10 hit album or song since his *Dancing on the Ceiling* album dominated the charts in 1986. *Dancing on the Ceiling* was a number 1 pop and number 3 R&B album that year. It included four top 10 R&B hits, including the number 1 crossover hit "Say You, Say Me," which topped the pop charts for four weeks.

Richie's first release of the 1990s was the 1992 compilation album *Back to Front*, which included songs from both his successful solo career and as part of the Commodores along with three new tracks: "Love, Oh Love,"(Did not chart) "My Destiny" (56), and "Do It to Me." Music critic and writer Simon Sweetman commented that "*Back to Front* captures Richie's 1980s (and some late 1970s) achievements and it freezes them." "Do It to Me" was the album's breakaway hit. It signaled to the music world that Richie was still a hitmaker and gained him a new generation of fans that missed his heyday.

In the years since, Richie has released new material but has mainly focused on his highly successful international tours and stints on television, including the popular competition show American Idol.

No Ordinary Love

Artist: Sade
Album: Love Deluxe
Year: 1992
Writers: Sade Adu, Stuart Matthewman
Producers: Sade, Mike Pela
Highest R&B Chart Position: 9
Highest Hot 100 Chart Position: 28

The English band Sade, which takes its name from its Nigerian-born lead singer, Helen Folasade "Sade" Adu, is comprised of members Adu, Stuart Matthewman, Paul Denman, Andrew Hale, Dave Early, and Paul Cooke. The band formed in 1982 as an offshoot of the English band Pride when Adu and the others left that band to form Sade.

In 1982, Sade was signed to Epic Records, where they released their debut album, *Diamond Life*. It became one of the best-selling albums in 1985 on the strength of the now classic songs "Smooth Operator," "Hang On to Your Love," and "Your Love Is King." Each song became a top 40 R&B hit, reaching numbers 5, 14, and 35 respectively. The album also garnered Sade the 1985 Grammy Award for Best New Artist.

The *Diamond Life* album—which contained elements of jazz, soul, and R&B—along with the band's subsequent releases are credited as forerunners of the neo-soul movement, which became popular in the mid-1990s.
Sade's second album, *Stronger Than Pride* (1988), included the song "Paradise," which became an R&B number 1, and the number 3 hit "Nothing Can Come Between Us."

Stronger Than Pride was Sade's last release until 1992's *Love Deluxe*. *Love Deluxe* included the runaway hit song "No Ordinary Love," which was released as the album's lead single. "No Ordinary Love," which had Sade's classic R&B/jazzy sound, announced the band's triumphant return to hitmaking after a four-year hiatus from the studio. The song became their first top 10 R&B hit since 1985's "The Sweetest Taboo," reaching this achievement in spite of new jack songs dominating the charts in 1992. "No Ordinary Love" would earn Sade its second Grammy win, this time for Best R&B Performance by a Duo or Group. The song would also make *Rolling Stone* magazine's list of 500 best songs of all time in 2021.

Carried by "No Ordinary Love," the album's other singles, "Cherish the Day" (45) and "Kiss of Life" (10), moved *Love Deluxe* to 4× platinum sales. Following an eight-year hiatus, Sade released their fifth studio album, *Lovers Rock*, in 2000. The album, which included the number 41 single "By Your Side," has since been certified triple platinum. Ten years later the band released its final album, *Soldier of Love*, which peaked at number 6.

Somebody Loves You Baby (You Know Who It Is)

Artist: Patti LaBelle
Album: Burnin'
Year: 1992
Writers: Eugene Curry, Bunny Sigler
Producers: Eugene Curry, Bunny Sigler
Highest R&B Chart Position: 2
Highest 100 Chart Position: Song did not chart

"Somebody Loves You Baby (You Know Who It Is)" was the product of a collaboration between two Philadelphia legends, singer Patti LaBelle and writer-producer Bunny Sigler. By the start of the decade, Patti LaBelle, born Patricia Louise Holte, already had three decades in the industry and had done it all, from glam rock to funk to Broadway to gospel [she would add Super Bowl halftime show performer at Super Bowl XXIX in 1995]. Patti Labelle had her first hits with the girl group the Bluebelles in the early 1960s with the song "I Sold My Heart to the Junk Man" (13) and the ballad "Down the Aisle" (14). The songs were released in 1962 and 1963 respectively.

This was the first of a handful of chart successes in the 1960s by the Bluebelles, which consisted of LaBelle, Cindy Birdsong, Nona Hendryx, and Sarah Dash.

In 1965, after their record label folded, the group signed with Atlantic Records. In 1967, Cindy Birdsong left to join the Supremes, and by 1970 the group was dropped from Atlantic.

The group then signed with Warner Bros. Records. It was there that they adopted a new name, simply LaBelle, a new persona and released their self-titled debut album in 1971. The record contained a mix of psychedelic soul, glam rock, funk, soul, and gospel rhythms, which was a far cry from their earlier sound.

LaBelle would go on to record their most acclaimed album to that point, *Moon Shadow* (1972). Their follow-up, *Pressure Cookin'* (1973), failed to generate a hit.

In 1974, LaBelle signed with Epic Records, where they released the *Nightbirds* album, which kept their psychedelic soul, funk, glam, and rock sound. This album included the smash "Lady Marmalade" (1). The song has since been inducted into the Grammy Hall of Fame. LaBelle released two more albums, *Phoenix* and *Chameleon*, in 1975 and 1976 respectively. However, although the albums produced R&B favorites "Isn't It a Shame" (18) and "What Can I Do For You" (8), none of the singles issued on those albums ever crossed over to the pop charts.

By 1976 it was reported that Patti LaBelle wanted the group to record more soul, while member Nona Hendryx wanted them to go further into funk rock, and third member Sarah Dash wanted to record songs in a more disco direction. The group would separate later that year. Patti LaBelle would sign a solo contract with Epic Records in 1977, where she recorded four albums starting with her critically acclaimed debut album, *Patti LaBelle*, which included the song "You Are My Friend" (61). It was during this time that Patti did a stint on Broadway starring in the musical *Your Arms Too Short to Box with God*.

In 1984, Patti LaBelle, now with the Philadelphia International Records label, worked with Bunny Sigler on her breakthrough solo album, *I'm in Love Again*, which included her first solo top 10 R&B single, "Love, Need and Want You" (10), written and produced by Sigler, and her first number 1 single as a solo artist, "If Only You Knew."

The year 1984 would turn out to be a big one for Patti as she recorded the songs "New Attitude" (3) and "Stir It Up" (5) for the soundtrack to the Eddie Murphy film *Beverly Hills Cop*. In 1986, her duet with Michael McDonald, "On My Own," became an R&B number 1.

She returned to the R&B top 10 with her 1989 *Be Yourself* album and its singles "If You Ask Me To" (10) and "Yo Mister" (6).

Entering the 1990s, Patti LaBelle cemented her status as an R&B diva with 1992's *Burnin'*, which included three top 10 singles: "When You've Been Blessed" (4), "Feels Like Another One" (3), and "Somebody Loves You Baby (You Know Who It Is)." With its heavy gospel rhythm, "Somebody Loves You Baby" was an instant success, reaching number 2 on the R&B chart.

This success led to Patti winning her first Grammy Award in the Best Female R&B Vocal Performance category in 1992.....sort of. In a rare Grammy tie Labelle had to share the award with singer Lisa Fischer, who also won for her R&B number 1 ballad "How Can I Ease the Pain." Patti's 1994 album, *Gems*, also went gold and featured the hit "The Right Kinda Lover" (8). In total, Patti LaBelle has sold more than 50 million records and has been included in *Rolling Stone's* list of 100 Greatest Singers.

Believe in Love

Artist: Teddy Pendergrass
Album: A Little More Magic
Year: 1993
Writers: Steve Beckham, Reggie Calloway, Vincent Calloway, Teddy Pendergrass, Keith Robertson
Producers: Reggie Calloway, Vincent Calloway
Highest R&B Chart Position: 14
Highest Hot 100 Chart Position: Song did not chart

Like Patti LaBelle, Theodore DeReese Pendergrass, a.k.a. Teddy Pendergrass, hailed from Philadelphia, and both were label-mates at Philadelphia International Records in the 1980s. Patti once recalled, "We were like sister and brother.

We were just always together. He lived not far from me, and he would come to all of my shows and sit in the front row. I'd see him and I'd get chills."

As the early 1980s saw LaBelle's career ascend to new heights, Pendergrass would experience the opposite, beginning in 1982 after having reached a level of R&B stardom and sex appeal that was rivaled only by his contemporary and fellow musician, the legendary Marvin Gaye. Pendergrass was involved in a single-vehicle car crash in the East Falls section of Philadelphia, which left him confined to a wheelchair as a tetraplegic (paralyzed from the chest down) for the remainder of his life.

Following the accident, Pendergrass faced an enormous amount of physical and emotional challenges, the burden of which caused him to fall into a deep depression as he had to learn to live with his life-changing injury. Philadelphia International Records released two albums in the months following the singer's car crash, *This One's for You* in 1982 and 1983's *Heaven Only Knows*, both of which included material Pendergrass had recorded prior to the crash. Neither album was a success for Pendergrass. These releases also completed Pendergrass's contract with Philadelphia International Records, which meant he no longer had a record label.

By 1984, Pendergrass was undergoing physical therapy, working through his depression, and looking to get back into the studio. However, major record labels were apprehensive about investing in a sex symbol who was now paralyzed from the chest down.

Undeterred, Pendergrass signed a deal with Asylum Records and began his comeback. His album *Love Language* was released in 1984. It reached number 4 on the R&B Albums chart and included the R&B number 15 hit song "You're My Choice Tonight," which was produced by Luther Vandross and featured singer Cissy Houston. However, Houston was outdone by her then unknown daughter Whitney Houston, who sang opposite Pendergrass on the album's biggest hit, "Hold Me" (5), which was also included on Whitney's self-titled debut album.

Pendergrass would release two more albums in the 1980s: 1985's *Workin' It Back* and 1988's *Joy*. The latter album included the song "Joy," which became his first number 1 single since 1978's "Close the Door." It was also his final Hot 100 charting single, peaking at number 77.

The 1990s saw Pendergrass's record label, Asylum, operating under a new name, Elektra, but with the same old results. His 1991 album *Truly Blessed* peaked as the number 4 R&B album in the country and included the number 1 hit "It Should've Been You." The aptly titled *A Little More Magic* (1993) was just that. It capped off an improbable run for Pendergrass as it climbed to become the number 13 R&B album in the country and included his last top 20 hit, "Believe In Love," which was a hip-hop-leaning track that he co-wrote. As writer Michele Johnson of *Classic Rock History* described, "This style of music is different for him. He's out of his comfort zone because he didn't sing songs like this, but he sings it as if he performed songs like this all of the time. Since this isn't his wheelhouse, you may not recognize that it's Teddy Pendergrass right away. Once you hear his smooth and velvety voice, there's no mistaking that it's Teddy Pendergrass. The funky guitar riffs are infectious. The drumbeat is hard and thumping, which gives the song its tempo. The groove is perfection."

In 1997, Pendergrass released his final studio album, *You and I,* which failed to produce any notable hits. Pendergrass passed away in January 2010 at the age of fifty-nine. His death prompted his friend, former label-mate and "play sister" Patti LaBelle, to recall the first time that she heard him sing. "We were on the same label and I heard him sing and his voice floored me," she said. "There'll never be another Teddy."

Practice What You Preach

Artist: Barry White
Album: The Icon Is Love
Year: 1994
Writers: Gerald LeVert, Edwin Nicholas, Barry White
Producers: Gerald LeVert, Edwin Nicholas, Barry White
Highest R&B Chart Position: 1
Highest Hot 100 Chart Position: 18

"Practice What You Preach" was the pinnacle of a steady comeback by R&B legend Barry White. White has been a staple of R&B music as a songwriter, producer, and vocalist ever since he produced, wrote, and arranged his first platinum seller, the 1972 classic "Walkin' in the Rain with the One I Love." The song, which was performed by the female group Love Unlimited, became a number 6 R&B hit. White's distinctive deep voice, which he had since the age of fourteen, can be heard in the song as he plays the lover who answers the phone call from the female lead. Since then, White has produced numerous other classics like the R&B number 1 hits "I'm Gonna Love You Just a Little More Baby" (1973), "Love's Theme" (1974), "Can't Get Enough of Your Love, Babe" (1974), and "It's Ecstasy When You Lay Down Next to Me" (1977).

As the 1970s closed and styles changed, the consistent hitmaker appeared as though he had failed to adapt. Between 1979 and 1987, he produced only one song in the top 100, that song being 1982's "Change" (12). Things improved in 1987 with the release of the single "Sho' You Right," which peaked at number 17. White would follow with his 1989 album *The Man Is Back!,* which had three top 40 singles: "Super Lover" (34), "I Wanna Do It Good to Ya" (26), and "When Will I See You Again" (32). Additionally, White was the anchor on Quincy Jones' smash 1990 song "The Secret Garden."

However, it was the single "Practice What You Preach" from 1994's *The Icon Is Love* that gave White his final number 1 hit album and first number 1 solo hit song in over two decades, en route to the album going double platinum. The album's production credits read like a who's who of early '90s R&B, with names like Gerald LeVert, Chuckii Booker, Jimmy Jam, and Terry Lewis. "Practice What You Preach" spent three weeks at number 1 on the R&B chart and reached number 18 on the pop chart. White's final album, 1999's *Staying Power*, resulted in his last hit song, "Staying Power," which reached number 45 on the R&B charts. While the song failed to break the top 40, the single won White two Grammy Awards in the categories of Best Male R&B Vocal Performance and Best Traditional R&B Vocal Performance.

Body and Soul

Artist: Anita Baker
Album: Rhythm of Love
Year: 1994
Writers: Rick Nowels, Ellen Shipley
Producer: Anita Baker, Barry Eastman
Highest R&B Chart Position: 4
Highest Hot 100 Chart Position: 36

So far we have learned that Anita Baker missed out on the number 1 song "Kissing You," which launched the career of Keith Washington and the number 2 song "Love Should'a Brought You Home," as well as the number 3 hit "You Mean the World to Me," both of which launched the career of Toni Braxton. But maybe Baker was content.

By the dawn of the 1990s, she had already cemented herself as one of the top voices in R&B. At the end of the 1980s, the gifted Baker—who began her career as a Detroit nightclub singer at the age of sixteen and whose first solo album, 1983's *Songstress*, had already sold in the millions—had five top 10 hits and three Grammys under her belt.

Her 1990 album *Compositions,* which had Baker more involved in the songwriting and production process, is where she began incorporating more jazz elements than on previous albums. The album contained the singles "Talk to Me" (3), "Fairy Tales" (8), and "Soul Inspiration" (16) and sold over a million copies.

After the end of the album's touring and promotion schedule in 1991, Baker took a break from the business to settle down with her husband, later having two children.

Following her four-year break, Baker released *Rhythm of Love* in 1994. The album, which featured "Body and Soul," her first pop hit since 1989, was an instant success.

"Body and Soul" was written by Rick Nowels and Ellen Shipley. In a 2019 interview with *Songfacts.com*, Shipley described what the song was about, how it was written with the singers Daryl Hall and John Oates (Hall & Oates) in mind, and how it came to be recorded by Baker, saying "'Body and Soul' has a classic old-time feel that also works now," ... "This is where people are afraid of commitment if they don't know for sure what the other person feels. It's a really simple song where she wants to know because she's in it, she's deep in it, and she wants to know what he feels, because we don't always know. . . . Melodically, lyrically, it's passionate." She added, "It's clear: It's got one thought and it's a lot of what people feel. It's commitment: Am I going to commit to this person? I've got to know how they feel first." Somewhere in the creative process, Nowels and Shipley realized the song was better suited for Baker's voice than Hall and Oates and they created a demo using a singer that sounded a lot like Baker. Reportedly, Baker chose the song as soon as she heard it.

The second single, the mid-tempo "I Apologize," won Baker her eighth Grammy. The album eventually sold over 2 million copies, becoming her fourth consecutive platinum-selling album. *Rhythm of Love* was Baker's last album of the 1990's. She did not release another project until 2004's *My Everything*, which reached number 1 on the R&B Albums chart.

Eye Hate U

Artist: Prince
Album: The Gold Experience
Year: 1995
Writer: Prince
Producer: Prince
Highest R&B Chart Position: 3
Highest Hot 100 Chart Position: 12

Each of us can relate to this song. Whether you met your soulmate in elementary school and have been together ever since or you consider yourself a heartless player who will never be tied down, this song—which explains why the singer hates his lover because he loves her so much—hits home.

Shortly after Prince's death in 2016, his former girlfriend Carmen Electra revealed details about their relationship and the role this song played in Prince's breakup with her.

Prince first met Electra, then Tara Leigh Patrick, when she auditioned for a girl group he was assembling. While she did not make the group, she did become one of Prince's "protégés." In fact, it was Prince who gave Carmen her name, as she recalled to *US* magazine: "I received a call from Prince saying I think you should be your own artist and not back up anyone else. I'm going to write you a song and if you like it, you can record it . . . The name of the song was 'Carmen on Top.' My name is Tara, so I was confused. I loved the song. I loved it, but he said, 'You're not a Tara. You're not Tara. You're Carmen.'"

Tara,… I mean Carmen, then began a romantic relationship with Prince. That relationship ended in unique fashion, In 2016 Electra told *GQ* magazine that "He [Prince] called me and said, 'I have a flight booked for you tomorrow morning to Minneapolis.' I packed up my little tiny suitcase, and I had maybe $20 and four or five outfits. As soon as I landed, a purple limo was waiting outside. He wasn't there, but he called and he said, 'Do you have a lot of clothes?' He made a kind of sarcastic comment, said, 'I'm gonna have my brother take you shopping.' He specifically said what he wanted it to be: 'I want you to buy something white—a white dress or white leggings and a top.' So we're on a mad hunt in a little tiny mall in Minneapolis for something white. I stayed at his house for a little while—I thought I was going to go to a hotel. But he was a gentleman. . . . And during that time I went out with a guy—I hadn't slept with this person—and Prince found out. He said, 'I wrote this song about you,' and then he played 'I Hate U.' It was hard to hear. And it was even harder to hear the parts of the song that said it could have been a completely different way. Then to say, 'I hate you because I love you'—I literally cried in front of him. I think he just wanted me to hear it and know that he was really upset. Then he flew me back to Los Angeles."

Now it must be noted that those closest to Prince are in solidarity with the fact that he was notorious for telling women that songs were about them. His former personal assistant Ruth Arzate told the *Questlove Supreme* podcast, "I've heard him lie to women and say that the songs were about one and that he wrote it about another, typical rock star response to music." Perhaps Prince's biographer Duane Tudahl described it best saying, "He may be inspired by one person, that doesn't mean everything in the song is inspired by that one person you know. 'wonderful ass' may be about Vanity, but it also may be about Susana Melvoin [Prince's former girlfriend] . . . could [also] be about the cat having a wonderful ass.

A Rose Is Still a Rose

Artist: Aretha Franklin
Album: A Rose Is Still a Rose
Year: 1998
Writer: Lauryn Hill
Producer: Lauryn Hill
Notable Samples: Super Hoe, Boogie Down Productions, (1987)
Highest R&B Chart Position: 5
Highest Hot 100 Chart Position: 23

By 1998, Aretha Franklin had reigned as the Queen of Soul for over three decades and showed no signs of stopping. While most of her contemporaries were long retired and resting on their laurels in the form of greatest hits albums, the Queen recorded seven top 40 R&B hits in the decade, which matches the output of '90s favorites Monica and Faith Evans, and is only two less than Aaliyah, who had nine. For *A Rose Is Still a Rose*, Franklin called upon her most talented subjects to support the cause and they delivered, culminating with her last gold album consisting mainly of original material. It contains cuts produced by hitmakers Jermaine Dupri, Sean Combs, Dallas Austin, and Narada Michael Walden, among others. But it was the Lauryn Hill written and produced track "A Rose Is Still a Rose" that would become the album's biggest hit.

Hill wrote and produced "A Rose Is Still a Rose" a few months before releasing her multiplatinum, multi-Grammy Award–winning album *The Miseducation of Lauryn Hill*. The song achieved a flurry of positive reviews. One such review by Jim Farber of Parade lauded Hill's vocal backing of Franklin on the recording as well as her adding a refrain from the Edie Brickell & New Bohemians hit "What I Am [/ is what I am.]"... Franklin's voice and stature as the element that made the song a chart maker capping one of the most consequential and honored careers in music history." Farber also keenly observed the use of Hill's lyrics that "cast the Queen as a romantic sage reminding a young woman of her value despite some previous failings in love." This was a subject that Franklin could relate to. As reported in her 2014 biography *Respect* written by David Ritz, Franklin had two children by the age of 15, was later physically abused by her first husband, and frequently battled alcohol abuse. In a 2021 interview with *Vanity Fair*, Liesl Tommy, the director of the screen adaptation of Respect, commented, 'Her childhood had so much heartbreak, that helps you to understand how she was able to sing with such emotional intensity, and how she was able to bring so much pain and power to the renditions of the songs she chose to sing.'"

In her *Andscape* article, writer Soraya Nadia McDonald echoed this sentiment in commenting, "'A Rose Is Still a Rose' was more than just lyrical balm for a woman who realizes she's been used and discarded. It's a rejection of slut-shaming, of the idea that a woman's worth depreciates with every instance she dares uncross her legs. "A Rose Is Still a Rose" would give Franklin her last top 20 hit. A reissue of her 1967 number 1 "Respect" just missed the top 20, peaking at number 21 shortly after her death in 2018.

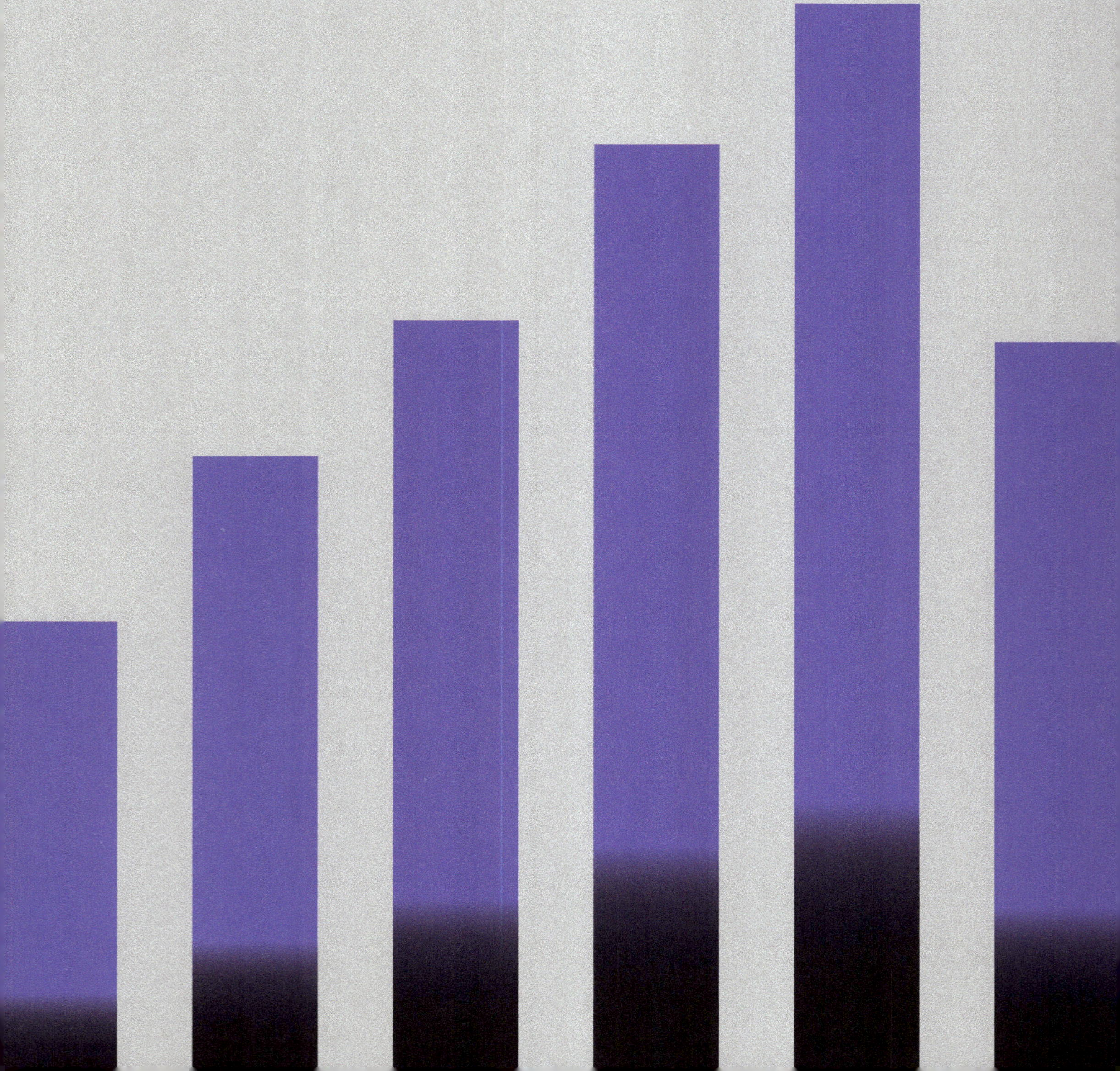

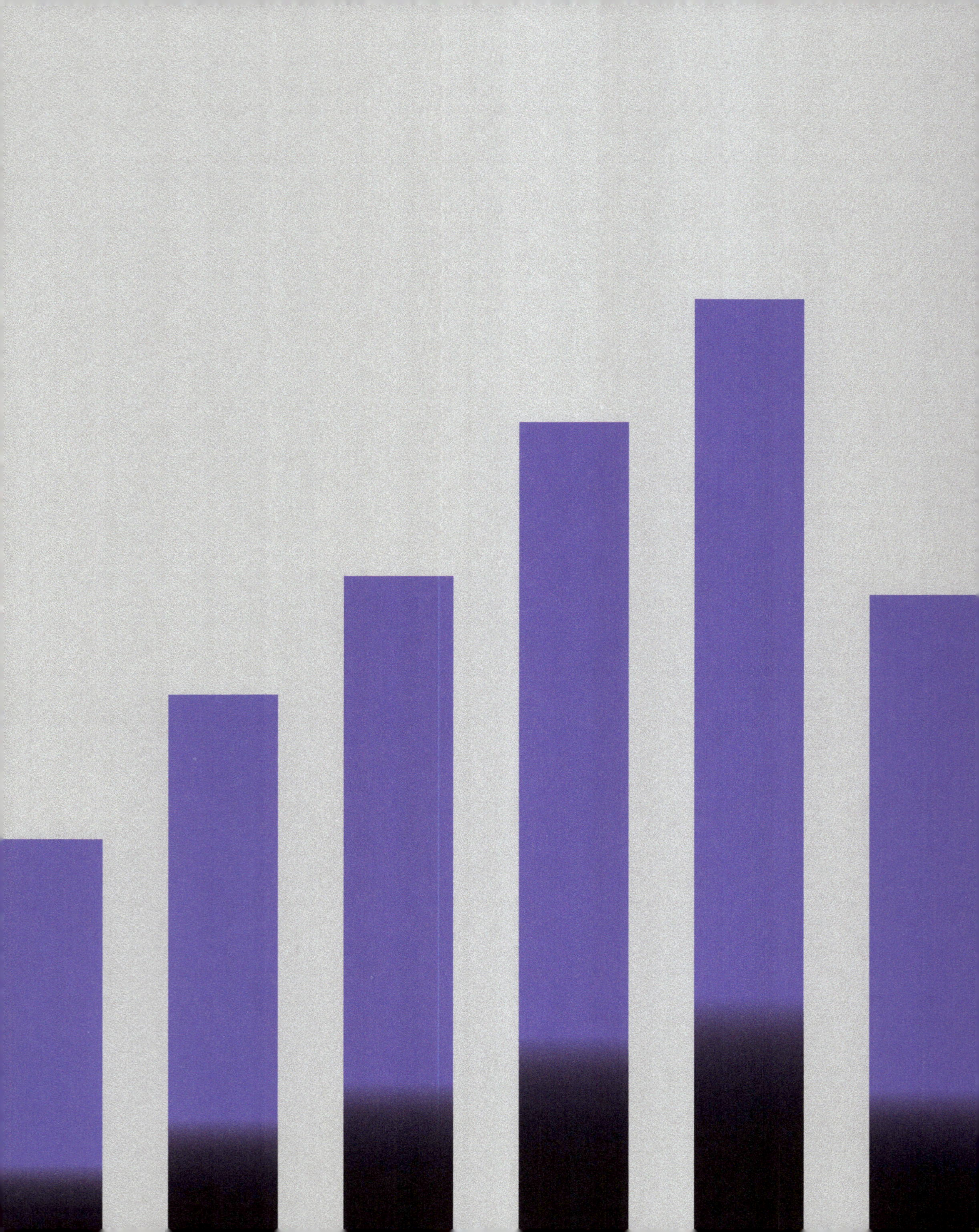

Where My Girls At?: Females Take Over R&B 1992 - 1996

Save the Best for Last
My Lovin' (You're Never Gonna Get It)
You Remind Me
Interlude: Jermain Dupri Gets So So Def
Baby-Baby-Baby
Just Kickin' It
Weak
Creep
Soon as I Get Home
Freak Like Me
Un-break My Heart
One in a Million
Interlude: Janet Jackson Dominates the Charts
That's the Way Love Goes
If
Scream
Got 'til It's Gone
Interlude: Prince of Petty, The Emancipation of Jimmy Jam and Terry Lewis
Artist Profile: Mariah Carey
Vision of Love
One Sweet Day
Fantasy (Bad Boy Fantasy)
Always Be My Baby
When You Believe
Interlude: Mariah Carey vs. Mary J Blige

Where My Girls At? Females Take Over R&B | 1992 - 1996

The '90s saw female artists on equal footing as males. Artists like TLC and SWV were generating strings of hits and sales numbers that rivaled those of Jodeci and Boyz II Men. This period also saw the rise of Mary J. Blige, Aaliyah, and Monica as certified hitmakers. This was also the period when Whitney Houston became an icon and Janet Jackson continued to dominate the charts with every album release.

Save the Best for Last

Artist: Vanessa Williams
Album: The Comfort Zone
Year: 1992
Writers: Phil Galdston, Jon Lind, Wendy Waldman
Producer: Keith Thomas
Highest R&B Chart Position: 1
Highest Hot 100 Chart Position: 1

Vanessa Williams is probably one of the most underrated entertainers of her generation. That's right—I said it! While the knee-jerk reaction is to disagree, let's see if I can make the case. Consider this: Williams has two platinum albums (*The Comfort Zone*, 1991, and *The Sweetest Days*, 1994); seven top 10 singles, including three number 1 singles; eleven Grammy nominations; three Emmy nominations (all for playing Wilhelmina Slater on the television series *Ugly Betty*); and a Tony nomination (for playing the Witch in the Broadway play *Into the Woods*). Oh, and did we mention she is a former Miss America? All of this and most millennials only know her for her proactive commercials.

This success story began as the child of two music teachers. Williams grew up studying drama and dance and played multiple instruments. She enrolled in Syracuse University and joined the Department of Drama, a part of the College of Visual and Performing Arts, as a musical theater major. She stayed at Syracuse through her second year until she was crowned Miss America in 1984. This accomplishment came thirty-three years after African Americans were allowed to compete in the contest. (Prior to 1950, the contest rules required contestants to "be of good health and of the white race.") That triumph led to racist letters and death threats. Near the end of her term, Williams was forced to resign her title when *Penthouse* magazine announced plans to publish unauthorized nude photographs of the beauty queen, photos which were taken years earlier and sold to the magazine without her knowledge or consent.

It was around this time that Williams hired public relations expert Ramon Hervey to do some damage control. Hervey became Williams's manager (and later her husband) and helped her to land a record deal with the PolyGram subsidiary, Wing Records. Williams released her debut album, *The Right Stuff*, in 1988. R&B fans weren't expecting much, but the first single, "The Right Stuff," peaked at number 4 on the R&B chart. The single "Dreamin'" was an R&B number 1 (number 8 on the Hot 100), and the slow-tempoed "Darlin' I" peaked at number 10. The album has since gone platinum.

The first singles from her second album, 1991's *The Comfort Zone*, were up-tempo tracks. "Running Back to You" was a number 1 hit, and "Work to Do," a cover of the Isley Brothers 1972 hit, peaked at number 3.

It was the album's third single that to this day Williams calls her favorite song. It would also be the biggest song of her career. "Save the Best for Last" was the product of a collaboration of three veteran songwriters: Wendy Waldman, Phil Galdston, and Jon Lind. Waldman described the song as being about "someone you love surprising you by confessing they love you, too," much like (as the lyrics say) the snow coming down in June or the sun going around the moon. Once complete, Waldman, a '70s folk singer, sung the demo, and the trio unsuccessfully shopped the song to various artists until Ed Eckstine of PolyGram Records and Vanessa Williams pounced on it. Allegedly when Williams heard the demo, she told her record company that it was the song she'd "been waiting for her whole life."

"Save the Best for Last" was a monster. It was an R&B number 1 and topped the Hot 100 chart for five weeks and was ranked fourth on *Billboard's* Top 100 hits of 1992 list. ASCAP named it Song of the Year in 1992. It was also nominated for the Grammy Awards for Song of the Year and Record of the Year in 1993.

My Lovin' (You're Never Gonna Get It)

Artist: En Vogue
Album: Funky Divas
Year: 1992
Writers: James Brown, Denzil Foster, Thomas McElroy John Starks, Fred Wesley
Producers: Denzil Foster, Thomas McElroy
Notable Sample: The Payback, James Brown (1973)
Highest R&B Chart Position: 1
Highest Hot 100 Chart Position: 2

En Vogue was styled as the first female R&B super-group, the brainchild of writers and producers Denzil Foster and Thomas McElroy. By 1990 the duo were already R&B veterans, having produced Timex Social Club's number 1 hit "Rumors" in 1986, becoming founding members of the band Club Noveau, and producing hits for the band Tony! Toni! Toné!, including tracks on the group's second album, 1990's *Revival*, which went double platinum. Foster and McElroy described their thought process in forming En Vogue in a 2012 *SoulCulture.com* interview, saying, "When Tommy and I were in Club Nouveau, we were talking about what we wanted to do once we started producing . . . One thing we kept talking about was, there wasn't a super girl group in the mainstream. There were the Supremes-like groups that had one lead singer and the rest were background singers. I can't remember an all-girl group where they all had powerhouse vocals and could sing lead. So, when we left Club Nouveau and finished working with Toni, Tony, Toné! we were able to get another production deal and we were looking for acts to sign. This is when we decided to put the group together."

After several audition calls, Foster and McElroy selected Cindy Herron, Maxine Jones, and Dawn Robinson to become the members of the newly titled group "For You." "Tommy and I went back and forth on our decision. We were sold on Cindy and Max, but we kept going back and forth between Dawn and Terry [Ellis] because both Dawn and Terry were so versatile and had such range with their vocals. One day, Tommy said, 'Who said it had to be three?' . . . Then the lights went off and I said, 'Yeah, you're right.' This is how it ended up being the four girls instead of three." Once complete the group's name was changed to Vogue. After learning that another group already had that moniker, Foster and McElroy changed the name to En Vogue."

The physical beauty of En Vogue's members was complemented by their vocal talents. Their debut album, *Born to Sing*, went platinum and drew comparisons to the Supremes. On their sophomore effort, *Funky Divas*, En Vogue experimented with their sound.

The track "My Lovin' (You're Never Gonna Get It)" is built on a sample of the James Brown song "The Payback." According to Foster, it was built in stages. "'My Lovin" was one of the most difficult songs to make," he says. "It was three songs before it became one because we kept rewriting it over and over again.

"We would get to a point where we would add something and say, 'Yeah, now we're getting somewhere.' …but we felt like everything we would put down on the track sounded whack." …"Tommy and I kept going back and forth with ideas. Finally, I said we didn't have a signature a cappella thing going on like we did at the beginning of 'Hold On.' Tommy started playing a set of chords and I said, 'Yeah, like that!'… It sounded so cool and I came up with the lyrics 'never gonna get it . . .' At that moment, I thought, yeah, this is going to set it off really nice." Foster was right, the addition of the a cappella breakdown did "set the song off", so much that a generation of R&B fans know exactly what's coming after they hear the announcer say 'and now it's time for a breakdown.'"

"My Lovin' (You're Never Gonna Get It)" went on to peak at number 2 on the *Billboard* Hot 100 chart and number 1 on the R&B chart. It charted in nine different countries and propelled sales of the *Funky Divas* album after it was released in the spring of 1992.

You Remind Me

Artist: Mary J. Blige
Album: What's the 411?
Year: 1992
Writers: Dave "Jam" Hall, Eric Milteer, Prince Markie Dee, Cory Rooney
Producer: Dave "Jam" Hall, Cory Rooney
Notable Samples: Remind Me, Patrice Rushen (1982)
Biz Dance Part 1, Biz Markie (1988)
Highest R&B Chart Position: 1
Highest Hot 100 Chart Position: 29

"You Remind Me" was Mary J. Blige's first single from her aptly named debut album, 1992's *What's the 411?* The song gave the former 411 operator her first number 1 song.

It was with "You Remind Me" that Blige began to hone the new jack formula of classic soul vocals and subject matter over hip-hop beats. It was a formula that she would repeat several times throughout her career, culminating in her coronation as the Queen of Hip-Hop Soul.

As for the song's production, Cory Rooney remembered how it all came together, stating, "'You Remind Me' was the first record we did together . . . I was a big Biz Markie fan and I sampled his song, 'Pickin' Boogers.' I sampled it and chopped it up and then I put a real pretty song on top of it . . . A writer that I used to work with back then by the name of Eric Milteer wrote this song. We went to church together. . . . I used some ideas from another artist that I loved by the name of Patrice Rushen. She had a song called 'You Remind Me' and I liked the tone of her song. I took some of the influences from there . . . The song came out well, but the label didn't really understand it, though. I really don't think they understood the whole project besides Diddy [Sean Combs]. He was a minor A&R at the label back then but had the ear and vision for what he wanted to do."

At the time, however, Blige was an afterthought at her label, Uptown Records. According to Rooney, "You Remind Me" was the exact song that compelled Andre Harrell, founder of Uptown Records, to craft a Blige solo album immediately. Rooney says, "She kind of sat around for a while and then Uptown did the movie soundtrack for the movie *Strictly Business*. Kurt Woodley pressed Andre about putting her on the soundtrack for the movie. They thought Mary was the next Stephanie Mills [Mills already had a track on the soundtrack]. This is how they were pitching her to us. When the *Strictly Business* soundtrack came together, Kurt Woodley told Andre that he had to give Mary a shot. . . . The song really took off and it jump-started the process for Mary's album. It was the most popular record on the radio, so Andre and everyone said it was time to put an album together right now for Mary. She went from being an artist on the shelf to Puffy [also Sean Combs] literally having weeks to put an album together."

"You Remind Me" topped the R&B chart for one week in 1992 and launched Blige's stardom. For what it's worth, Stephanie Mills' song on the *Strictly Business* album, "I Just Want Love," failed to chart.

Interlude
Jermaine Dupri Gets So So Def

Atlanta native and music mogul Jermaine Dupri got his introduction to hip-hop while a kid dancer (twelve years old) on the famed Fresh Fest Tour, which was a 1980s hip-hop tour that featured the genre's biggest acts, such as Run DMC, Whodini, the Fat Boys, and Kurtis Blow.

Dupri would later tell *Entrepreneur.com,* "I was taught so much through my relationships with Run DMC, Houdini, Grandmaster Flash, and these New York guys in hip-hop . . . It put me dead in the face of hip-hop in an era where you can never be taught by better people. I learned deejaying, graffiti, emceeing, and everything. I learned it all."

An enamored Dupri moved from Atlanta to New York City, where he learned the art of production and mastered turning break beats into full tracks. When he returned to Atlanta, he began to produce music. His first big break came in 1989 when the teenage Dupri produced the female rap group Silk Tymes Leather (whom he met on the Fresh Fest Tour) and their hits "Do Your Dance (Work It Out)" (1990) and "It Ain't Where Ya From . . . It's Where Ya At" (1990). Later he would meet teenagers Chris Kelly and Chris Smith at an Atlanta mall. He would turn the duo into the group Kris Kross, which would go on to sell 8 million records in large part due to their debut rap single "Jump," which Dupri produced using a sample of the Jackson 5's 1969 hit "I Want You Back" (1). "Jump" topped the *Billboard* Hot 100 for eight weeks.

On the strength of the 8 million sold and crossover success by Kris Kross, Sony Music offered Dupri a record deal that enabled him to start his So So Def record label. But despite the millions in sales and number 1 song, Dupri would soon find out that the work was just beginning. He recalled a humbling encounter with mega-producer Babyface, whose LaFace label was also located in Atlanta, saying, "I remember being a cocky young producer with a number one song. Then, I met Babyface, who said, 'You're the guy with the little Kris Kross song.' It disturbed me at first, but then he told me, 'It's cool to have a number one record, believe me, but it's cooler to do it multiple times.' He taught me to listen and learn and not get caught up in the moment of success."

This is a lesson Dupri would put into action as he and So So Def would go on to defy the odds and become a major force in R&B and hip-hop in the midst of stiff competition from rivals like LaFace, Bad Boy, Death Row, Arista, and later No Limit Records for the same audience.

Although So So Def's success was improbable, the results have been undeniable. Dupri would go on to discover R&B hitmakers TLC and Xscape and produce 1990s hits like "Just Kickin' It" (Xscape, 1993), "My Boo" (Ghost Town DJ's, 1996), and "You Make Me Wanna" (Usher, 1997) as well as breaking through the limitations of genre by producing, writing, or co-writing multiple Hot 100 number 1 songs and dozens of top 40 hits for some of music's biggest hitmakers, including Mariah Carey, Monica, and Alicia Keys.

Baby-Baby-Baby

Artist: TLC
Album: Oooooooohhh . . . On the TLC Tip
Year: 1992
Writers: Kenneth "Babyface" Edmonds, Antonio "L.A." Reid, Daryl Simmons
Producers: Kenneth "Babyface" Edmonds, Antonio "L.A." Reid, Daryl Simmons
Highest R&B Chart Position: 1
Highest Hot 100 Chart Position: 2

According to Jermaine Dupri, 2nd Nature, the first iteration of TLC, was formed in his living room when the trio of Crystal Jones, Lisa "Left Eye" Lopes and Tionne "T-Boz" Watkins were introduced to Dupri by mogul Ian Burke. In fact, it was Dupri who gave T-Boz her signature sound, which occupies the lead on the song "Baby-Baby-Baby." Dupri told the *Questlove Supreme* podcast, "The way T-Boz sings is the Jermaine Dupri style of singing, like the way she sounds, the reason why she sounds ahhhhhh [singing], that's me. You can hear me, that's me . . . that's how she sounds because I demo'd the songs and I told her that she should sing like me. . . . it just became the cool thing for her."

The trio would leave Dupri and sign with Pebbitone, a management and production company owned by Perri "Pebbles" Reid. Reid renamed the group TLC, an acronym for the names Tionne, Lisa, and Crystal, and arranged an audition for them with LaFace Records, a record label which was run by Kenneth "Babyface" Edmonds and Reid's then husband, Antonio "L.A." Reid.

Antonio Reid replaced Jones with Rozonda "Chili" Thomas, who was an aspiring singer and part-time backup dancer for LaFace artist Damian Dame. Jones has said that the reason for her departure was her unwillingness to sign Perri Reid's management contracts. She told *RollingOut.com*, "I turned to Pebbles and I asked if I could take mine home and have my mom look it over and she said 'absolutely not.' So I chose not to sign my contract . . . They kept having meetings without me and all of a sudden, they told me they didn't want me in the group anymore."

In February 1992, TLC released their debut album, *Oooooooohhh . . . On the TLC Tip.* The album was a commercial success, with three of its four singles making it into the top 10 of the R&B charts: "Baby-Baby-Baby" (1), "Ain't 2 Proud 2 Beg" (2), and "What About Your Friends" (2). The single "Hat 2 da Back" charted at number 14. The album has since been certified quadruple platinum.

"Baby-Baby-Baby" was the album's second single. It was the only number 1 song on *Oooooooohhh . . . On the TLC Tip,* staying at number 1 on the R&B chart for two weeks in June of 1992. It was also a major crossover success, reaching number 2 on the Hot 100, where it was kept out of the number 1 spot for six weeks by Boyz II Men's "End of the Road," which like "Baby-Baby-Baby" was also written by Babyface and L.A. Reid.

TLC's sophomore album, 1994's *CrazySexyCool*, was a monster. It topped the immensely successful *Oooooooohhh . . . On the TLC Tip* in becoming TLC's best-selling album, reaching diamond certification on the strength of the singles "Creep" (1), "Red Light Special" (3), "Waterfalls" (4), and "Diggin' on You" (7).

That year TLC sued LaFace Records and Pebbitone, claiming they were paid only $50,000 each between 1993 and 1994 despite having sold 11 million copies of *CrazySexyCool* and generating over $100 million in sales for LaFace/Arista. The case ended in a settlement amount that included a clause barring either side from commenting on the financial details or other specifics of the agreement. The judge also voided TLC's contracts with LaFace and Pebbitone. With new life, TLC recorded their third and final album of the 1990s, *FanMail* (1999). It did not disappoint, selling 6 million records and including the hits "No Scrubs" (1) and "Unpretty" (4).

Lisa Lopes died tragically in an automobile accident in Honduras in 2002. Lopes' legacy and the legacy of TLC continues as the undisputed best-selling female group of the 1990s.

Just Kickin' It

Artist: Xscape
Album: Hummin' Comin' at 'Cha
Year: 1993
Writers: Jermaine Dupri, Manuel Seal
Producers: Jermaine Dupri
Notable Samples: Show Me, Howard Hewett (1990)
Highest R&B Chart Position: 1
Highest Hot 100 Chart Position: 2

Xscape was formed in Atlanta, Georgia, in 1991 with original members Kandi Burruss, Tameka "Tiny" Cottle, LaTocha Scott, Tamika Scott, and Tamera Coggins-Wynn. Tamera Coggins-Wynn left the group in 1992.

Like TLC the group was managed by Jermaine Dupri. Xscape met Dupri when they were invited to his birthday party by Ian Burke. Dupri recalled that when the group sang him a version of "Happy Birthday," he told them that when he got his label he would sign them. True to his word, when Dupri founded So So Def, he signed Xscape as the label's first group. Dupri also wrote their first song, "Just Kickin' It." The song spent four weeks at number 1. Dupri said of the early success, "'Just Kickin' It' went number one on the R&B charts. It's been out for five weeks, and they're the first group on my label. So, me to have a first group to go number one in five weeks, I can't be more than happy." Dupri styled Xscape as a "hip-hop version of En Vogue," foregoing the glamorous dresses in favor of masculine baggy pants and jerseys. The tomboyish nature of the group is evidenced by Burruss' deep voice providing the lead vocals on the track. Her tone and cadence were modeled after Dupri's singing style on the "Just Kickin' It" demo. Dupri had previous success with this method with T-Boz of TLC. He told the *Questlove Supreme* podcast, "I made Kandi sing just like I made T-Boz sing; that's why she's low on that song."

In 1993 the group released their debut album, *Hummin' Comin' at 'Cha,* which Dupri produced. The album, which also included the number 1 hit "Understanding," is a 7× platinum seller worldwide.

Xscape's second album, *Off the Hook* (1995), also went multiplatinum carried by the singles "Feels So Good," which peaked at number 8, and a remake of the 1979 Jones Girls classic "Who Can I Run To," which gave Xscape another R&B number 1.

Xscape released their final album, *Traces of My Lipstick*, in 1998, which was also a platinum seller. The highest charting singles were "The Arms of the One Who Loves You," which peaked at number 4, and "My Little Secret," which was a number 2 hit.

Weak

Artist: SWV
Album: It's About Time
Year: 1993
Writer: Brian Alexander Morgan
Producer: Brian Alexander Morgan
Highest R&B Chart Position: 1
Highest Hot 100 Chart Position: 1

Sisters with Voices (SWV) originally consisted of members Cheryl "Coko" Gamble, Tamara "Taj" Johnson, Leanne "Lelee" Lyons, and a fourth member only identified years later as "Samantha". The group minus Samantha was signed to RCA Records in 1991, where the label envisioned them as the girl version of the popular male group Guy. Ditching Samantha wasn't the only change the group would make before signing with RCA. Apparently SWV went through a few name changes, including briefly adopting the name "TLC" (for Taj, Lelee and Coko) before Pebbles, TLC's manager, (the T-Boz, Left Eye and Chili version) hit them with a cease and desist order to change the name.

Once settled on name SWV, the group was teamed with producer Brian Alexander Morgan for their first album.

Morgan had just produced a number 1 dance track "Give It to You" for singer Martha Wash when Kenny Ortiz of RCA A&R approached him about writing songs for SWV.

Morgan, an accomplished musician, was looking for a record deal for himself and had written and demo'd several songs. One of the songs was "Weak," which he wrote in 1989. The lyrics describe Morgan's infatuation with singer Chanté Moore. Moore was dating Morgan's boss, Jay Records label owner, Jay King at the time. Morgan said in an interview with *Complex* magazine, "During that time we became friends; she and I kinda became close, but it was bad timing because Jay King was seeing her, and I didn't want to be anywhere in between that. She probably didn't know how much of a crush I had on her. So out of that frustration, I wrote a private little song called 'Weak.'"

Morgan sent Ortiz several music demos for the label to consider for SWV, but he did not include "Weak" because he intended to use it for himself. Morgan told the *Questlove Supreme* podcast, "Kenny [Ortiz] had no idea that I had these other songs. But this guy named Jeff Bowens, who used to work for Jay King, ended up working for RCA." According to Morgan, Bowens was a janitor at Jay Records, and he stole "Weak." Then Bowens got hired at RCA, where he played "Weak" in the RCA office, and Kenny Ortiz heard it. Ortiz asked Bowens where the song came from, and Bowens told him that it came from Morgan. Ortiz then called Morgan and said, "You holding out on me—you didn't tell me you had these songs!"

Morgan continued, "So he [Ortiz] sends me this FedEx package of these girls singing these demos, and I heard Coko's voice and I was like, 'Uh-oh. This girl gonna be a problem.' And again, I thought about the connection between 'Computer Love' and 'Weak.' I wrote the song for Charlie [Wilson to sing], but I thought Coko's voice sounded like Shirley Murdock, who was on 'Computer Love.' So Kenny is like, 'Would you come to New York and record them.'" Once in New York and production began, Coko did not like "Weak" initially, but thankfully she later grew to appreciate the song.

"Weak" was released as the third single from SWV's debut album, *It's About Time*. It peaked at number 1 on both the R&B and Hot 100 charts in 1993. The album's first two singles, "Right Here" and "I'm So Into You," reached numbers 13 and 2 respectively on the R&B chart. "Weak" was followed by the album's fourth single, "Right Here (Human Nature Remix)," which sampled Michael Jackson's 1982 hit "Human Nature." The song gave SWV their second consecutive R&B number 1, where it would stay for seven weeks. The album's final single, "You're Always On My Mind," peaked at number 8. The popular track "Downtown" was not released as a commercial single.

SWV's second album, *New Beginning*, was released in 1996 and included the singles "You're the One," another SWV number 1 song, the Neptunes-produced track "Use Your Heart," which reached number 6, and the album's last single, "It's All About U," which SWV member Taj sang lead on. The song peaked at number 32. In 1997 SWV released their third album, *Release Some Tension*, and it broke into the top 10 with the singles "Rain" (7) and "Someone" (5). The group split in 1998 and would reunite and separate on and off throughout the next several years.

Creep

Artist: TLC
Album: CrazySexyCool
Year: 1994
Writer: Dallas Austin
Producer: Dallas Austin
Notable Sample: Hey Young World, Slick Rick (1988)
Highest R&B Chart Position: 1
Highest Hot 100 Chart Position: 1

"Creep" shows the maturity of TLC following their first album 1992's *Ooooooohhh the TLC Tip*. The song was recorded for their second album, *CrazySexyCool* (1994). Writer and super-producer Dallas Austin wrote the song from a female's perspective after TLC's lead singer, T-Boz, told him about a cheating boyfriend she had. (The boyfriend was Mr. Dalvin of Jodeci.) In a 2015 interview with *Billboard,* T-Boz spoke about the concept of the song, saying, "'Creep,' unfortunately, was one of my true stories . . . You're with a guy and he's not showing you attention, so another guy comes along and you're like, 'Hey, if you were where you were supposed to be, he couldn't be showing me attention right now!' I was in the middle of this drama, because the other guy was [my boyfriend's] friend, and my boyfriend was just not getting it together." This story also literally hit home for Austin who was experiencing remarkably similar relationship issues of his own. In a 2019 interview with *Songwritersuniverse.com* Austin explained more about the inspiration for "Creep" saying "At the time, I had a girlfriend who I'd known for a very long time. We were friends first. So when we started to date, it kind of messed it up for a while (laughs). And I knew I hadn't been home, and I hadn't been around, and it was one of those things where the relationship was kind of going south. Then I found out that she was cheating on me with a friend of mine through a poetry book that he wrote (laughs). He wrote poems about her. So I thought…this sounds like my girl. So I go back to her and say, "Hey, are you messin' around with that guy?" And she said, "Yeah, you haven't been here…I didn't want to hurt your feelings and I needed some attention. Hey we're friends and I love you, but you haven't been here." In Atlanta, we could call it "the late night creep," when you would go and see a girl late at night after 11 o'clock. And so I took that, and just told the story that she told me, [and I wrote "Creep"].

Austin held on to the song for six months because, as he said, he thought it might be "too lame," but when he couldn't get the tune out of his head, he decided to have TLC record it. Lisa "Left Eye" Lopes, the group's rapper who was on probation for setting her boyfriend's (pro football player Andre Rison) house on fire, was opposed to the song. She disagreed with its message, saying, "I was like, 'If a girl is gonna catch her man cheating,'…'instead of telling her to cheat back, why don't we tell her [to] just leave?'"

As a result, Left Eye didn't initially contribute a rap to the song. Austin elaborated, "The reason there's not a rap on it is because Lisa said, 'Dallas, I don't want this to offend people personally. I don't want it to interfere with my relationships. If he thinks I'm doing this, it's going to cause problems and I'm making a record out of it.'"

Left Eye wasn't the only one who was not a fan of the song. The label didn't think it would be a hit either. T-Boz told *Billboard* that LaFace Records head L.A. Reid "flipped out" when he heard the song and was not going to release it. Fortunately, Clive Davis the head of Arista records which handled distribution for LaFace, intervened and green-lit the song for release. Davis would tell Dallas Austin, "L.A. is wrong" adding "and that little Miles Davis horn sound you have in there is going to get you a Grammy!" (Miles Davis is not playing horn on the song).

The song was a major crossover hit that was all over radio in 1994 and 1995. After it blew up Left Eye would eventually contribute a rap verse that was added to the songs remixes.

The iconic video depicting the group dancing in pajamas, (which was the third video shot for the song) was inspired by Salt-N-Pepa and En Vogue's video for their 1993 song "Whatta Man" (3). After seeing it, TLC contacted Matthew Rolston, who directed the En Vogue video, to film their video for "Creep."

"Creep" was TLC's first number 1 on the Hot 100 and did in fact win a Grammy for Best R&B Performance by a Duo or Group with Vocals.

Soon as I Get Home

Artist: Faith Evans
Album: Faith
Year: 1995
Writers: Sean Combs, Faith Evans, Chucky Thompson
Producers: Sean Combs, Chucky Thompson
Highest R&B Chart Position: 3
Highest Hot 100 Chart Position: 21

"Soon as I Get Home" was the second single from Faith Evans's debut album *Faith* (1995). Faith loves this song, she chose it as one of her favorites, stating, "I've heard many people say this song is a timeless love song. It's one of my faves from my first album, and I love the energy the audience gives me every time I perform it live."

Faith Evans was born to a mother who was a professional singer and a musician father. She began her music career in Los Angeles as a backing vocalist for other R&B artists like Al B. Sure! and Christopher Williams. It was there that she caught the attention of Sean Combs, the head of the Bad Boy Entertainment record label. Combs signed her as Bad Boy's first female solo artist. Evans wrote "Soon as I Get Home" about her relationship with her label-mate and husband Christopher Wallace, a.k.a. The Notorious B.I.G. As she told Will Levith of *Medium.com* in a 2021 interview, "I was writing it from the perspective of 'this is what I wish [Biggie] would be saying to me,' because he was on the road a lot at the time. We didn't have a lot of time in the beginning once we got married; B.I.G. sorta just blew up, so that was kind of the perspective I was singing from: I wish he would be saying this to me when he's calling me from out of town."

Combs added his influence and got a piece of the writer's credit for the hit. As Evans recalled, she and the song's co-writer Chucky Thompson "were at the Hit Factory studio, and I think Puff probably changed one or two words. The song was finished. Back then, I was like, 'oh, ok, [Puff] wrote it, too.' But whatever . . . it's all good. He was going to get credit anyway as a producer [laughs]. But I just remember Chucky playing these three or four chords, and I said, 'Just repeat those chords over and over; that sounds good.' And he did it with a tempo behind it, and I just started singing, 'Soon as I get home . . .' and that was how it started."

While that may have been how it started, it ended with "Soon as I Get Home" breaking into the top 5 and *Faith* the album going platinum. Evans's second album, *Keep the Faith* (1998), was also a platinum seller.

Freak Like Me

Artist: Adina Howard
Album: Do You Wanna Ride?
Year: 1995
Writers: Alita Carter, George Clinton Jr., Gary Cooper, William "Bootsy" Collins, Eugene Hanes, Livio Harris, Loren Hill, Kim Spikes, Marc Valentine
Producer: Mass Order
Notable Samples: All Night Long, Mary Jane Girls (1983)
Summer Madness, Kool & the Gang (1974)
I'd Rather Be with You, Bootsy's Rubber Band (1976)
Sing a Simple Song, Sly and the Family Stone (1968)
Highest R&B Chart Position: 2
Highest Hot 100 Chart Position: 2

In 1995, Adina Howard burst onto the music scene with her debut single "Freak Like Me." Howard got her start in the mid-1990s when she was introduced to manager-producer Livio Harris, who helped her record several demos, which led to a record deal with EastWest Records.

"Freak Like Me" samples Sly and the Family Stone's "Sing a Simple Song" and "I'd Rather Be with You" by Bootsy's Rubber Band, hence both are credited as joint writers and composers. One of the songs principal writers (all of whom are male), Loren Hill, described to the *The Baltimore Sun* how the song came into existence in a 1996 interview. He recounted how Howard's managers wanted a sexy image for their artist, so they requested that Hill write a sexually charged song. Hill stated, "The lyrics almost came out of frustration, Like, 'ok, you want a freak song, we'll give you a freak song.'" The duo did more than that; they gave us a freak anthem that dominated radio airplay and skyrocketed to number 2 on the R&B and pop charts with only Montell Jordan's megahit "This Is How We Do It" keeping it out of the number 1 spot on both charts. The song's popularity even got the attention of the Republican presidential nominee, Senator Bob Dole, who simply called the song "indecent."

However controversial, the song did lead to a level of success that even its writers didn't see coming. Hill added, "We'd hoped it would go gold, but we didn't expect it would go almost double platinum." "Freak Like Me" was by far Howard's biggest hit and her only platinum seller. Her follow-up singles from her album *Do You Wanna Ride?* included "My Up and Down" (32) and "It's All About You" (58), neither of which broke into the R&B top 30.

In 1997, Howard recorded her second album, *Welcome to Fantasy Island,* but it was shelved by her new label Elektra Records. One of the album's tracks, "T-Shirt & Panties," a collaboration with comedian-actor and musician Jamie Foxx, ended up on the soundtrack for the 1998 film *Woo*. "T-Shirt & Panties" was not released as a commercial single, therefore it was not eligible for the charts.

Some of Howard's other minor hits (all of which have the same theme) include "(Freak) And U Know It" (32), "Nasty Grind" (95), and "Freaks" (with Play-N-Skillz and Krayzie Bone) (52).

None of Howard's subsequent releases broke the top 30.

Un-Break My Heart

Artist: Toni Braxton
Album: Secrets
Year: 1996
Writer: Diane Warren
Producer: David Foster
Highest R&B Chart Position: 1
Highest Hot 100 Chart Position: 2

"Un-Break My Heart" is by far Toni Braxton's biggest commercial success. The song topped the Hot 100 and R&B charts for eleven weeks and one week respectively.

It was released as the second single from Braxton's sophomore album *Secrets,* which is one of the top-selling R&B albums of the decade at 8 million sales. The single has sold over 10 million copies worldwide.

The song's writer, Diane Warren, speaking about "Un-Break My Heart," told *The Wall Street Journal* in 2010, "It popped into my head, and I thought, 'I don't think I've heard that before, that's kind of interesting.' I started playing around on the piano with these chords and did a key change, and then I knew, 'ok, this is magic.'"

Braxton reportedly did not like the song when she first heard it because she feared being pigeonholed as a heartbreak queen. Her most popular songs to that point had all been about cheating or relationship problems. Her successful debut album included the songs "Seven Whole Days" (1), where her lover ghosted her for a week; "Love Should'a Brought You Home" (2), where her lover stays out all night with another woman; "Breathe Again" (4), where she threatens to stop breathing if she loses her lover; and ironically enough "Another Sad Love Song" (2).

Thankfully, Braxton agreed to record the track, which ultimately became her signature song.

One in a Million

Artist: Aaliyah
Album: One in a Million
Year: 1996
Writers: Missy Elliott, Timbaland
Producer: Timbaland
Highest R&B Chart Position: Song did not chart
Highest Hot 100 Chart Position: Song did not chart

Aaliyah, like Usher Raymond is another *Star Search* loser who would go on to immense success. Less than five years after losing on the show in November of 1989, she would have the number 1 song in the country.

Aaliyah began her professional singing career under the tutelage of her mentor, artist R. Kelly. Both Kelly and Aaliyah were signed to Jive Records, and it was Kelly who wrote and produced the majority of Aaliyah's 1994 debut album, *Age Ain't Nothing but a Number.* The album was a huge success, generating triple-platinum sales. Its lead single, "Back and Forth," was number 1 for three weeks, and her remake of the Isley Brothers' 1976 classic "(At Your Best) You Are Love" peaked at number 2. In 1994, it was discovered that the twenty-seven-year-old Kelly was involved in an intimate relationship with the then fifteen-year-old Aaliyah. The duo briefly married in 1994, but the marriage was quickly annulled.

Following this revelation, Jive released Aaliyah from her contract and she signed with Atlantic Records. Once signed to Atlantic, she began to work on her image and maturing her sound. An especially gifted artist, she was granted an immense amount of control over the direction of the album.

During the recording process for *One in a Million*, Atlantic received a demo of a song called "Sugar and Spice," which was produced by then unknown Producers Timothy "Timbaland" Mosley and Missy "Misdemeanor" Elliott. The duo had recently took a leap of faith and were working independently after fleeing DeVanté Swing of Jodeci's Swing Mob label, where they were reportedly underpaid and not properly credited for their work.

Timbaland says of the demo, "We sent her a song called 'Sugar and Spice'; this how dope Aaliyah was, she said, 'I don't like the song 'Sugar and Spice,' but I want to work with the producer and the writer who wrote that record' . . . and she flew us up the next day. She didn't like the record, but she knew it was something special in me and Missy." The duo then met Aaliyah and Atlantic Records chairman and CEO Craig Kallman. Kallman said of the meeting, "This young kid came in. His name was Tim Mosley. He started playing me beats and I thought 'This doesn't sound like anything that's out there. It had really super exciting and electric, just dynamic properties."

The album was recorded from August 1995 through early 1996. According to *Songfacts.com*, "Missy Elliott recalled to *Billboard* that she and Timbaland were called in to work on just one song with Aaliyah. However, that one track turned into eight, and the *One in a Million* album was birthed. The record was Aaliyah's breakthrough and a major milestone in the careers of Missy Elliott and Timbaland." Aside from Timbaland and Missy Elliott, who both wrote and produced the majority of material, the album featured a wide range of producers, including Barry Hankerson and Jomo Hankerson, who served as the executive producers, and Jermaine Dupri, Rodney Jerkins, Daryl Simmons, and KayGee. Additionally, Aaliyah was more involved with crafting the material by taking co-writing credits and assisting in the creative direction of the project.

Elliott told *Billboard* she wrote "One in a Million" in a rap-singing style, as back then she didn't know how to write songs for singers. "I was scared," she said. "I don't know if Tim was scared when we first played it because it was a different sound. It was a different way to attack records because people were really singing then; that world of rap-singing didn't really exist." However, Aaliyah loved the song. "She had an ear and she knew what that music made her feel like. She was next level to understand that this is some next level [music]. This is not just the sound that's going on right now—this is a new sound that is being created. This whole movement is new."

"If Your Girl Only Knew," written and produced by Timbaland and Missy Elliott, was the first single released from the album. It reached number 1 on the R&B chart. After the album's second single, "Got to Give it Up," a remake of Marvin Gaye's 1977 hit produced by Vincent Herbert and Craig King, received a less positive reception and failed to chart, the album's third single, "One in a Million," also produced by Timbaland and Elliott, was released. Like "If Your Girl Only Knew," Timbaland and Elliott delivered again, and "One in a Million" topped the R&B charts for two weeks and reached number 11 on the Hot 100. The album produced three more singles, "Hot Like Fire" and the ballads "4 Page Letter" and "The One I Gave My Heart To," with only the latter charting, reaching number 8 on the R&B chart.

One in a Million outperformed expectations en route to reaching triple-platinum status and cementing Aaliyah's legacy as a superstar.

Aaliyah would later comment, "I faced the adversity, I could've broken down, I could've gone and hid in the closet and said, 'I'm not going to do this anymore.' But I love singing, and I wasn't going to let that mess stop me. I got a lot of support from my fans and that inspired me to put that behind me, be a stronger person, and put my all into making *One in a Million*."

Interlude
Janet Jackson Dominates The Charts

Janet Jackson shot into music super-stardom in the mid-1980s, first with the release of her third album, *Control*, in 1986 and her fourth, *Rhythm Nation 1814*, in 1989. Both smashes were produced by hitmakers Jimmy Jam and Terry Lewis and contained a combined eight number 1 hits. As the 1990s began, Janet (Ms. Jackson, if you nasty) was still riding high from *Rhythm Nation's* success with five songs still in the top 10. In fact, the last single from the *Rhythm Nation* album to exit the charts would be "Love Will Never Do Without You" (3) in April of 1991, nearly two years after the album's release.

Jackson's success did not come without some criticism from those in the media, who saw her as the product of her production team and not her musical talent. In 1993, *The New York Times* published a review in which a critic called Jackson "a producer-dependent artist—i.e., someone who relies on others to make her sound interesting and trendy." The article further stated, "She also lacks a sharply defined personality, both as an artist and celebrity." According to *Stereogum.com,* the critic also noted that "Janet didn't have the massive voice of a Whitney Houston or a Mariah Carey" and that "in dance-pop, musical style can become dated overnight." While the statement comparing Jackson's voice to Whitney Houston's or Mariah Carey's is indisputable, so is Janet's talents as a vocalist and entertainer. She released two albums in the 1990s, 1993's *Janet* and 1997's *The Velvet Rope*. Both were not only highly successful, they also showcased Jackson's undeniable talent as a writer, producer, and recording artist, able to carry R&B and pop ballads alongside up-tempo jams. A selection of some of her '90s hits are profiled here.

That's the Way Love Goes

Artist: Janet Jackson
Album: Janet
Year: 1993
Writers: Charles Bobbitt, James Brown, Janet Jackson, Jimmy Jam, Terry Lewis, John Stark, Fred Wesley
Producers: Janet Jackson, Jimmy Jam, Terry Lewis
Notable Samples: Papa Don't Take No Mess, James Brown
Impeach the President, The Honey Drippers
Highest R&B Chart Position: 1
Highest Hot 100 Chart Position: 1

In coming up with the song, producer Jimmy Jam channeled his inner James Brown as he recalled, saying, "I'm a huge James Brown fan and I always thought it'd be cool to take something funky he did but actually make a song out of it. So that was the intention."

With James Brown in mind, Jam and Lewis sampled his number 1 1974 hit "Papa Don't Take No Mess" and turned it into "That's the Way Love Goes." But when Jam and Lewis played the song for Janet, she was not impressed. Jam says, "She kind of said, 'Eh, it's ok,' and so we moved on—because we were working on a ton of other things, too." Jam added, "When we took a break around the Christmas holidays she said, 'Put a cassette together for me,' and I put that track on there because, in my mind, it was still a viable track. She went to Anguilla and when she came back, the first thing she said was, 'We've gotta work on that track' and she immediately came up with the title."

"That's the Way Love Goes" was the first single from the *Janet* album. The label wanted to release the up-tempo song "If" as the first single, but Jimmy Jam and Terry Lewis thought that "If" was what everyone expected from Janet and they fought for releasing "That's the Way Love Goes" first. Jam recalled, "We had Chuck D. [of the rap group Public Enemy] and Hank Shocklee in the studio and we said: 'Can we get your opinion?' It was about three in the morning, but we played 'That's the Way Love Goes' and then we played 'If' and said: 'So, which one?' Chuck was like, '"If," man, that's a Janet record. But that other one, that's like when Sade releases a record, and there's no hype about it, it's just all-of-a-sudden in front of you.' And so Janet looked at him, and she said: 'ok, it's "That's the Way Love Goes."'" Jam, Lewis, and Chuck D. were right. "That's the Way Love Goes" was released first, and it peaked at number 1 on both the R&B and Hot 100 charts and is the longest running number 1 single for any member of the Jackson family on the Hot 100. "If" peaked at number 3 on the R&B chart and number 4 on the pop chart.

If

Artist: Janet Jackson
Album: Janet
Year: 1993
Writers: Jackey Beavers, John Bristol, Harvey Fuqua, Janet Jackson, Jimmy Jam, Terry Lewis
Producers: Janet Jackson, Jimmy Jam, Terry Lewis
Notable Samples: Someday We'll Be Together, Diana Ross & the Supremes (1969)
Hihache, Lafayette Afro Rock Band (1973)
Highest R&B Chart Position: 3
Highest Hot 100 Chart Position: 4

In case you missed it, "If" was the second single released from the *Janet* album. Jimmy Jam described the song as "very loud" and "metallic," calling it "basically like the tail-end of Rhythm Nation."

The up-tempo track stayed on the R&B chart for thirty weeks, peaking at number 3. The song seemingly sprung forth out of nowhere as Janet recalled saying, "Jimmy [Jam] was watching a ball game and playing around on the keyboards. I asked him to play the chords he was playing again. 'If' turned out to be funkier, grittier." Jackson told *Q* magazine, "The song is about fantasizing. I've had those feelings. 'If' is about a girl who goes to a club and fantasizes about this guy: serious fantasies about the things she'd do to him if she was his girl—the positions and things like that. But she's not, so she can't, so she gets pretty frustrated in the second verse."

Scream

Artist: Michael Jackson, featuring Janet Jackson
Album: HIStory: Past, Present and Future, Book I
Year: 1995
Writers: Janet Jackson, Michael Jackson, Jimmy Jam, Terry Lewis
Producers: Janet Jackson, Michael Jackson, Jimmy Jam, Terry Lewis
Highest R&B Chart Position: 2
Highest Hot 100 Chart Position: 5

"Scream" is the lead single from Michael Jackson's ninth studio album, *HIStory: Past, Present and Future, Book I*. The song is a duet between Michael and Janet Jackson. It is said to have been written by Michael, Jam, and Lewis in response to Michael's frustrations with events he was going through at the time—events that included accusations of child molestation and constant scrutiny from the media. Although a bona fide hit, the song is probably best remembered for its video, which at the time was the most expensive music video ever made, costing $7 million.

The track showcased a bit of sibling rivalry, as Jimmy Jam and Terry Lewis explained to *The Breakfast Club* in 2020. Although Jam and Lewis have a recording studio in Minneapolis, Minnesota, they met Michael and Janet in New York, City to record "Scream," with Michael and Janet scheduled to record their parts separately in the same studio. According to Jam and Lewis, Michael went into the recording booth first while Janet watched from the control room with Jam and Lewis. Well, Michael murders his take, leaving Jam, Lewis, and Janet in awe, and according to Lewis, Janet "just leans into him and says: 'I'll do my vocal in Minneapolis.' She wanted no part of following Michael."

Got 'til It's Gone

Artist: Janet Jackson, Q-Tip
Album: The Velvet Rope
Year: 1997
Writers: René Elizondo, Janet Jackson, Jimmy Jam, Terry Lewis, Joni Mitchell, Q-Tip
Producers: Janet Jackson, Jimmy Jam, Terry Lewis
Notable Samples: Big Yellow Taxi, Joni Mitchell (1970)
        Feel So High, Des'ree (1991)
Highest R&B Chart Position: Song did not chart
Highest Hot 100 Chart Position: Song did not chart

"Got 'til It's Gone" was the first single from Jackson's sixth studio album, *The Velvet Rope* (1997). The song was not released as a commercial single, making it ineligible for the R&B and Hot 100 charts. However, it topped the R&B airplay charts that year. "Got 'til It's Gone" prominently features a sample of Joni Mitchell's 1970 hit "Big Yellow Taxi" and lines by rapper Q-tip. Q-Tip and Jackson originally met in 1992 on the set of the movie *Poetic Justice*. Q-tip told the *The Source* magazine that he was originally set for the role of Lucky, which was ultimately played by Tupac Shakur, but Q-Tip ended up playing the role of Jackson's boyfriend in the movie. When the two later connected on "Got 'til It's Gone," they began dating. Q-Tip recounted, "We started dating after that. It be cool 'n s***. She be making eggs 'n s*** and I'll be chilling like, 'Yo, that's Penny!' to myself. I love her to death and it's like she's a Jackson. That's black royalty."

Apparently, America was not that into black royalty at the time. Producer Jimmy Jam observed that "it was interesting in this country because pop radio didn't touch it. Probably the video didn't help." In the video, Jackson portrays a lounge singer in apartheid South Africa. Inspired by a blend of '60s and '70s African culture, the video depicts freedom and prosperity, opposing racial segregation and white supremacy. It ends with bottles thrown at Afrikaans segregation signs. Jam added, "Mark Romanek [the video's director] did such a beautiful job, but it was so ethnic . . . It just wasn't what people were feeling."

Interlude
Prince of Petty, The Emancipation of Jimmy Jam and Terry Lewis

Mega-producers James "Jimmy" Jam and Terry Lewis first met while both were high schoolers in Minnesota in the 1970s. Growing up in Minneapolis, they each played in rival bands that were vying for dominance in the crowded local music scene, which included a third rival, Prince. In the late 1970s, Lewis, Harris, and their band Flyte Tyme would morph into "The Time" with the addition of members Morris Day and Gary "Jellybean" Johnson as a result of a deal struck between Day and Prince whereby Day gave Prince the track for the song "Party Up" in exchange for Prince helping him put a band together and getting Day and The Time a record deal. The newly minted band, The Time would get signed by Warner Bros. and would go on to tour with Prince as his opening act.

It was while they were with The Time that the ambitious Jam and Lewis looked to delve further into songwriting and production. They began creating and shopping demos of their work, one of which got the attention of record executive Dick Griffey, founder of SOLAR Records.

There was just one problem: Prince strictly forbade the side work. Things came to a head when Jam and Lewis were doing side work producing for the S.O.S. Band in Atlanta, Georgia, and a rare snowstorm closed the Atlanta airport, causing the duo to miss a concert. Prince then terminated the pair as members of The Time. As Jam recalled for *Vibe.com* in 2022, "So when we got to the studio, it was Prince, Morris, Jesse, and Terry and myself. And he [Prince] said, 'I told you guys not to produce outside acts and you did, so you're fired.'"

After being dismissed from the band, Jam and Lewis devoted their time to songwriting and production. Thankfully their first major production credit apart from The Time was the track "Just Be Good to Me" (1983), which they were working on prior to being fired by Prince. The song, which was recorded by the S.O.S. Band, entered the *Billboard* Hot Black Singles chart at number 2 and the Hot 100 chart at number 55 in 1983 en route to becoming a smash hit. The duo has been in high demand ever since and has produced multiple gold, platinum, multi-platinum, and diamond-selling albums, over forty *Billboard* Top 10 songs, and twenty-six number 1 R&B hits.

One of the duos biggest early projects was Janet Jackson's 1986 smash album *Control*. Songs from the *Control* album were all over the radio in the mid-1980s, and it made Jimmy Jam and Terry Lewis the hottest producers in music. According to Lewis, this didn't go unnoticed by Prince, who, in a major act of pettiness, drove by Lewis' home and threw a copy of the *Control* album out of his car window.

Artist Profile
Mariah Carey

Mariah Carey's influence on '90s R&B is undeniable. She burst onto the scene with her self-titled debut album in 1990 and has since released some of the best-selling albums of all time. She had nineteen top 10 R&B hits in the 1990s, including seven number 1's. Her God-given talent had her poised to rival R&B's greatest legends. However, for years her management prevented her from embracing the R&B/hip-hop fan base for fear of hurting her pop image and their bottom line. That was until she rebelled in the form of hip-hop collaborations that would become classics and set the tone for the next generation of R&B music.

Vision of Love

Artist: Mariah Carey
Album: Mariah Carey
Year: 1990
Writers: Mariah Carey, Ben Margulies
Producers: Rhett Lawrence, Narada Michael Walden
Highest R&B Chart Position: 1
Highest Hot 100 Chart Position: 1

"Vision of Love" was Mariah Carey's first single. She was working as a waitress to support her music career when she met the song's co-writer, Ben Margulies. They wrote "Vision of Love" between late 1988 and early 1989 while trying to secure a record deal with Columbia Records after her demo tape had impressed studio executives. While many interpret it as a love song, in a 1991 interview with *Ebony* magazine, Carey explained how the lyrics reflected her success in overcoming the hardships of a difficult childhood which included difficulties encountered from growing up as a biracial child and the struggles she would encounter and overcome in making it in the music industry.

Prayed through the nights /
Felt so alone /
Suffered from alienation /
Carried the weight on my own /
Had to be strong /
So I believed /
And now I know I've succeeded /
In finding the place I conceived.

Listening to the verses now, it is clear that this is more of a motivational track than a love ballad.

Once the deal with Columbia was secured, Carey was sent to Los Angeles to meet with producers Narada Michael Walden and Rhett Lawrence. Lawrence said of when he first heard Carey's voice, "I literally got goose bumps on my arms when I heard her sing. I couldn't believe the power and maturity in her voice." That power and maturity would wow audiences when the single was released in May of 1990 on the way to becoming an R&B number 1 in August of that year.

Carey built her stellar career off the song's success and became the top-selling female artist of the decade. Her debut album alone has sold over 17 million copies around the world, and "Vision of Love" won Carey the 1990 Grammy for Best Pop Vocal Performance, Female. She also won the award for Best New Artist that year.

One Sweet Day

Artist: Mariah Carey
Album: Daydream
Year: 1995
Writers: Walter Afanasieff, Boyz II Men, Mariah Carey
Producers: Walter Afanasieff, Boyz II Men, Mariah Carey
Highest R&B Chart Position: 2
Highest Hot 100 Chart Position: 1

This song was the product of tragedies experienced by Mariah Carey and Boyz II Men. Each had written songs independently in response to their respective losses. It was not until they came together that they realized they were

Interlude
Mariah Carey vs. Mary J. Blige

First off, let us start by saying that much like Carey's "rivalry" with Whitney Houston, her supposed rivalry with Mary J. Blige is also largely media and fan driven and that both of these ladies also openly express adoration for one another as artists and women. Now with all respect to the greatness of Whitney Houston, it is Mariah Carey's comparison to Mary J. Blige that continues to draw the most enthusiastic reactions. Whichever side you are on, you don't believe this is even a contest. Both have numerous classic songs, albums, and collaborations, and both have immensely influenced the genre. Mary is the undisputed Queen of Hip-Hop Soul, with the legacy of Aretha Franklin being the only thing standing between her ruling R&B altogether. And while Mariah does not have the title or the love from R&B fans like Mary, she did far better on the charts and in the sales numbers, particularly in the 1990s where Carey produced two of the top 10 best-selling albums of all time. Ironically, however, it must be noted that the sales were largely due to Carey's crossover appeal as a pop/adult contemporary artist.

Mariah Carey	Mary J. Blige
Number 1 Songs	
7	4
Top 10 Songs	
22	11
Charting Songs	
22	11
Top Selling Albums	
Daydream (1995) 11 Million	Share My World (1997) 5 Million

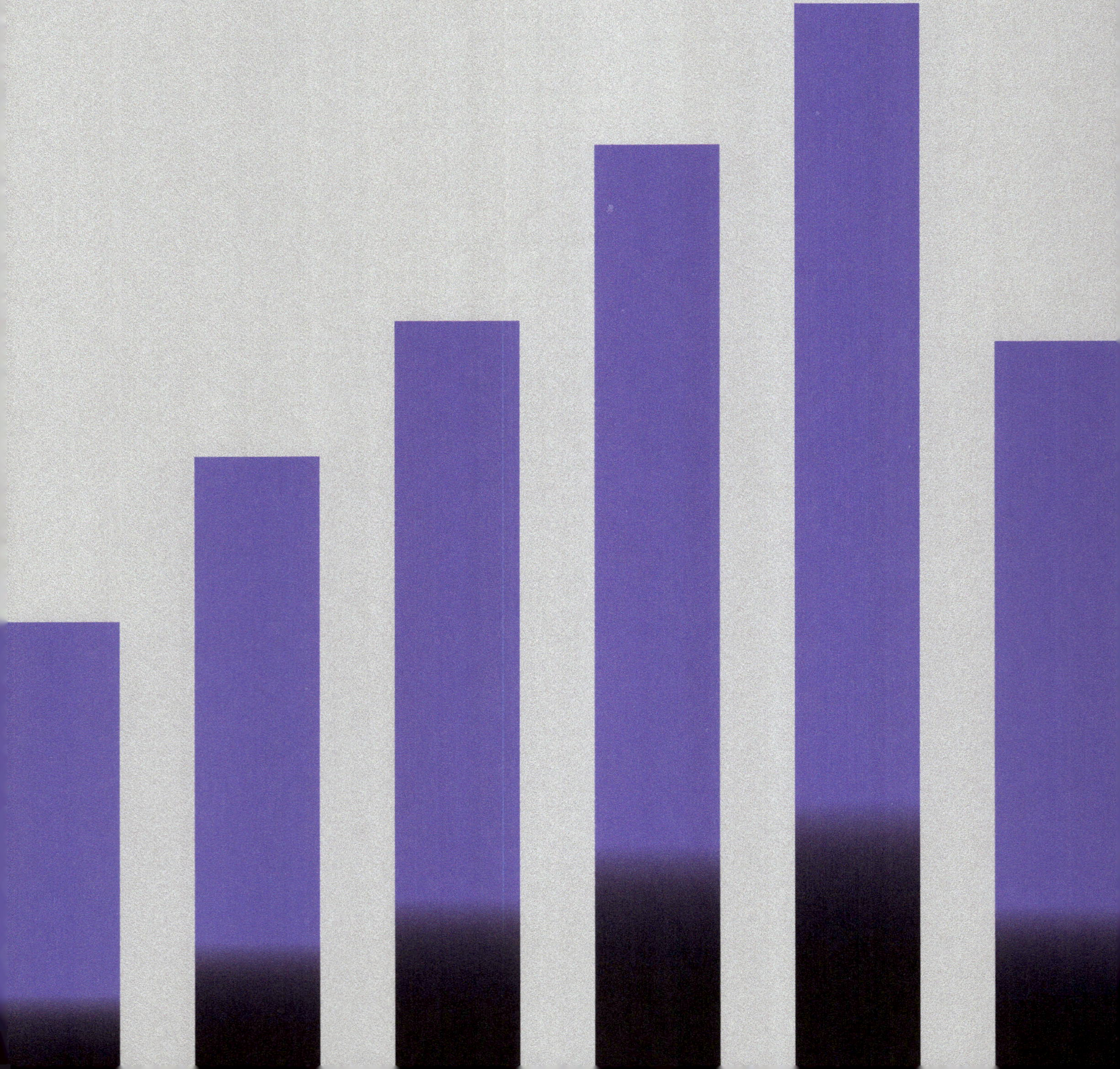

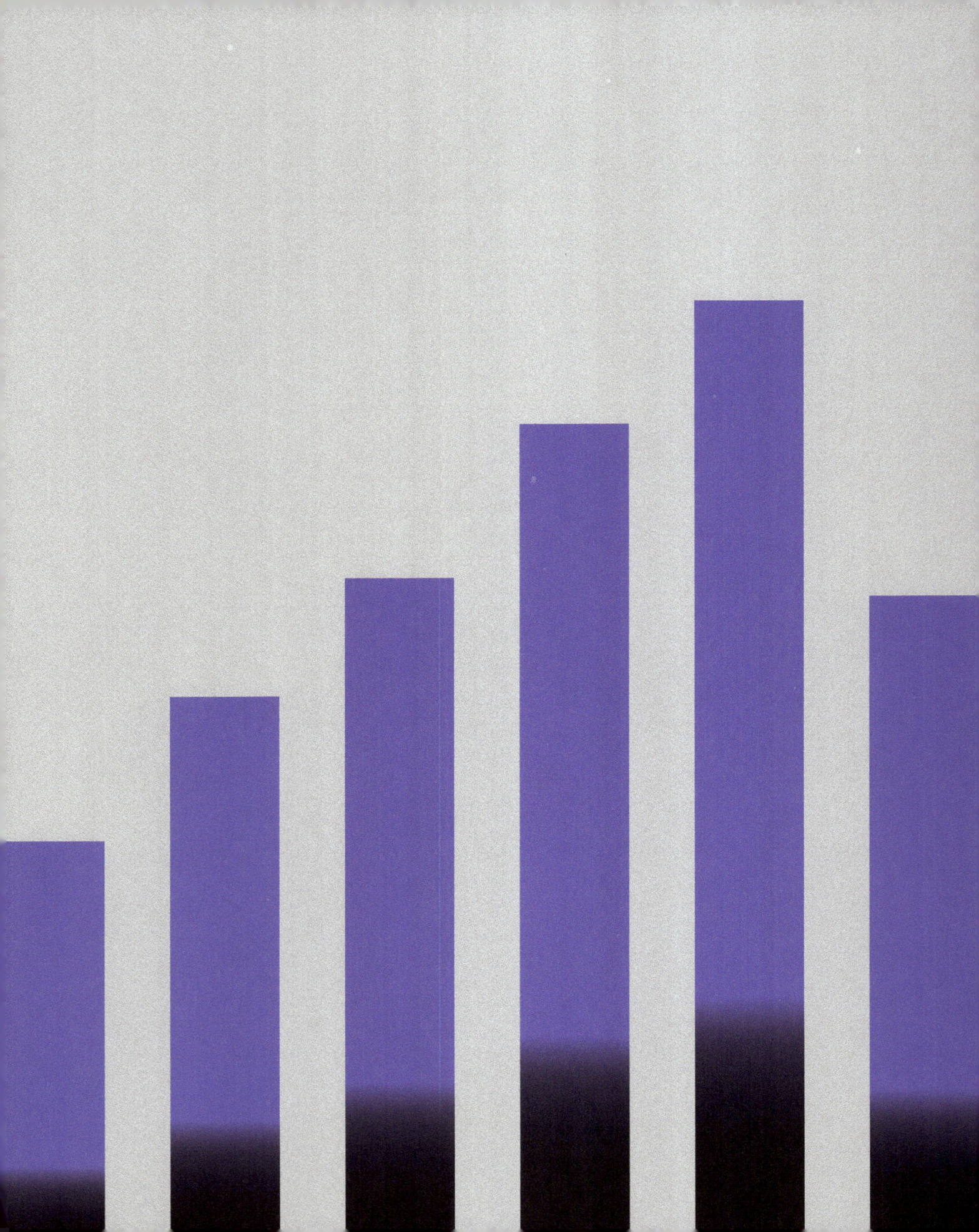

This is How We Do It: The Hip-Hop Hybrid Era
1994 - Present

Anything (Old School Party Mix)
I Wanna Be Down (The Human Rhythm Hip Hop Mix)
This Is How We Do It
Freek'n You Remix (Mr. Dalvin's Freek Mix)
Can't You See
Only You
I Gotta Be
No, No, No Part 2
Are U Still Down
Breakdown
Let's Ride
Artist Profile: R. Kelly

This is How We Do It: The Hip-Hop Hybrid Era | 1994 - Present

Somewhere in the great expanse of the music universe, the celestial beings of Rap and R&B collided, and that big bang gave life to what became the hip-hop hybrid. After years of image-conscious record labels drawing a clear line to prevent rappers and R&B singers from co-mingling in public, fearing career suicide, suddenly it was ok for rappers to jump on R&B love songs and provide interludes and singers could now provide hooks in between rap verses. The result increased the popularity of both genres and powered each to sales numbers and influence that had never been seen before.

Anything (Old School Party Mix)

Artist: SWV, Wu-Tang Clan
Album: It's About Time, Above the Rim soundtrack
Year: 1994
Writers: Ol' Dirty Bastard, Brian Alexander Morgan, U God, Method Man
Producers: Allen Gordon, Brian Alexander Morgan
Notable Samples: Get Up and Dance, Freedom (1979)
C.R.E.A.M., Wu-Tang Clan (1993)
Highest R&B Chart Position: 4
Highest Hot 100 Chart Position: 18

The original version of SWV's "Anything" was released for their 1992 debut studio album, *It's About Time*. This version was a typical early '90s R&B slow jam complete with lead singer Coko's soulful open to the track, SWV's tight harmonies throughout, and a slow piano set against a grooving bass line. Despite being a groove, this version failed to break the R&B top 40.

The remix and rebirth of "Anything" would occur on the *Above the Rim* movie soundtrack. The film is the story of the challenges faced by a promising high school basketball player played by Duane Martin and his relationship with his two brothers, one a drug dealer played by rapper Tupac Shakur and the other a former basketball player who is battling personal demons played by Leon.

Marion "Suge" Knight, the head of Death Row Records, was the executive producer of the film's soundtrack. Death Row was headquartered in Los Angeles, and while it had a formidable stable of more than capable west coast artists, it faced the daunting task of building an authentic soundtrack to a film set in Harlem, New York.

Enter New York natives SWV. To build the song, the producer of the original "Anything," Brian Alexander Morgan, collaborated with fellow producer Allen Gordon Jr., a.k.a. Allstar, and the two remixed "Anything" for the soundtrack. They transformed the ballad into a fast-paced jam, still showcasing SWV's harmonies with Coko as the centerpiece but in a quicker tempo and adding thumping old-school rap samples and killer verses from New York–area rappers from the Wu-Tang Clan. As Bandini of *AmbrosiaForHeads.com* wrote, "The song fell into a new groove, the perfect juxtaposition of street and soft, with samples of Grandmaster Flash & The Furious Five, which covered 'Get Up and Dance' by Freedom or the drums and horns and the hottest new rap group, Wu-Tang Clan—sprinkled verses. Breakout group star Method Man, clique jester Ol' Dirty Bastard, and the mahogany-voiced U-God splashed the track with fast musings that were a chest-pass away from the song's R&B roots. In a Death Row soundtrack to a film set in Harlem, New York—this mix had lots of Uptown flavor."

The soundtrack was released by Death Row/Interscope Records in March 1994 and would eventually become the number 1 R&B album in the country. The "Anything" single, one of many standouts on the *Above the Rim* soundtrack, went gold and became SWV's fifth pop hit and their sixth top 10 R&B hit. However, it was outperformed in sales by another song from the soundtrack, rappers Warren G and Nate Dogg's smash "Regulate," which went double platinum.

The combination of Morgan, Allstar, and SWV had a thing for successful remixes. So much so that the trio would release a remix album later in 1994 that would include the "Anything" remix as well as remixes for their hits "Weak," "Right Here," and "I'm So into You." The album went gold.

I Wanna Be Down (The Human Rhythm Hip Hop Mix)

Artist: Brandy, Queen Latifah, MC Lyte, Yo-Yo
Album: Single
Year: 1994
Writers: Keith Crouch, Kipper Jones, Queen Latifah, MC Lyte, Yo-Yo
Producer: Keith Crouch
Notable Sample: U.N.I.T.Y., Queen Latifah (1993)
Highest R&B Chart Position: Song did not chart
Highest Hot 100 Chart Position: Song did not chart

"I Wanna Be Down" is the debut single by Brandy Norwood, a.k.a. Brandy, from her self-titled debut album released in 1994. The song was about as successful as a debut could be, reaching number 1 on the R&B chart and charting in several countries.

While Norwood liked the song, she didn't initially like the idea of "I Wanna Be Down" being her first single. In 2012 she told *Complex* magazine, "I didn't really get it at first, but I was young and I didn't really know what worked at radio or what it was. I liked the song, but I just didn't get it being the first thing that people heard from me. Once it was released and I saw how everyone responded to the title phrase, I understood why!" Brandy added, "Everyone started using the phrase 'I wanna be down . . .' and I had an 'aha' experience!"

Upon the song's release and success, Atlantic Records head Sylvia Rhone came up with the idea of re-recording the song with a group of female rappers. She recruited Yo-Yo, Queen Latifah, and MC Lyte to add to the remix. MC Lyte needed little convincing. She was already a Brandy fan, as she would recall years later. Prior to being approached to do the remix, Lyte had seen Brandy (who already had a starring role on the short-lived 1993 ABC sitcom *Thea* and would go on to play the title character Moesha Mitchell on the hit TV show *Moesha*) in an interview where she said she wanted to do it all—act and sing. An impressed MC Lyte, who was already a hip-hop legend, jumped at the opportunity to do the record. Her memorable verse, which included the line, "You be that brother that I wanna sink my teeth in / Make me wanna ask 'Where the hell you been?'" was so formidable that it prompted Queen Latifah to rewrite her verse for the song. When the artists reunited on the set of *The Queen Latifah Show* in 2014 for the almost twenty-year anniversary of the remix's release, Queen Latifah recalled, "I thought it was a Brandy record, but Lyte made me rewrite my part!"

Brandy, who was sixteen at the time of recording, recalled her groupie experience with the hip-hop legends, saying of the remix in 2012, "The hip-hop remix meant the world to me. I'm fresh out of the box and these superstars are a part of my first single! They are my mentors and I looked up to them. I was a huge Queen Latifah fan. I'm thinking, 'Oh my God . . . I can't believe this is happening to me.' I got the chance to vibe with all three of them. They embraced me as a little sister. I was one of the first R&B artists to welcome hip-hop onto an R&B beat. It had never been done before quite like that [. . .] I knew it was a special record." The remix was released as a B side to Norwood's follow-up single "Baby" and soon became a smash of its own and a staple of R&B radio in 1995.

The four artists have performed the remix together live a number of times, most recently at the 2018 Essence Festival.

This Is How We Do It

Artist: Montell Jordan
Album: This Is How We Do It
Year: 1995
Writers: Montell Jordan, Oji Pierce, Slick Rick
Producers: Montell Jordan, Oji Pierce
Notable Sample: Children's Story, Slick Rick (1988)
Highest R&B Chart Position: 1
Highest Hot 100 Chart Position: 1

"There are two kinds of people in this world: people who roll their eyes to the point of pain when 'This Is How We Do It' comes on at a party and people who are ready to scream-sing the song's very first 'sha-la-la-la-la-la-la' as soon as the beat hits." That quote from writer Clarence Loberfeld describes every cookout since the summer of 1995.

"This Is How We Do It" was released as Montell Jordan's debut single from his debut album, *This Is How We Do It.* Jordan, who graduated summa cum laude from Pepperdine University in 1991 with a degree in communications, is a musician at heart. Like so many other R&B artists, he grew up playing music in church before making the transition to secular music. He was signed to Def Jam Recordings in 1995 after a mix tape he recorded got the attention of Def Jam executives. Jordan, who maintains that he was signed as a rapper, is officially credited as only the second R&B artist signed to Def Jam. Oran "Juice" Jones, most well known for his single "The Rain" (1), was the first in 1986. Jordan describes the song as "an eternal party anthem" and as a "direct reflection of what street life was for a good kid growing up in the neighborhood." This is a song that all of us could relate to.

Loberfeld remarked, "There are so many memorable lines in this song! Whether he was reaching for his 40, or seeing the 'summertime skirts, and the guys in Kani,' Montell painted a picture of a fun carefree night out. He even made sure he had a designated driver, so you know he was tryna get it in that night! It's the responsibility for me! But the best line . . . 'You gotta get your grooooove on . . .' You can't tell me when he sings that part, it doesn't touch your soul." Or that you aren't reminded of when Martin Lawrence sang it over and over in outtakes from his television show Martin. The song stayed at number 1 for seven consecutive weeks and remains one of the definitive songs of the decade.

"This Is How We Do It" doesn't give the deserved credence to the rest of Jordan's career. He would build quite a catalog following up the success of the *This Is How We Do It* album with three more gold albums during the decade. He spent the latter half of the '90s on the R&B and pop charts with singles from his first three albums, like the 1998 number 1 "Let's Ride" and the 1999 number 1 "Get it On Tonight." Jordan was also a songwriter for other artists, most notably penning Deborah Cox's ubiquitous 1998 hit "Nobody's Supposed to Be Here" (1).

Jordan later became a born-again Christian and left the music industry in 2010 to become a minister.

Freek'n You Remix (Mr. Dalvin's Freek Mix)

Artist: Jodeci, Ghostface Killah, Raekwon
Album: The Show, the After-Party, the Hotel
Year: 1995
Writers: Dalvin DeGrate, Ghostface Killah, Raekwon, DeVanté Swing
Producer: Dalvin DeGrate
Highest R&B Chart Position: Song did not chart
Highest Hot 100 Chart Position: Song did not chart

The original "Freek'n You" by Jodeci was released as the first single from the group's third studio album, 1995's *The Show, the After-Party, the Hotel.* Jodeci could do no wrong (on the charts) at this point, and "Freek'n You" became one of the best-selling singles of 1995. The success prompted the recording of a remix of the song, which was a popular tactic at the time, as in the mid-1990s labels would record and release remixes of popular songs to extend the hit's shelf life and sales.

The official remix of "Freek'n You," like the original, was produced by Dalvin "Mr. Dalvin" DeGrate of Jodeci. The song features Raekwon and Ghostface Killah of the rap group the Wu-Tang Clan. In August 2020, Mr. Dalvin told *AllHipHop.com* that he called Wu-Tang member RZA to get Method Man on the remix because "Method Man was first coming out of the Wu-Tang camp, the only one everyone was familiar with," but unfortunately Method Man was in Tokyo at the time. Mr. Dalvin added, "RZA said, 'I got these two new guys coming out next in line, Raekwon and Ghostface Killah. They're not known yet but they're next, trust me.' I said ok. Anybody from Wu-Tang because I like Wu-Tang. Sent them guys to the studio, they've never been on an R&B record."

Wu-Tang brought a different kind of vibe than the original "Freek'n You." They brought the full-on street vibe that Jodeci had only flirted with up until that point. The song was a perfect marriage of rap and R&B. Mr. Dalvin said, "The funny thing about them is they didn't know what to expect from me, and I didn't know what to expect from them. They came with forty dudes with machetes, these masks on in the studio. I didn't know what was going to happen." What did happen was the creation of a song that properly introduced Raekwon and Ghostface to the world, and the hit became almost as popular as the album version. As Mr. Dalvin put it, "I came up with the beat, they got on it, and it was history."

Can't You See

Artist: Total
Album: New Jersey Drive, Vol. 1 soundtrack
Year: 1995
Writers: James Brown, Sean Combs, Joseph Howell, Herb Middleton, Ghostface Killah, Mark South, John Starks, Fred Wesley, Terri Robinson, Christopher Wallace
Producer: Sean Combs
Notable Sample: The Payback, James Brown (1973)
Highest R&B Chart Position: 3
Highest Hot 100 Chart Position: 13

The trio known as Total (Kima Raynor, Keisha Spivey, and Pamela Long) was the first female group signed to Bad Boy Records. Their journey to Bad Boy started when friends Kima and Keisha decided to form a duo. Kima told *Essence* magazine, "She heard me singing Mariah Carey in the car one time and said, 'Let's start a group!' So, she saw something in me that I didn't see in myself. She gave me that confidence and encouragement."

The duo became a trio when a producer introduced them to Pam. Keisha recalled, "One day, our producer was like, 'I think y'all should hear this other girl, she's got a dope sound and I think y'all would all sound great together.'" The producer was right and Total was born. The newly formed trio were introduced to Bad Boy CEO Sean Combs by their manager, who arranged a meeting. They sang for Combs, but he didn't seem impressed according to Keisha, who said, "He asked us a few questions and then after we answered them, he was like, 'You girls are really good. I wish you a lot of luck. Just stay together and don't give up.' We kind of felt a little bad when we left. . . . I remember when we got the call later on that night. So, Total, B.I.G., and Craig Mack were the first artists that he signed to Bad Boy and the rest is history."

Once signed, the group provided background vocals for some of Bad Boy's biggest early rap hits, including The Notorious B.I.G. classics "Juicy" (14) and "One More Chance (Hip-Hop Mix)"(1).
When Total released their debut single "Can't You See" for the *New Jersey Drive* movie soundtrack, The Notorious B.I.G. returned the favor by providing a verse on the song. The song, which was also featured on Total's self-titled debut, would reach number 3 on the R&B chart.

The album produced three more R&B top 20 singles—"No One Else" (4), "Do You Think About Us" (20), and the Raphael Saadiq–penned "'Kissing You" (6)—and achieved platinum sales.

Prior to recording their second album, Total again provided memorable background vocals to songs like LL Cool J's "Loungin'/Who Do Ya Luv?" (4) and Mase's "What You Want" (3). The group also reunited with The Notorious

B.I.G. in providing the hook for his number 1 rap hit "Hypnotize."

Total's follow-up album, 1998's *Kim, Keisha & Pam*, was certified gold and produced Total's last two top 20 R&B hits, with the songs "Sitting Home" (10) and "Trippin'" (3), which was a collaboration with rapper Missy Elliott.

Only You

Artist: 112
Album: 112
Year: 1996
Writers: Mason Betha, Harry Wayne Casey, Sean Combs, Stevie J., Richard Finch, Daron Jones, Michael Keith, Nashiem Myrick, Quinnes Parker, D. J. Rogers, Christopher Wallace
Producers: Sean Combs, Stevie J., Nashiem Myrick
Highest R&B Chart Position: 3
Highest Hot 100 Chart Position: 13

112 group members Daron Jones, Michael Keith, Marvin Scandrick, and Quinnes "Q" Parker met as teenagers in Atlanta, Georgia. The group then known as Forte did their rounds on the competitive Atlanta talent show circuit until their demo, which was produced by fellow Atlantan Dallas Austin, made its way to Sean Combs, who was impressed by what he heard and requested to hear the group sing live. Combs was going to be at Atlanta's Club 112, and the group did not want to let the opportunity pass. However, the location for the audition presented a problem for the high schoolers, who were too young to get into the club. So they did what any aspiring artist would do—they sang a cappella for Combs in the club's parking lot.

Combs later signed the quartet to Bad Boy, changed their name to 112 (after the club), and moved them to New York City to record their debut album. The Atlanta natives were welcomed by the Bad Boy family, which at the time had marquee acts like Total, Faith Evans, and Junior M.A.F.I.A. But by far the biggest impression was left by Bad Boy artist The Notorious B.I.G. As 112 member Michael Keith recalled to *AllHipHop.com*, "This is when we realized how dope Big really was. One day in the studio at Diddy's house, we had a session in the SSL room. Somebody told us, 'Yo Big in the other room, he wanna holler at y'all.' Not really on anything, to say what up. We went into the room and from here on up, you couldn't see anybody because it had so much smoke. At the time, 112 didn't partake in anything like that. We went in and saw Big, he said, 'What up?' Jay-Z and Charli Baltimore sitting over in the corner. Everybody's enthralled with being in the room with Big. Big's sitting in the room smoking, he's not moving. A couple hours had passed, he's listening to all these stories. We're in there talking, Junior M.A.F.I.A., Lil' Cease. All of a sudden he gets up and tells the engineer he's ready. Dude went in the booth; you know that song 'I Got a Story to Tell'? The line "My 112, CD blast, I was past / She came twice, I came last." That originated in the room, that's how ill he is. He didn't write anything down."

Looking to make an impression themselves, 112 recorded their debut album *112* with B.I.G. leading off with a verse on their first single "Only You." Quinnes Parker remembered, "We wrote that song five times, only to go back to the first way we wrote it. We wanted that record to be the best it could be. Of course we had the original but when we got out with the remix, Stevie J. did the production. Being in the studio when B.I.G. put his rhyme on there, it was instant. We heard the words and it was perfect, wow. What Mase put on there was the sprinkling on top. Definitely a momentous occasion, can't forget that. History."

Being a Stevie J. production, the song has a bold hip-hop tone to it. This sound was a bit of a departure from what the group envisioned. According to Keith, "We wanted so badly to be known as R&B-singing crooners. When Puff came in with the idea of doing hip-hop and R&B, we said, 'Nah, bro, that's going to diminish what we got going on. We're real singers, it's going to take away from the true artistry.' Puff said, 'Yeah, I hear you. Slim, go in there and sing this R&B section real quick.' He already knew. He already had the template and the blueprint of what he wanted *112* to be and that it was going to be really special. . . . We're extremely proud."

The album, which also included the hits "Come See Me" (15) and "Cupid" (2), peaked at number 2 on the R&B chart and would go double platinum.

I Gotta Be

Artist: Jagged Edge
Album: A Jagged Era
Year: 1997
Writer: Brandon Casey, Brian Casey, Jermaine Dupri, Manuel Seal
Producers: Jermaine Dupri, Manuel Seal
Highest R&B Chart Position: 11
Highest Hot 100 Chart Position: 23

Like 112, Jagged Edge was also based out of Atlanta, Georgia. The group consists of identical twin brothers Brandon and Brian Casey, Kyle Norman, and Richard Wingo. Jagged Edge was born out of the Brandon and Brian Casey duo group Twin AK. Shortly following Norman joining the group, they changed their name to Jagged Edge. With the addition of Richard Wingo, the trio became the chart-topping quartet that we recognize today.

Although Xscape singer and hit songwriter Kandi Burruss is credited with discovering Jagged Edge, member Brian Casey contends that equal credit should also be given to Burruss' Xscape bandmate Tameka "Tiny" Cottle. Jagged Edge member Richard Wingo went to high school with Burruss. The group had become popular on the Atlanta talent show circuit and had cut a demo, hoping to land a record deal. They brought the demo to Burruss to get her thoughts. At the time Burruss was beginning to branch out and become more than just a singer. She was so impressed with the demo that she took on the role of becoming the group's manager. According to Casey, Burruss and Cottle took the demo to So So Def label head Jermaine Dupri. The demo led to an audition with Dupri, which resulted in the group's record deal with Columbia/So So Def Recordings.

Prior to signing with Dupri, Jagged Edge entertained deals with star-makers like Michael Bivins, Rico Wade of Organized Noize, and Dallas Austin's Rowdy Records, all of which fell apart before being finalized. According to Casey, what separated Dupri and So So Def was Dupri's willingness to let the group write their own material. This would prove beneficial to Dupri, as the Casey twins would contribute to hits for Jagged Edge and other So So Def artists like Usher Raymond's number 1 "Nice & Slow."

Jagged Edge also influenced Burruss in becoming a chart-topping writer. As Casey put it, "We influenced each other because when we got with her, she wasn't a writer . . . so we kind of opened her mind to becoming a songwriter and we would sit in her house, in her garage and we would all put stuff together and she would run things by us and it always sounded good."

Jagged Edge would go on to write the majority of the material for their ten-plus studio albums that would follow over the next twenty years, which included seven top 20 hits and three R&B number 1's. Only two of those albums were released in the 1990s, *A Jagged Era* (1997) and *J.E. Heartbreak* (1999). However, with classic songs like "Promise" (1), "Let's Get Married" (1), and "He Can't Love You" (3), those two albums left an indelible mark on late '90s and early 2000s R&B.

But this fantastic run almost didn't happen. Dupri believed so strongly in Jagged Edge that the label invested hundreds of thousands of dollars into recording and promoting their first single, "The Way That You Talk." So much so that when the song underperformed, only peaking at 34 on the R&B chart, Columbia Records executive Bart Phillips informed the group that if their second single "I Gotta Be" didn't work, "There would be no more Jagged Edge." Thankfully the song—which according to Burruss was written about her and her romantic relationship with Jagged Edge member Brandon Casey (which was ongoing while she was the group's manager)—was the highest charting single on the album, reaching number 11 on the R&B charts.

The song not only saved the group's record deal, but Brian Casey credits "I Gotta Be" with giving birth to Jagged Edge's first number 1 hit, 2000's "Let's Get Married" from their multiplatinum sophomore album *J.E. Heartbreak*. According to Casey, "When we did 'Gotta Be' it was so many people sending our label videos and things, getting married to our song . . . so once we saw the effect of that, JD [Jermaine Dupri] said to us, he was like, 'Look, man, people really out here getting married off this song. Why don't you all really give them a song to get married to?' We was like, 'What you mean?' He was like, 'Just make a song called "Let's Get Married!"' So we took that concept, we wrote the record, and you know it's just one of those things."

With a hit in "I Gotta Be" under their belt, Jagged Edge started touring with the popular up-and-coming female group Destiny's Child. By this time Burruss and Brandon Casey had ended their relationship on amicable terms. While on tour, Brandon began a relationship with Destiny's Child member LaTavia Roberson, and Brian Casey began a relationship with her bandmate LeToya Luckett.

The chemistry is not so obvious in the second music video for "I Gotta Be." The first video featured Jagged Edge donning suits and singing to the camera in various scenes. The second video featured them paired with their tour mates Destiny's Child as their love interests. In the video, which takes place over several scenes, Brandon is paired with Roberson, but Brian is paired with Kelly Rowland and not his real-life girlfriend LeToya Luckett. Both scenes are fairly sterile, featuring Brandon and Roberson getting into an SUV after shopping and Brian pushing Rowland on a swing. The relationships between the teenage members of Destiny's Child and the more mature members of Jagged Edge, who were in their early twenties, did not sit well with Destiny's Child's image-conscious manager Mathew Knowles. It is not certain whether these relationships were the reason or simply a reason why Luckett and Roberson were dismissed from the tour following an incident where Jagged Edge, Luckett, Roberson, and Roberson's mother were removed from the tour. According to Knowles, Jagged Edge was removed because they had harassed group members Beyoncé Knowles and Kelly Rowland. But according to Jagged Edge, they were removed from the tour for simply sticking up for Roberson and her mother following an altercation. Roberson and Luckett were subsequently dismissed from Destiny's Child altogether later that year.

Brandon Casey and Roberson's romantic relationship continued for eight years and inspired at least one R&B number 1 hit, 2000's "Promise," which Roberson told TV One was written by Casey about her. (Much like Kandi Burruss did in saying that the Jagged Edge song "I Gotta Be" was written by Casey about her/their relationship).
Despite the setback on tour, Jagged Edge would gain popularity and go on to mega stardom with their follow-up albums, 2001's platinum seller *Jagged Little Thrill* and 2003's *Hard,* which has been certified gold. Both albums would reach number 1 on the R&B Albums chart. In 2003, Jagged Edge mentor and longtime producer Jermaine Dupri left Columbia. The group was still contractually obligated to the label until 2006, when they were released from their contract following production of their fifth album, *Jagged Edge*. Although that album and the follow-up, *Baby Makin' Project,* would both break the top 10, Jagged Edge was never able to recapture their chart dominance, as only one single, "Good Luck Charm" from *Jagged Edge,* would break the top 20, settling at number 13.
In an interesting twist, before Roberson (who was dating Brandon Casey) and Luckett's dismissal from Destiny's Child, Kandi Burruss (Casey's ex) showed immense maturity and business acumen in exercising the writing skills she'd honed while working with Casey and Jagged Edge in spectacular fashion. She wrote two monster hits for Destiny's Child, the Hot 100 and R&B number 1 "Bills, Bills, Bills" and the R&B number 13 hit "Bug a Boo," both of which appeared on Destiny's Child's 1999 multiplatinum smash album *The Writing's on the Wall*.

No, No, No Part 2

Artist: Destiny's Child, Wyclef Jean
Album: Destiny's Child
Year: 1997
Writers: Beyoncé, Mary Brown, Rob Fusari, Calvin Gaines, Vincent Herbert, Wyclef Jean, Barry White
Producer: Wyclef Jean
Notable Samples: Strange Games and Things, The Love Unlimited Orchestra (1976)
Highest R&B Chart Position: 1
Highest Hot 100 Chart Position: 3

In 1993, long before Jagged Edge entered the picture, the six-member girl group Girl's Tyme lost on the television show *Star Search* to their competition, Skeleton Crew. Girl's Tyme member Kelly Rowland was devastated and surprised by the loss. In 2018 she told *Yahoo*, "I'll never forget my experience on *Star Search* and knowing what that 'no' felt like . . . We just cried so hard, because we were so excited about the opportunity and everything . . . But also beyond that, we still felt there was something inside that was just like, 'No, we're still going to make it.' . . . We believed in each other, we believed in ourselves, and we did it."

The loss was also a surprise to the management of Girl's Tyme, who had packed a separate hotel room full of costumes anticipating a long run on the show. The disappointment prompted Mathew Knowles, the father of Girl's Tyme member Beyoncé Knowles (he was not the group's manager at the time), to approach *Star Show* host Ed McMahon. As he recalled to the *Questlove Supreme* podcast in 2021, "I said to Ed, 'These kids are crying their hearts out; what do I do?' And he said, 'I don't know why, Mr. Knowles, but everyone that consistently wins on this show professionally goes on to do nothing....It's the people that lose—Aaliyah, Justin Timberlake, Usher, Alanis Morrissette—they go on and be successful because they recommitted, rededicated, change their organization, and I never forgot those words." Mathew Knowles—who was already a stellar salesman having been the top earner at the company Xerox for nearly two decades—pivoted and refocused his efforts on getting the group a record deal and making Girl's Tyme the hottest group in the world. Knowles, who has an MBA in strategic planning and organizational culture and a PhD in business administration, enrolled in Houston Community College and took classes in artist management, music production, and publishing. He also "went to every seminar he could. Knowles recalled, 'I quit my job at the time. . . . I had to prepare myself as a manager and prepare [Beyoncé] as an artist. I made sure we built a very good team—from entertainment attorney, booking agent, road manager, I wanted to surround her with a really great team.'"

By 1996, Girl's Tyme was down to four members—Beyoncé Knowles, Kelly Rowland, LaTavia Roberson, and LeToya Luckett—and their name had changed from Girl's Tyme to "Something Fresh" to "Destiny" before settling on Destiny's Child. Knowles then formed his own management company and began to formally manage the group, but not until after he signed his first artist, Houston-area rapper Lil' O, fresh off his regional 1997 hit "Can't Stop," which featured Destiny's Child as backing vocalists.

Destiny's Child then signed with Elektra Records. But Elektra had its fair share of girl groups at the time, including one of the hottest of the decade in En Vogue. Elektra eventually cut ties with Destiny's Child before recording an album. In 1997, Knowles secured a deal with Columbia Records, where Destiny's Child recorded their self-titled debut album. It was released in 1998.

The group's first single was entitled "No, No, No Part 1." They recorded two versions of the song, both of which were included on the album. Part 1 was styled as a mid-tempo ballad blending contemporary R&B with "lush" 1970s soul. This version fit perfectly on any late '90s quiet storm playlist, but it only performed modestly. In contrast, "No, No, No Part 2" (the remix), which was produced by Wyclef Jean of the hip-hop group The Fugees, was more up-tempo. Jean also provided some vocals on the song, which performed much better than "No No, No Part 1." In fact, it was "Part 2" that would give Destiny's Child their first hit and change R&B and hip-hop forever.

Wyclef, who was coming fresh off the 1996 Fugees megahit "Killing Me Softly," recalled how the collaboration with Destiny's Child was orchestrated in a 2018 *DazeDigital.com* interview, saying, "I was approached by Sony Music/Columbia Records. They were like, 'There's these four girls you gotta go check them out.' I went to see them in the hotel because before I can do a song, I have to hear the artist raw, you know what I mean? Like, no piano, no nothing, just a cappella. The best I could describe it was raw talent. I said to them, 'I'm from the church, sing a church song for me,' and they started singing. Beyoncé of course was on lead. I just fell in love with the group. Because they were from Texas, I had this idea to rewrite it ["No, No, No Part 1"], but have them sing it, double-time it—at the time there wasn't a lot of girl groups doing that. To actually take a rap flow pattern and put it in an R&B scheme. Today it's more common. I just saw them being the biggest thing on earth. Not only did I know it, it's documented in the remix, like if you listen to the rap I say they went from 'a dream to the young Supremes.'"

Wyclef was onto something. While blending melodic singing and rapping was nothing new as the artist Domino had achieved success with the formula nearly 5 years earlier with his hits "Ghetto Jam" (4) and "Sweet Potato Pie"(13), the success of the much more rapid double-time singing in a rap flow pattern was an evolutionary development that further blurred the lines between Rap and R&B and became Destiny's Child's signature sound. It not only laid the groundwork for "No, No, No Part 2" to succeed, but it was prominent on the hits from Destiny's Child's, 8-times platinum selling, sophomore album, 1999's *The Writing's on the Wall,* specifically the songs "Bug a Boo", a number 15 hit and the smash "Bills, Bills, Bills" which spent virtually the entire summer of 1999 (from July to September) in the number 1 spot on the R&B chart. The juxtaposition of "No, No, No, Part 1" and "Part 2" displays the tipping point where double-time syncopation transformed the genre far beyond Domino's laid back melodic rhyming. With all respect to Domino who was truly ahead of his time, it was the immense popularity and crossover success of "No, No, No

Part 2" and *The Writings on the Wall* that led record companies to invest in artists who could successfully blend rap and R&B into crossover success. This tactic laid the path for artists like rapper Nelly and his 2000 debut single "Country Grammar" (an R&B number 5, Hot 100 number 7) and his follow-up R&B number 1, "Ride wit Me" (a number 3, Hot 100 hit) to reach the top of the charts using this double-time syncopation. Both of Nelly's songs are considered rap songs by the way, despite reaching the top 10 on both the R&B and Pop charts. In the years that followed, this rap/singing or sing/rapping would be copied by 50 Cent, T-Pain, and most notably Drake before becoming commonplace in modern Rap and R&B by 2010.

Destiny's Child's journey from *Star Search* losers to having the number 1 song in the country and changing R&B took eight years, and yet the girls were still only teenagers when "No, No, No Part 2" dropped. Kelly Rowland described what it was like when the group members first heard the song on the radio. She was in Houston, Texas driving Beyoncé, Luckett, and Roberson on their way to pick up Beyoncé's little sister, Solange Knowles, from school when the song came on. "We were like, 'Oh my God, oh my God!'" she recalled to *Radio.com*. "We started running around the courtyard at Solange's school and she hops out of the school and is like, 'Why are y'all embarrassing me?'" The girls explained what was happening, and Beyoncé's little sister started running around the courtyard too. "It was beautiful moment," Rowland said. "We were just really happy."

Riding the success of "No, No, No Part 2," *Destiny's Child* went platinum despite not producing any other hits. For a time, the success of "No, No, No" appeared to be an outlier, and many critics believed Destiny's Child's fifteen minutes of fame were close to being over. That is until the release of their second album, T*he Writing's on the Wall,* in 1999, which included the aforementioned crossover number 1's "Bills, Bills, Bills" and "Say My Name." The album became one of the best-selling albums of the decade, selling 8 million units in the U.S.

This late 1990s quote from *The Washington Post* summarizes how the group was viewed in the time post "No, No, No Part 2" and prior to *The Writing's on the Wall*: "After their debut single, 'No, No, No (Part II),' became a major hit in '97, Texas natives Destiny's Child were a one-hit wonder in waiting. The group's first album failed to produce any more hits despite high-profile cameos by Jermaine Dupri and Master P. And their corny ads for sensitive-scalp hair relaxer only intensified their potential as future joke fodder. Many people would have bet against Destiny's Child's ever having another hit or making a great album. But with the release of the group's sophomore effort, *The Writing's on the Wall*, these naysayers would be broke."

While the album positioned Destiny's Child to dominate the first half of the 2000s, the success of *The Writing's on the Wall* could not shield the group from internal issues that caused lineup changes and lawsuits, resulting in the dismissal of Luckett and Roberson, followed by the brief addition and exit of Farrah Franklin and the addition of singer Michelle Williams.

The trio, Destiny's Child released their fourth and final album, the multiplatinum *Destiny Fulfilled,* in 2004. After embarking on a world tour, the group announced their split in 2005, saying in a statement that they wanted to leave "on a high note, united in our friendship and filled with an overwhelming gratitude for our music, our fans, and each other."

Destiny's Child won two Grammys, had ten top 10 R&B hits, and has sold more than 60 million records worldwide

Are U Still Down

Artist: Jon B, 2Pac
Album: Cool Relax
Year: 1998
Writers: Jon B, Johnny Jackson, Tupac Shakur
Producers: Johnny Jackson, Tupac Shakur
Highest R&B Chart Position: 2
Highest Hot 100 Chart Position: 29

In 1996, Jon B and Tupac were both stars in the music industry. Tupac was already considered one of the greatest rappers ever, and Jon B. had achieved success as a songwriter and artist having written songs for R&B acts like After 7, Color Me Badd, Toni Braxton, and Michael Jackson. Jon B. also achieved success as an artist following his 1995 release

Bonafide, which sold over 1 million copies. In 1996, Tupac was coming off his multiplatinum double CD *All Eyez on Me* when the two met during the video shoot for Tupac's single "How Do U Want It." As Jon B. explained to *VladTV* in 2019, He [Jon B.] was visiting the set of the video when he encountered some trouble getting into the shoot due to the East Coast, West Coast beef. When Eric B. [no relation] met him and got into Jon B.'s car, Jon was playing a song he was working on called 'Down and Out, On Lonely Street.' Eric B. heard the song's beat and suggested that Jon play it for Tupac.

Jon B. went on to describe meeting Tupac, saying, "Oh man, Pac was on the bus, he had this RV that he had, you know one of those film RVs that they have for the movies when they are filming videos and stuff like that. . . . It's all love, and I'm sittin' there, and Tupac comes out and starts freestyling to one of my beats and I was like 'Yooo!' . . . so he starts rocking to this beat, and Sway and Tech and everybody, we're all listening to him, and he goes, 'How the hook go, how the hook go?' And I'm like, 'Down and out, on lonely street. Down and out, on lonely street.' So he starts going, 'ok, ok, you got me down and out, on lonely street.' And I was like, 'That's straight.' It was like on the spot, like ok, Jon B. and Tupac gotta get it on in the studio in a real way, because this is magic right now. And K-Ci & JoJo were on the side going 'aaaahhh dammnnn!!' . . . Two weeks later we were in the studio and three hours after being in the studio, we had penned the track. It was Tupac who came up with the hook [replacing "Down and out, on lonely street"] with 'Girl it's alright, baby.' And I was like 'Yo, what is that!' And he's like that's how it goes, that's the melody right there."

With track in hand, Jon was eager to put it on his album, but the label was concerned about how a collab with Tupac would negatively affect Jon B's image. Jon had found success as a smooth R&B singer, and he had just come off a platinum album and Grammy-winning duet on "Someone to Love" (7) with Babyface and seemed to be the face of '90s blue-eyed soul. So the label was slow-rolling the song until they could figure out what to do with it.

Then Tupac is killed in Las Vegas. In an instant everything Tupac related was hotter than it already was. Not wanting to miss out, the label now wanted to release the song quickly. However, in a bit of role reversal it was Jon B. who now did not want to release the song, and he had no plans to do so until Tupac's mother, Afeni Shakur, gave him her blessing. "Are U Still Down" was released on Jon B.'s *Cool Relax* album in 1998. The single peaked at number 29 on the Hot 100 and number 2 on the R&B chart and drove the album to double-platinum status in sales.

Breakdown

Artist: Mariah Carey, Bone Thugs-n-Harmony
Album: Butterfly
Year: 1998
Writers: Krayzie Bone, Wish Bone, Mariah Carey, Stevie J.
Producers: Mariah Carey, Sean Combs, Stevie J.
Highest R&B Chart Position: 4
Highest Hot 100 Chart Position: Song did not chart

"Breakdown" was released from Carey's sixth studio album, *Butterfly*, in 1997. The song was limited as a promotional single and therefore not widely available and not eligible for the Hot 100 chart. That did not stop this collaboration between superstar Mariah Carey and rappers Krayzie Bone and Wish Bone from the rap group Bone Thugs-n-Harmony from reaching number 4 on the R&B charts.

The limited release of such an obvious hit caused many to speculate that it was Columbia CEO and Carey's ex-husband Tommy Mottola's attempt to sabotage his ex-wife, who was still contractually bound to his label.

Columbia and Mottola had carefully guided Carey's career progression since the early 1990s. Following the immense success of her debut and sophomore albums, both of which were R&B, pop, and adult contemporary successes, Columbia and Mottola steered Carey's career toward the latter two genres and avidly avoided associations with hip-hop. Shortly before her divorce from Mottola, Carey began plotting her career closer and closer to hip-hop and R&B audiences, culminating with the remix to her song "Fantasy," which became a 1995 number 1 collaboration with Wu-Tang

Clan rapper Ol' Dirty Bastard.

In 2012, Mariah told *Complex* magazine, "Everyone swung it like I didn't want to put something out because I wouldn't accept less than a number 1 pop single. That's not even true. . . . I wanted to put out 'Breakdown' with Bone Thugs-n-Harmony. That was a no-brainer. Release it. I'll always be upset 'Breakdown' never got its shot."

Carey recorded "Breakdown" at the Hit Factory in New York City throughout 1997. The song's producer, Stevie J. recalled to the website *Youknowigotsoul.com* how Carey's collaboration with Bone Thugs-n-Harmony came to being saying, "I was in the studio with a friend of mine named Eric Williams out of Buffalo, and we were sitting down in the studio with Mariah, and she was like, 'I want to do something like Bone Thugs type of, you know simple but effective.' So I sat down and played her some melodies and put different drum patterns down, and she wrote the song . . . and she was actually like she wanted to get Bone on the record. So, after she finished doing what she did, she called up Bone, got them on the record, and that was history."

Krayzie Bone added, "We got to the studio and you know how people say they laid it out on a silver platter . . . She literally had a silver platter with Hennessy and marijuana for us. So we were like, 'Ah s**t. Ah man. Mariah cool as hell.' So we are so excited. We feeling the atmosphere now. We meet Stevie J., Puff even stopped by for a minute. So we indulged on the Hennessey and marijuana and then we actually passed out in the studio. And she came in and asked our manager, 'Is this normal?' And he was like, 'Yeah, yeah, they'll be up in a minute. Trust me.' So he came and woke us up. And we woke right up, she played the beat for us, and as soon as she played it, we were like, 'Oh, this is our lane right here. Like, this is perfect for us.' So me and Wish [Bone] just got to collabing . . . We were shocked that she had so much knowledge of who we were. She was like, 'I had to meet the guys who were blocking me on the charts.' She was very laid-back and like one of the homies."

Let's Ride

Artist: Master P., Montell Jordan
Album: Let's Ride
Year: 1998
Writers: Montell Jordan, Percy Miller, Vyshonn Miller
Producer: Teddy Bishop
Highest R&B Chart Position: 1
Highest Hot 100 Chart Position: 2

This song is evidence that there was a time in history when Master P. had the Midas touch. Everything he touched went at least gold. With "Let's Ride," even at the time of its release, examining the juxtaposition between the song and its immense success proved that the song overachieved. This is no shade to Master P., who was in the middle of directing the No Limit hip-hop/business takeover, nor Montell Jordan, who had already proven himself as a worthy artist and writer by striking platinum and gold respectively with his first two albums, *This Is How We Do It* (1995) and *More* (1996).

"Let's Ride" was the lead single released from Jordan's third album, *Let's Ride*. The song, which was produced by Teddy Bishop and arranged by R&B singer Case, came about by accident as Jordan told *MTV* in 1998, saying, "When I heard the track, he's [Teddy Bishop] got this vocal thing, he uses like a slowed-down tape sound that says, 'That's right.' And it goes, 'That's right, that's right, that's right . . .' And when I heard it, I thought it was saying, 'Let's ride,' and so I was like, 'Oh! Let's ride!' So, it came about by accident."

Jordan added No Limit Records rapper-CEO Master P. and P's brother, artist Silkk the Shocker, on the song. No Limit Records was one of the hottest labels at the time, and it blew up from there. Powered in part by No Limit's immense popularity, "Let's Ride" spent three nonconsecutive weeks at number 1 on the R&B chart and quickly became a platinum seller only two months after its release.

R

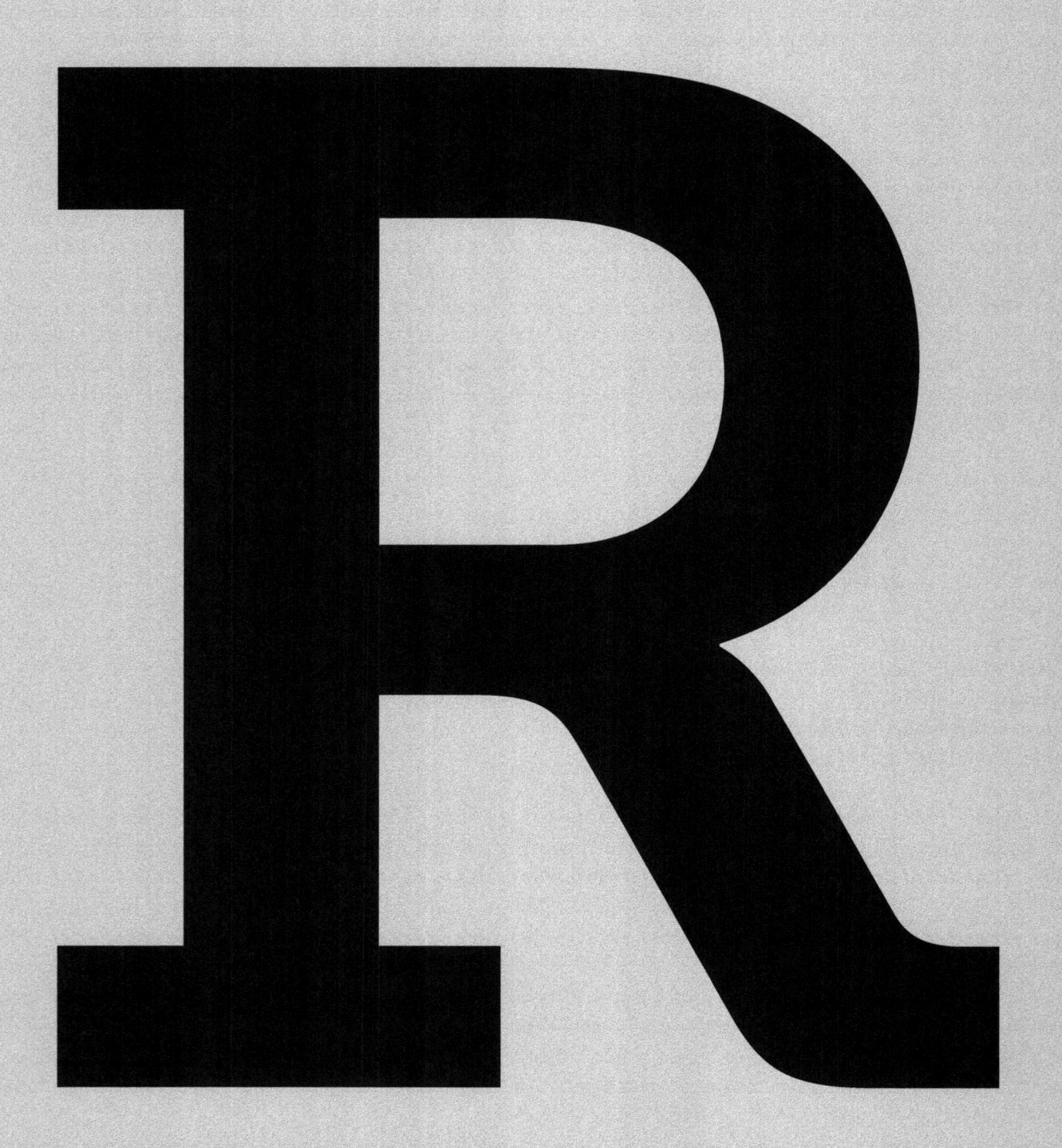

Artist Profile
R. Kelly

Fans of R&B will have difficulty reconciling the man's criminal actions with his music for years to come. The truth is that R. Kelly's spectacular contributions to and influences on the genre cannot be forgotten, though since his disgusting deeds are not just unforgettable but traumatizing, his achievements cannot be celebrated.

His legacy is more than just complicated. He is an illiterate felon, but he has also influenced R&B more so than anyone in his generation. His catalog of masterpieces is undeniable to many, much like the fact that it was him in the 2005 video urinating on an underage girl. But he got a pass because he was the man behind "Bump and Grind" (1), "Sex Me, Parts 1 and 2" (8), and "Age Ain't Nothing but a Number" (35). Ironically, those same hits that protected him from persecution fueled his prosecution and conviction of federal racketeering and sex crimes charges in 2021 and child pornography charges in 2022.

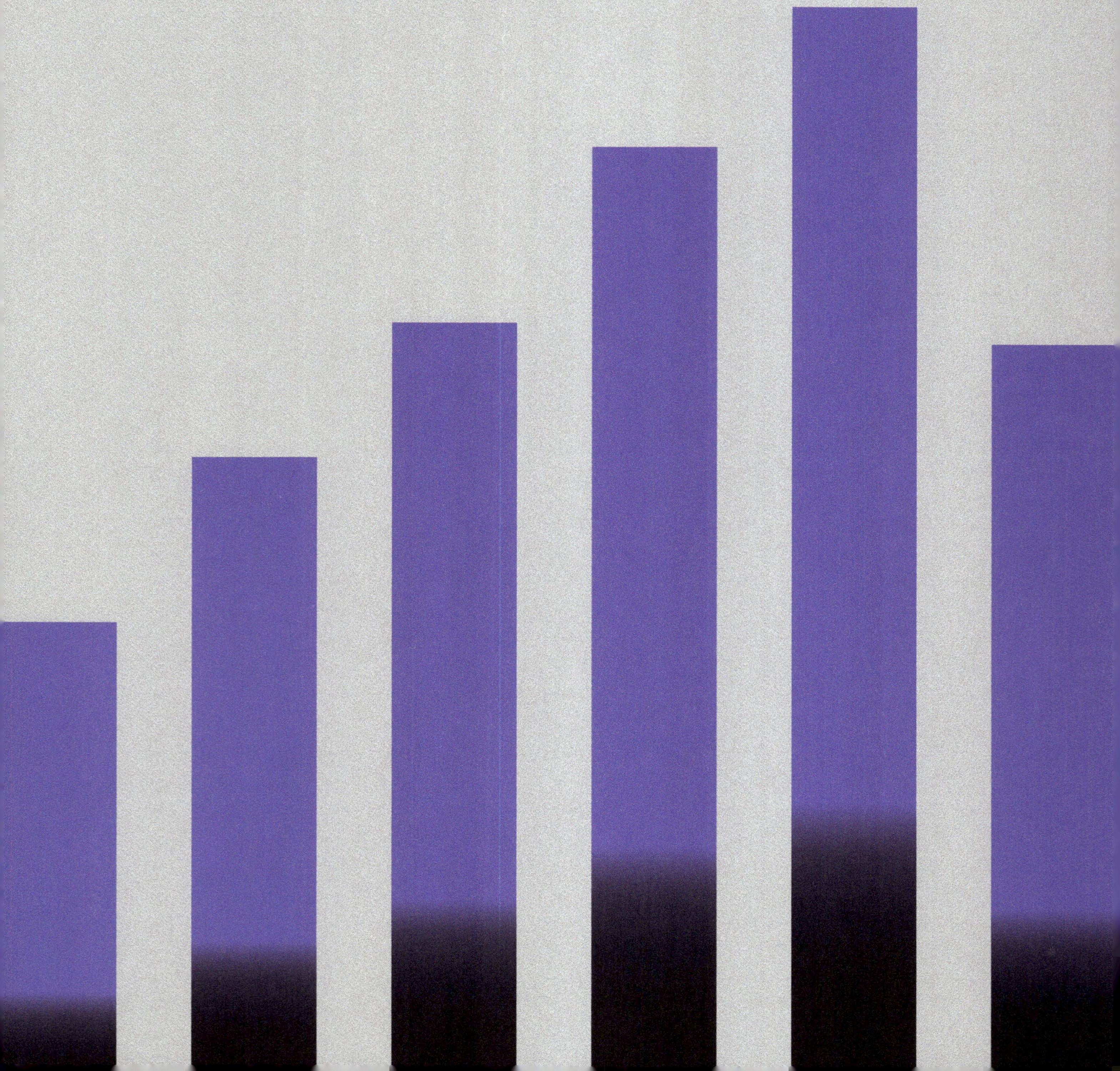

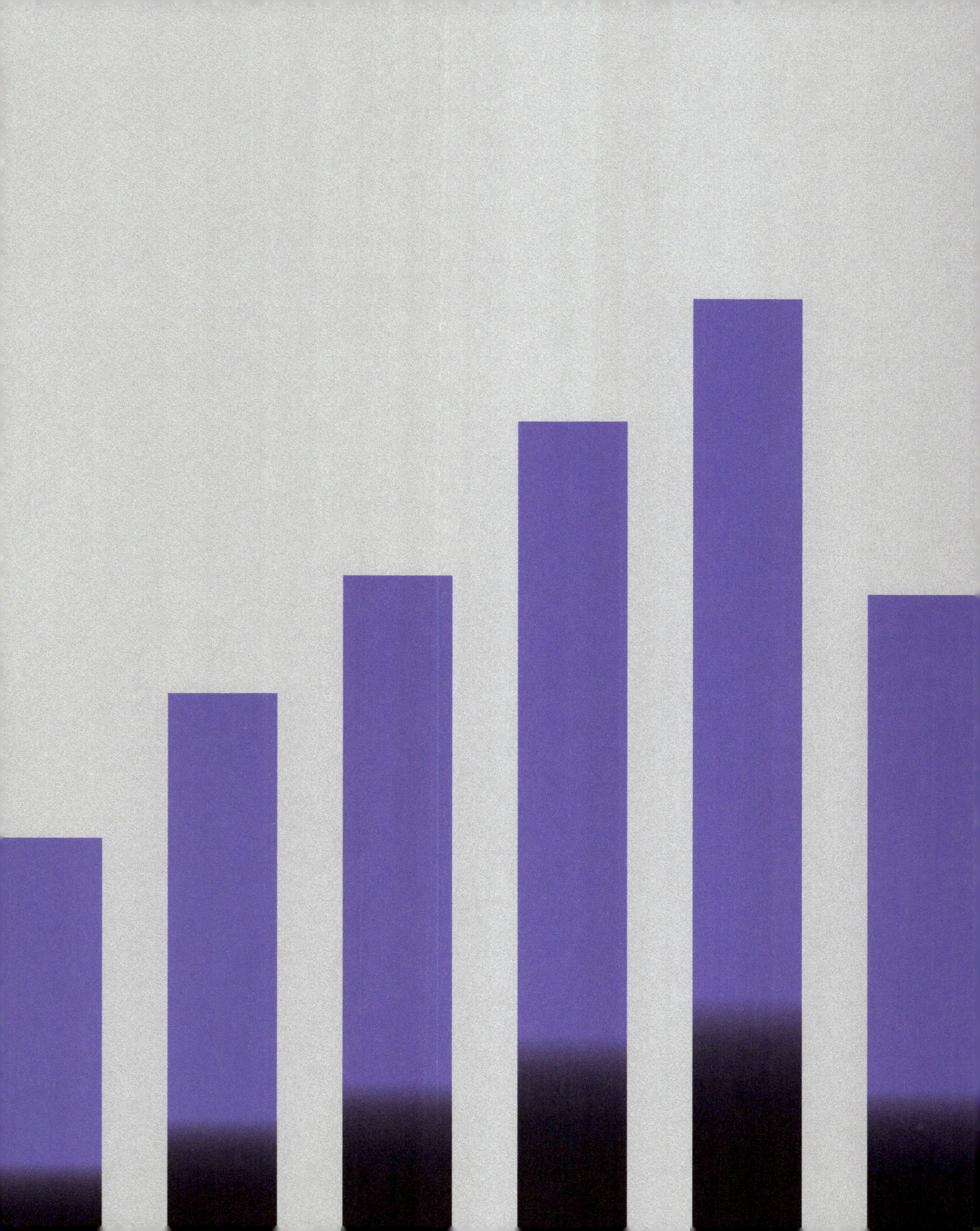

Soul Searchin': The Dawn of Neo Soul
1996 - Present

Soulquarians
A Touch of Jazz
Ascension (Don't Ever Wonder)
Tyrone
Hopeless
Makeda
Ex-Factor
Artist Profile: Meshell Ndegeocello
Outside Your Door
If That's Your Boyfriend (He Wasn't Last Night)
Soul Searchin' (I Wanna Know If It's Mine)
Stay

Soul Searchin: The Dawn of Neo Soul | 1996 - Present

In the mid-1990s, several R&B artists began to abandon the production-heavy sound ushered in with the new jack era in favor of exploring elements of funk, jazz fusion, and acoustic music and combining it with hip-hop. But instead of the hard-core lyrics that were popular in hip-hop at the time, the music focused on a more conscious-driven style, and thus neo-soul was born. Though the genre would not dominate the charts in the way that new jack or traditional R&B had during the earlier part of the decade, neo-soul greatly elevated the artistry and consciousness of the genre.

Soulquarians

The Soulquarians were a collective of artists established during the late 1990s that collaborated on some of neo-soul's biggest songs and albums. Founding members D'Angelo, Ahmir "Questlove" Thompson, James Poyser, and J Dilla originally converged at Electric Lady Studios in New York City for the purpose of working on D'Angelo's sophomore album, Voodoo. The collective would eventually turn the space into a collaborative mecca of creativity for like-minded artists seeking the freedom to produce music that was considered unconventional at the time. The name Soulquarians comes from the original members either sharing or being born close to the Aquarius zodiac sign's season. Members would eventually expand to include Erykah Badu, Roy Hargrove, Bilal, Pino Palladino, Q-Tip, Mos Def, Talib Kweli, and Common.

The members worked collaboratively on writing and production and even recorded in adjacent rooms where they would pop in on each other, adding new sounds to each of their respective sessions.

The Soulquarians would produce platinum new-soul albums like the Roots' Things Fall Apart (1999), D'Angelo's aforementioned Voodoo (2000), and Erykah Badu's Mama's Gun, (2000).

Although the collective would cease to exist by the mid-2000s, the run of artistry and creativity left a lasting impression on the artists themselves and neo-soul fans alike.

A Touch of Jazz

Philadelphia would become ground zero for the neo-soul explosion in large part because of the creativity spawned by local Philly artists. This creativity was made possible by Philly and hip-hop legend DJ Jazzy Jeff and his A Touch of Jazz studios.

Seeking a place to allow more artist control, DJ Jazzy Jeff opened A Touch of Jazz in downtown Philadelphia in the mid-1990s. As he told *Youknowigotsoul.com* in a 2020 interview, "It was just certain things about the music industry that just did not make sense. I systematically tried to break a lot of that stuff down. The first thing that I really tried to break down is the creative freedom. Let me save my money up and get a building and put a studio in it that we could go in and basically make music without someone telling us what we should make . . . It was extremely satisfying because it made me feel like the music we were doing without someone telling us, people really liked it. It made me feel like I was on the right path."

Being true to his vision, Jeff also established A Touch of Jazz Production Company and recruited a stable of producers, songwriters, musicians, and artists to make his vision a reality. With artist like Jill Scott, Musiq Soulchild, and Floetry and producers and songwriters like Carvin Haggins, Ivan Barias, Andre Harris, Vidal Davis, Keith Pelzer, and Darren Henson, A Touch of Jazz became the premier force that would carry R&B and neo-soul well into the 2000s.

Ascension (Don't Ever Wonder)

Artist: Maxwell
Album: Maxwell's Urban Hang Suite
Year: 1996
Writers: Maxwell, Itaal Shur
Producer: Maxwell
Highest R&B Chart Position: 8
Highest Hot 100 Chart Position: 36

Gerald "Maxwell" Rivera along with fellow musicians Erykah Badu and D'Angelo are considered part of the first wave of neo-soul artists.

Maxwell taught himself to play various instruments starting with a Casio keyboard that he borrowed from a friend in the 1980's. By 1991 he was performing in New York City–area clubs and had written and recorded hundreds of songs. He was signed to Columbia Records in 1994.

With Maxwell being an unknown commodity, Columbia executives assigned Sade band member Stuart Matthewman to the project. Maxwell also assembled a group of R&B veterans to complete the team. Matthewman recalled to *Rolling Stone* that the singer "was very enamored with the Sade album *Love Deluxe*" at the time, but also singer-songwriter-producer Leon Ware and Wah Wah Watson, a guitarist whose résumé included Marvin Gaye's *Let's Get It On* and Michael Jackson's *Off the Wall*. Maxwell told *Rolling Stone*, "I was a 22-year-old kid flying to meet guys who were 50, 60 years old . . . For all intents and purposes, they thought the industry was done with them. I was walking in like, 'I think you're incredibly valid.'"

Maxwell's Urban Hang Suite was a concept album that tells a story about a couple meeting on the second track, then falling in love and becoming committed to one another by the album's end. Maxwell recalled, "I was just writing songs. However, I knew in the back of my mind that I wanted to sequence them in a particular way so you could put the record on and just let it play."

Theingroove.com described the resultant album as "a mellow, groove-based sound with elements of funk, jazz, smooth soul, and quiet storm. A concept album, *Maxwell's Urban Hang Suite* was composed as a song cycle that focuses on an adult romance, based in part on Maxwell's personal experiences."

The completed album was reportedly presented to Columbia Records in 1995, but it was shelved for nearly a year, in part due to record executives' doubts about its commercial potential.

Maxwell's Urban Hang Suite was eventually released in 1996. The album spawned four singles, the first of which, "Til the Cops Come Knockin'," debuted at number 87 on the R&B charts and would eventually peak at number 79. The second single, "Ascension (Don't Ever Wonder)," debuted at number 11, eventually peaking at number 8. The album's third and fourth singles, "Sumthin' Sumthin'" and "Suitelady (The Proposal Jam)," peaked at numbers 23 and 64 respectively.

It was "Ascension (Don't Ever Wonder)" that was the album's highest charting single and the track that put the album and Maxwell on the map. As Elias Leight of *Rolling Stone* notes, "'Ascension' sold more than a million copies, and it's not hard to understand its allure: There's the gliding economy of the groove, which seems to walk on water; the reckless falsetto run from Maxwell that opens the song; the strangely sticky lyrical construction of the hook, which swings from questioning to emphatic ('Shouldn't I realize / You're the highest of high / If you don't know, then I'll say it / So don't ever wonder'); and the subtle tumble of drums that precedes the chorus every so often."

In a *Songfacts.com* interview, co-writer Itaal Shur described the process for writing the song: "We wrote a few songs in a little teeny room in Brooklyn where I used to live, and one of them was 'Ascension,' which we changed two or three times until we came up with the right bass line. Then when we got in the studio we put down the track, which had Jonathan Maron who was the bass player from the Groove Collective, which is one of the most memorable bass lines. Also, Matthewman played the guitar. I played the keyboards and did the drum programming. Max had the verses for that song and didn't have a chorus. He went through three or four choruses until he finally came up with the one that worked."

Maxwell's Urban Hang Suite was ranked as one of the year's top 10 best albums by *Time*, *Rolling Stone*, and *USA Today*. The album was certified 2× platinum, Maxwell's first of four consecutive platinum-selling studio albums along with *Embrya* (1998), *Now* (2001), and *BLACKsummers'night* (2009).

Prior to the decade's end, Maxwell would also successfully release "Sumthin' Sumthin': Mellosmoothe" for the *Love Jones* movie soundtrack in 1997. That year he also recorded and released a cover of Kate Bush's hit "This Woman's Work" for *MTV's Unplugged* series. Neither of these songs were released as commercial singles. In 1999, Maxwell's best-performing single of the decade, "Fortunate," which was written by R. Kelly, was released on the *Life* movie soundtrack. The song was an R&B number 1.

Tyrone

Artist: Erykah Badu
Album: Live
Year: 1997
Writer: Erykah Badu
Producers: Erykah Badu, Norman Hurt, Kedar Massenburg
Highest R&B Chart Position: Song did not chart
Highest Hot 100 Chart Position: Song did not chart

Erykah Badu's music career reached hyper-speed after she opened a show for singer D'Angelo in 1994 in Fort Worth, Texas. Record label executive Kedar Massenburg was highly impressed with her performance and signed her to Kedar Entertainment. Her first album, *Baduizm*, was released in 1997 and contained the hits "On & On" (1), "Appletree," "Next Lifetime," and "Other Side of the Game," with the latter three songs not being released as commercial singles. The album has since been certified triple platinum.

Badu's Live album, which has since been certified double platinum, contained the song "Tyrone," which began as a joke but became a hit. Badu later told *Clutch* magazine, "It was a song I literally made up on stage in London in 1997. It was a spontaneous thing." Speaking with *The Breakfast Club* in 2015, Badu provided a bit more detail, saying, "In rehearsal a lot of times we'd just play around and do stuff like 'call me!' [Singing]. But I didn't know it was going to turn into 'Tyrone.' So the background vocalists were prepared because they kind of know the joke. But it just kind of turned into a song that was totally freestyled."

Badu continued, "Later, I looked around and saw they were having debates about it on TV and radio. They said I was male bashing. I had no idea that it would have such an impact. I was just making it up as I was going along. As the song blew up, I realized that I had to take some kind of stance. I began to challenge all the 'Tyrones' to do better. The song 'Tyrone' did its job musically and socially. Women loved it because that's how they felt and men hated it because that's how they were. As a result, it became an anthem. I'm not apologetic for 'Tyrone.' It's the jam and I love it. It's one of my favorite songs to perform on stage and it's still hilarious to me."

With the song becoming popular on the heels of Badu's divorce from André 3000 of the rap group Outkast, many thought the song was about him. However, "3 Stacks" put that rumor to bed via a line in the 2003 track "A Life in the Day of Benjamin André" where he says:

When I was going through them phases trying to find /
Anything that seemed real in the world /
Still searching, but I started liking this girl /
Now you know her /
As Erykah on and on Badu /
Call Tyrone on the phone why you /
Do that girl like that boy you ought to be ashamed /
The song wasn't about me and that ain't my name.

"Tyrone" was played in heavy rotation on the radio but was not released as a commercially available single for purchase and thus did not place on either the R&B or pop singles chart. However, the song reached number 1 on the R&B Airplay chart.

Hopeless

Artist: Dionne Farris
Album: Love Jones soundtrack
Year: 1997
Writers: Dionne Farris, Van Hunt
Producers: Van Hunt, Randy Jackson, Dionne Farris
Highest R&B Chart Position: Song did not chart
Highest Hot 100 Chart Position: Song did not chart

Although Dionne Farris was never an official member of the group Arrested Development, her prominent vocals on their 1992 hit "Tennessee" were pivotal in the song reaching the top 10 on the R&B chart, becoming the number 1 rap single in the U.S., and winning the 1993 Grammy Award for Best Rap Performance by a Duo or Group. In total, Farris sang on three songs on the group's *3 Years, 5 Months and 2 Days in the Life of . . .* album: "Fishin' 4 Religion," "Give a Man a Fish," and "Tennessee." Of these songs, "Tennessee" was the only one to chart.

At the time Farris and Arrested Development were signed to the same management company, and the success of "Tennessee" prompted Chrysalis (the label to which Arrested Development was signed) to offer Farris a solo deal. However, the deal was said to be contingent upon Speech of Arrested Development producing the project. The independent-minded Farris rejected the offer in search of a deal where she would have artistic control.

This and other business-related issues caused tension between the group and Farris, which ultimately led her to seek a record deal of her own with Columbia Records, where she was signed by Randy Jackson (who later became well known as a judge on American Idol). It was at Columbia where Farris recorded her debut album, *Wild Seed—Wild Flower,* which was released in the summer of 1994, spawning the hit pop single "I Know," which reached number 4 on the Hot 100 chart and was nominated for the Grammy Award for Best Female Pop Vocal Performance in 1996. The song did not reach the R&B chart.

Farris's success got the attention of none other than Prince, and he became her mentor of sorts as she told *RnbJunkieOfficial.com* saying, "Well, back at the start of my solo career in '95 I was in concert and my manager at the time comes to me and says, 'Prince was watching your show and wants to meet you,' and I was like, 'You're kidding, right?' [Laughs] So sure enough we met, talked, exchanged numbers, and we kept in touch I'd say for about three years having conversations about the music industry. At the time he was fighting to get his master tapes, and I would talk to him about the situations I was having at the time with my label. For someone who's been in the business as long as he had and one that was respected, I knew he knew what he was talking about and so I listened, giving him my full attention, and because of that I'm sure about the artist I am today. It opened me up to a lot of knowledge."

The knowledge would be needed as tensions over creative control grew between Farris and Columbia, which ultimately led to her sophomore album being shelved by the label.

In 1996, Farris and another colleague of Prince, musician-songwriter Van Hunt, collaborated on a song for the *Love Jones* movie soundtrack. She recalled, "Van Hunt who wrote that song sat down with me and we discussed what was going on and of course we watched the *Love Jones* movie and my story just gelled in with the storyline and that's how 'Hopeless' came about."

The song was one of many gems on the soundtrack, which featured hits by Lauryn Hill ("The Sweetest Thing") and Maxwell ("Sumthin' Sumthin': Mellosmoothe"). Neither "Hopeless" "The Sweetest Thing" nor "Sumthin' Sumthin': Mellosmoothe" were released as commercial singles.

Following the success of "Hopeless," Farris took a hiatus from the music industry. However, in 2007 she released her sophomore album, *For Truth If Not Love.* She also founded the independent label Free & Clear Records, where she released her third album, *Signs of Life,* in 2011.

Makeda

Artist: Les Nubians
Album: Princesses Nubiennes
Year: 1998
Writer: Mounir Belkhir, Les Nubians
Producer: Les Nubians
Notable Sample: Suite Revenge, Herbie Hancock (1974)
Highest R&B Chart Position: 48
Highest Hot 100 Chart Position: Song did not chart

In 1998, Les Nubians climbed the R&B charts with the French language neo-soul hit "Makeda." The duo, sisters Hélène and Célia Faussart, are from France via Cameroon. In the 1990s the pair began singing a cappella, producing poetry slams in Bordeaux and Paris and singing background vocals for various artists worldwide.
In 1998 they were signed to Virgin Records as Les Nubians, using the name as a way to pay homage to their African heritage. They would say of their name, "It was also a way to talk about Pan-Africanism and not only speak about Cameroon but to explore and share the whole diaspora."

It was at Virgin that the duo released their debut album, *Princesses Nubiennes,* and its best-known single "Makeda." Named after the Queen of Sheeba in Ethiopic *biblical* texts, "Makeda" tells the story of a royal mixed-race couple.
In the historical context, Makeda, the Queen of Sheba, appears as a prominent figure in the Ethiopian text *Kebra Nagast (Glory of King)*, and although the story of her visit to King Solomon is told in the *Bible* and *Quran,* it is only in this Ethiopian text that she becomes pregnant by Solomon and returns to her kingdom, where she bore Solomon an interracial son, Menelik, who would become king of Ethiopia. Menelik's royal Solomonic dynasty would rule Ethiopia until the deposition of Haile Selassie I in 1974.

With this in mind, the song, which is a groove, takes on deeper meaning when you translate the lyrics.

They want to make us believe lost myths /
The passages of history falsified and revised /
From Ramses to Mandela, the truths that were killed /
In ignoring the start, they wander aimlessly /

Makeda was queen, beautiful and powerful /
Solomon dreamed of her black skin /
I sing to revive the memories /
To dig up the knowledge /
That the spiral of time erases /

The queen of Sheba lives in me /
Makeda lives in me.

In offering insight into the song, Les Nubians says, "We're basically saying that if you don't know where you're from, you don't know where you're going, and we know that intermixing exists since the beginning of time: since the Queen of Sheba and King Solomon . . . We also speak about historical falsification: How the Queen of Sheba from the *Bible* for example, in *Cantique des Cantiques,* is depicted as beautiful but black. Why couldn't she be beautiful and black? So there are so many misinterpretations and misrepresentations. The song is also about celebrating our beauty, celebrating who we are through love."

Despite being regarded as one of the most successful French-language musical groups in the U.S., Les Nubians failed to strike another R&B hit.

Ex-Factor

Artist: Lauryn Hill
Album: The Miseducation of Lauryn Hill
Year: 1998
Writer: Lauryn Hill
Producer: Lauryn Hill
Highest R&B Chart Position: 7
Highest Hot 100 Chart Position: 21

"The Fugees were on the road in the summer of '96 and Lauryn called me like, 'I can't believe these muthaf***ers. I've been talking about making my solo record for the longest and they're doing everybody's solo record but mine! I'm leaving the group, I've had it.' I was like, 'Call [then Sony chairman] Donnie Ienner.' And she was like, 'I don't wanna f**k with them, I just wanna get a whole new crew.'" According to Lauryn Hill's former manager Jayson Jackson, this was the conversation that began Hill's solo career and was the beginning of the end of the highly successful Fugees. However Sony, the Fugees label, had other plans. According to producer Gordon "Commissioner Gordon" Williams, Sony never wanted Hill to make a solo record. He believes they wanted her to make another Fugees record. Undeterred, Hill and her new crew began work on her solo album *The Miseducation of Lauryn Hill*, which took about a year and a half to record. Hill, as she put it, "wanted to write songs that lyrically move me and have the integrity of reggae and the knock of hip-hop and the instrumentation of classic soul." Hill's longtime companion and father of her five children, Rohan Marley, recalled to *Rolling Stone* in 2008 that Lauryn and her mom took [early versions of] her album to Sony Records and they [Sony] said, "'This is coffee table music. What is this s**t? Coffee table music.' She took her s**t and walked outta there."

Hill wrote the majority of *Miseducation* at the young age of twenty-three, during her pregnancy with first child Zion and after The Fugees split. She cites her pregnancy as sparking her creativity, saying, "When some women are pregnant, their hair and their nails grow, but for me it was my mind and ability to create. I had the desire to write in a capacity that I hadn't done in a while. I don't know if it's a hormonal or emotional thing . . . I was very in touch with my feelings at the time." Of the early writing process, Hill said, "Every time I got hurt, every time I was disappointed, every time I learned, I just wrote a song."

"Ex-Factor" personifies the tone of the *Miseducation* album. Hill is the sole writer and producer of the song, and she is bearing her soul in an intimate way in addressing her failing relationship. However, millions of us could relate to the trials of love and heartbreak. As a critique at the *Song Meanings + Facts* blog noted, "Her incredibly honest lyrics trace the confusion that comes with separating from someone who you both love deeply and have been hurt by. It's rare to hear those internal and external battles articulated so powerfully in a song."

The song has been claimed to be about Wyclef Jean, Hill's former boyfriend and bandmate who was married to model Claudinette Jean at the time. Wyclef provided the details over a decade later in his 2012 memoir *Purpose: An Immigrant's Story*, writing, "I was married and Lauryn and I were having an affair, but she led me to believe that the baby was mine, and I couldn't forgive that. . . . She could no longer be my muse. Our love spell was broken." According to *MTV.com*, "Jean also revealed that Hill began dating the father of her children, Rohan Marley, during the period when she was still romantically involved with him. In the book, Wyclef admits that he was jealous of Hill's new relationship, despite having his own marriage", adding "when it became clear that Marley was the father of Hill's first son, things were never quite the same."

According to Vada Nobles, a producer and programmer for *Miseducation*, "Ex-Factor" wasn't the only song about Jean. She told *Rolling Stone*, "There was a female group called Ex Factor signed to Arista and we did a song called 'Ex-Factor' for them. And then we started working on a song called 'Loved Real Hard Once'—the title got switched [to "When It Hurts So Bad"]. Those were the first two records that we worked on. We were making songs for other people, and the songs started becoming too personal and we were like, wait a minute, this is your story. We were having a conversation about her relationship in the little studio in her attic in South Orange, and that's how 'I Used to Love Him' came about. It was about 'Clef."

The Miseducation of Lauryn Hill was a massive success, reaching diamond sales and sweeping the 1998 Grammy

Awards, where the album received ten nominations and five awards, including awards for Best R&B Album and Album of the Year. The album was even placed on the *Rock and Roll Hall of Fame's 200 Definitive Albums of All Time* list, and in 2015, *The Miseducation of Lauryn Hill* was deemed "culturally, historically, or aesthetically significant" by the U.S. Library of Congress and selected for inclusion in the National Recording Registry.

Despite the immense success, *The Miseducation of Lauryn Hill* would be Hill's last studio album. In 2021 she explained to *Rolling Stone* that her label never reached out to her to record a second album, stating, "The wild thing is no one from my label has ever called me and asked how can we help you make another album, ever . . . ever. Did I say ever? Ever!" That and the combination of pressure to follow up on the enormous success of *Miseducation* and a "deep disillusionment with the music business" led Hill to take a lengthy hiatus from the industry.

Artist Profile
Meshell Ndegeocello

Although Meshell Ndegeocello is not a household name, unapologetically our writers have pronounced her as the queen of neo-soul. The singer-songwriter, rapper, and bassist, born Michelle Lynn Johnson, would adopt the surname Ndegeocello, which means "free like a bird" in Swahili, at the age of seventeen. Ndegeocello was educated in Washington, D.C., and attended the prestigious Duke Ellington School of the Arts. She refined her skills and style in the D.C. Go-Go scene working with legendary groups like Rare Essence, Prophecy, and Little Benny & the Masters. In a 2018 interview with *Washingtonian Magazine*, Ndegeocello reflected on how this experience influenced her music, stating that "it made me a much better musician. You have to be in tune with the audience. Rare Essence was my favorite band, and their bass player truly inspired me. He's one of the first people to give me pointers. To me, you can only experience Go-Go live. Very few recordings truly [capture] how it feels to be in that room with sweaty bodies moving to the music. There's nothing like that feeling."

It was at Maverick Records that Ndegeocello released her debut album, *Plantation Lullabies*. The album featured the songs "Outside Your Door" and "If That's Your Boyfriend (He Wasn't Last Night)."

Her music has been described as incorporating "a wide variety of influences, including funk, soul, jazz, hip-hop, reggae and rock. She has received significant critical acclaim throughout her career, being nominated for eleven Grammy Awards, and winning one. Her style of blending spoken and sung verses over jazz, hip-hop and R&B textures speak to some of the hallmarks of the neo-soul movement that was to come."

During her thirty-plus-year career, Ndegeocello has worked with everyone from Chaka Khan and Madonna to the Rolling Stones and the Blind Boys of Alabama and has been featured in a number of film soundtracks, including *How Stella Got Her Groove Back*, *Batman & Robin*, *Love Jones*, *Love & Basketball*, *The Best Man*, *Higher Learning*, *Down in the Delta*, and *The Hurricane*.

So why don't most R&B fans know her by name? Well, it's complicated. First, she is notoriously reclusive and seemingly not overly concerned with the publicity machine of the music industry. Secondly, she has always done her own thing regardless of the controversy perceived by others. In doing so she has defied the industry that has tried to put her in a box.

NPR's Michel Martin astutely describes Ndegeocello as "one of the most unique recording artists around. She's made a career challenging the conventions around her. When most women musicians were being promoted as sex symbols, she shaved her head and played the bass and when many artists tried to earn indie cred by shunning mainstream music, she scored widespread praise, critical success collaborating with artists ranging from John Mellencamp and Chaka Khan and contributing to movie soundtracks." To put it bluntly, she is successful in spite of the industry and not because of it, and she has sacrificed aspects of her fame for the creative freedom to express herself on her terms.

Outside Your Door
Artist: Meshell Ndegeocello
Album: Plantation Lullabies
Year: 1993
Writer: Meshell Ndegeocello
Producers: David Gamson, Meshell Ndegeocello
Highest R&B Chart Position: 41
Highest Hot 100 Chart Position: Song did not chart

If That's Your Boyfriend (He Wasn't Last Night)
Artist: Meshell Ndegeocello
Album: Plantation Lullabies
Year: 1993
Writer: Meshell Ndegeocello
Producers: André Betts
Highest R&B Chart Position: 23
Highest Hot 100 Chart Position: 73

Soul Searchin' (I Wanna Know If It's Mine)
Artist: Meshell Ndegeocello
Album: Higher Learning soundtrack
Year: 1995
Writer: Meshell Ndegeocello
Producers: David Gamson, Meshell Ndegeocello
Highest R&B Chart Position: Song did not chart
Highest Hot 100 Chart Position: Song did not chart

Stay
Artist: Meshell Ndegeocello
Album: Peace Beyond Passion
Year: 1996
Writer: Meshell Ndegeocello
Producers: David Gamson
Highest R&B Chart Position: 67
Highest Hot 100 Chart Position: Song did not chart

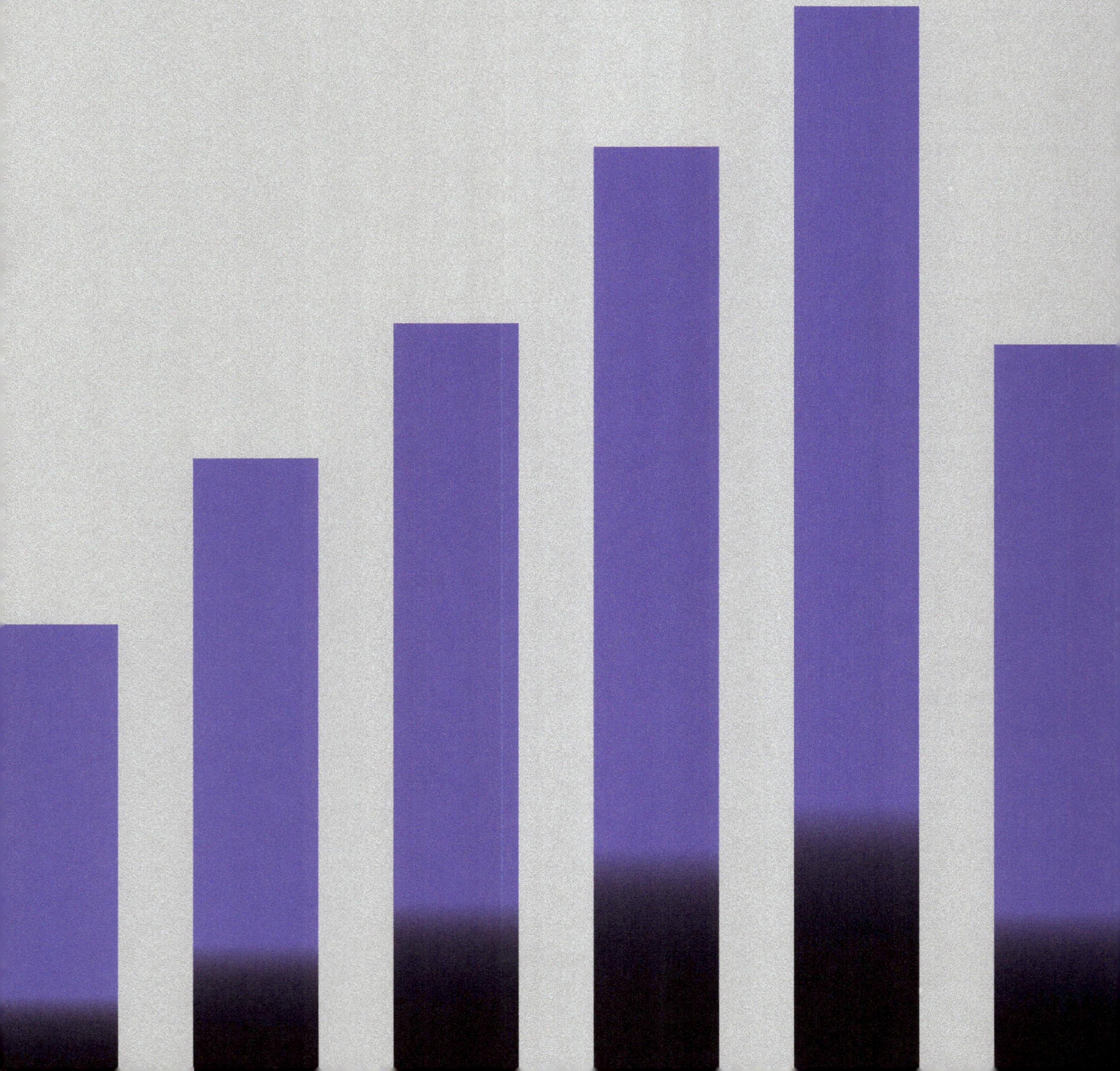

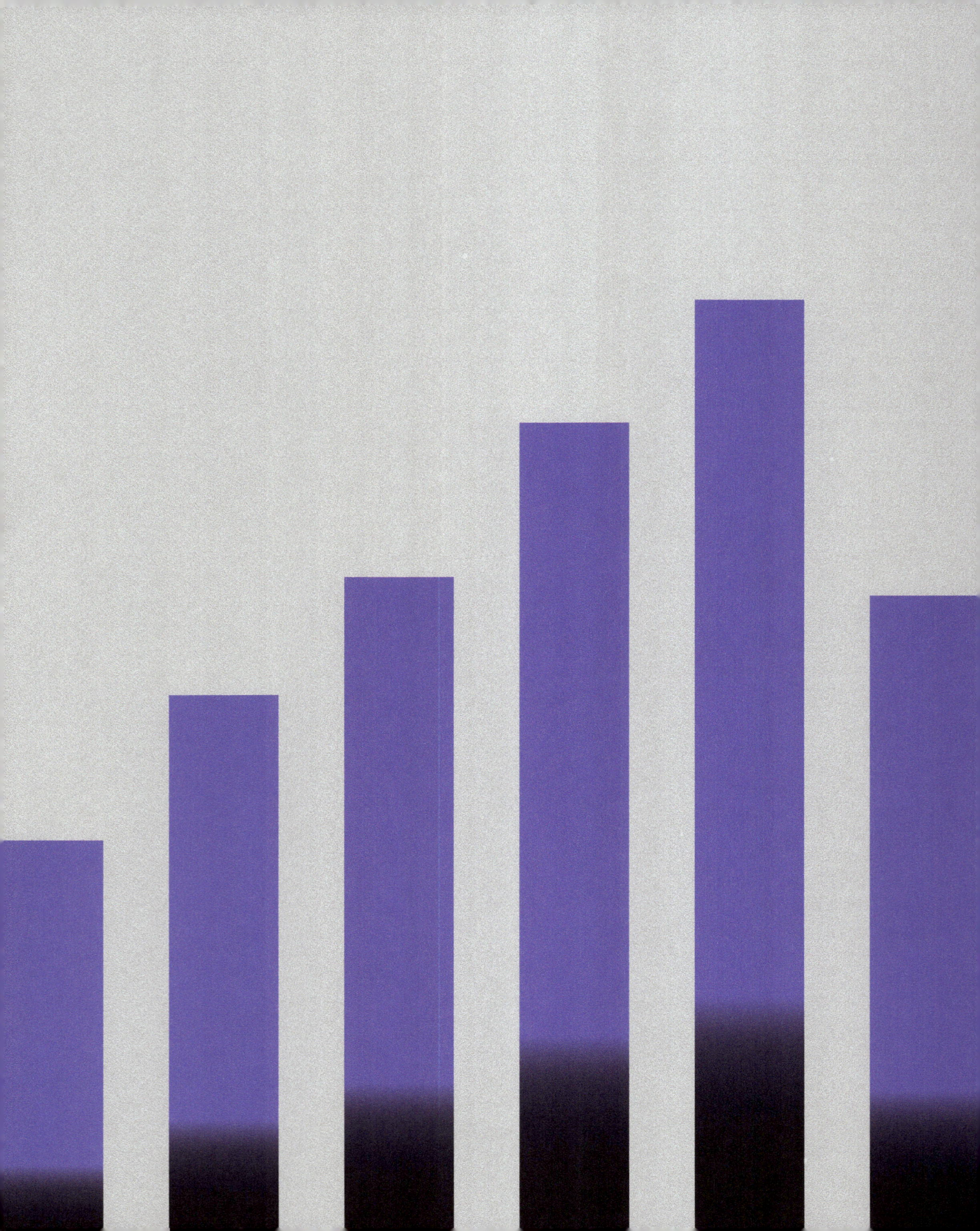

The One Hit Wonders

Ghetto Jam
Tell Me
My Boo
You
Caught Out There

The One Hit Wonders

As with any other genre and in any other decade, 1990s R&B was full of artists that had hits but for one reason or another could never duplicate that success. There is no industry-wide definition of a one-hit wonder, so the criteria used here is as follows:
1. The artist or group had to have sang lead on at least one top 10 R&B hit.
2. The artist had no other top 10 R&B hits during the decade.

These criteria may sound like a daunting task, but with R&B's explosion of popularity in the 1990s, it was fairly difficult for an artist to not score at least one follow-on hit after reaching the top 10, as the sheer presence of a top 10 song on an album would drive airplay and sales of at least one lesser song by the artist to top 10 status. Take for example the artist Rome, who struck gold with his 1996 number 2 hit "I Belong to You (Every Time I See Your Face)" but eluded this list by his rather forgettable follow-up song "Do You Like This," which reached number 10. Then there is the artist Trey Lorenz. Lorenz had a number 5 hit with 1992's "Someone to Hold," which he co-wrote with Mariah Carey and Walter Afanasieff. He would have avoided one-hit wonder status had he released the song "Tell Me," which he recorded but passed on including on his debut album. The duo Groove Theory would take "Tell Me" to number 5 with Lorenz's ad-libs from his original recording still on the track. In Lorenz's case, he literally had to refuse to release a top 10 hit to become a one-hit wonder.

Here we highlight some of the other artists and songs that we classify as one-hit wonders.

Ghetto Jam

Artist: Domino
Album: Domino
Year: 1993
Writers: Battlecat, Domino
Producers: Battlecat, Domino
Highest R&B Chart Position: 4
Highest Hot 100 Chart Position: 7

Domino (Shawn Ivy) arrived in the mid-1990s with an innovative sound that blended rap and R&B to funk rhythms. He was truly ahead of his time as his melodic style which was unusual in 1993 would become commonplace with artists like Nelly and Drake climbing the charts with tuneful verses in the 2000's. Domino's abstract flow was intentional, as he told David Ma of *Passionweiss.com* in a 2020 interview: "I wanted to do it in a way that others weren't doing. We had streets full of hip-hop dudes and all of us came up doing battle rap s**t. But the difference with me is that I wanted to do all of that and wanted to stand out with a style that was obviously different or new. That's why I stuck with the singing, melodic s**t."

The Long Beach, California, native burst onto the scene around the same time as legendary rapper Snoop Dogg, who is also from Long Beach. But the similarities would not end there. Domino's Godfather Leon Haywood produced the original 1975 track "I Want'a Do Something Freaky to You" (7) that Dr. Dre sampled for his rap song "Nuthin' but a 'G' Thang" (1993), which was the track that introduced the casual rap fan to Snoop Dogg. Also, both released their debut singles only a month apart with Domino's "Ghetto Jam," which was released in November 1993, outperforming Snoop's "Who Am I (What's My Name)?," which was released in October of the same year. On the R&B/hip-hop chart the songs were numbers 4 and 8 respectively. On the Hot Rap Songs chart where "Who Am I (What's My Name)?" was the number 1 song for three weeks, Ghetto Jam replaced Snoop's song and held the number 1 spot for six weeks.

Although "Ghetto Jam" and Domino's follow-up "Sweet Potato Pie" (13) were both hits, initially labels weren't willing to take a gamble on Domino and his unique melodic sounds. As he said, "The thing about it was, the style was so new and wasn't proven so no one wanted it. We're sitting there and trippin'. The whole thing was these record labels kept saying it wasn't a proven sound and that everything needed to sound gangster and hard. Ice Cube and Dre's sound was what everyone wanted. So, we decided to do the record independently, and we would take the song to swap meets and play it all day long. All of a sudden, people started to come every Saturday just to hear it."

It would ultimately take some indirect help from the musical legend Stevie Wonder for Domino to break through. As he recounted, "Stevie Wonder had a radio station he owned in Southern California [KJLH] and one of the DJ's was a friend of mine who one day said, 'Hey, Stevie wants us to play a hip-hop record on air.' Apparently it was because they never played any rap on the show before. So, they had this 'Make It or Break It' segment on the show to see what the response was and if the public was with it. One day they put it on and it won. Then it won another two times! And so on. After that they wanted to add it to the rotation, and that's when things blew up. That's when all the labels that had passed on it started to hit me up. We ended up selling the distribution rights to Russell Simmons, and that was the beginning of the world knowing about Domino."

In the months that followed, "Ghetto Jam" was everywhere and it was the quintessential west coast vibe. Today the song functions as a time machine that to this day, no matter where you are when you hear it, it transports you to wherever you were in 1993.

But by late 1994 Domino's style failed to catch on with mainstream music execs who, despite the success of the song still didn't grasp the game-changing potential of his music. The blending of rap and R&B in a rap-singing style would not catch on until the end of the decade. Most notably with Destiny's Child singing in a double-time rap flow pattern on their hits "No, No, No Part 2" (1) and the crossover number 1's "Bills, Bills, Bills" and "Say My Name." from their 8 times platinum selling album *The Writings On the Wall* (1999).

In 2020, Domino and Snoop collaborated on the song "Baby So West Coast," which is a song that has been described as a "bouncy track about sun and girls that sounds like a conversation among old friends."

Tell Me

Artist: Groove Theory
Album: Groove Theory
Year: 1995
Writers: Darryl Brown, Rick James, Amel Larrieux, Bryce Wilson
Producer: Bryce Wilson
Notable Samples: All Night Long, Mary Jane Girls (1983)
Highest R&B Chart Position: 3
Highest Hot 100 Chart Position: 5

"Tell Me" has been described as one of the '90est songs of the '90s. It's a mid-'90s song that transcends the era and would be a hit among neo-soul and later R&B sounds that would come to rule the end of the 1990s and early 2000s. As one critic noted, "The song is striking in its simplicity." Wilson used a simple drum pattern, threw in some "Christmas bells," and added the bass line from the Mary Jane Girls' "All Night Long" (1983).

Groove Theory artists Amel Larrieux and Bryce Wilson met while both were employed at the publishing company Rondor Music in New York City in 1993, Larrieux as a receptionist-intern and the singer-songwriter Wilson as a producer. The duo would team up to form Groove Theory and would co-write "Tell Me" for up-and-coming singer Trey Lorenz, who had garnered attention for his vocals opposite Mariah Carey on her Unplugged version of the Jackson 5 hit "I'll Be There." Lorenz laid some vocals on the song, but it did not make his album.

After getting little traction elsewhere, Groove Theory's label, Sony, insisted that the duo record the song for their upcoming album, but Larrieux wasn't feeling it. She would say, "Sony turned around to us and said in the midst of finishing and recording the *Groove Theory* album, 'We want you to record that song that you wrote for Trey,' and I was like, 'That's a song for a guy. I didn't write that for myself.' It was very black and white. I was like, 'I wrote this song for this purpose and that is it,' and they were like, 'Yeah, we think this is going to be a hit. You should do it.' So we did and they were right. They put their machine behind it, the Sony machine, and it resonated with people. And I just had no idea."

Groove Theory rerecorded the song, with Larrieux singing lead. However, Trey Lorenz's ad-libs, including the "Oh, tell me, tell me, baby" toward the end, were kept on the song, and many listeners assumed the male voice was Wilson's. In the decades since its release, Larrieux has come to embrace the song and its effect, saying, "It didn't mean anything to me personally because I really hadn't written it for myself but . . . I live an experience because of that song. It's in every conversation I have with a person who has related to that song for that many years. . . . Instead of being this song that feels so impersonal and I'm trying to sing it and make it mean something, it means something because of the experience I have with the audience who is like jumping out of their skin to sing it with me saying, 'Wow, I remember what I was doing in '95.' It's pretty great and it ["Tell Me"] made it possible."

"Tell Me" would be Groove Theory's only top 10 hit. Their singles "Keep Tryin'" and "Baby Luv" peaked at number 24 and 23 respectively. The group would break up before releasing new material. As Wilson stated to *Blackdoctor.com*, "Me and Amel Larrieux began not to see eye to eye. When you're in it, you don't understand what you have, so you don't fight to protect it and fight to keep it. I think that Amel had her views of what she wanted, and I was like I started this. I had produced a lot of things. It just got to the point when she wanted to go her way and I wanted her to go; it wasn't working anymore."

Despite the breakup, Larrieux and Wilson have remained on good terms. Larrieux told *Complex* magazine, "Because I knew him before we started making music together—we were working together for three years before *Groove Theory* even came out—the relationship between us never changed. It evolved, but it never ended." And both have gone on to successful careers. Larrieux is a successful recording artist, and Wilson would go on to produce for artists like Mary J. Blige and Toni Braxton and work with songwriters and producers like Babyface. As reported by *SoulBounce.com*, Wilson's production sales have exceeded 50 million since his exit from Groove Theory, and he has won two Grammy Awards.

My Boo

Artist: Ghost Town DJ's
Album: Single
Year: 1996
Writers: Carlton Mahone, Rodney Terry
Producers: Jermaine Dupri, Lil Jon, Carlton Mahone, Rodney Terry
Highest R&B Chart Position: 18 (1996), 10 (2016)
Highest Hot 100 Chart Position: 13 (1996), 27 (2016)

The song, which was originally called "I Wanna Be Your Lady" before rapper-producer Lil Jon changed the title to "My Boo," has the distinction of being one of only a few songs to chart above its initial peak position on the Hot 100 years after its initial release. The resurrection of this song on the charts was due to teenagers remixing a '90s-era dance called "the Running Man" in a series of #RunningManChallenges set to the tune of "My Boo" and the whole thing going viral.

Ghost Town DJ's consisted of singer Virgo Williams, DJ and producer Greg Street, producer Rodney Terry, DJ Demp, and Jermaine Dupri. Their original release in 1996 appeared on the So So Def Bass All-Stars compilation, and despite the success of the record, to this day "My Boo" is the only single that is credited to the Ghost Town DJ's. The sound is enduring, mainly because it is comprised of simple yet effective contrasts, a slow record over a fast beat that was typical in cities like Atlanta and Miami at the time but unknown to the rest of the country. As Lil Jon told *Spin.com*, "Back in the day, Atlanta DJs would take a bass track and then would take, say, Shai's 'If I Ever Fall in Love' and put it over a bass beat. Because it's really double time. [Doing that] was really popular with all the DJs."

The group was formed when Lil Jon, then of So So Def A&R, was given the assignment as his "first main project." Looking for a hit, he teamed with Rodney Terry, who worked promotions at Def Jam Recordings. DJ Demp was added when it was time to do stage shows, and Virgo Williams, who was initially only intended to provide backup vocals, became the track's lead singer when circumstances with the original lead singer changed.

According to Lil Jon, "When the [first] girl came in to sing it she just couldn't do it. We were like, 'Let's just use Virgo,' because she sounded good. So Virgo kind of got in by accident because she was the background singer and then she ended up being the main singer. Everything kind of just happened."

With the project well underway, Rodney Terry provided the group's name. He says, "I came up with the name Ghost Town DJ's. The words 'ghost town' to me means heard and not seen. That's why no one's ever, ever seen us, but they are definitely feeling us."

The explanation of the group's name could also apply to the song's video, which does not include all the group's members. "It wasn't necessarily about Ghost Town at the time," Virgo recalled. "I didn't even know the video was going on until it was being shot. I was actually called by a friend of mine at that point who also helped me with the background vocals for that track. And he's like, 'Do you guys have a video going on?' I was like, 'Nope.' And he was like, 'Well, there's a video.'" Virgo added, "I think the concept was to put out the song and to push the album, and that's why we don't see anyone [from the group] actually in the video singing the song. It's just a barbecue pool party on a nice summer day. It's not really about Ghost Town, but the song."

The song did the equivalent of going viral in 1996 thanks to group member Greg Street. As producer Rodney Terry told *Spin.com*, "Because he [Street] played the record during Freaknik [a popular gathering/pilgrimage made by young people across the south to Atlanta in the mid-1990s], he was the first person to ever play the record, and he played it during Freaknik, so there were a lot of people in the town who heard the record and one thing led to another. So without any sign of a doubt, Greg Street is the individual who broke the record. Period." From Freaknik it spanned the country and the charts, reaching the top 40 on both the R&B and Hot 100 charts.

Despite the song's success, the Ghost Town DJ's would disappear just as quickly as they came onto the scene. It was largely due to label and management disputes involving the artists, who were signed to different labels.

As for the song's resurgence, Virgo noted, "I knew it would play continuously just because it is good music, but how this generation has adapted it and taken it in as its own and went off with it is amazing. I just love the fact that they're loving it and enjoying it the same as we did in 1996."

You

Artist: Jesse Powell
Albums: Jesse Powell, 'Bout It
Year: 1999
Writers: Jesse Powell, Carl Roland
Producer: Carl Roland
Highest R&B Chart Position: 2
Highest Hot 100 Chart Position: 10

Jesse Powell is best known for his single "You," which was included on his first and second albums. Powell got his start in the industry when record executive Louil Silas spotted him at an artist showcase and signed him to his Silas Records imprint. None of the songs on Powell's self-titled first album broke the top 30, including the original iteration of "You."

Powell would reach number 25 with the track "I Wasn't With It" from his second album, 1998's *'Bout It*, which also included a re-release of "You." "You" dropped as the album's second single in early 1999. This time "You" became Powell's biggest hit and his signature song, peaking at number 2 on the R&B chart, number 10 on the Hot 100 chart and powering *'Bout It* to be certified gold. Powell's third and fourth albums, *JP* and *Jesse*, would fail to make any waves.

Caught Out There

Artist: Kelis
Album: Kaleidoscope
Year: 1999
Writers: Chad Hugo, Pharrell Williams
Producers: The Neptunes
Highest R&B Chart Position: 9
Highest Hot 100 Chart Position: 54

In a 2013 interview with *The Independent*, songwriter and producer Pharrell Williams of the Neptunes informed us all that the track for Kelis' hit "Caught Out There" was originally intended for Busta Rhymes. Pharrell said, "At the time, we sat at an office at Elektra Records, and I played him that beat and I was sure he was gonna love it. And he was just, like, reading a sports magazine, listening to these tracks. And I was honored, because it was Busta. In full pigtail dreads, you don't understand. He was like the king to me. All these people! They were like deities. It was like being on Mount Olympus, where Apollo and the gods were, to be around these people. Think about it: Busta's voice is not ordinary. You don't go to school with a guy like that, and you don't know anybody's dad that sounds like that. But here he is. And he's chewing gum, not even looking up one time."

With an unimpressed Busta Rhymes passing on the track, the song was offered to up-and-coming writer-artist Kelis, who was then signed to Virgin Records, and "Caught Out There," which she recorded for her debut studio album *Kaleidoscope*, became one of her biggest hits.

Written and produced by Kelis and the Neptunes, the song was released as the album's lead single in 1999. While only peaking at number 54 on the Hot 100 chart, it was a bigger R&B and international hit, peaking inside the top 10 in the U.S., Canada, Iceland, Italy, the Netherlands, Sweden, and the U.K.

Although Kelis would have later success in 1999, singing the hook on Ol' Dirty Bastard's rap hit "Got Yo Money" and in the 2000's with her solo songs "Milkshake" (a 2003 number 4 R&B, number 3 Hot 100 hit) and 2006's "Bossy", (an R&B number 11), she believes the drama behind "Caught Out There" tainted the rest of her career. In 2012 she told *The Guardian*, "I think it set the tone for my entire life," with its decibel-piercing screams and savage refrains ("So sick of your games / I'll set your truck to flames"). "Also, within the industry, I've got a reputation because I really don't care enough. They take that aloofness as bitchiness. The music industry is a world of smoke and mirrors:

they tell you exactly what they think you want to hear. And they are bare-faced lying. I tend to stay away from that." In a bit of foreshadowing, in 2020 Kelis alleged that she was "blatantly lied to and tricked" by the Neptunes (Pharrell Williams and Chad Hugo), saying she was told "we were going to split the whole thing 33/33/33, which we didn't do." To this day the Neptunes are credited with writing most of the tracks that make up *Kaleidoscope* with Kelis co-credited with the pair on only two of them: "Ghetto Children" and "Suspended." Neither "Ghetto Children" nor "Suspended" charted.

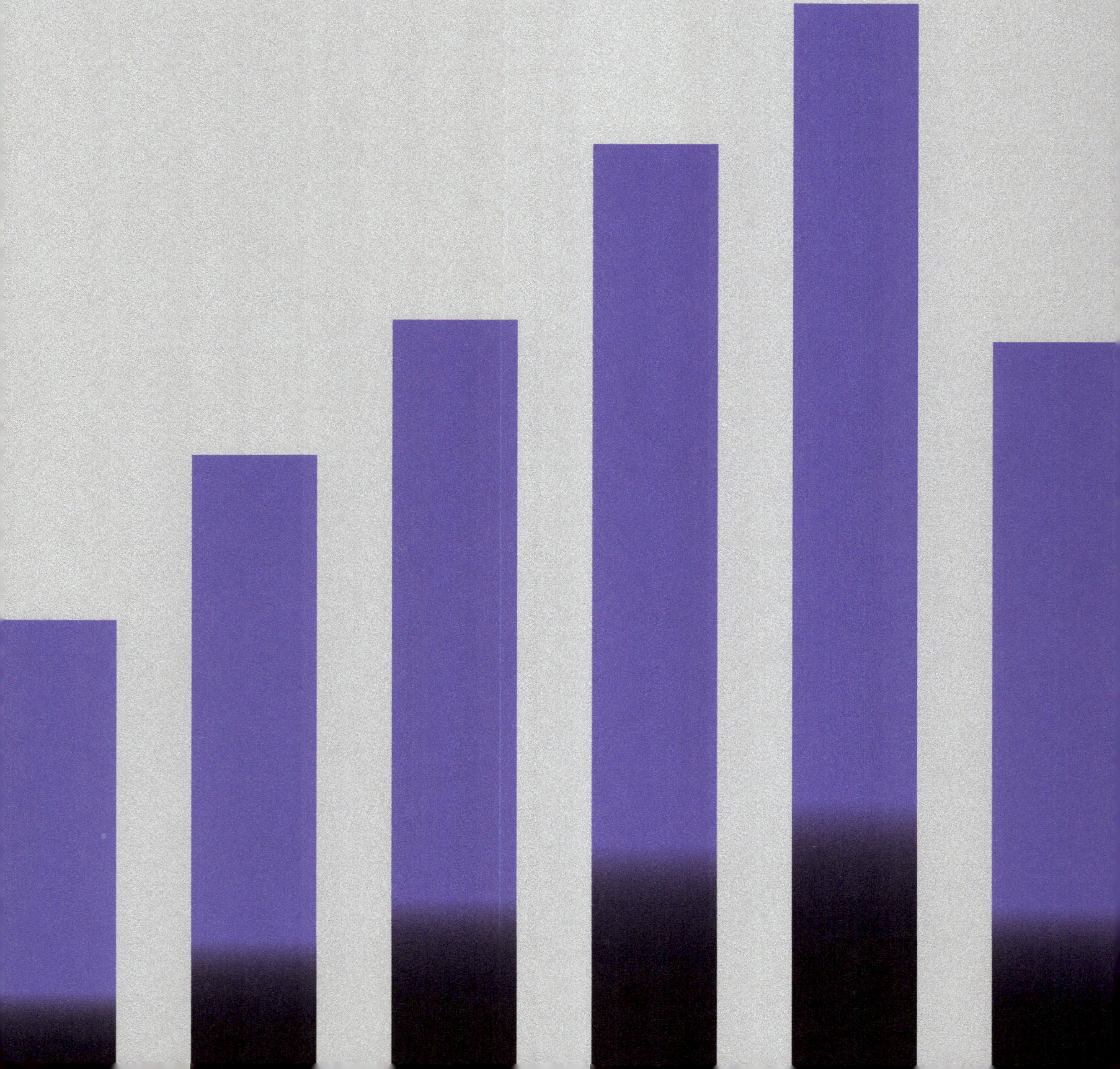

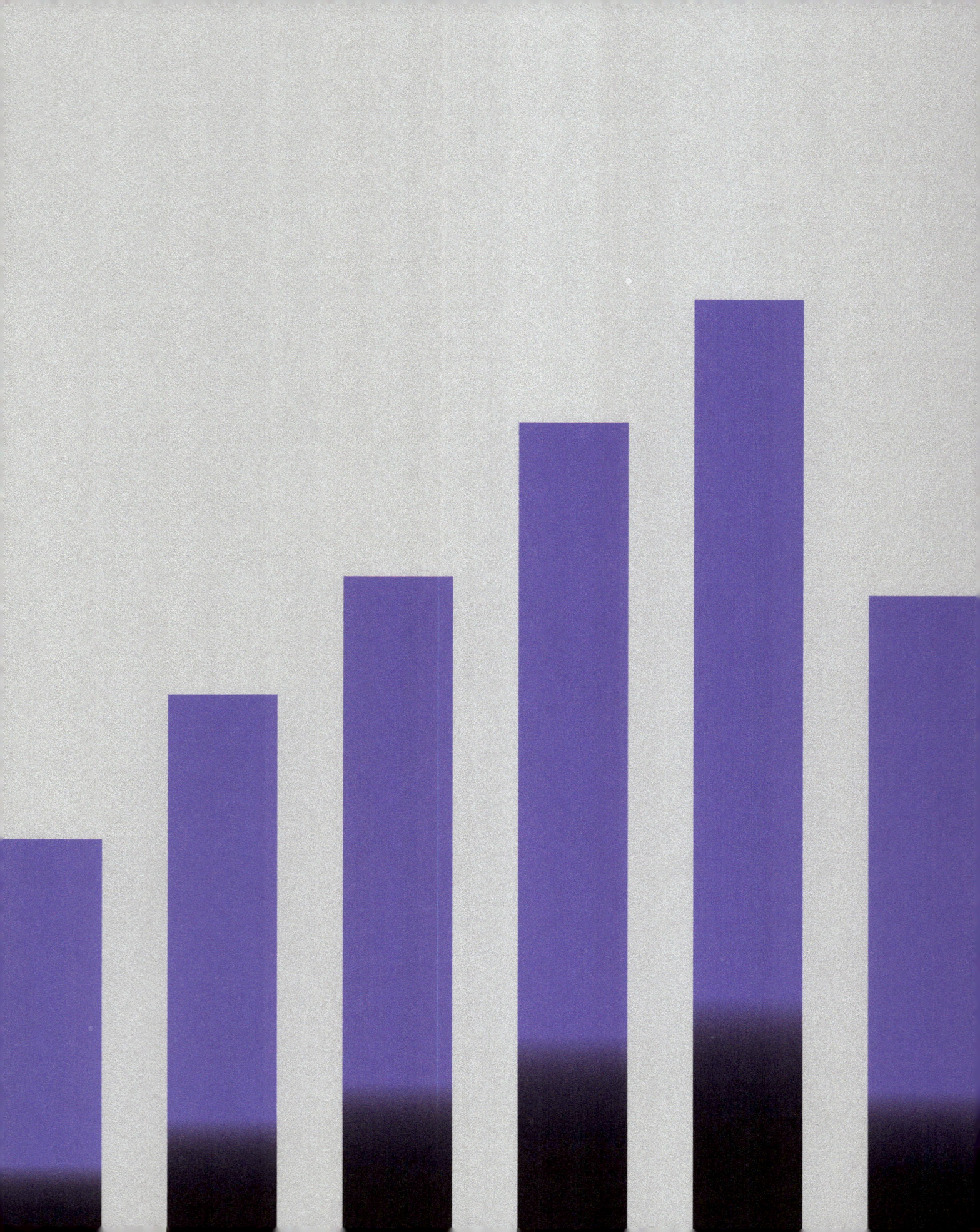

The Remakes

Yearning For Your Love
It's So Hard to Say Goodbye to Yesterday
Baby, I'm for Real/Natural High | Baby, I'm for Real
I Will Always Love You
I'll Be There
Giving Him Something He Can Feel | Something He Can Feel
I'm Every Woman
Lately
Sweet Thing
If You Think You're Lonely Now
If I Was Your Girlfriend
At Your Best (You Are Love) | (At Your Best) Your Are Love
Cruisin'
Love Don't Live Here Anymore
Killing Me Softly | Killing Me Softly with His Song | Killing Me Softly with His Song
Thin Line Between Love and Hate
Knocks Me Off My Feet
Betcha By Golly Wow
All Cried Out
Slow Jam
The Beautiful Ones
Honorable Mention

The Remakes

We've all heard and maybe even used the phrase "flattery will get you nowhere." But while that may apply in most of life's circumstances, the opposite is true in music, where the saying "imitation is the sincerest form of flattery" seems to be a better fit. Unlike other art forms like painting and poetry, where reproducing a Picasso or remixing a Maya Angelou poem would be equivalent to heresy, in music the remake can be a surefire way to score a hit for both new and established artists. Here some of the decade's biggest remakes are highlighted.

Yearning for Your Love

Artist: Guy
Album: The Future
Year: 1990
Writers: Oliver Scott, Ronnie Wilson
Producer: Teddy Riley
Highest R&B Chart Position: Song did not chart
Highest Hot 100 Chart Position: Song did not chart

Artist: The Gap Band
Album: The Gap Band III
Year: 1981
Writers: Oliver Scott, Ronnie Wilson
Producers: Oliver Scott, Ronnie Wilson
Highest R&B Chart Position: 5
Highest Hot 100 Chart Position: 60

This song "Yearning for Your Love" was penned by Gap Band keyboardists Oliver Scott and Ronnie Wilson in 1981 and was said to be dedicated to Wilson's wife. Guy remade the song less than a decade later for their highly successful sophomore album *The Future*.

It's So Hard To Say Goodbye To Yesterday

Artist: Boyz II Men
Album: Cooleyhighharmony
Year: 1991
Writers: Freddie Perren, Christine Yarian
Producer: Dallas Austin
Highest R&B Chart Position: 1
Highest Hot 100 Chart Position: 2

Artist: G. C. Cameron
Album: G.C. Cameron
Year: 1975
Writers: Freddie Perren, Christine Yarian
Producer: Freddie Perren
Highest R&B Chart Position: 38
Highest Hot 100 Chart Position: Song did not chart

The original song was written for the 1975 movie *Cooley High*, which is about students at a predominately black Illinois high school. It was written by the Motown producer and songwriter Freddie Perren and his wife, Christine Yarian. Perren co-wrote many Motown hits of the '60s and '70s, including the Jackson 5 number 1 "ABC" (1969) and Gloria Gaynor's number 4 hit "I Will Survive" (1978). "It's So Hard to Say Goodbye to Yesterday" was originally sung by G. C. Cameron, who was a member of The Spinners before the group left Motown Records and he stayed with the label as a solo artist. Cameron's original has a lush arrangement with strings and piano, but the Boyz II Men version, which was released as the second single of their debut album *Cooleyhighharmony,* is sung a cappella, proving they could carry a song without any production tricks. This tactic was important, as Boyz II Men's first single, "Motownphilly," was a heavily produced new jack track. Boyz II Men would later dedicate performances of this song to their tour manager, Khalil Rountree, after he was killed in Chicago when the band was on tour with MC Hammer in 1992.

Baby, I'm for Real/Natural High | Baby, I'm for Real

Title: Baby, I'm for Real/Natural High
Artist: After 7
Album: Takin' My Time
Year: 1992
Writers: Ana Gordy Gaye, Marvin Gaye, Charles McCormick
Producers: Daryl Simmons, Vincent Herbert
Notable Samples: (Interpolations) Natural High, Bloodstone (1973)
Highest R&B Chart Position: 5
Highest Hot 100 Chart Position: 55

Title: Baby, I'm for Real
Artist: The Originals
Album: Green Grow the Lilacs
Year: 1969
Writer: Ana Gordy Gaye, Marvin Gaye, Charles McCormick
Producers: Marvin Gaye, Richard Morris
Highest R&B Chart Position: 1
Highest Hot 100 Chart Position: 14

In 1968 the group the Originals were seasoned Motown backing singers, having provided harmonies for hits such as Jimmy Ruffin's 1966 song "What Becomes of the Brokenhearted" (6) and David Ruffin's 1969 number 2 hit "My Whole World Ended (The Moment You Left Me)." However, the Originals had failed to gain any traction on their own singles. Enter Marvin Gaye, who had become friends with the group members while they served as his background singers, and Gaye was looking to become more involved in production of his own material at Motown. Gaye saw helping the group to score a hit as an opportunity for him to showcase his writing and production skills to the Motown brass.

Gaye and his wife wrote the lyrics to a song called "The Bells I Hear" for the Originals. He would later rework the song as "Baby, I'm for Real" and its follow-up, "The Bells." Gaye also produced both songs. For "Baby, I'm for Real," he had each member of the band provide a lead vocal on each of the verses while also singing along in the background. With Gaye at the helm of production, "Baby, I'm for Real" reached number 1 on the Top Black Singles chart and reached number 14 on the Pop Singles chart, eventually selling over 1 million copies and putting the Originals on the map for a brief period as recording artists. The song's success paved the way for more Gaye-helmed productions at Motown, including his own classics. After 7's remake also included a portion of the hook from the group Bloodstone's 1973 hit "Natural High" (4), hence the title "Baby I'm for Real/ Natural High." After 7 released the song on their second album, *Takin' My Time*, which also included the hits "Kickin' It" (6) and "Can He Love U Like This" (22).

I Will Always Love You

Artist: Whitney Houston
Album: The Bodyguard Movie Soundtrack
Year: 1992
Writer: Dolly Parton
Producer: David Foster
Highest R&B Chart Position: 1
Highest Hot 100 Chart Position: 1

Artist: Dolly Pardon
Album: Jolene
Year: 1974
Writer: Dolly Parton
Producer: Bob Ferguson
Highest R&B Chart Position: Song did not chart
Highest Hot 100 Chart Position: 53
(Was a number 1 Country hit)

This song is perfect, whichever version you prefer. The original, penned and performed by Dolly Parton was a country ballad hit on her highly acclaimed *Jolene* album. Parton wrote the song as a farewell to her business partner and mentor Porter Wagoner after her decision to pursue a solo career. The original version was a certified hit, topping the Country charts in June 1974 and earning Parton the Female Vocalist of the Year award at the 1975 Country Music Awards.

In the years between Parton's release and Houston's, the song was covered by other artists, most notably Linda Ronstadt, who released a pop version for her 1975 album *Prisoner in Disguise*.

However, one famous country-adjacent artist who sought to cover the song but did not do it was "the King" himself, Elvis Presley. In 1974, Presley's manager Colonel Tom Parker, reached out to Parton to cover the song. Parton recalled that she was honored until Colonel Tom told her that it was standard procedure for the songwriter of every song Elvis covered to sign over half of their publishing rights to him. Parton refused. Recalling the incident years later, she said, "I cried all night. I mean, it was like the worst thing. You know, it's like, oh, my God . . . Elvis Presley. And other people were saying, 'You're nuts. It's Elvis Presley.' . . . I said, 'I can't do that. Something in my heart says, "Don't do that."' And I just didn't do it . . . He would have killed it. But anyway, so he didn't. Then when Whitney [Houston's version] came out, I made enough money to buy Graceland."

Another R&B artist also had a chance to record the song but refused. Parton offered Patti LaBelle an opportunity to cover the song because she thought LaBelle's voice was perfect for it, but LaBelle admittedly kept putting off the opportunity. She regretted that decision after she heard Houston's rendition.

In 1982, a Parton re-recording of "I Will Always Love You" would reach the top of the Country charts again, this time from the soundtrack for the movie *The Best Little Whorehouse in Texas*.

In 1991 when filming *The Bodyguard*, which was to be Whitney Houston's big-screen starring debut, recording "I Will Always Love You" was likely the furthest thing from the singer's mind. Houston, who was already tapped to do several songs on the film's soundtrack, intended to cover Jimmy Ruffin's "What Becomes of the Brokenhearted" (6) as the lead single. But that song was already attached to the 1991 film *Fried Green Tomatoes*. It was her co-star Kevin Costner, who was also *The Bodyguard's* producer, who recommended "I Will Always Love You" as a replacement.

According to *Songfacts.com*, "When the decision was made to record it for the movie, David Foster, the producer of Houston's version, went to a record store and bought the Linda Ronstadt version so Houston could learn the song. When he called Dolly Parton to let her know they were using her song, Dolly told him something very important: the Ronstadt version leaves out the last verse ("I wish you joy and happiness . . ."), which changes the tone of the song. Parton gave Foster the full lyrics and Houston recorded the full version. Foster had to tell the film's director, Mick Jackson, that he needed an extra forty seconds of screen time, as the song had been placed in the film minus the last verse. Houston's version was an instant smash. It remained at number 1 on the Hot 100 chart for fourteen weeks, which was a record at that time. That record was eventually broken by a 1995 collaboration on the song "One Sweet Day" by Mariah Carey and Boyz II Men, which held the top spot for sixteen weeks.

In an interview with *Q* magazine years later, Parton recalled that she "was blown away" by Whitney's version. She said, "The way she took that simple song of mine and made it such a mighty thing, it almost became her song. Some writers say, 'Ooh, I hate the way they've done that to my song or that version wasn't what I had in mind.' I just think it's wonderful that people can take a song and do it so many different ways."

I'll Be There

Artist: Mariah Carey
Album: MTV Unplugged
Year: 1992
Writers: Hal Davis, Berry Gordy, Willie Hutch, Bob West
Producers: Walter Afanasieff, Mariah Carey
Highest R&B Chart Position: 11
Highest Hot 100 Chart Position: 1

Artist: The Jackson 5
Album: Third Album
Year: 1970
Writers: Hal Davis, Berry Gordy, Willie Hutch, Bob Bob West
Producer: Hal Davis
Highest R&B Chart Position: 1
Highest Hot 100 Chart Position: 1

"I'll Be There" was first recorded by the Jackson 5 and released by Motown Records in 1970 as the first single from their *Third Album*. It would become the Jackson 5's fourth consecutive number 1 hit after "I Want You Back," "ABC," and "The Love You Save," making them the first group to have their first four singles reach number 1 and the first black male group with four consecutive number 1 pop hits.

Michael Jackson is on the lead vocal, with his brother Jermaine coming in on the bridge. This was typical of the division of vocal labor in the group. At one point during the song Michael hollers, "Just look over your shoulders, honey." He had been instructed by Berry Gordy to sing "just look over your shoulder" (as an allusion to what Levi Stubbs said in the Four Tops' song "Reach Out I'll Be There"), but Michael fluffed the line and it was allowed to remain in the final mix.

It is difficult to believe now but Carey suffered from stage fright early in her career, which led to speculation that she was a studio singer and could not reproduce her trademark range live. In part to address these doubts she booked an appearance on *MTV Unplugged,* which presented artists "unplugged" or in a stripped-down setting devoid of studio equipment. "I'll Be There" was originally a last-minute addition to her *MTV Unplugged* set list after she had been informed that most acts on the show commonly perform at least one cover. Carey's version was performed as a romantic duet, with her singing Michael Jackson's lines and background singer Trey Lorenz, who had provided background vocals on her *Emotions* album, performing Jermaine Jackson's part.

Carey's live performance put all doubts to rest. After the show aired, her record label received numerous requests to release "I'll Be There" as a single. The label relented and the single, which was co-produced by Carey and her frequent collaborator Walter Afanasieff, became her sixth number 1 single in the U.S. The song would also launch the career of Trey Lorenz, who would land a record deal based on his performance on the song. Lorenz would produce one '90s hit, "Someone to Love," which reached number 5 in 1992.

Carey's version earned triple-platinum certification, and the song was inducted into the Grammy Hall of Fame.

Giving Him Something He Can Feel | Something He Can Feel

Title: Giving Him Something He Can Feel
Artist: En Vogue
Album: Funky Divas
Year: 1992
Writer: Curtis Mayfield
Producers: Denzil Foster, Thomas McElroy
Highest R&B Chart Position: 1
Highest Hot 100 Chart Position: 6

Title: Something He Can Feel
Artist: Aretha Franklin
Album: Sparkle Movie Soundtrack
Year: 1976
Writer: Curtis Mayfield
Producer: Curtis Mayfield
Highest R&B Chart Position: 2
Highest Hot 100 Chart Position: 28

Curtis Mayfield wrote this song for the soundtrack to the 1976 musical drama *Sparkle.* The film, starring actresses Lonette McKee, Irene Cara, and Dwan Smith, followed an aspiring all-girl singing trio's named Sister and the Sisters and their struggle for fame in 1960s Harlem. "Something He Can Feel" was part of the group's sexy nightclub act. Mayfield told *Billboard* the song was based on "how I thought a woman might feel when she loves a man."

The actresses behind the Motown-inspired group, called Sister and the Sisters, expected their renditions of the songs in the movie to be featured on the soundtrack album, but Mayfield had someone else in mind, saying, "I had written all these songs for the youngsters who were acting in *Sparkle* . . . What is funny is how the depth of my writing made me think of Aretha [Franklin]." Franklin loved the songs and, backed by the female vocal group Kitty & the Haywoods, recorded them accompanied by Mayfield on guitar. Franklin's version of "Something He Can Feel" was a number 1 R&B hit.

The song and the *Sparkle* soundtrack's success was a much-needed boost for Franklin, who hadn't released a gold album since 1972's *Young, Gifted and Black.* "It also caused a rift between Franklin and her sister Carolyn, who sang on many of the singer's early hits, including the number 9 hit 'Ain't No Way'" (1968), which Carolyn wrote. Struggling to carve out a solo career of her own since the late '60s, Carolyn wanted to sing the Sparkle songs and in fact she claimed Mayfield approached her first before Franklin stepped in. Upon the soundtrack's release, Carolyn's own album *If You Want Me* flopped, and RCA dropped her from her contract. The sisters eventually made up, but Carolyn never recorded another album.

I'm Every Woman

Artist: Whitney Houston
Album: The Bodyguard Soundtrack
Year: 1993
Writers: Nick Ashford, Valerie Simpson
Producer: Narada Michael Walden
Highest R&B Chart Position: 5
Highest Hot 100 Chart Position: 4

Artist: Chaka Khan
Album: Chaka
Year: 1978
Writers: Nick Ashford, Valerie Simpson
Producer: Arif Mardin
Highest R&B Chart Position: 1
Highest Hot 100 Chart Position: 21

By 1978 the husband-and-wife songwriting duo of Nick Ashford and Valerie Simpson had already achieved legend status for crafting some of Motown's biggest hits like the number 1's "Ain't No Mountain High Enough" (1967) and "You're All I Need to Get By" (1968). When the duo was pegged to write a song for Chaka Khan on her debut solo project, they were seeking a major hit for the dynamic vocalist. The twenty-five-year-old Khan had already proven herself as well, having several top 10 hits under her belt as the lead singer of the band Rufus.

Of course, you would expect that it would be Valerie Simpson who took lead on writing the female anthem's lyrics. However, as she explained to Oprah Winfrey in a 2020 interview, that was not the case. Valerie says that during a writing session, "I started playing these chords and he [Nick Ashford] says 'I'm every woman' and I said yeah! And he said, 'I can't feel the verse,' then I said, 'Put your hand on your hip,' and he did and it just came out. I'm every woman, it's all in me. The song took only a couple of days to complete." Simpson told *People* magazine, "It was one of those things that just all came together."

Khan initially did not like the song. Years later she would disclose that she felt awkward saying the words "I'm every woman," saying, "I thought how dare somebody say that they're every woman. I was just not mentally there yet. It's a song that I grew into." Thankfully the song's producer, Arif Mardin, convinced Khan to record the song, which became a number 1 hit for her in 1978. "That song," says Simpson, "became very much a woman's anthem. With Chaka, she just is like a dynamo, unstoppable, very sexy person. Her persona is just all woman, which is why she did 'I'm Every Woman' so well."

Whitney Houston recorded the song in 1993, taking it to number 4 and introducing it to a new audience. Her version appeared on the soundtrack to the movie *The Bodyguard*. *The Bodyguard* album is still the best-selling soundtrack of all time, with worldwide sales of over 44 million. In her version of "I'm Every Woman," Houston pays tribute to Khan by yelling "Chaka Khan" twice near the end of the song. In an ironic twist, Whitney's mom Cissy Houston sang backing vocals on Chaka Khan's original version of the song.

Lately

Artist: Jodeci
Album: Uptown MTV Unplugged (Single)
Year: 1993
Writers: DeVanté Swing, Stevie Wonder
Producer: DeVanté Swing
Highest R&B Chart Position: 1
Highest Hot 100 Chart Position: 4

Artist: Stevie Wonder
Album: Hotter Than July
Year: 1980
Writer: Stevie Wonder
Producer: Stevie Wonder
Highest R&B Chart Position: 29
Highest Hot 100 Chart Position: 64

Jodeci covered the Stevie Wonder song, which is about a man piecing together the signs of his lover's infidelity, for the "*Uptown MTV Unplugged*" album release in 1993.

The arrangement for Jodeci's version of "Lately" was originally composed by Al B. Sure!. K-Ci & JoJo were demo singers for Al B. Sure! at the time, and the group was working on songs for Tevin Campbell's debut album T.E.V.I.N.. Al B. Sure! thought the Stevie Wonder hit would be a good fit for Campbell's album and had K-Ci & JoJo record a demo of the song. K-Ci & JoJo had not heard the song prior to Al B. Sure! playing it for them. "Lately" was not selected for Campbell's album, and as far as Al B. Sure! was concerned the song was abandoned until he saw Jodeci's *Unplugged* performance where they performed the song as he had arranged it. Jodeci's version was a smash, and Andre Harrell, who is credited as the producer for the track, called it Jodeci's "End of the Road," referencing the hit by Boyz II Men. Jodeci's rendition would become the group's fourth R&B number 1 hit.

Sweet Thing

Artist: Mary J. Blige
Album: What's the 411?
Year: 1992
Writers: Chaka Khan, Tony Maiden
Producers: Prince Markie D, Cory Rooney
Notable Sample: I'm Gonna Love You Just A Little More Baby Barry White (1973)
Highest R&B Chart Position: 11
Highest Hot 100 Chart Position: 28

Artist: Rufus
Album: Rufus featuring Chaka Khan
Year: 1975
Writers: Chaka Khan, Tony Maiden
Producers: Rufus, Russ Titelman
Highest R&B Chart Position: 1
Highest Hot 100 Chart Position: 5

Chaka Khan wrote this song with her boyfriend at the time, Tony Maiden, who was also the guitarist in the band Rufus. Khan was the band's lead singer. She told LaShonda Barnett in *I Got Thunder: Black Women Songwriters and Their Craft*, "I told all of my boyfriends around that time that it was them that inspired the song. In fact, I think Tony was my real boyfriend at the time. That song was just spontaneous. Tony and I were just sitting around and it happened—really. We had that kind of chemistry, and it was that kind of situation. We wrote the song in five minutes. It's all really chemistry when it boils down to it. Rufus and I had an amazing chemistry. That's what was underneath it all and the love we had for each other."

"Sweet Thing" became a number 1 for Rufus and the group's second gold single. Funny thing is, while most of us and our parents interpreted the groove as an innocent love song, the truth is that Khan and Maiden wrote the song about infidelity. It is a story of an affair told from the perspective of a side piece who wishes she could have her lover to herself. Hence the lines:

I will love you anyway / Even if you cannot stay /
I think you are the one for me / Here is where you ought to be /
I just want to satisfy you / Though you're not mine / I can't deny you.

Blige's version was released as the fifth single from her debut album *What's the 411?*, and became her fourth top 25 song. In total, *What's the 411?* would produce seven top 25 songs.

If You Think You're Lonely Now

Artist: K-Ci & JoJo
Album: Jason's Lyric Movie Soundtrack
Year: 1994
Writers: Richard Griffin, Patrick Moten, Sandra Sully, Bobby Womack
Producer: James Mtume
Highest R&B Chart Position: 11
Highest Hot 100 Chart Position: 17

Artist: Bobby Womack
Album: The Poet
Year: 1981
Writers: Richard Griffin, Patrick Moten, Sandra Sully, Bobby Womack
Producer: Bobby Womack
Highest R&B Chart Position: 3
Highest Hot 100 Chart Position: Song did not chart

"If You Think You're Lonely Now" was originally released as a B side to Womack's song "Secrets" from his 1981 album *The Poet*. However, it was "If You Think You're Lonely Now" that became the far bigger hit and eventually became Womack's signature song, reaching number 3 on the R&B charts. Jodeci member K-Ci Hailey was a huge Bobby Womack fan and jumped at the opportunity to cover the Rock and Roll Hall of Famer's signature classic for the soundtrack to the 1994 movie *Jason's Lyric*. K-Ci & JoJo's version earned them a top 20 R&B hit.

If I Was Your Girlfriend

Artist: TLC
Album: CrazySexyCool
Year: 1994
Writer: Prince
Producers: Sean Combs, Chucky Thompson
Notable Sample: Computer Love, Zapp (1985)
Highest R&B Chart Position: Song did not chart
Highest Hot 100 Chart Position: Song did not chart

Artist: Prince
Album: Sign O' the Times
Year: 1987
Writer: Prince
Producer: Prince
Highest R&B Chart Position: 12
Highest Hot 100 Chart Position: 67

"If I Was Your Girlfriend" was originally part of Prince's planned triple album titled *Camille Project* that the artist was to release under the name of his alter ego/adopted female persona "Camille" in 1986. Three of the tracks from that abandoned project made it into 1987's *Sign O' the Times* album: "If I Was Your Girlfriend," "Housequake," and "Strange Relationship." Only "If I Was Your Girlfriend" would chart.

The song was released as the album's second single. It is delivered from an androgynous male perspective to a woman, wherein Prince explores the possibilities of a more intimate relationship if he were his lover's girlfriend. It is believed that "If I Was Your Girlfriend" deals with the jealousy Prince felt at the close bond shared between his then girlfriend/fiancée Susannah Melvoin and her twin sister Wendy. Allegedly four songs on *Sign O' the Times* are about Melvoin: "If I Was Your Girlfriend," "Forever in My Life," "Strange Relationship," and "Adore."

The production of "If I Was Your Girlfriend" shows how much of a genius Prince truly was. The opening seconds, which are rarely played on radio, feature a sound collage that includes an orchestra tuning up, a salesman, and a sample of Felix Mendelssohn's "Wedding March."

The track itself features Prince's androgynous vocals over a sparse bass and drum machine pattern, punctuated by a keyboard line. According to Prince's sound engineer Susan Rogers, a rare technical error on her part led to distortion—albeit only on certain words. As recounted in Alex Hahn's book *Possessed: The Rise and Fall of Prince*, Rogers stated, "[I] thought Prince was going to rip my head off" for the mistake. Yet after hearing the playback, Prince loved the effect, which is featured on the released version." The product of an accidental board malfunction turned into a R&B hit. The song was released in the spring of 1987 and reached number 12 on the R&B chart. TLC, which had covered another Prince-penned song in 1993 with a version of his 1981 hit "Get It Up" on the *Poetic Justice* soundtrack, remade "If I Was Your Girlfriend." Their cover—which featured T-Boz's deep voice produced in a somewhat distorted sound—was not released as a commercial single.

Beyoncé sang a few lines of the song in 2002's "'03 Bonnie and Clyde" with her then boyfriend, now husband, Jay-Z, which earned Prince a writing credit for that track.

At Your Best (You Are Love) | (At Your Best) You Are Love

Title: At Your Best (You Are Love)
Artist: Aaliyah
Album: Age Ain't Nothing but a Number
Year: 1994
Writers: The Isley Brothers, Chris Jasper
Producer: R. Kelly
Highest R&B Chart Position: 2
Highest Hot 100 Chart Position: 6

Title: (At Your Best) You Are Love
Artist: The Isley Brothers
Album: Harvest for the World
Year: 1976
Writers: The Isley Brothers, Chris Jasper
Producers: The Isley Brothers
Highest R&B Chart Position: Song did not chart
Highest Hot 100 Chart Position: Song did not chart

The original was written by the Isley Brothers as a display of their deep appreciation to their mother. The line "You're a positive motivating force within my life" is sung throughout, showing their appreciation for the love and strength she brought them.

Aaliyah's version of the song was produced by R. Kelly in conjunction with Barry Hankerson. It was released as the second single from her debut album.

Cruisin'

Artist: D'Angelo
Album: Brown Sugar
Year: 1995
Writers: Smokey Robinson, Marv Tarplin
Producer: D'Angelo
Highest R&B Chart Position: 10
Highest Hot 100 Chart Position: 53

Artist: Smokey Robinson
Album: Where There's Smoke
Year: 1979
Writers: Smokey Robinson, Marv Tarplin
Producer: Smokey Robinson
Highest R&B Chart Position: 4
Highest Hot 100 Chart Position: 4

When Smokey Robinson heard the music to "Cruisin'" he recalled, "I loved it. It was so sensual, so sexy. It did something to my soul. I played it forever—in my car, when I got home, over and over. I wrote two or three other songs to that music, but they didn't work. Nothing fit this music. This song came in bits and pieces. 'Cruisin'' took five years to write." In an interview with *The Guardian's* 1000 *Songs Everyone Must Hear* supplement, Smokey recalled that his guitarist, Marv Tarplin, had already written the music. Smokey added, "He put it on cassette and gave it to me to write the lyric. As it turned out, I had the music . . . but I couldn't get the words. Then one day I got: 'You're gonna fly away and I'm glad you're coming my way.' And then I was driving my car down Sunset Boulevard, and I heard that song by the Rascals, 'Groovin',' and I thought, 'That's it! Grooving.' But then, no, it wasn't intimate enough, it wasn't sensual enough for the music, and that's when I thought of 'Cruisin'.' You'd be surprised by how many people speculate on what cruisin' means. Cruisin' is a word that I leave up to the listener. When you're with the person you're with, and you feel you're cruisin', it's whatever you want it to be."

Neo-soul artist D'Angelo would release "Cruisin'" as a single on his debut album *Brown Sugar* in the summer of 1995. The track peaked at number 10 on the R&B charts. *Brown Sugar* would spawn four charting singles: "Brown Sugar" (5), "Cruisin'" (10), "Lady" (2), and "Me and Those Dreamin' Eyes of Mine" (25).

Love Don't Live Here Anymore

Artist: Faith Evans featuring Mary J. Blige
Album: Faith
Year: 1995
Writer: Miles Gregory
Producers: Prince Charles Alexander, Diddy, Mark Ledford
Highest R&B Chart Position: Song did not chart
Highest Hot 100 Chart Position: Song did not chart

Artist: Rose Royce
Album: Rose Royce III: Strikes Again
Year: 1978
Writer: Miles Gregory
Producers: Paul Buckmaster, Norman Whitfield
Highest R&B Chart Position: 5
Highest Hot 100 Chart Position: 32

"Love Don't Live Here Anymore" was written by Miles Gregory of the band Rose Royce and is said to be based on the musician's real-life marital strife. In 2015, Rose Royce's lead singer Gwen Dickey, the voice that turned the song into a classic, told the music website *SoulandJazzandFunk.com* that the song grew out of Gregory's wife's frustration with the band's frequent studio sessions. According to Dickey, the band's legendary producer, Norman Whitfield, was a taskmaster who demanded every ounce of time and dedication from them in the studio" — often keeping them in the studio for three or four days in a row). Dickey continued "You had to come to the studio with an overnight bag because you didn't know when you were going to get to leave."

After one of these all-nighters, Gregory's wife had had enough and gave him an ultimatum, telling him, "The next time you go to the studio and you stay in there for twenty-four hours and you don't come home, I won't be here when you come back because I've had enough of this!"

Well, Gregory either dismissed his wife's threat or didn't believe she would leave him, because a few weeks later he, Whitfield, and the band hit the studio again for another marathon session.

The next morning when Gregory arrived at his home he saw that his wife and all of his furniture were gone. However, she did leave him a few things in the bedroom—"some clothes hanging in the wardrobe, his guitar in a corner"— and a message written in lipstick on a mirror in the bedroom that read, "Love Don't Live Here Anymore." According to Dickey, "Gregory sat down and wrote 'Love Don't Live Here Anymore' right there in tears." Along with Faith Evans, the song has also been covered by Madonna, Morrissey, Seal, and many others.

Killing Me Softly | Killing Me Softly with His Song

Title: Killing Me Softly
Artist: Fugees
Album: The Score
Year: 1996
Writers: Charles Fox, Norman Gimbel, Lori Lieberman
Producers: Fugees
Notable Samples: Bonita Applebaum, A Tribe Called Quest (1990)
The Day Begins, The Moody Blues featuring the London Festival Orchestra
Highest R&B Chart Position: Song did not chart
Highest Hot 100 Chart Position: Song did not chart

Title: Killing Me Softly with His Song
Artist: Lori Lieberman
Album: Lori Lieberman
Year: 1972
Writers: Charles Fox, Norman Gimbel, Lori Lieberman
Producers: Charles Fox, Norman Gimbel,
Highest R&B Chart Position: Song did not chart
Highest Hot 100 Chart Position: Song did not chart

Title: Killing Me Softly with His Song
Artist: Roberta Flack
Album: Killing Me Softly
Year: 1973
Writers: Charles Fox, Norman Gimbel, Lori Lieberman
Producer: Joel Dorn
Highest R&B Chart Position: 1
Highest Hot 100 Chart Position: 2

If you were anywhere around a radio in 1996, you were inundated with this song. It was on heavy rotation on top 40, hip-hop, and R&B stations during that summer. The Fugees' version with lead vocals by Lauryn Hill, fresh off her acting role as Rita Louise Watson in *Sister Act 2*, gave new life to the Lori Lieberman hit that Roberta Flack made into a timeless classic.

So how improbable was this hit in 1996? Well, it turns out that lightning struck twice for this song decades apart. The original "Killing Me Softly with His Song," written by Lori Lieberman and Norman Gimbel, was inspired by "American Pie" singer Don McLean when in 1971 a twenty-year-old Lieberman saw McLean in performance at the Troubadour nightclub in Los Angeles. At the time "American Pie" was a folk/rock hit, but it was his song "Empty Chairs" that drove Lieberman to write "Killing Me Softly with His Song." Lieberman was said to have scribbled notes of poetry on a napkin while McLean was singing. Following the concert, she read the notes to the song's co-writer Gimbel. Gimbel said in 1973 that "her conversation fed me, inspired me, gave me some language and a choice of words." Lieberman released her version of the song in 1972, but it did not chart.

Roberta Flack first heard the song while on an airplane via the an-flight audio program. Flack recalled, "The title, of course, smacked me in the face. I immediately pulled out some scratch paper, made musical staves [then] play[ed] the song at least eight to ten times jotting down the melody that I heard. When I landed, I immediately called Quincy [Jones] at his house and asked him how to meet Charles Fox. Two days later I had the music." Shortly afterward Flack rehearsed the song with her band, but did not record it then.

Two weeks later Flack was on tour with Jones. During a performance at the Greek Theater in Los Angeles, California, after performing her prepared songs the crowd was clamoring for an encore. Jones then said to Flack "Ro do something." Flack recalled how she responded to PBS in an episode of the *American Masters* documentary television series saying "Well, I got this new song I've been working on. So I started with 'strumming my pain with his fingers'" [singing]." After I finished [the song] the audience would not stop screaming and Quincy said 'Ro don't sing that dang-on song no more until you record it.'"

Taking Jones' advice, Flack headed to the studio and made some changes to the Lieberman/Gimbel/Fox version. As she described it, "My classical background made it possible for me to try a number of things with [the song's arrangement]. I changed parts of the chord structure and chose to end on a major chord. [The song] wasn't written that way." Flack's version was released in 1973 as the opening track of her *Killing Me Softly* album and spent more weeks at number 1 than any other song of 1973 (five nonconsecutive weeks). It won the 1974 Grammy for Record of the Year and Best Female Pop Vocal Performance and earned Lieberman, Gimbel, and Fox the Grammy for Song of the Year. In 1996, a house remix of Flack's version went to number 1 on the U.S. dance chart, and in 1999 Flack's version was inducted into the Grammy Hall of Fame.

As for the Fugees, "Killing Me Softly" was the last song they recorded for their second album, *The Score*. Their first album, 1994's *Blunted on Reality*, did not chart well so the pressure was on for a hit. "Killing Me Softly" was recorded at group member Pras' suggestion to cover the song. The Fugees version sampled the 1990 song "Bonita Applebaum" by A Tribe Called Quest and included that band's sample of a riff from the song "Memory Band" from the psychedelic soul band Rotary Connection and their 1967 eponymous debut album. The Fugees version, became an international hit, reaching number 1 on the U.S. top 40 chart and number 2 on the U.S. Airplay chart. The song was not released as a commercial single and was ineligible for the R&B chart. It also won the 1997 Grammy for Best R&B Performance by a Duo or Group with Vocal. The song has been certified 3× platinum, and both the Fugees' and Flack's versions were placed on the list of *Rolling Stone's* 500 Greatest Songs of All Time.

Thin Line Between Love and Hate | A Thin Line Between Love and Hate

Title: Thin Line Between Love and Hate
Artist: H-Town (featuring Roger Troutman and Shirley Murdock)
Album: A Thin Line Between Love and Hate Movie Soundtrack
Year: 1996
Writers: Jackie Members, Richard Poindexter, Robert Poindexter
Producer: Roger Troutman
Highest R&B Chart Position: 6
Highest Hot 100 Chart Position: 37

Title: A Thin Line Between Love and Hate
Artist: The Persuaders
Album: A Thin Line Between Love and Hate
Year: 1971
Writers: Jackie Members, Richard Poindexter, Robert Poindexter
Producers: Richard Poindexter, Robert Poindexter
Highest R&B Chart Position: 1
Highest Ho 100 Chart Position: 15

Songs about domestic violence don't typically have much chart or sales success. This tune is an exception. Originally released by the R&B group the Persuaders in 1971, it details a man taking his woman for granted and ending up "in the hospital, bandaged from feet to head" as a result. It reached the top of the R&B charts in 1971. Houston, Texas–based group H-Town was tapped to remake the song for the Martin Lawrence film *A Thin Line Between Love and Hate*, which was released in 1996. Lawrence's story centers around a ladies' man who falls victim to an obsessive woman played by Lynn Whitfield and ultimately ends up nearly dying as a result. The key takeaway from both versions of the song and from the film is "the sweetest woman in the world can be the meanest woman in the world if you make her that way."

Knocks Me Off My Feet

Artist: Donell Jones
Album: My Heart
Year: 1996
Writer: Stevie Wonder
Producer: Darin Whittington
Highest R&B Chart Position: 14
Highest Hot 100 Chart Position: 49

Artist: Stevie Wonder
Album: Songs in the Key of Life
Year: 1976
Writer: Stevie Wonder
Producer: Stevie Wonder
Highest R&B Chart Position: Song did not chart
Highest Hot 100 Chart Position: Song did not chart

"Knocks Me of My Feet" is a song from Stevie Wonder's much celebrated *Songs in the Key of Life* album, which many consider to be one of the greatest albums of all time. It earned Wonder his third Album of the Year Grammy Award in a four-year span. Jones released his version of the song on his debut album *My Heart*. In doing so, he faced stiff competition from some R&B veterans. Artists Luther Vandross and Tevin Campbell, both of whom had already scored number 1 R&B hits earlier in their careers, also released covers of the song that same year. But it was Jones' version that stood out among fans, as his rendition became a top 20 R&B hit while neither the Vandross nor Campbell versions broke the top 50.

Betcha by Golly Wow

Artist: Prince
Album: Emancipation
Year: 1996
Writers: Thom Bell, Linda Creed
Producer: Prince
Highest R&B Chart Position: Song did not chart
Highest Hot 100 Chart Position: Song did not chart

Artist: The Stylistics
Album: The Stylistics
Year: 1972
Writers: Thom Bell, Linda Creed
Producer: Thom Bell
Highest R&B Chart Position: 2
Highest Hot 100 Chart Position: 3

The song was written by Thom Bell and Linda Creed, the duo behind some of Philadelphia International Records biggest hits, like The Delfonics song "Didn't I (Blow Your Mind This Time)" (3) and The Spinners 1972 number 1, "I'll Be Around." "Betcha by Golly Wow" was originally titled "Keep Growing Strong" and was first recorded by the white pop singer and actress Connie Stevens in 1970. Stevens was no stranger to the R&B charts, having scored a top 10 R&B hit ten years earlier with her 1960 song "Sixteen Reasons." So it should not be surprising that Stevens delivered a more soulful rendition of the song than expected. Stevens' version failed to chart as the song may have been too soulful for pop fans and too pop for R&B fans. In 1971 Bell and Creed changed the songs name from "Keep Growing Strong" to "Betcha By Golly Wow" and formatted the arrangements to create a full on R&B ballad for the group The Stylistics to record. The Stylistics version was a success and became the group's fourth top 10 R&B single between 1971 and 1972.

During this run The Stylistics were the definition of cool, but the songs new title was, well…..corny. Bell, the songs principal writer, came up with the title because, as he put it "I'm the only one crazy enough to come up with something like that. It takes a nut! All of those words are elements of expression, of surprise, Golly! Gee! Wow! Ooh! and they were elements of expression, so I wondered if I can put those words together." He added "In the history of songwriting there have been many songs written of I love you and a lot of different versions of those same words or any reasonable facsimile of those same words, but there's only one "Betcha by Golly Wow.'"

Prince's release of "Betcha by Golly Wow" was surprising because for the majority of his nearly four decade long career he did not do remakes. Prince's version was not released as a commercial single, thus was not eligible for the R&B and Hot 100 charts. However, it did reach number 10 on the R&B airplay charts.

All Cried Out

Artist: Allure, 112
Album: Allure
Year: 1997
Writers: Paul Anthony, Curt Bedeau, B-Fine, Baby Gerry, Bow-Legged Lou, Shy Shy
Producers: Walter Afanasieff, Mariah Carey, Cory Rooney
Highest R&B Chart Position: 9
Highest Hot 100 Chart Position: 4

Artist: Lisa Lisa & Cult Jam
Album: Lisa Lisa & Cult Jam with Full Force
Year: 1985
Writers: Paul Anthony, Curt Bedeau, B-Fine, Baby Gerry, Bow-Legged Lou, Shy Shy
Producers: Full Force
Highest R&B Chart Position: 3
Highest Hot 100 Chart Position: 8

Lisa Lisa, a.k.a. Lisa Velez, was discovered by Cult Jam drummer Mike Hughes while dancing at the Fun House club in Manhattan, New York. Hughes spotted her, found her attractive, and asked her to audition for the Full Force production team. Velez, who was only sixteen at the time, lied to Full Force, telling them she was eighteen at the audition. The audition went well, and Velez was teamed with Hughes and Alex "Spanador" Moseley, forming Lisa Lisa & Cult Jam. Soon after they recorded their debut single, "I Wonder If I Take You Home" (6), which was written by Full Force member B-Fine and produced by Full Force, they released it as an independent single. B-Fine specifically wanted a Latin American female to sing the song. Full Force member Bow-Legged Lou told the *Questlove Supreme* podcast, "At that time there was no . . . Puerto Ricans or Spanish girls doing anything resembling dance R&B and hip-hop combo, not one. This was before Gloria [Estefan], this was before Shakira, this was before J. Lo, this was before Ricky Martin, any Spanish person." The release with Lisa Lisa singing lead was a success, which led to Columbia Records signing the group.

The album that followed, *Lisa Lisa & Cult Jam with Full Force*, yielded two freestyle/club hits that were released as it's first two singles including a re-release of "I Wonder If I Take You Home" and the song "Can You Feel the Beat," which peaked at number 40. Yearning for a chance to showcase Velez's vocals, the band released the ballad "All Cried Out" with Velez as the lead and Full Force's Paul Anthony and Bow-Legged Lou also contributing vocals, singing from the perspective of Velez's apologetic ex. According to Bow-Legged Lou on his *Memories and Flashbacks* YouTube channel, Paul Anthony wrote the lyrics drawing off inspiration from a female friend of his who was complaining to him about her unfaithful boyfriend when she told him she was "all cried out," Paul Anthony took note of the term and as Bow-Legged Lou put it, the rest is songwriting history.

Velez jumped at the chance to sing the ballad. In 2020 she told *NJArts.net*, "It was a chance to let people hear my talent . . . it was very important for me to get 'All Cried Out' out there. I wanted people to see and hear what I can do." Velez recalled that she could relate to the heartbreak in the song, stating, "I hear so many stories from people. The one I hear the most is from the females. 'You helped me through my breakup with your song, "All Cried Out." You kept me alive and moving.' Well, whatever I can do to help is cool with me, because when we were doing the song, I was going through the same thing. . . . We all universally go through the same first breakup experience." The song eventually went platinum.

Allure which consisted of members Alia Davis, Akissa Mendez, Lalisha McClean and Linnie Belcher was the first group signed to Mariah Carey's Crave Records label, which she created with her then husband Tommy Mottola in 1997. Carey, Cory Rooney, and Walter Afanasieff produced the remake of "All Cried Out," which was included on Allure's self-titled debut album. To date, "All Cried Out" is Allure's highest charting single, which they covered as a duet with the male group 112. Crave Records would fold in 1998 following Carey's divorce from Mottola. Allure would continue to record new music as late as 2018, but to date the group's highest charting single since "All Cried Out" is 2001's "Enjoy Yourself," which peaked at 50.

Slow Jam

Artist: Usher and Monica
Album: My Way
Year: 1997
Writers: Sidney DeWayne, Kenneth "Babyface" Edmonds, Belinda Lipscomb, Bo Watson
Producer: Kenneth "Babyface" Edmonds
Highest R&B Chart Position: Song did not chart
Highest Hot 100 Chart Position: Song did not chart

Artist: Midnight Star
Album: No Parking on the Dance Floor
Year: 1983
Writers: Sidney DeWayne, Kenneth "Babyface" Edmonds, Belinda Lipscomb, Bo Watson
Producer: Reggie Calloway
Highest R&B Chart Position: Song did not chart
Highest Hot 100 Chart Position: Song did not chart

Kenneth "Babyface" Edmonds invented the term for the genre he would come to dominate with this song. "Slow Jam" was his first major credit as a songwriter for hire. Unfortunately, his last name is misspelled as "Edmunds" on the LP's side-two label. Babyface also produced this reboot with Monica and Usher for Usher's *My Way* album.

The Beautiful Ones

Artist: Mariah Carey featuring Dru Hill
Album: Butterfly
Year: 1997
Writer: Prince
Producer: Mariah Carey, Cory Rooney, DeVanté Swing
Highest R&B Chart Position: Song did not chart
Highest Hot 100 Chart Position: Song did not chart

Artist: Prince and the Revolution
Album: Purple Rain
Year: 1984
Writer: Prince
Producer: Prince
Highest R&B Chart Position: Song did not chart
Highest Hot 100 Chart Position: Song did not chart

The legend that persisted for decades was that Prince wrote "The Beautiful Ones" for the woman who would eventually become his girlfriend, Susannah Melvoin. Melvoin was seeing someone else at the time, and this was said to be Prince's attempt to steal her from him. It was only in 2015 during an interview with *Ebony* magazine that Prince revealed that the song was really about Denise Matthews, a.k.a. Vanity. Prince told the magazine, "I was talking to somebody about 'The Beautiful Ones.' They were speculating as to who I was singing about—but they were completely wrong . . . If they look at it, it's very obvious. 'Do you want him or do you want me'—that was written for that scene in *Purple Rain* specifically, where Morris [Day] would be sitting with [Apollonia] and there'd be this back and forth. And also, 'The beautiful ones you always seem to lose,' Vanity had just quit the movie."

For her version, Mariah Carey brought in R&B group Dru Hill and performed the song as a duet with Dru Hill member Sisqó singing lead opposite Carey. This track was produced by DeVanté Swing of Jodeci. Sisqó recalled that he did not know the record and was literally reading the lyrics from a piece of paper while recording. Label head Tommy Mottola was in the studio, though at the time he and Mariah Carey were in the process of ending their marriage. Sisqó recalled that while playing the song Mottola began crying because the song "really touched him like that."

Honorable Mention
Everything | You Are Everything

Title: Everything
Artist: Mary J. Blige
Album: Everything
Year: 1997
Writers: Thom Bell, Linda Creed, Jimmy Jam, Terry Lewis
Producers: Jimmy Jam, Terry Lewis
Notable Sample: The Payback, James Brown (1973)
Highest R&B Chart Position: 5
Highest Hot 100 Chart Position: 24

Title: You Are Everything
Artist: The Stylistics
Album: The Stylistics
Year: 1971
Writers: Thom Bell, Linda Creed
Producer: Thom Bell
Highest R&B Chart Position: 9
Highest Hot 100 Chart Position: 10

This song receives honorable mention because it technically isn't a remake. Like a lot of R&B hits of the era, it relies heavily on samples from a previous hit, with contemporary vocals and arrangements. However, the story behind the original, which shows the genius of Philadelphia songwriters Thom Bell and Linda Creed, is one that had to be told. In a 2021 interview, Bell told NPR's Terry Gross the origin of the original song, saying, "One day, [Linda] Creed and I couldn't come up with anything, we would just get up and walk on the street. So we're walking down the street. We're looking around because there's always something in the street to write about. There's always events. And I happened to see this guy—I was at Broad and Chestnut. And I saw this guy crossing. We were all crossing. And the guy stopped in the middle of the street and looked back. And he went a couple more, but then he looked back again. He's looking at this woman. And he called out this girl's name. 'Hey, so-and-so'—I couldn't hear the name—[and] was chasing her. The girl looked at him like he was crazy. He said, 'Oh, I'm sorry. I'm sorry.' But he couldn't believe it wasn't who he thought it was.

"I was watching this. I said, 'Creed, I got it, I got an idea . . . [we] went back and wrote it. 'Today, I saw somebody who looked just like you, walk like you do. I thought it was you. And she turned the corner. I called out her name. I felt so ashamed when it wasn't you.' I saw that because you're everything. Everything—I saw that happen. It's like we saw that when 'People Make the World Go Round,' a trash man didn't get my trash today, those things happen. . . . that we weren't abstract writers. And we were futuristic and very real. Very rarely did we write anything that was odd, things that were nonrealistic."

Blige's take on the song which was produced by Jimmy Jam and Terry Lewis added a sample of James Brown's 1973 hit "The Payback" (1) and peaked at number 5 on the R&B chart.

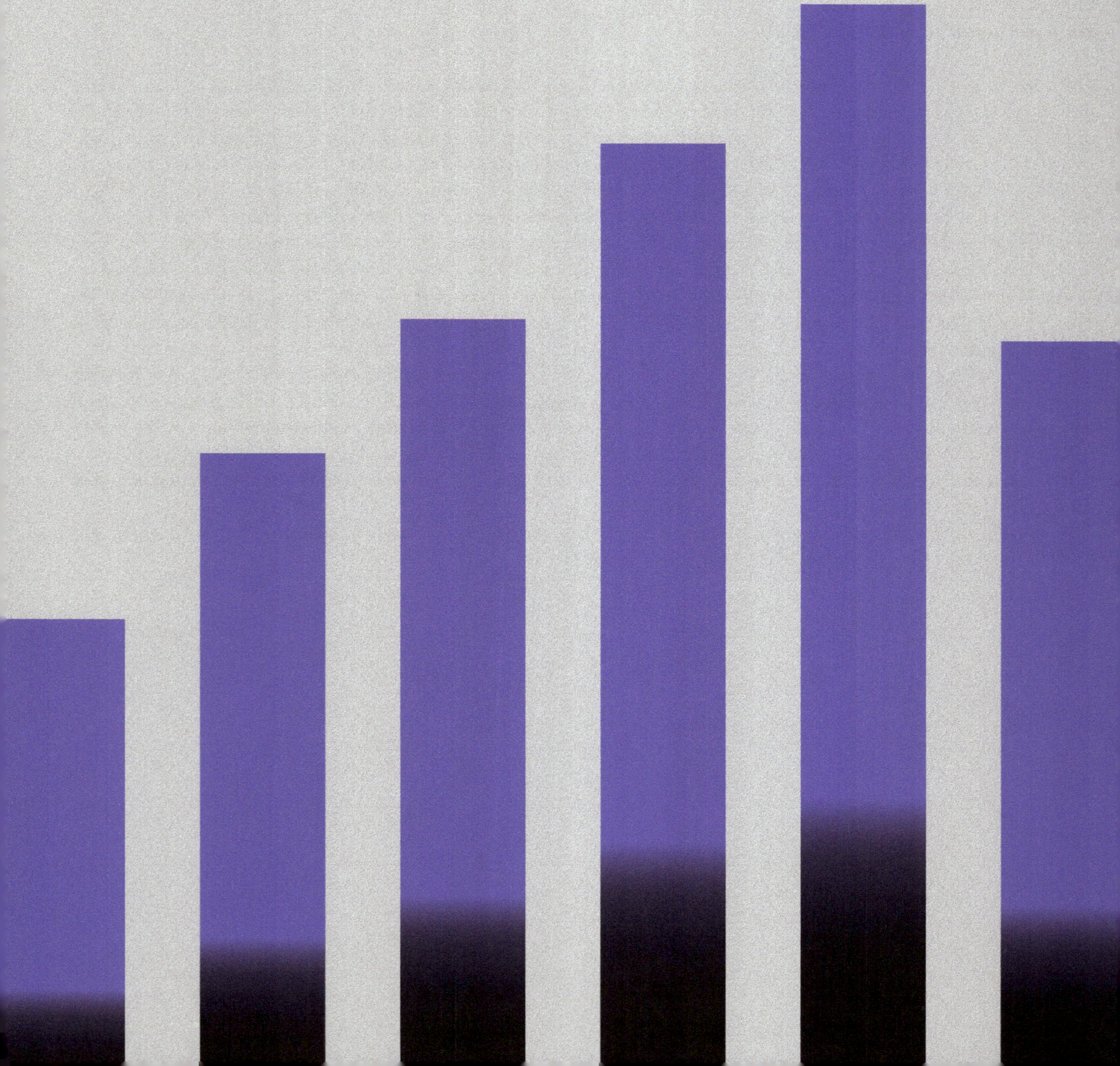

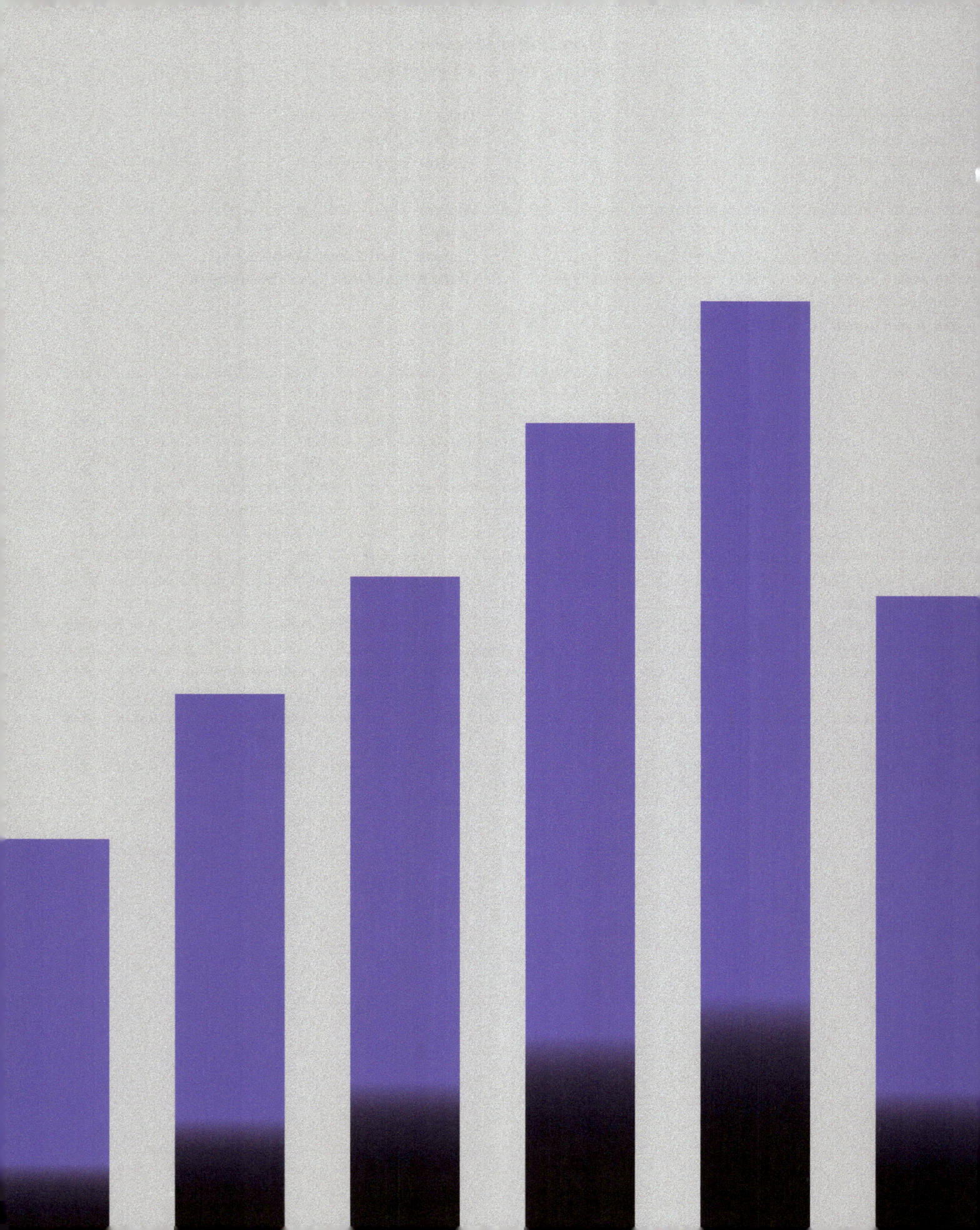

I'll Be Missing You: The Tribute Songs

So Alone
Gangsta Lean
I Miss You
I Miss My Homies

I'll Be Missing You: The Tribute Songs

In this section we highlight some of the songs that made us reflect on the ones we loved and lost.

So Alone

Artist: Men at Large
Album: Men at Large
Year: 1992
Writers: Gerald LeVert, Edwin Nicholas
Producers: Gerald LeVert, Edwin Nicholas, Rude Boys
Highest R&B Chart Position: 5
Highest Hot 100 Chart Position: 31

Discovered by the late Gerald LeVert, the Cleveland-based group Men at Large was composed of singers Dave Tolliver and Jason Champion. Their big break came via the "Cleveland connection" with their fellow Ohioan LeVert. As Tolliver explained to *The Hype Magazine* in 2019, "The first time he saw us, man, was in 1986 in Cleveland. One of the DJs that work for this radio station was doing music. He [LeVert] sang and had a concert and then he had an after-party at his crib. We were at the crib and Gerald came. We would always run around with this Casio keyboard with tape on the back to hold the batteries in . . . he came, we sang, and he was like, 'Yo, I'm gonna hook ya'll up.'" That was in '86. LeVert then went on tour, and it wasn't until three years later that the three men would meet again by chance. Tolliver continued, "We were in a studio and we were coming out of the house and Gerald was coming in and he was like, 'Yo, I had been looking for you. I have this idea for a group with three big guys that can sing, dance, and were cute. Two weeks later we went to the studio, we auditioned, and it took us about three years to get everything together." Men at Large was born, the group name being an obvious play on their size.

The group was signed by EastWest Records and issued a self-titled album in 1992. In the interim, as Tolliver put it they spent time touring with LeVert and "going through all of the business stuff, rehearsing and making sure that we were the best that we could be." In May 1992 the group's first single, "Use Me," dropped, and eventually it would chart at number 9.

Men at Large followed up their first album two years later with another cleverly named album, *One Size Fits All*, and issued their signature song "So Alone."

The song is a ballad, a love song written to the memory of Tolliver's mother, who he shouts out toward the song's end of the song, a fact lost to a lot of its fans. As Tolliver explains, "I was singing to my mother. My mother had passed away . . . Cats that were born in the '70s and '80s, they used to call their ladies 'momma.' 'Come here, momma.' But I was really talking to my momma. 'Can't nobody take your place. There will never be another like you.' But it still relates to those same subject matters. I've had people on the road come up to me like, 'Man, I used to get so much ass off of that.' And I used to be like, 'That's dope. But you know that was about my mom?' Then you get the response 'Oh, my bad, dog. I'm sorry.'"

Gangsta Lean

Artist: Dirty Rotten Scoundrels (DRS)
Album: Gangsta Lean
Year: 1993
Writers: Chris Jackson, DRS
Producers: Chris Jackson, Delaney McGill, The Whole 9
Highest R&B Chart Position: 1
Highest Hot 100 Chart Position: 4

Dirty Rotten Scoundrels (DRS) was a Sacramento, California–based rap group made up of members Chris Jackson, E. Jay Turner, Ian Knowles, J. B. Brown, and LaMarr "Deuce" Lubin. In a 2021 interview, Deuce Lubin recounted that the group's most popular song, "Gangsta Lean," came about as a result of the death of a friend of the group, Y-B, who was killed during a home robbery. Y-B's mom asked the group to sing Boyz II Men's version of "It's So Hard to Say Goodbye to Yesterday" for his funeral. When considering the song, the group members collectively thought, "Y-B would've been like, 'Negroes don't sing that song at my funeral.'" It was at that point that the group members decided to make a "song for the hood," and while Lubin thought the song was certain to be an underground hit, he didn't think it would reach chart status. To his surprise, what started out as a "song for the hood" ended up being a nationwide hit. "Gangsta Lean" was released as the first single from DRS's debut studio album of the same name. The song spent six weeks at number 1 on the R&B chart and peaked at number 4 on the Hot 100 chart en route to going platinum.

In the process of making "Gangsta Lean," a few friends and relatives of DRS members also died. The group gives them and Y-B shout-outs during one of the song's interludes:

This song is dedicated to homies in that gangsta lean /
Tommy from master's touch /
My boy Y-B /
And my boy Eibere /
And whoever else out there /
That's gotta homie that's in a gangsta lean.

The group's success was short-lived, as the popularity of "Gangsta Lean" drew exposure to some of DRS's other songs, including "Strip," which contains a graphic description of rape. "Strip" drew heavy criticism, and DRS's follow-up album, *Skoundrels Get Lonely*, was a sales and chart failure.

I Miss You

Artist: Aaron Hall
Album: The Truth
Year: 1994
Writers: Gregory Cauthen, Aaron Hall
Producer: Gregory Cauthen
Highest R&B Chart Position: 2
Highest Hot 100 Chart Position: 14

Aaron Hall achieved mega success as one third of the group Guy. "I Miss You" was the fourth of five singles released from his solo debut album *The Truth*. The song is remembered in part for its immensely sad video that features Hall and his wife's relationship told through a series of flashbacks and culminating with his pregnant wife being rushed into a hospital where she dies while giving birth to their son. The video ends with Hall and his son visiting his wife's grave. Although it has been reported that the song and video are inspired by the death of Hall's first-born son shortly after his birth, that could not be confirmed.

I'll Be Missing You

Artist: Puff Daddy & the Family
Album: No Way Out
Year: 1997
Writers: Albert Brumley, Faith Evans, Todd Gaither, Sting
Producers: Sean Combs, Stevie J
Notable Samples: Every Breath You Take, The Police (1983)
                           I'll Fly Away, Albert E. Brumley (1940)
                           Adagio for Strings, Samuel Barber (1936)
Highest R&B Chart Position: 1
Highest Hot 100 Chart Position: 1
Highest Hot Rap Songs Chart Position: 1

This song is the only song in this book to reach number 1 on the R&B, Hot 100, and Rap charts. It was recorded under the name Puff Daddy & the Family, which consisted of artists on the Bad Boy Record label brought together to celebrate the life of The Notorious B.I.G., who was killed March 9, 1997.

    The murder of his colleague and friend left Sean Combs ready to leave the music industry. He would say, "I was ready to quit; I wasn't gonna put out any more [Bad Boy] records. Then I was watching TV one day—you know, one of those times of despair where nobody is around, and you're like crying on the floor. The self-pity is at an all-time high, and you're asking God, 'Why?' And then I just heard 'Every Breath You Take' by the Police. I just took it as a sign. Sometimes you just need that little bit of light to be able to express yourself. But I [then] thought that the best thing I could do was not give up. I was down, and I was out, but I wasn't finished. All I could do was get up and start to fight. That's the way B.I.G. would've wanted it. . . . That song really kinda saved my life. . . . I just wanted to express the pain. . . . That song humanized us. We could be at our lowest point, and still have hope."

    The song was released as the second single from Puff Daddy & the Family's debut album, *No Way Out*. It won the Grammy Awards for Best Rap Performance by a Duo or Group and Best Rap Album. The single spent eleven weeks atop the U.S. Hot 100 chart en route to becoming one of the best-selling singles of the year, 3 million copies in the U.S. to be exact. It was also a bona-fide international hit, topping the charts in numerous countries across the world. The enduring popularity was evident as the K-pop band BTS covered the song twenty-five years after its release during their BBC Radio 1 Live Lounge debut in July of 2021.

    "I'll Be Missing You" samples the Police's 1983 hit song "Every Breath You Take" with an interpolated chorus sung by The Notorious B.I.G.'s wife Faith Evans. The song also interpolates the 1929 Albert E. Brumley hymn "I'll Fly Away" and features a spoken intro over a choral version of Samuel Barber's "Adagio for Strings." Unfortunately, Combs didn't sort out any of the legal issues related to using these songs until after his song was released. Sting, who wrote "Every Breath You Take," was granted a writer's credit, resulting in substantial royalties ($20,000 a day according to a 2014 report at *UltimateClassicRock.com*). Police guitarist Andy Summers says the first he knew about the hit single that sampled "Every Breath You Take" was when his son heard it on the radio. He said, "My ten-year-old came in the house and came over. He goes, 'Hey Dad, I want you to come listen to my radio in the room, there's a guy who is completely doing your guitar thing' . . . I went in and it was the first time I'd heard Puff Daddy and whatever he called that song. I went, 'Oh my God.' . . . We went from there and called the manager." Summers continues, "I think we ended up settling out of court and we got some kind of royalty."

    Combs was also sued and settled with Albert E. Brumley & Sons, a gospel and country music publishing company that owned the rights to the song "I'll Fly Away," which contained the line, "Some glad morning when this life is over," which Evans sings in the songs chorus.

I Miss My Homies

Artist: Master P.
Album: Ghetto D
Year: 1997
Writers: Pimp C, Percy Miller, Vyshonn Miller
Producer: Mo B. Dick
Notable Sample: Brandy, The O'Jays (1978)
Highest R&B Chart Position: 16
Highest Hot 100 Chart Position: 25
Highest Hot Rap Songs Chart Position: 2

This song reached the top 20 on the R&B charts and number 2 on the Rap charts, as it is technically a rap song. However, the success of the song combined with heavy reliance on the chords and melody via the obvious sample of The O'Jays' 1978 classic "Brandy" (21) make it worthy of mentioning.

We cite that sample as obvious because apparently Mo B. Dick, the producer of "I Miss My Homies," either didn't know or didn't care about the O'Jays coming up with the melody nearly two decades earlier, as No Limit, Master P.'s label, did not clear the song with "Brandy's" original writers Joe Jefferson and Charles Simmons. As a result, Master P. was sued. The suit charged that "I Miss My Homies" copied the verse and chorus structure of The O'Jays' "Brandy," and it sought $1.5 million in compensation. The suit also claimed that on the late-night talk show *Vibe*, Master P. said that he and his colleagues Pimp C. and Silkk the Shocker had written the song. Being the savvy businessman that he is, Master P. via his lawyer admitted his oversight, saying that his camp "had been in negotiations with the writers of 'Brandy' and that the omission of the writers' names in the songwriting credits of 'I Miss My Homies' was a total error."

While Master P. appeared to have learned his lesson, apparently he hadn't. He would repeat the error in June 1998 on his 4× platinum-selling album *MP Da Last Don* when he did not clear the use of the melody from SWV's hit "Rain," which was released nine months earlier. This error again resulted in a financial settlement with that song's writer, Brian Alexander Morgan.

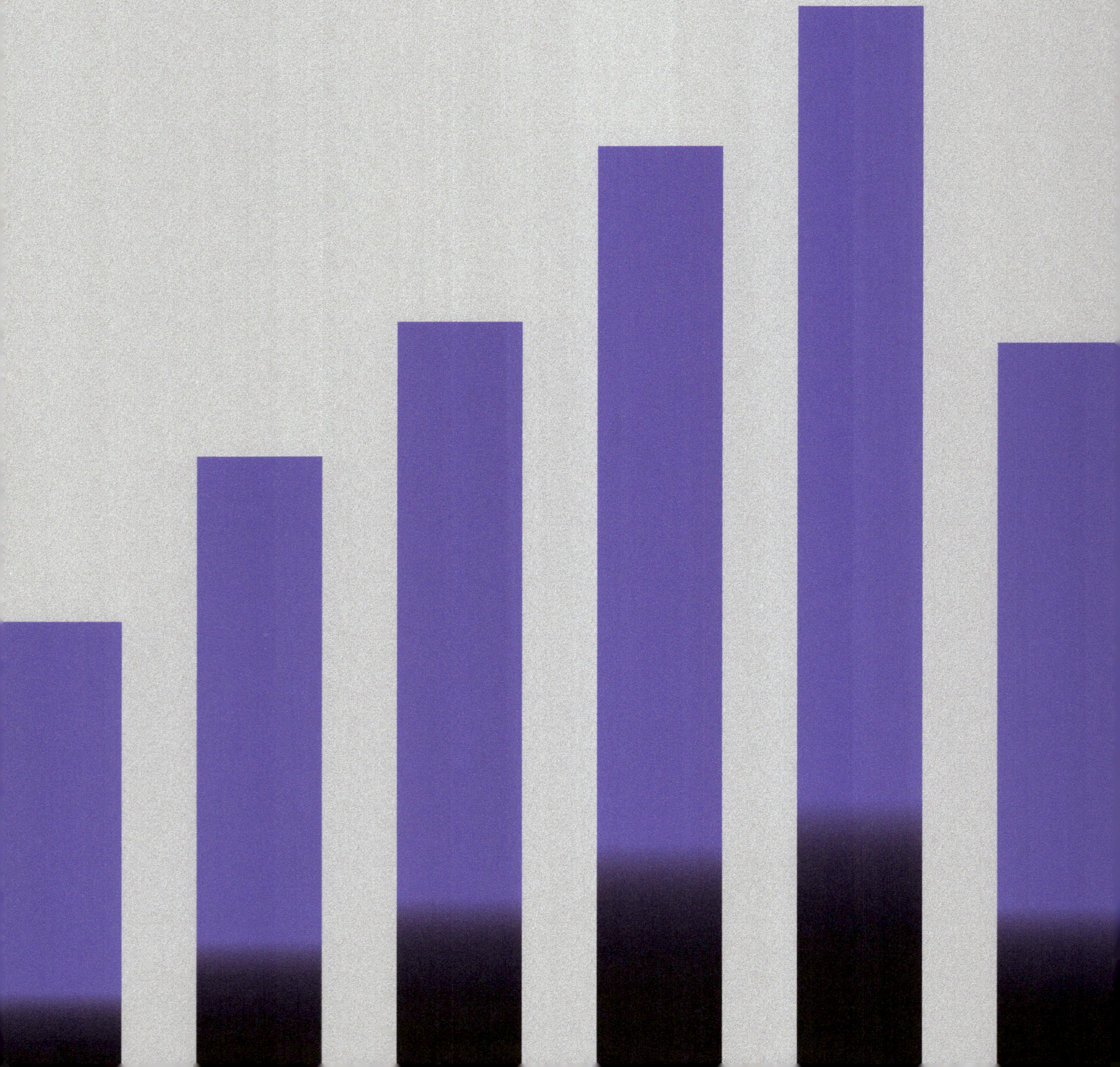

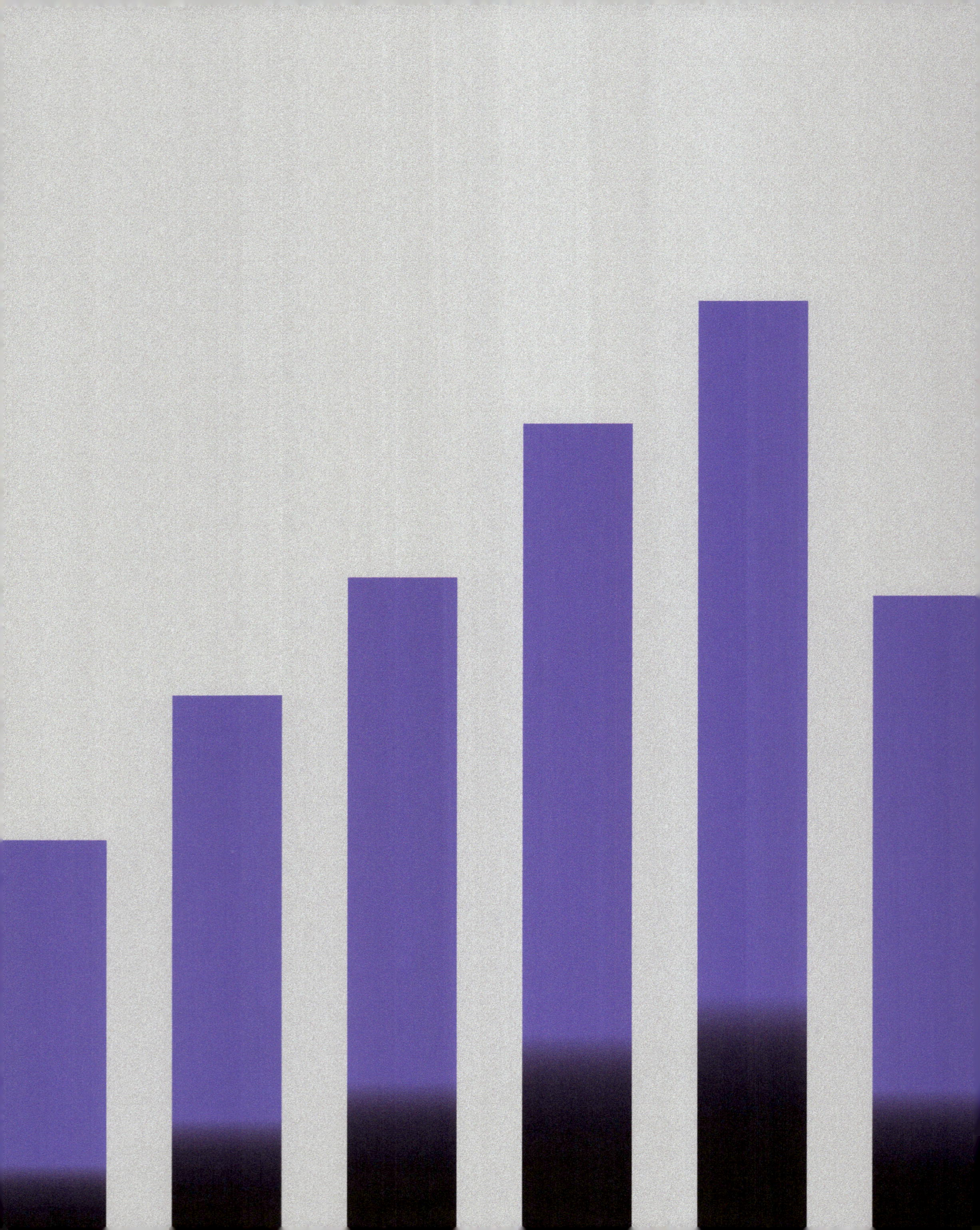

In Case You Missed It

(Lay Your Head on My) Pillow
Age Ain't Nothing but a Number
Brown Sugar
Don't Take it Personal (Just One of Dem Days)
Rain
Too Close

In Case You Missed It

Many of us learned later in life that some of our favorite songs may have had hidden meanings, like The O'Jays song "Brandy" being about a dog or the rumor that Cameo's 1986 number 1 hit "Candy" was about cocaine. In this section we highlight some popular songs with hidden meanings. Think less TLC's "This Is How It Works," which describes step-by-step how to do it, and more "Mary Jane" by Rick James, which you didn't understand until you were older.

(Lay Your Head on My) Pillow

Artist: Tony! Toni! Toné!
Album: Sons of Soul
Year: 1993
Writer: Tony! Toni! Toné!
Producer: Tony! Toni! Toné!
Highest R&B Chart Position: 4
Highest Hot 100 Chart Position: 31

The song has been described as a mid-tempo love ballad that features "tender, seductive lyrics." This is absolutely true, but what most reviews leave out of the critique is that most of the song is a prelude to the eventual climax where the narrator performs cunnilingus on his female partner. Because the lyrics are a bit more subtle than SWV's "Downtown," which was released the same year, the reference to oral sex in "Pillow" flew over many of our heads, despite the rather obvious language. Judge for yourself.

Won't you pull back the sheets and lay down /
Put your head upon my shoulders /
Let me tell you how I wanna feel /
You're the girl that knows my pleasure /
So let me go down and find my treasure /
Let me see where my pearl is at /
Lay your head on my pillow /
And just relax, relax, relax.

The song also features a "country-influenced pedal steel guitar." The rumor is that the guitar was a last-minute addition on the track after Tony! Toni! Toné! discovered that the country band that had used the Paradise Recording Studio prior to them had left it behind.

Age Ain't Nothing but a Number

Artist: Aaliyah
Album: Age Ain't Nothing but a Number
Year: 1994
Writer: R. Kelly
Producer: R. Kelly
Highest R&B Chart Position: 35
Highest Hot 100 Chart Position: 75

We missed this one. The song was written and produced by R. Kelly. At the time, the twenty-seven-year-old Kelly was likely already engaged in a secret intimate relationship with the fourteen-year-old Aaliyah, which culminated in their brief marriage in August 1994 and swift annulment in February 1995. R. Kelly's habit of sexually abusing women/girls makes this song far more creepy than entertaining, as it appears that the hidden meaning here was Kelly's bragging about his abuse of the teenaged Aaliyah.

Brown Sugar

Artist: D'Angelo
Album: Brown Sugar
Year: 1995
Writers: D'Angelo, Ali Shaheed Muhammad
Producers: D'Angelo, Ali Shaheed Muhammad
Highest R&B Chart Position: 5
Highest Hot 100 Chart Position: 27

"Brown Sugar" is not a song about a woman but rather a love song to Mary Jane à la Rick James. The song was created by accident when D'Angelo was noodling around on the piano while the production engineer was fixing a computer problem. "At first, it sounded like intermission music," Ali Shaheed Muhammad, the track's co-producer, told *Waxpoetics.com* in 2010. "But then he [D'Angelo] started playing this chord progression, and I stopped and looked at him. Even he wasn't aware of what exactly he was playing; he just had his hands on the keyboard. When I asked him what he was playing, he said, 'Nothing.'" Luckily, Muhammad was recording the "nothing" and within the next fifteen minutes, he was programming a beat and D'Angelo was adding bass over the chords and throwing in some lyrics of what would shortly become "Brown Sugar." Now the lines make sense.

I met her in Philly and her name was Brown Sugar /
See, we be making love constantly /
That's why my eyes are a shade blood burgundy.

    Philly was the popular brand of cigar used to roll blunts, the smoking of which often results in bloodshot eyes.

Skin is caramel with the cocoa eyes /
Even got a big sister by the name of Chocolate Thai.

    Chocolate Thai being an infamous strain of cannabis.

Brown sugar, babe /
I gets high off you love /
Don't know how to behave.

    In a bit of life imitating art, in the years following the song's release, D'Angelo had a few episodes of behaving badly that included a 2005 arrest and guilty plea for marijuana possession.

Don't Take It Personal (Just One of Dem Days)

Artist: Monica
Album: Miss Thang
Year: 1995
Writers: Dallas Austin, Willie James Baker, James Brown, George Clinton, Quincy Jones, LL Cool J, Monica, Carlton Ridenhour, Eric Sadler, Hank Shocklee, Derrick Simmons
Producer: Dallas Austin
Notable Samples: Back Seat (of My Jeep), LL Cool J (1993)
Bring the Noise, Public Enemy, (1988)
Highest R&B Chart Position: 1
Highest Hot 100 Chart Position: 2

The song was released as Monica's debut single in early 1995. A major success, it sold 1.2 million copies domestically, going platinum in the U.S., where it spent two weeks at number 1 on the R&B chart and peaked at number 2 for three nonconsecutive weeks on the Hot 100 chart. "Don't Take It Personal (Just One of Dem Days)" also reached the top 10 in Australia and New Zealand, where it was certified gold and platinum respectively. The song, alongside the follow-up single "Before You Walk Out of My Life," made Monica the youngest solo recording artist to have two consecutive number 1 hits on the R&B chart.

Ever since its release, the song has elicited speculation that it was about female menstruation. Why else would a teenage girl be singing these lines?

Just one of dem days, that a girl goes through /
When I'm angry inside, don't want to take it out on you /
Just one of dem days, don't take it personal /
I just wanna be all alone, and you think I treat you wrong.

It seems obvious, right? But over two decades later, Twitter put the rumor to bed. In 2018, user @norvis_boy reached out to Monica, writing:

"Dear Monica, Me and a Friend are having a little debate about "Don't Take It Personal," we both agree that it's about a women being on a period, and not wanting to be bothered . . . can you please confirm?" – @norvis_boy."

Monica responded:

"@norvis_boy Not at all, I didn't even have one back then. I was 12 when we recorded that song. It was about a BAD DAY lol RT"

Rain

Artist: SWV
Album: Release Some Tension
Year: 1997
Writer: Brian Alexander Morgan
Producer: Brian Alexander Morgan
Highest R&B Chart Position: 7
Highest Hot 100 Chart Position: 25

SWV's song "Downtown" was pretty clear. Many of us correctly assumed the song was about oral sex, right? "You gotta go downtown, that's the way to my love." Group member Lelee confirmed that the song was about oral sex in a

TV One *Unsung* episode that profiled the group, stating, "I knew that the song wasn't about going shopping, but we wanted to make oral sex special for married people." The group has since tried to distance themselves from the song, and on their reality show *SWV Reunited*, they clashed over performing it. In a 2015 interview with Kiss 103.5 FM in Houston, when asked why the group doesn't perform the song, lead singer Coko stated, "Back then I really didn't care, I would do and say anything. But I'm older now, I have kids, so I think before I put things out into the atmosphere." With a song like "Downtown" in their catalog and as a track on an album titled Release Some Tension, it was easy to deduce that SWV's song "Rain" was about a woman's climax, hence the lines:

Full as a dam at capacity /
My passion's about to explode, yeah /
I can't escape, it's surrounding me /
I'm caught in a storm/
That I don't need no shelter from.

SWV quelled this rumor during an appearance on *BET Her*, where they explained that those interpretations were not accurate:

Lelee: There has been so many speculations about the meaning of this song.
Coko: It's not true.
Lelee: Apparently, I had it wrong too.
Coko: Yeah, ya did.
Lelee: What is the meaning of "Rain"?
Coko: It's just rain. It's about love.
Lelee: A lot of people don't understand, they don't know rather that "Rain" was written for Brandy. And we're so happy that she did not want that song. Because it made our lives a lot easier.

Adding credence to "Rain" not being about sex was the fact that the song's writer-producer, Brian Alexander Morgan, came up with it in the shower [while he was alone]. He told the *Questlove Supreme* podcast in 2020, "I'm in the shower, a hook comes to me in its full entirety, a whole hook with the words and everything came to me as I was showering. Water's always involved in my s**t. The whole 'rain down on me, let your love just fall like rain' just came to me."

Too Close

Artist: Next
Album: Rated Next
Year: 1998
Writers: Kurtis Blow, Raphael Brown, Robert Ford Jr., KayGee, R.L., Denzil Miller, J. B. Moore
Producer: KayGee
Notable Sample: Christmas Rappin', Kurtis Blow (1979)
Highest R&B Chart Position: 1
Highest Hot 100 Chart Position: 1

Yes, this song is about a man getting an erection from dancing too close. On the song's intro the group—made up of Terry "T-Low" Brown, Robert "R.L." Huggar and Raphael "Tweety" Brown—confirm this with R.L.'s opening line, "I wonder if she can tell I'm hard right now"! But that line was scrubbed from radio airplay, leaving those who never heard the album version to wonder. In a recent interview with *Genius.com*, Tweety says that the song was inspired by a night out with hip-hop group Naughty By Nature, saying, "We had some females that were cool with us and we were dancing with them. We knew them, so we were getting a little close and pokes started coming through and we got shocked. We got shocked to learn that they actually purposefully make a guy get aroused on the dance floor to see what he's workin' with, to see if they want to take it any further than that."

In terms of turning this experience into a song, Tweety added, "It seemed like the song wrote itself. . . . We didn't think that it would be a big hit. That showed our lack of knowledge." The A&R team at Arista had another plan. "All the guys at Arista were like, '"Too Close" is gon' be our pop record.'"

R.L. cleared up another misconception about the opening line of the hook. Emphasizing that the line "Baby when we're grinding / I get so excited" inevitably gets botched, he said, "They always say, 'Baby no more crying' or something like that. Why would someone be crying on the dance floor?"

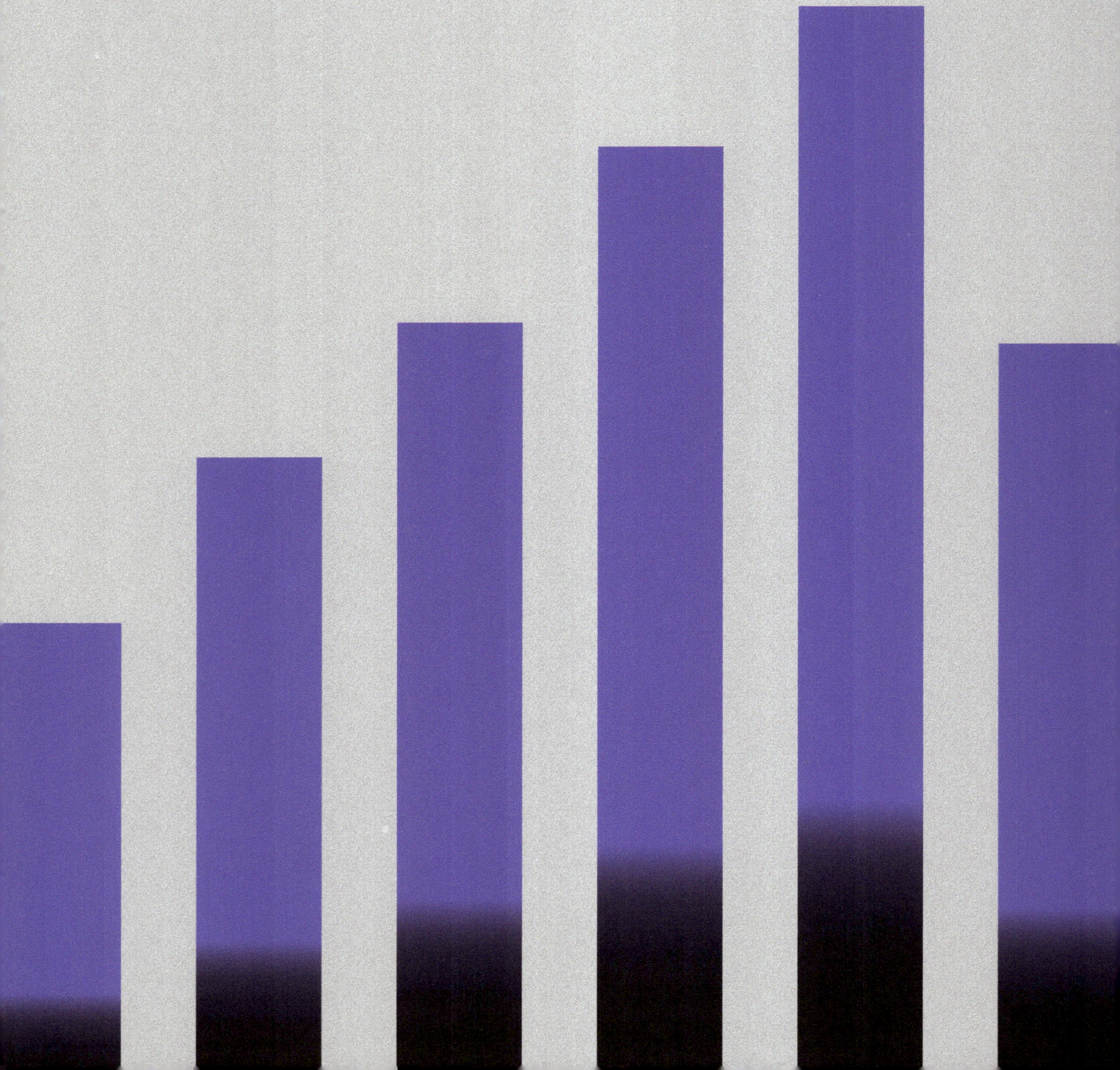

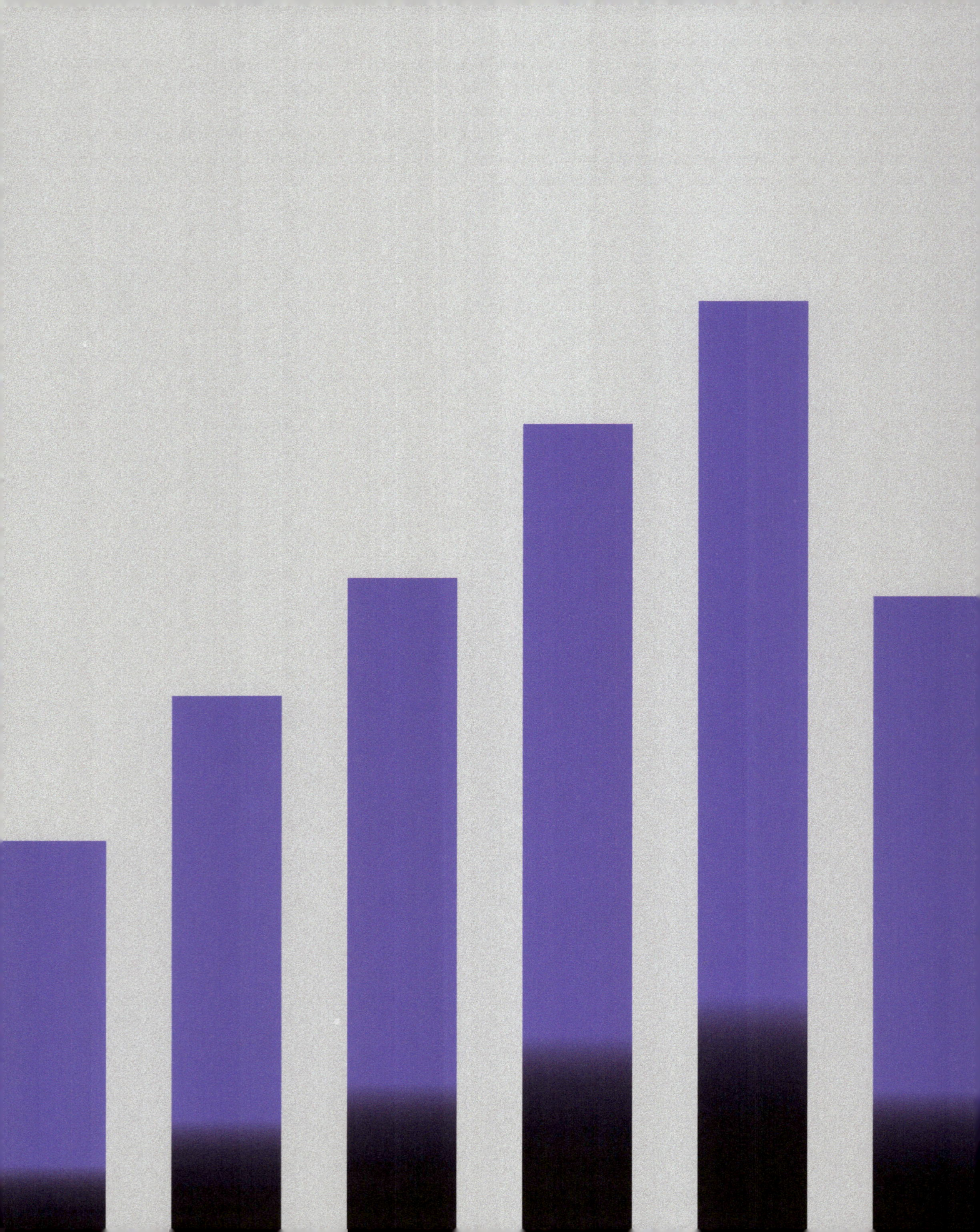

Happily Ever After: The Decade Closes
1996 - 1999

Pony
In My Bed
Cupid
Full of Smoke
No Diggity
All the Things (Your Man Won't Do)
My Body
Interlude: The Staying Power of Keith Sweat and Gerald LeVert
The Rain (Supa Dupa Fly)
I Belong To You (Every Time I See Your Face)
Get It Together
Don't Let Go (Love)
Anytime
Nice & Slow
The Boy Is Mine
The First Night
Sweet Lady
Nobody's Supposed to Be Here
Pushin' Inside of You
Bring It All to Me
Happily Ever After
No Scrubs
Where I Wanna Be
Thong Song

Happily Ever After: The Decade Closes | 1996 - 1999

This section highlights the songs that closed the decade that would become known as the golden age of R&B. The influence of these works ushered in the crop of R&B stars that would propel the genre into the 2000s.

Pony

Artist: Ginuwine
Album: Ginuwine . . . the Bachelor
Year: 1996
Writers: Stephen Garrett, Ginuwine, Timbaland
Producer: Timbaland
Highest R&B Chart Position: 1
Highest Hot 100 Chart Position: 6

"Pony" is singer Ginuwine's debut single. It was the first track his friend and collaborator Timbaland produced for him. It is also a great example of Timbaland's signature early production. The instrumentation features a start-stop rhythm pattern similar to drum and bass music, a bass line and melody formed by vocoded vocal samples, and a cartoon slide whistle.

Despite being instrumental in the production success of Jodeci's *Diary of a Mad Band* (1993) and *The Show, the After-Party, the Hotel* (1995) albums, this was Timbaland's first top 10 on the Hot 100 as a composer on which he got a composer credit.

In fact, Timbaland originally created the innovative "Pony" beat as an interlude for a Jodeci album. However, when Ginuwine heard it, he knew it would be a hit and snagged it for himself.

The beat was all Timbaland, and there's a lot of mythology around how he came up with that prominent burp-sounding bass sound while playing with his drum machine by accidentally turning the tempo knob down from 120 to 60, giving him a new sound. According to Timbaland's memoir published in 2016, the sound was likely the result of the producer intentionally warping the record. As reported in *Rolling Stone*, "Around the time Timbaland was making the beat that would ultimately become Ginuwine's 'Pony' . . . he developed an interest in degraded records." He told the magazine, "If you leave a record out in the sun, it will warp. It's going to have a strange, distorted sound. I love that sound and I started making beats with that vibe. I was thinking, warp it a little, when I added belching synthesizers to the beat I was working on."

While Timbaland perfected the beat, Ginuwine says he and producer Static Major (Stephen Garrett) went back and forth freestyling lyrics until it came together. "We started and I was like, 'I'm just a bachelor,' and he's like, 'Looking for a partner,' and that's how we did it, just went back and forth, line for line." As Ginuwine noted, "It was already a hit" and jokingly added, "Anybody could've sung anything to that song."

"Pony" was completed in 1994 but not released until 1996 because although Ginuwine instantly saw it as a hit, the production team thought of it as just another demo, one of hundreds in fact. As the song's production engineer Jimmy Douglas told *Revolt* in 2020, "At that time, Timbaland was on fire for two years. He was making tracks like that every day. The stuff wasn't going nowhere. We had 'Pony' ready for about a year. . . . We cut about three hundred songs in two years. For 'Pony,' Tim had done the crazy beat, Static started writing, and Ginuwine went, 'I have to have this, Static.' That night, we went downstairs and did it. Then we put it away because it was just another demo."

The success of the song earned Ginuwine a deal with 550 Music, a division of Epic, and he has since released five more albums and started his own label, Bag Entertainment. "Pony" became popular again over a decade later after being featured in the film *Magic Mike* (2012) and its 2015 sequel *Magic Mike XXL*.

In My Bed

Artist: Dru Hill
Album: Dru Hill
Year: 1996
Writers: Raphael Brown, Daryl Simmons, Ralph Stacy
Producer: Daryl Simmons
Highest R&B Chart Position: 1
Highest Hot 100 Chart Position: 4

Dru Hill (Mark "Sisqó" Andrews, Larry "Jazz" Anthony, James "Woody Rock" Green, and Tamir "Nokio" Ruffin) released "In My Bed" as the second single from their eponymous debut album.
The album's first single, "Tell Me," performed well, peaking at number 5 on the R&B chart and setting the stage for the group's first number 1, "In My Bed."

Daryl Simmons told *Songwriters Universe* about first meeting Dru Hill and writing the song. Saying "I fell in love with Sisqó. He reminded me of Bobby [Brown]. He had that energy . . . that voice. So, I did these two songs" ("In My Bed" and "Never Make a Promise").

Sisqó sang lead on "In My Bed" and initially did not want to record it due to the subject matter. He told TV One, "I absolutely did not want to sing 'In My Bed,' you know, singing about somebody cheating on me, I'm like, 'What kind of loser!' So, I channeled that anger of not wanting to sing the song into singing the f**k out of the song." In Sisqó's interview with *Unsung Live* he added, "We just put our all into it . . . If you listen to the beginning of the song, I was using the anger of not really wanting to sing the song and I just kinda used that energy to sing the song."

"In My Bed" spent three weeks at number 1 on the R&B chart, and the *Dru Hill* album included four top 10 hits: "Tell Me" (5), "In My Bed" (1), "Never Make a Promise" (1), and "5 Steps" (7). The album also sold 2 million copies. Following the success of *Dru Hill*, the group released the Babyface-penned crossover number 13 hit "We're Not Making Love No More" (2) from the *Soul Food* movie soundtrack.

Dru Hill solidified their status as a legitimate R&B force with the release of their second album, 1998's *Enter the Dru*, which gave the group their highest charting hit "How Deep Is Your Love." The song peaked at number 3 on the Hot 100 and became an R&B number 1. The album also included the hits "These Are the Times" (5), "You Are Everything" (24), and "Beauty" (27).

Following *Enter the Dru*, Dru Hill separated for a period from late 1999 to 2002, during which time group member Sisqó released his solo album *Unleash the Dragon* (1999), which included the number 1's "Thong Song" and "Incomplete" and group member Woody Rock released a gospel album, *Soul Music*, in 2002.

Dru Hill went through a lineup change and added fifth member Scola for their third album, 2002's *Dru World Order*, which went gold in large part due to the success of the singles "I Should Be . . ." (6) and "I Love You" (27). Shortly after *Dru World Order*, the group was dropped from their label Def Jam. They would separate, reunite, and go through a few lineup changes over the next two decades. During that time, they would release two albums, *InDRUpendence Day* and the holiday album *Christmas in Baltimore*, neither of which had any charting singles.

Cupid

Artist: 112
Album: 112
Year: 1996
Writers: Arnold Hennings, Daron Jones, Michael Keith, Quinnes Parker, Marvin Scandrick, Courtney Sills
Producers: Arnold Hennings, Daron Jones
Highest R&B Chart Position: 2
Highest Hot 100 Chart Position: 13

When 112 was signed to Bad Boy, each member of the quartet was still a teenager. They honed their musical skills on the road opening for established acts like the Isley Brothers, New Edition, Keith Sweat, and Whitney Houston. These experiences not only expanded the group's set list and catalog, it also expanded their knowledge of the business side of the industry. If you note, each 112 album has the group members credited as songwriters on multiple tracks. One of their biggest hits, "Cupid," is no exception.

112 wrote "Cupid" shortly after relocating from Atlanta to New York to work on their first album with Bad Boy Records. In 2022, 112 member Quinnes Parker told *Rolling Stone* that he and his group-mates wrote "Cupid" themselves because they couldn't afford songwriter and mega-producer Kenneth "Babyface" Edmonds, saying, "When you're first starting out, you don't have the big huge budgets . . . During that time, Babyface was the most sought-after producer and songwriter, but our first album budget wouldn't let us afford him." So inspired by Babyface, the group laid down the stair-step guitar riff that was common for Edmonds' songs of the time. The actual lyrics were drawn from the group members' relationships, which, as *Rolling Stone* writer Elias Leight put it, "are packed full of misunderstanding and pain." However, in spite of the lyrical content, Parker said, "It [Cupid] became a Valentine's Day record, a wedding song, an ask-my-girl-out-on-a-date song, an ask-my-girl-at-your-concert-to-marry-me song . . . That's the thing I marvel over: those lyrics came from seventeen-year-olds . . . How can these seventeen-year-olds write a song with so much substance?"

"Cupid" was the third single from 112's debut album following the hits "Only You" (3) and "Come See Me" (15), and it bested both of the previous singles in sales and on the charts, going platinum and peaking at number 2.

Full of Smoke

Artist: Christión
Album: Ghetto Cyrano
Year: 1997
Writer: Poetry Man
Producers: Kareem Burke, Damon Dash, Jay-Z
Highest R&B Chart Position: 15
Highest Hot 100 Chart Position: 53

Christión was a male duo consisting of members Kenni Ski and Allen Anthony. The pair had the distinction of being one of the first R&B acts to be signed to Damon Dash and Jay-Z's Roc-A-Fella label. "Full of Smoke" was their first single. The group recalled, "The song came while we were in the throngs of the neo-soul movement but offered something more." Edward Bowser of *SoulinStereo.com* describes the song as sounding as "good today as it does back then—the spooky, subdued beat and mellow, yet scratchy vocals are all the rage these days. The track was definitely ahead of its time."

The group—which had a moderately successful first album that produced three singles: "Full of Smoke," "Bring Back Your Love" (67), and "I Wanna Get Next to You" (32), a remake of the 1977 Rose Royce hit—would become the victim of mismanagement as the rap-heavy Roc-A-Fella label would have trouble adjusting to the learning curve in building Christión a R&B fan base.

As Kenni Ski recounted to *AllHipHop.com* in a 2004 interview, "They [Roc-A-Fella] were going to be successful and that's why I signed with them. What I didn't know was that the hip-hop promotion and marketing system is completely different from the R&B one. I don't think [Damon] knew it either. So, we tried to promote Christión as an act in the same avenues as hip-hop and for some reason we just weren't getting anywhere. There were a lot of people that didn't even know the album was out when it came out. We weren't in the public eye and [the label] couldn't figure out how to get us . . . we sold 150,000 copies of the album and 400,000 copies of the single. We needed to take it to the next level, but none of us knew how to do it. As an artist I didn't think it was my responsibility to sit in on Def Jam and Roc-A-Fella meetings. On one occasion they asked a room full of people if they had any marketing or promotion ideas for Christión and the whole office was silent!"

In the fast-paced world of music, the faulty promotion quickly left Christión as an afterthought with most R&B fans, and it would be seven years before the group would release a follow-up album, 2005's *Project Plato*. The album failed to produce any hits.

No Diggity

Artist: Blackstreet
Album: Another Level
Year: 1996
Writers: Dr. Dre, Chauncey Hannibal, Queen Pen, Teddy Riley, William Stewart, Richard Vick, Bill Withers
Producers: Teddy Riley, William Stewart
Notable Sample: Grandma's Hands, Bill Withers (1971)
Highest R&B Chart Position: 1
Highest Hot 100 Chart Position: 1

After Guy ended, Teddy Riley went on to pursue other successful ventures. He produced Wreckx-n-Effect's number 1 "Rump Shaker" and Michael Jackson's highly successful multi-platinum *Dangerous* album and developed his new group Blackstreet with members Riley, Chauncey Hannibal, Levi Little, and Joseph Stonestreet. However, Stonestreet was replaced with Dave Hollister before the group's first self-titled album was released.

Blackstreet released their debut album *Blackstreet* in 1994. The album was a platinum-selling success with the singles "Booti Call," "Joy," and "Before I Let You Go" reaching numbers 14, 12, and 2 respectively on the R&B chart. Following the success of the *Blackstreet* album, Hollister, who sang lead on "Joy" and "Before I Let You Go," left the group for a solo deal. He was replaced by Eric Williams and Mark Middleton.

Prior to working on Blackstreet's sophomore effort, it was a meeting with writer and producer Will "Skylz" Stewart at Riley's Future Recording Studios that led to the concept and development of "No Diggity." Riley heard Skylz experimenting with Bill Withers's 1971 song "Grandma's Hands" and wanted to add to the sample. He told *Vibe* magazine, "After I finished making the track, Will came in and was like, 'This record is a smash. But what do you want to write to it?' I gave him the melody to 'No Diggity.' I wanted the song to start with 'Shorty get down . . .' And then I thought, 'Well, can we add the words 'Good Lord' to the track?'" According to *Yahoo.com*, Stewart added, "She got game by the pound," then Riley had the idea to sample the line "I like the way you work" from the song of the same name on Blackstreet's debut album.

Once completed, Riley originally offered "No Diggity" to Guy as part of their short-lived reunion in 1996. When that fell through, he offered the song to Guy's former lead singer Aaron Hall, who also passed on it. Lastly, he offered Blackstreet a chance to record the song. However, Blackstreet almost let this one get away. In a 2010 interview Riley revealed, "None of the guys liked 'No Diggity.' None of them. They wouldn't even say it. That's why I'm singing the first verse. You know how they say they pushed the little one out there to see if it tastes good and see if he would get egged? Well, they pushed me out there—and it became a hit."

According to Riley, the label also wasn't impressed by "No Diggity," but Riley's longtime friend, rapper turned music executive Heavy D., who was the newly appointed CEO of Uptown Records, believed in the track and convinced the label to not only back it but release it as the lead single to Blackstreet's *Another Level* album.

Prior to finishing the recording, Riley saved a spot for his protégé, Brooklyn rapper Queen Pen, to contribute a few verses. Also, according to Riley, superstar rapper and producer Dr. Dre was an early believer in the song, and he contributed a verse himself. Around this same time Dr. Dre had launched his label Aftermath Entertainment after leaving Death Row Records in 1996.

Dre's departure did not sit well with his former Death Row label-mates. Upon the release of the finished recording by Blackstreet, rapper Tupac Shakur and Death Row responded with the diss track "Toss It Up" over an instrumental sampling of "No Diggity." The song featured K-Ci & JoJo of Jodeci and Riley's former Guy band-mate Aaron Hall, who initially passed on "No Diggity." "Toss it Up" devoted an entire verse to insulting Dr. Dre. But when Blackstreet hit Death Row with a cease-and-desist order, Tupac and Death Row re-worked the song, and the re-worked version would eventually be released under Tupac's alias "Makaveli" after his death in 1996.

But no dis could stop "No Diggity" from shining. It was an instant crossover hit, reaching number 1 on the R&B and Hot 100 charts. It also won the 1998 Grammy for Best R&B Performance by a Duo or Group, and it was universally applauded as the song that knocked Los del Río's worldwide smash "Macarena" out of the Hot 100 number 1 spot. Blackstreet would go on to release two more albums, neither of which were great successes, before a series of breakups, makeups, and remakes of the group. Ultimately *Another Level* was their most successful album and "No Diggity," the song that seemingly no one wanted, was by far their biggest hit.

All the Things (Your Man Won't Do)

Artist: Joe
Album: All That I Am
Year: 1996
Writers: Joe, Joshua Thompson, Michele Williams
Producers: Joe, Joshua Thompson
Highest R&B Chart Position: 5
Highest Hot 100 Chart Position: 11

Joseph Thomas, a.k.a. Joe, hails from Columbus, Georgia. He relocated to Atlanta and signed a record deal with Polygram Records in 1992, where he released his debut album *Everything*. The album peaked at number 105 on the *Billboard* 200 and number 16 on *Billboard's* Top R&B/Hip-Hop Albums chart.
All That I Am was Joe's second album, and it was also his breakthrough, released in 1997 on the Jive record label. Each of the album's first four songs—"All the Things (Your Man Won't Do)," "The Love Scene," "Don't Wanna Be a Player," and "Good Girls"—were '90's classics.

"All the Things (Your Man Won't Do)," which was originally featured on the soundtrack for the film *Don't Be a Menace to South Central While Drinking Your Juice in the Hood,* was also issued as the first track on *All That I Am*. It was co-written and produced by Joe and was the best-performing track on the album, reaching number 1 on the R&B chart and just missing the Hot 100 top 10, peaking at number 11.

"Don't Wanna Be a Player," which originally appeared on the soundtrack to the 1997 film *Booty Call*, became a number 5 hit. The song was sampled in Joe's collaboration with rapper Big Pun on Pun's number 6 hit "Still Not a Player." "Love Scene" was a number 7 hit, and "Good Girls" peaked at number 27. Both became R&B standards of late 1990s radio, and *All That I Am* reached number 4 on the Top R&B/Hip-Hop Albums chart.

So how big was Joe's record? Well, its chart success and platinum sales were enough to get the attention of the king of '90s R&B, R. Kelly. Both were label-mates on Jive, but according to Joe, his success may have threatened Kelly, which led to Kelly attempting to sabotage his career. Joe spilled the beans in a 2014 interview with DJ Vlad, stating that he'd received "credible information" from trusted sources that his then label-mate had been speaking to some mutual parties against him.

Joe elaborated: "It's funny because I was getting credible information from [program directors] and friends of mine as well. This guy had no idea these were my friends as well that you are talking to. And, as if they are really going to stop playing my record because you said, 'If you don't stop playing his record I'm never going to come back to this show.' . . . It was really one of those things like you can't really be serious. . . . No one man has all that power—trust me when I tell you."

Joe would follow his '90s success well into the 2000s. His third album, 2000's *My Name Is Joe,* topped the R&B/Hip-Hop Albums chart and included the song "I Wanna Know" (2) and the R&B and pop number 1 "Stutter." *My Name Is Joe* has since been certified triple platinum.

My Body

Artist: LSG
Album: Levert.Sweat.Gill
Year: 1997
Writers: Darrell Allamby, Lincoln Browder, Antoinette Roberson
Producer: Darrell Allamby
Highest R&B Chart Position: 1
Highest Hot 100 Chart Position: 4

R&B super-group LSG (Gerald LeVert, Keith Sweat, and Johnny Gill) literally started with a telephone call from Sweat to his friend and fellow superstar LeVert. Already a successful solo artist, Sweat wanted to join a group and he was already a big fan of both Gill and LeVert, so he pitched the idea to LeVert. LeVert and Gill had already done the group thing successfully, with LeVert having been the front man for the group "LeVert" that had numerous hits in the late 1980s and early 1990s and Gill having been a part of the highly successful group New Edition.

LeVert was on board and cold-called Gill with the proposal to complete the trio. They [LeVert and Gill] were already old friends, having sang together at various shows and even showing up unsuspecting acts on the same bill as them by "double-teaming" and outperforming them. With Gill's yes, Gerald LeVert, Keith Sweat, and Johnny Gill, each already superstars in their own right, reinvented themselves as LSG.

With R&B royalty serving as headliners, the group had no problem enlisting a stable of superstar producers and artists like Sean Combs and Jermaine Dupri and rappers LL Cool J., Busta Rhymes, and MC Lyte.
However, the album's biggest hit, "My Body," featured only LSG doing their thing over a Darrell Allamby–produced track. Allamby also co-wrote the song.

Allamby recalled the production process for creating "My Body" in a 2020 interview with *YouKnowIGotSoul.com,* saying, "Oh man, first and foremost, you know just being in the studio with three icons was just, it's a lot of respect just being able to be in the studio with them, but they were comfortable to allow this young kid to produce them and to direct their path because everything we did in that song was brand new for them, you know. Keith Sweat, his vibe and cadence are different. Johnny Gill has more vocal acrobatics, and Gerald is such a soul singer. I gave them like some youthful flavor."

"My Body" quickly reached number 1 and stayed there for four weeks, becoming a platinum seller. The group's debut album *LeVert.Sweat.Gill,* which was released in the fall of 1997, also quickly went double platinum. LSG would go on to release their second and final album, 2003's *LSG2,* which would peak at number 3 on the R&B Albums chart.

Interlude
The Staying Power of Keith Sweat and Gerald LeVert

Gerald LeVert and Keith Sweat each personify staying power in an industry where what's hot today is quickly forgotten by noon tomorrow. The two opened the decade with a collaboration as artists on Sweat's 1990 album *I'll Give All My Love to You* with the song "Just One of Them Thangs" and would later collaborate toward the end of the decade in forming the super-group LSG. Both were hitmakers in the late 1980s and early 1990s (LeVert with the group LeVert and Sweat as a solo artist), and both would acclimate to the changing face and tempo of 1990s R&B, remaining relevant from the death of new jack swing to the birth of neo-soul and beyond. Each adapted, becoming hit-making songwriters, producers, and managers for others while consistently reaching the top of the charts themselves throughout the decade.

Keith Sweat	Gerald LeVert
Make You Sweat **Artist:** Keith Sweat **Album:** I'll Give All My Love to You **Year:** 1990 **Writers:** Timmy Gatling, Keith Sweat, Bobby Wooten **Producers:** Keith Sweat **Highest R&B Chart Position:** 1 **Highest Hot 100 Chart Position:** 14	**Baby I'm Ready** **Artist:** LeVert **Album:** Rope a Dope Style **Year:** 1990 **Writers:** Gerald LeVert, Marc Gordon **Producers:** Gerald LeVert, **Highest R&B Chart Position:** 1 **Highest Hot 100 Chart Position:** Song did not chart
Why Me Baby **Artist:** Keith Sweat **Album:** Keep It Comin **Year:** 1992 **Writers:** LL Cool J, Teddy Riley, Keith Sweat **Producers:** Teddy Riley, Keith Sweat **Highest R&B Chart Position:** 2 **Highest Hot 100 Chart Position:** 44	**Baby Hold on to Me** **Artist:** Gerald LeVert **Album:** Private Line **Year:** 1991 **Writers:** Gerald LeVert, Edwin Nicholas **Producers:** Gerald LeVert, Edwin Nicholas **Highest R&B Chart Position:** 1 **Highest Hot 100 Chart Position:** 37
Twisted **Artist:** Keith Sweat **Album:** Twisted **Year:** 1996 **Writers:** Lavonn Battle, Athena Cage, Tabitha Duncan, Elliott McCaine, Keith Sweat, **Producers:** Elliott McCaine, Keith Sweat, **Highest R&B Chart Position:** 1 **Highest Hot 100 Chart Position:** 2	**abc-123** **Artist:** LeVert **Album:** For Real Tho **Year:** 1993 **Writers:** Gerald LeVert, Edwin Nicholas, Terry Scott **Producers:** Gerald LeVert, Edwin Nicholas **Highest R&B Chart Position:** 5 **Highest Hot 100 Chart Position:** 46
Nobody **Artist:** Keith Sweat **Album:** Keith Sweat **Year:** 1996 **Writers:** Keith Sweat, Scott Fitzgerald **Producer:** Keith Sweat **Highest R&B Chart Position:** 1 **Highest Hot 100 Chart Position:** 3	**Thinkin Bout It** **Artist:** Gerald LeVert **Album:** Love and Consequences **Year:** 1998 **Writers:** Darrell Allamby, Gerald LeVert, Antoinette Roberson **Producers:** Darrell Allamby **Highest R&B Chart Position:** 2 **Highest Hot 100 Chart Position:** 12

The Rain (Supa Dupa Fly)

Artist: Missy Elliott
Album: Supa Dupa Fly
Year: 1997
Writers: Don Bryant, Melissa Elliott, Bernard Miller, Ann Peebles, Timbaland
Producers: Timbaland
Notable Sample: I Can't Stand the Rain, Ann Peebles (1974)
Highest R&B Chart Position: 4
Highest Hot 100 Chart Position: Song did not chart

"The Rain (Supa Dupa Fly)" was Missy Elliott's first solo hit. It was produced by her longtime friend and collaborator Timbaland following their exit from DeVanté Swing's Swing Mob label/production company, where the duo experimented with many of the complex beats they would come to be known for. It also followed their breakthrough production of Aaliyah's multi-platinum second album, *One in a Million*. In fact, it was the success of *One in a Million* that drove Elektra, Elliott's record label, to give her and Timbaland the freedom to write, produce, and develop artists and pursue solo projects.

One of their first endeavors was Elliott's album *Supa Dupa Fly*, which they are said to have completed in two weeks. The track "The Rain (Supa Dupa Fly)" was the first release from the album, and it served as a formal introduction to Elliott and Timbaland's innovative style. As Rob Harvila of *TheRinger.com* put it, "the song features cricket sounds, multiple Wiki, wiki / icky, icky lyrics, as well as the now infamous line "Beep! Beep! Who got the keys to the Jeep! Vroooom"! "That Vroooom is amazing. Onomatopoeia is everything to Missy—she's a walking comic book. Every part of the comic book. The action, the costumes, the dialogue. And how the words sound means as much as what the words mean."

Perhaps the part that makes the song so memorable for many is the prominent sample of Ann Peebles' song "I Can't Stand the Rain," which has an interesting story behind it as well. Peebles wrote the song with her husband Don Bryant and friend DJ Bernard "Bernie" Miller in 1973. According to *The Guardian*, the song came about one evening in Memphis, Tennessee, when Peebles, Bryant, and friends were getting ready to go to a concert. When the time came for them to leave for the concert, it began raining, to which Peebles exclaimed, "I can't stand the rain." Bryant liked the reaction and turned it into a song. He sat down at the piano and started riffing on the rain theme. The song was finished that night, and the group never made it to the concert.

As for Missy Elliot and Timbaland, the album *Supa Dupa Fly*—which also included the hits "Sock It 2 Me" (4) and "Beep Me 911" (13) reached number 1 en route to platinum sales and was another major step in their careers. These steps would culminate in their both winning multiple Grammys, having multiple platinum songs, and being inducted into the Songwriters Hall of Fame.

Because "The Rain (Supa Dupa Fly)" was not initially released in a physical format, the song was not eligible for the Hot 100. However, *Billboard's* Hot R&B/Hip-Hop Songs chart did not have a similar requirement at the time, and the song reached the number 4 spot on that chart.

I Belong to You (Every Time I See Your Face)

Artist: Rome
Album: Rome
Year: 1997
Writers: Rome, Gerald Baillergeau
Producers: Gerald Baillergeau, Victor Merritt
Highest R&B Chart Position: 2
Highest Hot 100 Chart Position: 6

The musical journey of Jerome Woods, a.k.a. Rome, was the stuff of a classic Hollywood story. He came from a small town in the Midwest (Benton Harbor, Michigan), left school, and headed west with a dream of making it big in music. Once there, he toured as a background singer before getting a break when his demo made its way to RCA Records, where he got signed. In 1997, he released his self-titled debut album, which included the platinum seller "I Belong to You (Every Time I See Your Face)," one of the biggest R&B songs of 1997. The artist behind the song, Rome, who is also its primary writer, seemed poised for stardom following this massive hit. However he was never able to duplicate the success of "I Belong to You," although his follow-up single, "Do You Like This," made it to number 10.

With two hits under his belt, Rome began work on his sophomore album, but RCA shelved it for undisclosed reasons. Rome then sought to record under his own label; however RCA still held the rights to the music and would not release it. Rome would release two more albums in the early 2000s, *To Infinity (Thank You)* (1999) and *Do It* (2003), but neither reached the charts.

Get It Together

Artist: 702
Album: No Doubt
Year: 1996
Writer: Donell Jones
Producer: Donell Jones
Highest R&B Chart Position: 3
Highest Hot 100 Chart Position: 10

"Get It Together" was the second single released from 702's debut album *No Doubt* in 1996. The group was originally a quartet consisting of members Amelia Childs, identical twin sisters Irish and Orish Grinstead, and LeMisha Grinstead. But as their success grew there would be many lineup changes.

702 was named after the area code of their hometown, Las Vegas, Nevada, which is where the group then known as Sweeta than Suga was discovered by comedian Sinbad while they were singing in the lobby of the Caesar's Palace Hotel and Casino. It was Sinbad who persuaded the group's parents to allow them to travel to Atlanta to compete in a music competition, where they came in second place. Although they did not win the competition, the group did hit the jackpot in meeting Michael Bivins, who agreed to develop them. Bivins was a member of the highly successful groups New Edition and Bell Biv DeVoe, but most importantly for Sweeta than Suga, he had a successful track record of developing hitmaking groups like Another Bad Creation and Boyz II Men. Under Bivins' tutelage the name Sweeta than Suga was dropped and 702 was born.

Shortly after he began managing the group, Bivins felt that some lineup changes were needed. He dropped Amelia and Orish, not thinking their voices were good enough, and replaced them with singers Tiffany Villarreal and Kameelah Williams.

This iteration of 702 was tapped to provide vocals counter the male group Subway on their [Subway's] lead single "This Lil' Game We Play," released from Subway's only album, *Good Times*. The song was written and produced by

Gerald LeVert and Edwin Nicholas and reached number 4.

As production of 702's debut album moved forward, more changes were on the way. After six months in the group, Tiffany Villarreal departed for a solo career. Her departure led to the most well-known lineup as a trio consisting of Kameelah, LeMisha, and Irish. Through these lineup changes, Bivins continued to work with different producers and songwriters to get the right feel for 702's first album, including producer Missy Elliott, who co-wrote and produced four songs on the album, including the groups debut single "Steelo" (12) and its remix.

However, it was the group's third single, "Get It Together," that exploded, reaching number 3 on the R&B charts and number 10 on the Hot 100. Years later, singer Solange Knowles reflected on the group's influence by saying, "I know that there's no way to really explain the emotional and physical and mental reaction when you're at a party in seventh grade and a 702 record comes on. . . . Their music, often mid-tempo jams, struck the perfect balance between soulful pop and mature fun." "Get it Together" was just that type of track.

The Donell Jones–penned song became No Doubt's standout track. According to *Vibe.com*, "It dominated the charts throughout 1997. The single went on to sell 800,000 copies prompting *Billboard* to name it one of the best-selling records of that year." The Recording Industry Association of America (RIAA) certified the single gold on April 1, 1997, (no joke) less than three months after its release. The song not only provided 702 with a hit record, it also helped launch Jones' career as an up-and-coming R&B singer and songwriter.

After their gold debut album, 702 released their self-titled second album, *702*. The first single from the album, "Where My Girls At?" which was another song written and produced by Missy Elliott, reached number 4 on the Hot 100 and R&B charts. The album's remaining singles, "You Don't Know" (50) and "Gotta Leave" (58), failed to break the R&B top 40.

Later that year, group member LeMisha gave birth to a son and left the group to care for her newborn. Her sister Orish took her place during the absence. Soon after, however, Kameelah Williams left the group to pursue a solo career, eventually finding some success as a writer on Faith Evans's *Faithfully* album. She was replaced by Cree Le'More, but when Williams returned to the group, Le'More was out. The group's next release was the 2002 album *Star*, which was considered a failure by most critics and fans despite producer Pharrell Williams having written several of the songs on the album and the Neptunes producing its two lead singles.

In a 2004 interview with *The Washington Post*, Pharrell listed *Star's* "I Still Love You" (49) as one of his top ten songs because it takes him on "an emotional ride." The emotion in the song may be one of the reasons "I Still Love You" is often listed as one of 702's best songs even though it didn't reach the same heights as the most popular tracks in the group's discography.

The group disbanded in 2006 before regrouping again in 2017.

Don't Let Go (Love)

Artist: En Vogue
Album: EV3
Year: 1997
Writers: Sleepy Brown, Marqueeze Etheridge, Andrea Martin, Ivan Matias, Ray Murray, Rico Wade
Producers: Ivan Matias, Organized Noize
Highest R&B Chart Position: 1
Highest Hot 100 Chart Position: 2

"Don't Let Go (Love)" was written and produced for the *Set It Off* movie soundtrack in 1996. It also appeared on En Vogue's third album, 1997's EV3. This song showcased the talents of En Vogue member Dawn Robinson with her singing the lead and Maxine Jones singing the bridge.

"Don't Let Go (Love)" was an international hit, reaching the top 10 in several countries. It was also recognized by *Billboard* as one of the top 100 songs of the 1990s at number 83.

The immense success of "Don't Let Go (Love)" led En Vogue's label, Elektra, to get the group back into the studio to record their third album. However, Dawn Robinson had other plans. She made the decision to leave the group to pursue a solo career with Dr. Dre's Aftermath Entertainment. She departed En Vogue before the album was completed, leaving remaining members Maxine Jones, Cindy Herron, and Terry Ellis to perform as a trio, hence the *EV3* album title.

EV3 debuted at number 8 on *Billboard's* Top R&B/Hip-Hop Albums chart and produced the R&B hit singles "Don't Let Go (Love)," "Whatever" (8), and "Too Gone, Too Long" (25).

However, "Don't Let Go (Love)" would be the group's last number 1, as Robinson's exit was only the beginning of the end for En Vogue as hit-makers. There would be disagreements with management and labels, bankruptcies, disputes over the use of the En Vogue name, and numerous lineup changes in the years that followed.

Anytime

Artist: Brian McKnight
Album: Anytime
Year: 1997
Writers: Brandon Barnes, Brian McKnight
Producer: Brian McKnight
Notable Sample: Outside Your Door, Meshell Ndegeocello (1993)
Highest R&B Chart Position: Song did not chart
Highest Hot 100 Chart Position: Song did not chart

Brian McKnight has sold over 20 million albums and has seven platinum records and seven top 10 singles. He began writing songs as a teenager, and his unique voice and songwriting talents helped him to earn a recording contract with Mercury Records' subsidiary Wing Records at nineteen years old. In 1992, McKnight released his self-titled album *Brian McKnight*, which had two hit singles: his first, "The Way Love Goes," which reached number 11, and "One Last Cry," which reached number 8. The debut release was followed by two more albums for Mercury, *I Remember You* (1995) and *Anytime* (1997). The *Anytime* album sold 2 million copies. It was driven by its immensely popular first single of the same name, despite "Anytime" not being released as a commercial single.

The song was the product of McKnight and fellow songwriter Brandon Barnes, the duo that had created most of McKnight's hits. While attending Oakwood College, a Christian college near his hometown of Huntsville, Alabama, McKnight met Barnes. Both were employed at a local music publishing house that owned a studio.

McKnight recalled to *USA Today*, "I had written a couple of songs, but the publisher wasn't interested in me . . . But Brandon had a little four-track recorder, and he said he'd let me record my songs if I would sing his demos. The first song we ever wrote together was 'The Way Love Goes,' and that was the first song on my first album. We've gotten so good together that he still lives in Alabama, and I live in Los Angeles, and we were able to write 'Anytime' over the phone."

"Anytime" not only brought McKnight double-platinum sales but it also brought him a crossover audience, which he fully embraced. Prior to "Anytime," McKnight's songs were rarely heard outside of R&B stations; however since the release of "Anytime," he has enjoyed top 40 mainstream success.

The song's mega success did not come without controversy. "Anytime," which was released in 1997, contains a piano riff intro that is extremely similar to the piano riff intro from Meshell Ndegeocello's song "Outside Your Door" from her 1993 album *Plantation Lullabies*. As reported by *MTV,* "Spokespeople for Ndegeocello weren't all that concerned about McKnight's song, stating, 'Her music speaks for itself,'" while McKnight's spokespeople stated that he and Barnes composed the song "long before Meshell ever landed a recording deal." While that is quite likely, the McKnight song wasn't copywritten until 1998, five years after Ndegeocello's release. To date no lawsuits have been filed by Ndegeocello.

In 1999, McKnight released *Back at One* on Motown Records, which sold over 3 million copies. That album spawned the hit single "Back at One" (7), which went on to rival "Anytime" as one of McKnight's biggest songs.

Nice & Slow

Artist: Usher
Album: My Way
Year: 1997
Writers: Brian Casey, Jermaine Dupri, Usher Raymond, Manuel Seal
Producers: Jermaine Dupri, Manuel Seal
Highest R&B Chart Position: 1
Highest Hot 100 Chart Position: 1

Following the lukewarm reception of Usher's first album, 1994's *Usher*, and a failed project *The Book of Love* album with producer Dallas Austin, Usher was introduced to So So Def label head Jermaine Dupri, who would serve as lead producer on his sophomore album *My Way*. The aptly titled album got its name because on this album Usher did a lot of the writing and took an active role in defining his image. Dupri and Usher decided to steer Usher's sound into a different approach than Sean Combs had done on his previous album, which was released when Usher was sixteen years old. On *My Way*, the more mature approach was evident as Usher sings a lot about sex. "Nice & Slow" is the perfect example. The song was written by Usher along with Jermaine Dupri and Manuel Seal. Brian Casey from Jagged Edge was also a co-writer of the song, and Jagged Edge provided background vocals.

Of the song's four writers, it's not clear who wrote the opening line, which has since become a testament to how black you are. In fact, to this day if someone asks you where Usher was at seven o'clock on the dot and you don't respond with the right answer, (which is in his drop top cruisin the streets) you would have to surrender your black card on the spot.

Although not as catchy as the album's first single, the upbeat R&B number 1 "You Make Me Wanna," it was "Nice & Slow" that became Usher's first crossover number 1 single on the Hot 100 chart.

And it was Jermaine Dupri who pressed Usher to put a ballad on the album to "knock out the world." The composition and recording of "Nice & Slow" took four hours, according to Dupri. The song is a delicate balance of sex appeal without being too raunchy. Manuel Seal told *Stereogum.com*, "We didn't want too good a guy like Michael Jackson, and we didn't want too bad a guy like Bobby Brown, so we had to make [Usher] a nice guy but not too nice."
The balance was perfect. Although *My Way* was already certified platinum before "Nice & Slow" was released, the track drove sales to double-platinum status by the time the song reached number 1, en route to 6 million album sales.

The Boy Is Mine

Artist: Brandy, Monica
Album: The Boy Is Mine
Year: 1998
Writers: Brandy, LaShawn Daniels, Fred Jerkins, Rodney Jerkins, Japhe Tejeda
Producers: Dallas Austin, Brandy, Rodney Jerkins
Highest R&B Chart Position: 1
Highest Hot 100 Chart Position: 1

In 1982, music superstars Michael Jackson and Paul McCartney released the song "The Girl Is Mine" as the lead single from Jackson's *Thriller* album. The song was a hit, reaching number 1 on the R&B charts and number 2 on the Hot 100. The two would feud three years later in 1985 when Jackson bought the publishing rights to the majority of the Beatles song catalog. The catalog consisted of hit songs written by McCartney while he was a member of the Beatles, and he desperately wanted the catalog and the rights to his music. In the years that followed, McCartney would often complain about "having to pay" every time he performed his songs.

Sixteen years later, teenage stars Brandy and Monica released "The Boy Is Mine." The song was the lead single from both Brandy's *Never Say Never* album and Monica's *The Boy Is Mine* album.

Brandy and Monica's version was not a remake, and although this duet lacked the star power of Jackson and McCartney, the song became a far bigger hit than "The Girl Is Mine" by miles. "The Boy Is Mine" was the best-charting R&B female duet in history, topping the R&B chart for four weeks and the Hot 100 for an amazing thirteen weeks. In a bit of life imitating art, there were also rumors about the teenagers having a real-life beef. Rumors persisted about one of the stars being upset about the other using the song on their album. Thankfully, unlike Jackson and McCartney's beef, these rumors were all marketing and not real. Monica cleared things up in 1998, saying, "We didn't even know each other . . . I had never even seen her before. . . . From the time she was [first] released and I was [first] released, instantly people compared us, and I never understood it. It's like they chose the two of us out of the bunch to put at odds. They never did it with me and Aaliyah, or Brandy and Aaliyah. It was always Brandy and Monica. That's why we took the song and brought humor to a situation that people tried to make serious. We thought it would be really funny to show us feuding in the video and then come together at the end, because we wanted people to let go of the idea of us not liking each other—but of course, they haven't."

The song and the make-believe feud drove "The Boy Is Mine" to become the top-selling single in 1998 with over 2 million copies sold. It also earned the duo a Grammy win for Best R&B Performance by a Duo or Group with Vocals. As for McCartney and Jackson, the real-life feud would last for decades, prompting McCartney to remark in 2001 that "he [Jackson] won't even answer my letters, so we haven't talked and we don't have that great of a relationship." McCartney would regain a portion of the Beatles catalog in 2016 thanks to U.S. copyright law that restores rights to original songwriters after fifty-six years. Currently, McCartney has ownership rights restored for songs that he wrote up until 1962. He will be able to reclaim the rights to all his Beatles songs in 2026.

The First Night

Artist: Monica
Album: The Boy Is Mine
Year: 1998
Writers: Jermaine Dupri, Tamara Savage, Marilyn McLeod, Pam Sawyer
Producer: Jermaine Dupri
Notable Samples: Love Hangover, Diana Ross (1976)
Highest R&B Chart Position: 1
Highest Hot 100 Chart Position: 1

"The First Night" was released as the second single from Monica's album *The Boy Is Mine* on the heels of Monica and Brandy's immensely successful single of the same name. "The First Night" was also a major success for Monica, topping both the Hot 100 and R&B charts and becoming her first solo Hot 100 number 1. Monica commented about the song in a 1998 interview with *MTV News*, saying, "'The First Night' is not an experience of mine, but it's a record that Jermaine Dupri produced . . . It is basically about a guy making an approach towards a woman on the first date." The song was written by Tamara Savage and Jermaine Dupri, with Dupri providing production and additional vocals. The heavy sample of Diana Ross' 1976 recording "Love Hangover" (1) earned writing credits for that songs writers Marilyn McLeod and Pam Sawyer.

"The First Night" was Savage's breakthrough song. She was signed to EMI as a writer while still a student at the University of Southern California. She recalled the initial shock in going from a college student to working with hit-maker Jermaine Dupri on "The First Night," saying, "I went from working with [unknown] writers to working with Jermaine Dupri, I was so nervous."

As reported by *Songwriter Universe*, EMI chose Savage to work with Dupri on a song for the soundtrack for the movie, *South Park, Bigger , Longer, Uncut*, which would potentially be sung by Janet Jackson. But when Savage began working with Dupri, they decided to focus first on writing a song for Monica. She recalled, 'Jermaine and I went into the studio and wrote "The First Night," which was the first song we wrote together . . . When the song went number 1 R&B, I didn't know what to say. Before "The First Night," the only single that I had out was "Take Me There" from

The Rugrats Movie soundtrack. That was one of my first crossovers, but it didn't reach the Top 10, so when "The First Night" became a number 1 pop hit, I nearly died from shock. I was excited, but I really didn't know how to express myself. I don't think it had hit me yet.'"

"The First Night" would stay at number 1 on the R&B charts for six weeks. Savage would go on to write songs for superstars Deborah Cox, Destiny's Child, TLC, and most notably Whitney Houston with her number 1 hit song "Heartbreak Hotel" in 1998.

Sweet Lady

Artist: Tyrese
Album: Tyrese
Year: 1998
Writers: Johntá Austin, Charles Farrar, Troy Taylor
Producers: The Characters
Highest R&B Chart Position: 9
Highest Hot 100 Chart Position: 12

It may be hard to believe but heart-throb Tyrese Gibson once had a Jerry curl and no muscles. He got the idea for his signature bald head from the woman he describes as his "first love," "Candice", who told him that she would not date a guy with a curly top and no muscles. From there Tyrese shaved his head and hit the gym to create his new look. That move would pay off.

Gibson got his big break thanks to a stellar performance in a memorable Coca-Cola commercial that almost didn't happen. It was his high school music teacher that suggested he audition for the commercial; however the sixteen-year-old Tyrese didn't have a ride to the audition and by the time he got there, the casting agent was literally packing up and preparing to leave. She reluctantly let him audition and while he looked the part, he nailed the role when he sang for her. He ended up getting the commercial, which was a nationally aired thirty-second spot that featured Gibson as the central character singing the early '90s "Always Coca-Cola" jingle as he got on a city bus. From there Gibson was signed as a model for Guess and Tommy Hilfiger.

A singer at heart, Gibson parlayed his fame into a record contract with RCA Records at age nineteen. "Sweet Lady" was the third single released from his self-titled debut album in 1998. The song became his biggest hit, reaching number 9 on the R&B charts. "Sweet Lady" also earned Gibson a Grammy nomination for Best R&B Male Vocal Performance in 1998 en route to the album being certified platinum.

Although the song became Tyrese's signature song, he was not initially sold on it. He told TV One, "Anthony played a song for me called 'Sweet Lady.' I said to him, 'I don't like it.' He said to me, 'What?! This is it!'" But after much discussion, Tyrese relented and recorded the track. He added, "I literally fought them on that record. Clearly, I was wrong, and they were right."

To date, Tyrese has sold over 4 million records, and while he still records new material and performs his hits, he is also known as an accomplished actor, beginning with the lead role as the character Jody in the 2001 John Singleton film *Baby Boy* and continuing with his recurring roles as Robert Epps in the *Transformers* franchise and Roman Pearce in the *Fast & Furious* franchise.

Nobody's Supposed to Be Here

Artist: Deborah Cox
Album: One Wish
Year: 1998
Writers: Anthony Crawford, Montell Jordan
Producer: Anthony Crawford
Highest R&B Chart Position: 1
Highest Hot 100 Chart Position: 2

"Nobody's Supposed to be Here" was quite the pivot for the song's co-writer Montell Jordan, who had experienced immense success with the 1995 anthem "This Is How We Do it" and the 1998 number 1 hit "Let's Ride," a collaboration with rapper Master P. But as it turns out, Jordan and his former church band-mate Anthony "Shep" Crawford would go back to their roots to craft their biggest hit.

Crawford wrote "Nobody's Supposed to Be Here" for Patti LaBelle after seeing her perform at the Soul Train Awards, and as he told *Billboard* in 2018, "I said to myself, 'I need to write a really big song for Patti.' . . . But I didn't want to just have a happy song. I wanted to make sure it addressed the pain. You can listen to it whether you're in love or whether you're sitting at home with the shades down." With the idea and only a piece of the chorus in his head, Crawford reached out to Jordan and the two wrote the song with the mindset of what they thought LaBelle would sing. Crawford recounted, "So for the line 'This time, I swear I'm through / but if only you knew,' we wrote that because of Patti LaBelle's song 'If Only You Knew.'"

After the song was finished, the pair began shopping it and it didn't get picked up for over a year. Then seemingly all at once everyone wanted it. Def Jam wanted the song for Kelly Price, Sean Combs wanted it for Faith Evans, but the song would end up with Clive Davis at Arista, which at the time was home to Whitney Houston and Aretha Franklin. Arista eventually allotted it to the unknown Canadian recording artist Deborah Cox, who was supposed to be Davis's next Whitney Houston.

When Cox heard the song, she knew it was a hit. She would say, "I immediately knew the song was a smash. I just remember hearing it and going, 'Oh my God, this speaks to me!' I had just gone through the same thing: I was caught off guard with the love of my life, so it really resonated." While it may have resonated with Cox, Jordan and Crawford had reservations about their hit going to the singer, as Jordan told *Billboard* magazine: "Once we committed the song to Clive, he changes his mind and says, 'Well, I'm not going to give it to Whitney or to any of the others. I've got this newer artist named Deborah Cox.' It was like, 'Wait, we gave you the record because we thought it was going to be something for one of the bigger artists.'"

Those reservations faded away during the first studio session with Cox. As Jordan recalled, "I didn't feel confident until we got into the studio and heard Deborah open her mouth." Crawford remembered a similar feeling, saying, "While she was singing, I was standing there saying, 'Go girl, c'mon!' Like I was in church. She delivered it."
Deliver she did. Released as the lead single from Cox's second studio album, *One Wish,* "Nobody's Supposed to Be Here" is Cox's most successful song, peaking at number 2 on the Hot 100 for eight weeks and spending a then record fourteen weeks at number 1 on the R&B Songs chart.

The success of the song did not go unnoticed by Miss Patti, as Montell Jordan detailed: "I happened to meet Patti many years later, and she pulled me by my ear like an auntie: 'Come here, I want to talk to you.' She pulled me over to this group of people like, 'Tell them what you did, tell them who that song was for.' I said, 'Well, we originally wrote "Nobody's Supposed to Be Here" for you,' and she stopped for a second and said, 'And I couldn't hear it. Back then, my husband, my son, everybody was trying to tell me.'"

Pushin' Inside You

Artist: Sons of Funk
Album: The Game of Funk
Year: 1998
Writers: Sons of Funk
Producers: Sons of Funk
Highest R&B Chart Position: Song did not chart
Highest Hot 100 Chart Position: 97

Ok, so the title leaves little to the imagination in terms of what it is about. But that has been a typical Sons of Funk theme throughout their career, with raunchy titles like "Making Love to My Bi**h," "Big Butt," "Pull Out," and "Bust" prominently featured in their catalog. However, from the beginning the four members of the group (Rico, Lorenzo "Zo" Chew, Des, and G-Smooth) styled themselves as bad boys. In a 1997 interview with *Radio Free Richmond*, group member Zo explained, "The song is a perfect summary of what Sons of Funk are about. We was trying to take [the song] to a controversial level . . . A little something to show people what we're about." Group member Rico echoed the sentiment, explaining, "We have a different edge. We're not like Boyz II Men . . . People are looking for music that's smooth as silk, but they also want something sexual with a gritty rap edge. When you listen to a Sons of Funk record, that's what you get."

The group hails from Richmond, California. They got their big break via divine intervention from a few sources, most notably from a man who would become a rap god, but at the time was just an up-and-coming rapper and entrepreneur, Percy Miller, a.k.a. Master P., who signed them to his new label No Limit Records in 1996.

But it was back in Richmond nearly two years earlier when group member Rico first met Master P. As he explained, "Back then he was just going by Percy, but from the moment we met I knew we were gonna go far. I was at my friend Alamo's barbershop and this man walks in. He's about 6'5", large in stature, with about five guys behind him. He comes up to me and he says, 'Hey, you're Rico, I've heard about your music.' We get to talking, and eventually he says, 'How about this—if you ever make it big, you help me, and if I ever make it big, I'll help you.' At the time I was broke as hell, so I said, 'Sure!' And that was the beginning of our friendship."

By the time Sons of Funk and Master P. would cross paths again, Rico would have already penned "Pushin' Inside of You," which he came up with after praying to God to "put a song in his head that people will love," and Master P. would have inked a seven-figure record deal.

"This is the epic of it all," Rico explained. "I was working at Charles Schwab, and I heard this voice come from behind me. It said, 'Rico, if you don't go to Los Angeles within seventy-two hours, you'll never make it in the music industry.'" That day, he said he told his fellow group members to quit their jobs because they had to go to LA or they would never make it in the music industry.

Following Rico's message, the group members quit their jobs, packed some "chicken and bologna sandwiches," and headed to LA, where the voice told him to go to Priority Records. It was at Priority that Rico describes "all the sudden Master P. walks in with an entourage of like ten cats. C-Murder, Silkk, and some other cats" and P. remembered meeting Rico at the barbershop in Richmond. Rico said, "So by the time I see him in LA, No Limit is ridiculous. They were the biggest independent black record company in the world. I told him I was trying to get into the business, and he's like, 'You still singing?' I said yeah. So, we get on the elevator and he tells me that if he likes my music he's going to make us one of the biggest R&B groups that's out there. It won't be a problem, and he'll put a gang of paper in our pockets. So, I said ok. I was very, very confident in the songs that we had, so I gave him 'Pushin'' and he put the song on. I swear, it was like two seconds later and he was telling me to call my boys cuz we about to get signed up. He put the song out, and two weeks later it was platinum. P. had dropped us a gang of money apiece, and we was happy."

"Pushin' Inside of You" was an underground hit despite not reaching the R&B chart and only reaching number 97 on the Hot 100. Sons of Funk followed the song with a collaboration on another No Limit smash, this time a rap track, 1996's "*I Got the Hook Up,*" which peaked at number 11 on the R&B chart. The group also produced songs on Master P.'s *Ghetto D* and Silkk the Shocker's *Made Man* albums.

Bring It All to Me

Artist: Blaque
Album: Blaque
Year: 1999
Notable Sample: I Don't Wanna Be the Last to Know, Shalamar (1982)
Writers: Nidra Beard, Billy Lawrence, L.E.S., Cory Rooney, Violet Ruby, William Shelby, Kevin Spencer, Leon Sylvers, Linda Van Horssen
Producers: Cory Rooney, L.E.S.
Highest R&B Chart Position: 15
Highest Hot 100 Chart Position: 5

Consisting of members Natina Reed, Shamari DeVoe, and Brandi Williams, Blaque's self-titled debut album sold more than 1 million copies and was certified platinum. The group's debut included the platinum-selling R. Kelly–penned single "808" (4) and the international hit "Bring It All to Me" (15).

Blaque was formally discovered by Lisa "Left Eye" Lopes of TLC after her brother Ronald Lopes brought the group to her attention. Left Eye signed the group to her production company, Left Eye Productions, and served as their mentor and the "creative force behind their image and sound."

Blaque achieved crossover success having had two songs reach the Hot 100 top 10, touring with NSYNC and TLC, securing roles in the popular *Bring It On* movie franchise, and even being named the fourth Best New Artist for 1999 by *Billboard* magazine. However, with all this promise Blaque was unable to secure another R&B hit.

The group's second album, *Blaque Out,* which was set for release in 2001, was shelved by Columbia Records for unknown reasons. After Left Eye's death in a car crash in Honduras in 2002, the group signed with Elektra Records. In 2002 and 2003, they released three less successful singles: "Can't Get It Back" (91), "Ugly," which did not chart, and "I'm Good" (95). Blaque also worked on two unreleased albums in the mid- and late 2000s before going their separate ways in 2008. The group's 2012 comeback was cut short when member Natina died unexpectedly.

Happily Ever After

Artist: Case
Album: Personal Conversation
Year: 1999
Writers: Chris Henderson, Case Woodard
Producer: Chris Henderson
Highest R&B Chart Position: 3
Highest Hot 100 Chart Position: 15

Writer Chris Henderson told *SongbuildersTV.com* that the song that would become "Happily Ever After" started with a hook melody; then he built a piano arrangement around it. Then some time later he got a call from some friends from his hometown, who told him they were getting married. He had known the bride since elementary school and the groom since middle school. In fact, he hooked them up in the tenth grade. In the emotion of the moment, he asked if he could write them a wedding song. Then as he puts it, "The words to the hook just came easy to me so a few days later I called the bride and groom separately and asked the whole story: What day he proposed? What words were used? And they couldn't remember the exact dates so that ended up in the song." With the lines, "It was last May / don't know the exact day."

The song was originally a duet that Henderson never intended to be played outside the wedding. However, as he told *VoyageATL.com* in 2022, "A friend of mine convinced me to include it in a demo package that I had sent to Def Jam A&R, where it was quickly scooped up by the label and eventually presented to up-and-coming artist Case." It became one of Case's biggest records and is still considered a classic wedding song.

Speaking of weddings, the video for "Happily Ever After" included an up-and-coming female artist as the love interest. Interestingly, this artist would go on to become the love interest of millions en route to taking over the R&B and pop worlds. Trying to figure who should be cast as the love interest in the video, Case saw a Destiny's Child video and thought the group's lead singer would be perfect. He contacted Mathew Knowles, father of Beyoncé Knowles, then of Destiny's Child. Mathew asked to hear the song and loved it. According to Case, it was that simple to get Beyoncé in the video, but with one catch. The video originally had the pair kissing, but Mathew Knowles objected to his seventeen-year-old daughter kissing a grown man [Case], and the scene was cut from production. (At least Knowles was consistent. He had previously removed Jagged Edge from a tour with Destiny's Child following romantic relationships between two teenage members of Destiny's child with two adult members of Jagged Edge.)

Don't be surprised if you weren't the only one who didn't know about Beyoncé's stint as a video girl. Old heads sometimes forget that there is an entire generation that have only known Beyoncé as "Queen Bey." Take for example model and actress Karruechee Tran, who in 2012 "discovered" Beyoncé in the "Happily Ever After" video and tweeted "Beyoncé in Case's 'Happily Ever After' video? I've never seen this!" The tweet got a mixed bag of responses, from more mature respondents in the tone of "Girl you like twelve years late" to one presumably youthful respondent who asked, "WTF is Case."

No Scrubs

Artist: TLC
Album: FanMail
Year: 1999
Writers: Kevin Briggs, Kandi Burruss, Tameka "Tiny" Cottle, Lisa Lopes
Producer: Kevin Briggs
Highest R&B Chart Position: 1
Highest Hot 100 Chart Position: 1

Kandi Burruss began exploring writing for other groups when her time in the female group Xscape was ending. She reflected, "Because the group was falling apart [before their third album], I was in panic mode, meaning I didn't know what was going to happen with my career at the time. I was scared. I was just like, 'ok, if Xscape breaks up and we don't have another album coming, how am I going to take care of myself? How am I going to provide for myself?' I didn't have another way to make money."

"No Scrubs" grew out of personal experiences that Kandi Burruss and her Xscape groupmate Tameka "Tiny" Cottle were experiencing in the dating scene. Kandi told *Glamour* magazine, "At that particular time, I used to put titles in my notepads that I felt would be great song titles or concepts. So I had 'Scrubs' written in my notepad as a title I would want to use one day. I remember I was riding down the highway with a friend of mine. She was dating the brother of the guy that I was dating, and we were both talking trash about the guys. I started freestyling over a track that She'kspere [Kevin Briggs] had given me. So it was really me joking with my friend, freestyling, and talking trash about this guy. I wrote the verse, the B section, and the hook right there. Because we were in the car, it was on an old envelope." While Kandi and Tameka had written the song for themselves (after all, it was their experiences and they are artists), early versions of the track generated a lot of buzz. Cottle told *Rolling Stone* in 2014, the song's producer She'kspere "played it for some of the powers that be at LaFace [Records], and they immediately were like, 'We want this song for TLC,' and he came back to us, and we were kind of thinking about it. We were kind of like, 'This is a hit for us. Like, we really feel like we can make it off this song.'"

Ultimately the song would be recorded by TLC, but that did not necessarily mean that it would make their *FanMail* album. Cottle recalled, "They were going back and forth on what they wanted to do with the song because that's the first song that Chili sang lead on. So that's why I wasn't really sure if that song was going to be a first single, or even a single at all. Normally, T-Boz was the lead, so I didn't know if they were going to keep it."

Thankfully "No Scrubs" made the record. It became the third number 1 for TLC, was number 2 on *Billboard's* year-end Hot 100 singles chart, won two Grammys, and launched the writing careers of Burruss and Cottle.

Cottle isn't bitter about passing on recording the hit. She says, "It was probably the best thing we probably could have ever, ever did by giving TLC that 'No Scrubs' record . . . It gave me a Grammy and it put us in a different light than just being artists. It gave us another outlet, like, 'ok, these are songwriters. Grammy-winning songwriters.' So it was a different category, a different level for my life. I had been a successful artist but never a successful writer."

Where I Wanna Be

Artist: Donell Jones
Album: Where I Wanna Be
Year: 1999
Writers: Donell Jones, Kyle West
Producers: Donell Jones, Kyle West
Highest R&B Chart Position: 2
Highest Hot 100 Chart Position: 29

Where I Wanna Be is the title of Donell Jones' second studio album as well as the title track. The Chicago native began singing at age eight and by twelve, he wrote his first song, "Love Can't Win." It wasn't long before he was discovered in an unlikely place.

Jones told *TheBoomBox.com*, "I was working at McDonald's and the manager heard me singing one day. He was putting together a group, and he wanted me to try out. When I tried out, I made it." The group began performing together as Porché, making a name for themselves in the Chicago scene. Jones says, "Everything started from there. I was just doing everything I could with music, and I was around other people who were doing it, too, so I was soaking it all up like a sponge. We did a lot of shows around Chicago. We made a name for ourselves. It took about three or four years to really build that name up, and that's pretty much where we started at. We couldn't get a deal in Chicago, so that's why we went to the Black Radio Exclusive convention that was in Washington, D.C., in 1993."

Jones continued, "we had a showcase in Washington, D.C. Nobody came to it, so we just went outside the hotel and played for everybody who happened to be at the hotel at that particular time. Eddie F. happened to be one of those people, and he signed our group. Shortly after that, we had a song on his new record label entitled 'Make You Feel Real Good.' After that, the group broke up, and then I started working on writing for other people. I wrote some songs for myself, and Eddie [F.] played them for L.A. Reid, and that's how I pretty much got signed."

While at LaFace, Jones wrote Usher's hit song "Think of You," which became a number 8 hit in 1995. Soon after, label heads Babyface and Reid let him write and produce his debut album, *My Heart*. The album was a modest success, producing two top 25 hits: "In the Hood" (22), which Jones wrote, and "Knocks Me Off My Feet" (14), which was a remake of the 1976 Stevie Wonder classic.

Three years later, Jones got another opportunity with *Where I Wanna Be*. He stated, "My goal for going into *Where I Wanna Be* was, I wanted to make every song sound like it could be a single. So, whatever they put out, it wouldn't matter because it was going to be a good song. I think we accomplished that goal." The album would go platinum, spawning four singles and two classics, including the number 1 hit "U Know What's Up" and the title track "Where I Wanna Be."

Jones says the song came from his real-life relationship experience. He recalls, "That's what I was going through at the time. I was in a relationship with my children's mother, and we just grew apart. This particular song was something I was going through as I wrote it. I was on the plane coming back to Chicago because my dad's mom passed away. When I was on the plane, I was writing the song, but when I got to Chicago I forgot about it. But when I went home, everything started coming back to me. I think the reason why a lot of people fell in love with the song was because it was something that was true. I found out that it just wasn't me that was going through it. Half the world was going through the same thing . . . It just ended up being a really honest record that did great for me."

Thong Song

Artist: Sisqó
Album: Unleash the Dragon
Year: 1999
Writers: Mark Andrews, Desmond Child, Tim Kelley, Bob Robinson
Producers: Sisqó, Tim Kelley, Bob Robinson
Notable Samples: Eleanor Rigby, the Beatles (1966)
Livin' la Vida Loca, Ricky Martin (1999)
Highest R&B Chart Position: 2
Highest Hot 100 Chart Position: 3

Sisqó, whose real name is Mark Andrews, was the front man of the immensely popular '90s R&B group Dru Hill. Dru Hill was so popular that each of their commercial releases, including 1996's *Dru Hill* album and the follow-up, 1998's *Enter the Dru*, had achieved either platinum or multi-platinum status before the group's hiatus in 1999. As the first member of the group to release a solo project, the pressure was on Sisqó to come up with a hit. However, despite the group's immense sales, Sisqó had to borrow money from his manager Kevin Peck to fund the solo project.

To craft a track, Sisqó solicited producers Bob Robinson and Tim Kelley (Tim & Bob) for beats. The duo had previously worked with R&B acts Joe, Usher, and Boyz II Men. In 1999 they were looking to get onto Michael Jackson's upcoming *Invincible* album, so they were experimenting with out-of-the-box ideas when they discovered Wes Montgomery's cover of the 1966 song "Eleanor Rigby" originally recorded by the Beatles (which Michael Jackson owned the rights to). The production duo intended the track for MJ, but when Sisqó heard it he wanted it for himself.

The inspiration for the lyrics came to Sisqó from a date he went on with a woman who showed him her thong. As he recounted to *Vice*, "I had never seen one before, apparently none of my friends had actually seen one before, because in 1999, there wasn't a whole lot of thongs being worn unless it was in some sort of swimsuit ad. I just remembered first seeing one and it was like . . . you ever seen *The Ten Commandments*, when Moses went up and his hair was black, and then he came back down and his hair was all silver? That was literally the joke I was making with [my] silver hair. [The thong] was stone tablet-ed into my mind."

The famous "thong-th-thong-thong-thong" line came to Sisqó via his cousin, who recounted a date to Sisqó and some friends where a woman handed him her "thong-th-thong-thong-thong!" Sisqó appreciated the line and worked it into the song. He would later say, "We were laughing at first like it was a joke, but then later we laughed all the way to the bank."

"Thong Song" was all over R&B, pop, and top 40 stations that year, and the video, which rivaled 1991's "Pop That Coochie" video, was in heavy rotation despite not featuring a single thong, as the networks would not allow it. The song also received four Grammy nominations and the album, which also included the number 1 hit "Incomplete," went platinum.

However, Sisqós "laughing all the way to the bank" was short lived, as the majority of the publishing rights for "Thong Song" would become owned by writer Desmond Child, who authored Ricky Martin's "Livin' la Vida Loca," which is a line that Sisqó references throughout "Thong Song."

Since no one cleared the reference before the song's release, Child threatened to sue after "Thong Song" exploded in 2000. As reported by *Vice*, Tim & Bob apparently cautioned Sisqó about using the interpolation of Child's song without clearing it first. But Sisqó confidently told them that he had a relationship with Child, so it wasn't a big deal. The matter was ultimately settled out of court. As a result, today Desmond Child has more ownership of the song than anyone. "We just gonna have to take the L on this one," Sisqó added.

For their part, producers Tim & Bob did hear from Michael Jackson, as he reached out looking for them to make him something hotter than "Thong Song.

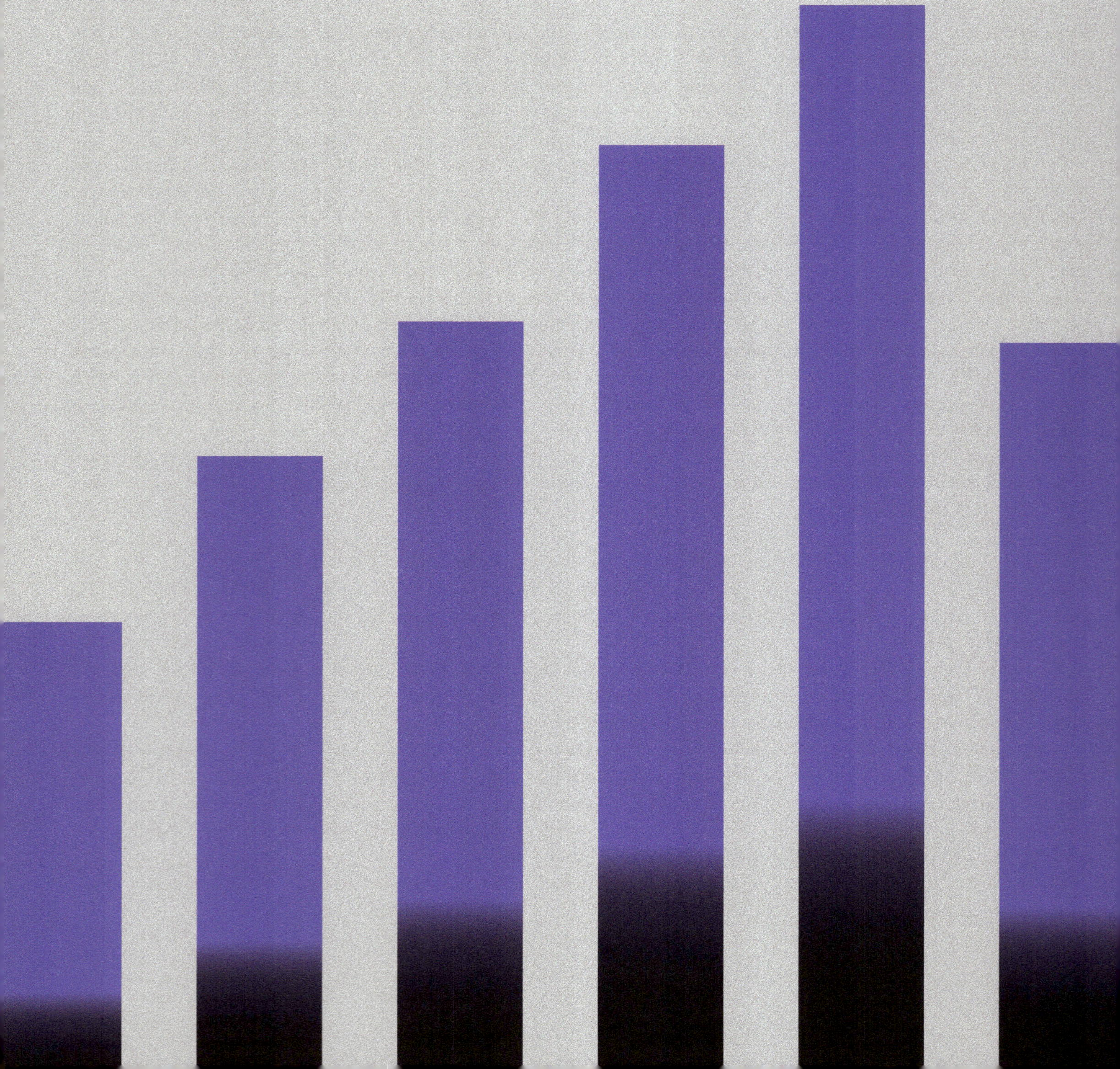

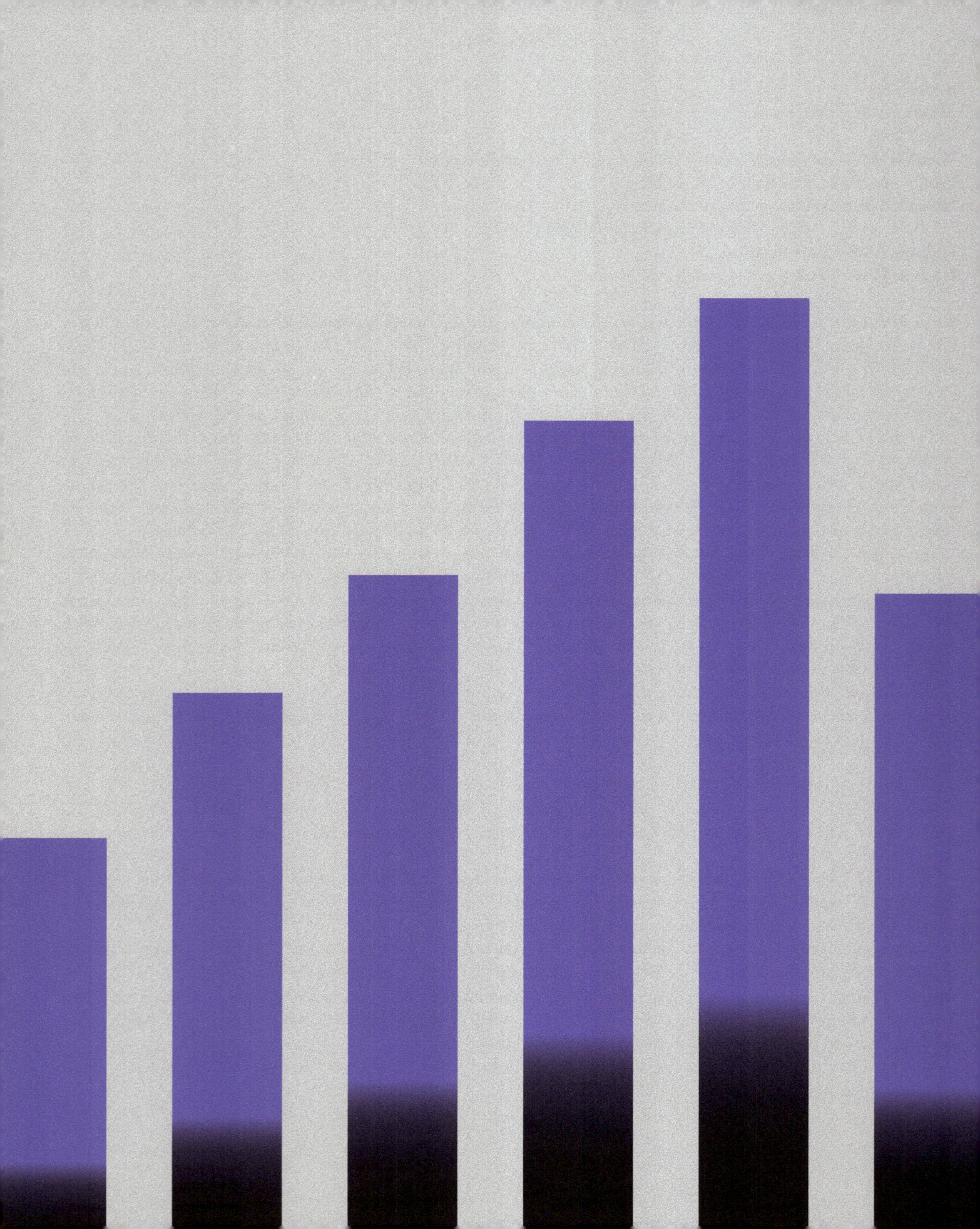

Debatable

Nothing Compares 2 U
Dreaming of You
I'll Be There for You/You're All I Need to Get By (Puff Daddy Mix)
Hey Lover

Debatable

In this the final part of our journey, it seems that we have come full circle. As we noted in the beginning of this book, with the explosion and expansion of R&B the question of what makes a song an R&B song can be rather difficult to answer. Is it determined by the artist? The melody? The demographic that likes it the most? Or is it something you just know when you hear it. Like the rest of the music world, our researchers also struggled with finding a definitive answer, with each person trusting their ears and experience to decide. In drafting this book, there were some rather spirited debates about which songs should make the cut. Ultimately we settled on creating this "Debatable" section and letting you the reader decide. So here are some profiles of a few of the songs that caused the most dissension and the arguments for why they should or should not be considered R&B songs.

Nothing Compares 2 U

Artist: Sinéad O'Connor
Album: I Do Not Want What I Haven't Got
Year: 1990
Writer: Prince
Producers: Sinéad O'Connor, Nellee Hooper
Highest R&B Chart Position: Song did not chart
Highest Hot 100 Chart Position: 1
Billboard Top Songs of the '90s: 21

"Nothing Compares 2 U" was one of the reportedly thousands of songs written and composed by Prince. While not only a hitmaker for himself, Prince had a knack for writing from the female perspective and lending songs to female artists that would turn into hits like "Manic Monday" by the Bangles, a number 10, Hot 100 hit, "The Glamorous Life" by Sheila E., a number 9 R&B hit and "I Feel for You" by Chaka Khan, an R&B number 1.

In term of "Nothing Compares 2 U," the story of this song as told by Prince's sound engineer Susan Rogers goes like this: "He wrote this during a very creative period when he was coming up with a song just about every day . . . he wrote it at his rehearsal space in Eden Prairie, Minnesota, where he vanished for an hour and emerged with the lyrics on a notebook. He recorded the song on the spot, playing the instruments himself."

As for the inspiration for the song, Prince never clarified it himself. While the song seems to linger as a plea to a departed lover, Rogers provided what is probably the best version of what the inspiration was. As she told the BBC, "The song was actually inspired by Prince's housekeeper, Sandy Scipioni, who left him to be with her family after her father died. Sandy was the person who made sure he had his favorite beverage, which was Five Alive, and she made sure the house was clean and that there were fresh flowers on the piano and that the socks and underwear were washed." Presumably those flowers could have come from the backyard, hence the line, "All the flowers that you planted in the backyard all died when you went away."

Prince recorded the song himself in 1984 but never released that version. It was ultimately released by Warner Bros. and Prince's estate in 2018 following the artist's death. The funk group the Family, which Prince put together and signed to his Paisley Park record label, recorded it for their self-titled debut album in 1985, but again the song was not released as a single and received almost no airplay.

In 1989, Irish singer Sinéad O'Connor's manager, Fachtna O'Ceallaigh, was looking for songs for the singer's second album, *I Do Not Want What I Haven't Got*, when he came across the song and presented it to O'Connor for her to do a cover. Producer Nellee Hooper changed the arrangement, and O'Connor recorded the song and released it in 1990. It became an international hit, charting all over the world, including number 1 spots in the U.K. and the U.S. The song did not reach the R&B charts, likely because O'Connor was considered an "alternative" artist, as evident by her version of the song winning the Grammy that year for Best Alternative Music Performance.

In 1993, Prince's version, which was arranged as a duet with soul singer Rosie Gaines, peaked at number 66 on the Hot R&B/Hip-Hop Songs chart.

Dreaming of You

Artist: Selena
Album: Dreaming of You
Year: 1995
Writers: Franne Golde, Tom Snow
Producer: Guy Roche
Highest R&B Chart Position: Song did not chart
Highest Hot 100 Chart Position: 22

How big was Selena? Well, imagine the Queen Bey herself, Beyoncé Knowles, being somewhat starstruck during their first meeting. In an interview with *MTV Tres*, Beyoncé opened up about what it was like meeting the music icon as a little girl at the Galleria mall in Houston, Texas. "I didn't say much to Selena because I wasn't a celebrity," she said, "and I just saw her and said hello and kept it moving. . . . Growing up in Texas, I heard her on the radio, and I think listening to her album, even though I didn't know exactly what she was singing, it helped me in the studio with my pronunciation." Beyoncé also praised Selena, calling her a "legend" and an inspiration: "She was so talented . . . I'm very happy that, even though she didn't know who I was, I'm still so excited that I got that opportunity."

Selena Quintanilla Pérez, a.k.a. Selena, was a singer, songwriter, spokesperson, model, actress, and fashion designer. She is still immensely popular decades after her death and is also still considered the queen of Tejano music.
In 2020, *Billboard* magazine put her in third place on their list of Greatest Latino Artists of All Time.

She began her career as a member of the band Selena y Los Dinos, with her elder siblings A. B. and Suzette Quintanilla. At sixteen she won Female Vocalist of the Year at the Tejano Music Awards in 1987. She would go on to win the award nine consecutive times from 1988 to 1996. She signed with EMI Latin in 1989 and released her self-titled debut album the same year, while her brother became her principal music producer and songwriter.

By 1994, Selena had already become the dominant force in Latin American music in the U.S. Her album *Selena Live!* (1993) won Best Mexican-American Album at the 1994 Grammy Awards. She was poised for major crossover success and recorded the *Dreaming of You* album with that in mind. However, Selena was shot and killed on March 31, 1995, prior to the album's release, by Yolanda Saldívar, her friend and the former president of her fan club, When *Dreaming of You* was released in 1995, it debuted at the top of the *Billboard* 200, making Selena the first Latin American artist to accomplish this feat.

"Dreaming of You" is the album's title track and first single. The song was recorded several weeks before Selena's death. By year's end *The Los Angeles Times* recognized it as one of the top 10 singles of 1995.

So why should "Dreaming of You" be considered as an R&B song? Well, the bass and rhythmic sound is reminiscent of an earlier '90s R&B sound—think Vanessa Williams or Tracie Spencer—and considering that the song was originally written in 1989 for freestyle/R&B group the Jets, who turned it down, it becomes clear why this song should be considered as an R&B gem. Accordingly, *Newsweek* magazine correctly called Selena's English-language recordings "a blend of urban pop and Latin warmth," and according to *Texas Monthly* magazine, Selena's brother modernized her music into a more "funk and hip-hop" sound, which is apparent on this track.

I'll Be There for You/You're All I Need to Get By (Puff Daddy Mix)

Artists: Method Man, Mary J. Blige
Album: Tical
Year: 1994
Writers: Ashford and Simpson, Robert Diggs, Clifford Smith, Christopher Wallace
Producers: RZA, Sean Combs
Notable Samples: You're All I Need to Get By, Marvin Gaye, Tammi Terrell (1968)
    Me & My Bitch, the Notorious B.I.G., (1994)
    Mona Lisa, Slick Rick (1988)
Highest R&B Chart Position: 1
Highest Hot 100 Chart Position: 3
Highest Hot Rap Songs Chart Position: 1

Although intertwined with a timeless R&B melody, this song is a rap song, thus it is relegated to our debatable section. The underlying track was written by the duo Nick Ashford and Valerie Simpson while at Motown Records and released as a single performed as a duet by Marvin Gaye and Tammi Terrell in 1968. The gospel backing of the song was inspired by Ashford and Simpson's gospel background (the duo met in church). The original became another in a long line of hits for the label, peaking at number 7 on the Hot 100 and number 1 on the Hot R&B/Soul Singles chart for five weeks in 1968. The song was so powerful that it added fuel to the speculation that Gaye and Terrell were romantically involved. However, they both stood by the notion that they were just good friends. (Terrell was romantically involved with David Ruffin of the Temptations at the time.)

RZA of the Wu-Tang Clan had the idea to use the song as a backing track on a song for his groupmate Method Man. Method Man's verses originated during a monthlong stay in San Francisco away from his then girlfriend, now wife of twenty-plus years, Tamika Smith. When Smith finally visited, she brought him inspiration. As Method Man recalled, "I was recording my album on the road and we lived in San Francisco for about three weeks. We had a little apartment out there. Being out on the road so long, I was missing my girl so I used my money and flew her out. Me and RZA had joining rooms. So he's in there making the beat and I swear on everything I love I wrote that record right there while she was laying next to me, asleep in the bed. I hadn't seen her in a month and I was just so happy to see her. I wrote the record, recorded the record, and wrote the hook."

It was Def Jam Recordings executives that had the idea to get Mary J. Blige on the song. "But to get Mary, you gotta go through Puffy," Method Man recalled. "So now here comes the dilemma: RZA's a producer and Puffy's a producer. Puff wants to do his version and RZA wants to do the track too. So what do we do here? How do we compromise? And the deal was struck: there would be multiple production versions of the song."

For their part, Method Man and Blige worked well together. The chemistry, while not as dynamic as Gaye and Terrell, was nonetheless magical. When Meth and Mary first met, she let him know that she woke up to [his song] "Bring the Pain" "every goddamn day." Method Man said, "I was like, 'Well s**t, I love the s**t out of Mary J. Blige!'" It was the success of "Bring the Pain" [a rap track] and Mthod Man's *Tical* album that would cause friction between Method Man and his label. *Tical* was released in 1994 with "Bring the Pain" as the first single. "Bring the Pain" was a success, charting at 30 on the R&B chart and number 4 on the Hot Rap Songs chart. Banking on keeping the success rolling, label executives wanted "You're All I Need" to be the second single off of the album, but Method Man and RZA weren't having it. They wanted the track "Release Yo' Delf" [also a rap track] to be released as the second single. Still riding high off the single "Bring the Pain," Method Man's star was ascending, and he did not want to chance losing his core rap audience. So when Def Jam was pressing him to release a love song with Mary J. Blige, he wasn't with it. During an interview with hip-hop insider Angela Yee, Method Man said the song was "Lyor Cohen's [Def Jam's] idea." Method Man was not on board, saying, "I refused to do it. I didn't want to do it because I saw something happening, and there was a trend in hip-hop whereas when you became a ladies' man . . . I'm looking at Kane [Big Daddy Kane] and people like that—even though Kane was a dope MC, what detracted from dudes really effing with Kane like that was the ladies were always screaming."

Initially Method Man and RZA got their way, and "Release Yo' Delf" was slated as the second single. However, while filming the video for "Release Yo' Delf," the image-conscious Method Man took issue with the feel of the project. He would say, "We go and do the 'Release Yo' Delf' video that Steve Carr shot. I was mad at him because I didn't like the look and the feel of the video. It was like he was trying to re-create 'Method Man,' and that wasn't gonna happen. Then the 'All I Need' s**t pops up again."

Method Man goes back to Def Jam, and this time "Cohen had RZA on board with releasing 'You're All I Need' as the second single." Method Man relented and the record exploded. "I'll Be There for You/You're All I Need to Get By," the version, produced by Sean Combs and Trackmasters and samples the lines "Lie together, cry together / I swear to God I hope we fu***n' die together" from the Notorious B.I.G.'s song "Me & My Bi**h," sold over 800,000 copies. It was eventually certified platinum and earned Method Man a Grammy for Best Rap Performance by a Duo or Group. The song also did wonders for Method Man's career. He remembered this, saying, "I realized, at first there were nothing but grimy ni**as at my shows. Once that record dropped, it was blonde hair and silver outfits all in the front! There were a bunch of little Mary J. Bliges' running all through the damn party . . . I remember the phone calls and getting called up to the office. I watched how we started from doing college tours to bars to theaters to outside venue festivals to arenas off this one fu**ing record . . . At the end of the day, we got the record done. Puffy [Combs] was happy, RZA was happy, people that got it were happy, and Lyor sat back with his cigar like, 'See, I told you! You should've done this record when I told you to.'"

Hey Lover

Artist: LL Cool J., Boyz II Men
Album: Mr. Smith
Year: 1995
Writers: LL Cool J., Rod Temperton
Producers: Trackmasters
Notable Samples: The Lady in My Life, Michael Jackson (1982)
　　　　　　　　　All Night Long, Mary Jane Girls (1983)
Highest R&B Chart Position: 3
Highest Hot 100 Chart Position: 3
Highest Hot Rap Songs Chart Position: 1

Like "You're All I Need to Get By," the song "Hey Lover" is also heavily infused with classic R&B melodies and harmonizing throughout, but it is still a rap song, thus it is also consigned to our debatable section.

However, unlike Method Man, by 1995 LL Cool J. had already proven that he was not concerned with losing male fans over more tender lyrics that female fans appreciated. Eight years earlier in 1987, LL released his song "I Need Love," which became a number 1 hit. He would say "I Need Love" was probably the first major rap love song that showed vulnerability. Although it would be followed by Rob Base's "Crush" a year later, rappers being vulnerable would not be the norm for some time. Hence Method Man's concerns over releasing "You're All I Need to Get By" in 1995, a full eight years after "I Need Love." As LL explained in a 2020 interview with *Revolt*, "I wanted to creatively be able to do all kinds of music. When we did 'I Need Love,' it was a huge hit. But at the same time, it got a lot of backlash . . . They didn't understand, at that time, that hip-hop could go there."

Following the success of "I Need Love," LL would "go there" again and achieve success, first with 1990's "Around the Way Girl" (5) which is a respectful celebration of girls from the neigborhood and "Hey Lover," releasing it as the first single from his sixth album, *Mr. Smith*.

That's right—LL Cool J had six charting albums by 1995. Which begs the question: Why is LL Cool J. not in more of our top five rappers conversations? He has just as many songs that are considered classics as his contemporaries, and he has consistently put up sales numbers that rival anyone in the rap game (with the exception of 1993's *14 Shots to the Dome*, which was a rather forgettable album). From 1985's *Krush Groove* (his acting debut) to playing his decade-plus role as Sam Hanna on the CBS series *NCIS: Los Angeles*, he has been a staple in the culture, and the genius of "Hey Lover" is an example of why he deserves to be on rap's Mount Rushmore.

Dissecting "Hey Lover's" lyrics today can be a bit tricky as the words appear to be begging to be "Me too-ed." Admittedly the song is a bit, well.....stalkerish by today's standards.

The opening line itself could have been taken from the climax of a Lifetime move: "I've been watchin' you from afar / for as long as I can remember . . . This is love, girl / this is more than a crush."

Additionally, every verse is about LL seeing the object of his affection in public, then fantasizing about sexing her.
Verse 1. He sees her at the Ruckers in Harlem (with her man), then he works out every day thinking about her and fantasizes about laying her on her stomach and caressing her back.
Verse 2. He sees her at the bus stop "waitin' everyday," comments about whether thats safe for her to do, then dreams about tonguing her down with vanilla ice cream and searching her body with his tongue all night.
Verse 3. Last week he saw her at the mall on a pay phone, then had a vision it was him on the other end of the call when she walks in and her dress falls to the floor and you get the rest.
At minute 3:58 he comes out and repeats, "Imma have that . . . imma have that."
In LL's defense, there was no *Tinder* or *Match.com* in 1995, so that is pretty much how you pursued a girl you liked back then.

The Trackmasters-produced song features vocals from Boyz II Men (the hottest vocal group at the time) and heavily samples Michael Jackson's "The Lady in My Life" from his 1982 hit album *Thriller*; thus Rod Temperton, the writer of "The Lady in My Life" was given credit as a writer "Hey Lover."

LL Cool J. explained the collaboration with Boyz II Men to *Entertainment Weekly,* stating, "I wrote this hook and I just thought it felt like Boyz II Men. They were on fire at the time, but more importantly it just felt like they were made to do it. We drove out to Philly and I played the record for the guys. They got in the truck with me and some friends, and they loved it. We went right to the studio that night and did the entire song in one take. Everything, it was just magical."

The song won LL Cool J. his second Grammy for Best Rap Solo Performance. His first Grammy was in the same category, for the song "Mama Said Knock You Out" from the 1990 album of the same name.

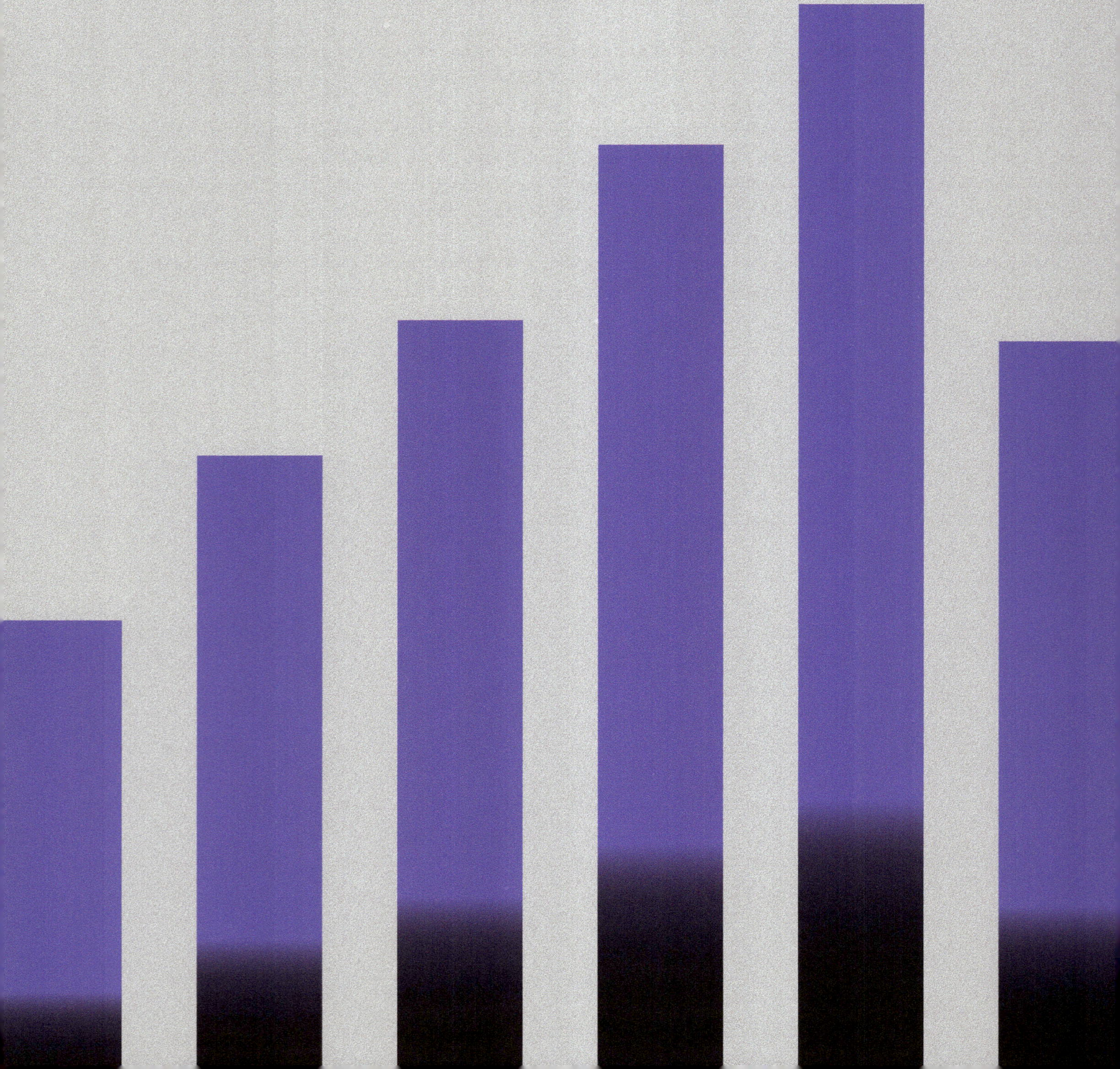

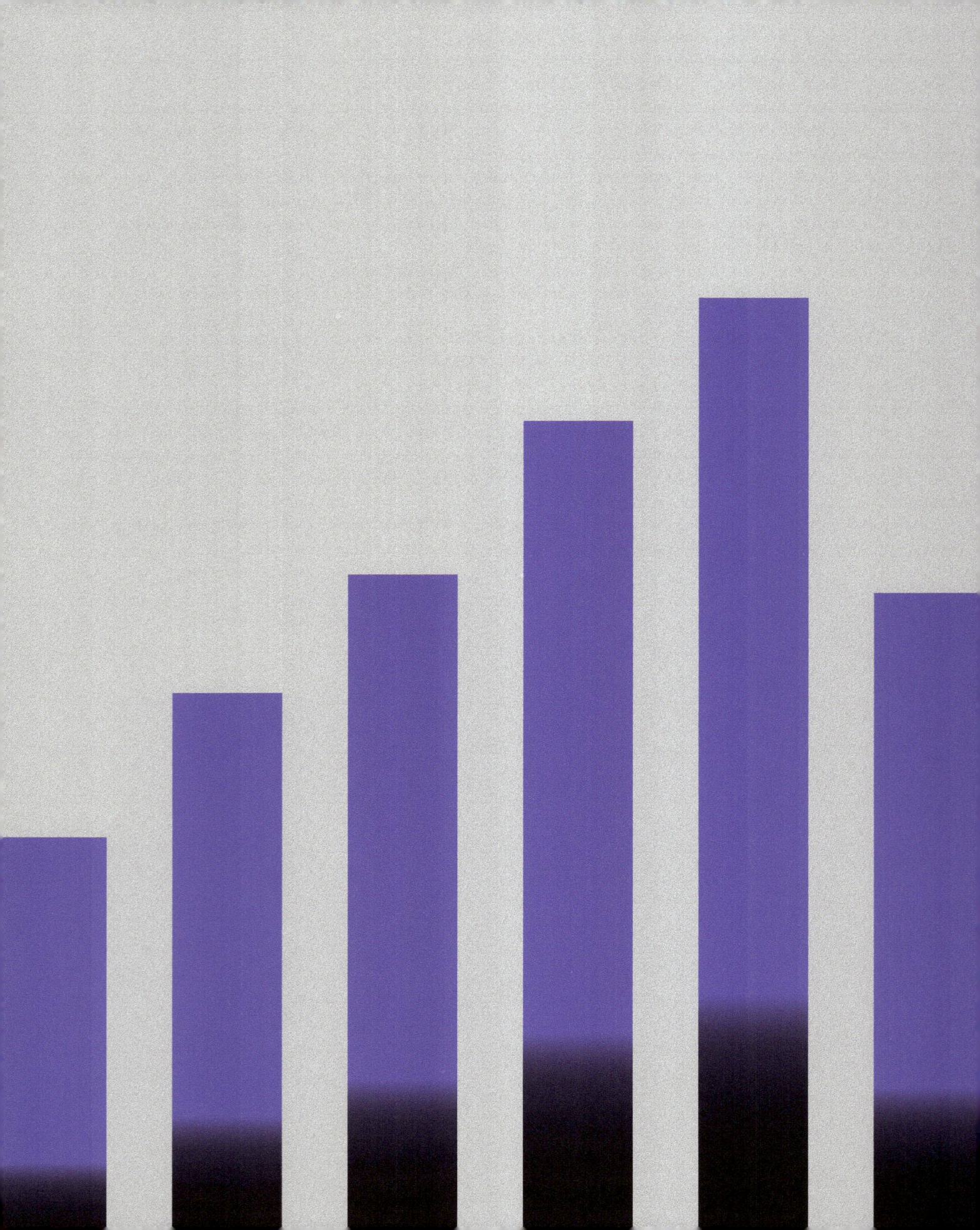

Charts & Numbers

The R&B Number Ones 1990 - 1999
Top 10 Charting R&B Artists of the Decade
R&B Songs That Spent the Most Weeks at Number One
Top 10 Best Selling R&B Albums of the Decade

The R&B Number Ones 1990 - 1999

1990

Week	Song Title	Artist
6 January	Tender Lover	Babyface
13 January	Rhythm Nation	Janet Jackson
20 January	I'll be Good to You	Quincy Jones featuring Ray Charles and Chaka Khan
27 January		
3 February	Make it Like it was	Regina Belle
10 February	Real Love	Skyy
17 February	It's Gonna be Alright	Ruby Turner
24 February	Where Do We Go From Here	Stacy Lattisaw and Johnny Gill
3 March		
10 March	Escapade	Janet Jackson
17 March	The Secret Garden (Sweet Seduction Suite)	Al B. Sure!, James Ingram, El DeBarge, Barry White
24 March	All Around the World	Lisa Stansfield
31 March		
7 April	Spread My Wings	Troop
14 April		
21 April	Ready or Not	After 7
28 April		
5 May	Poison	Bel, Biv, DeVoe
12 May		
19 May	Rub You the Right Way	Johnny Gill
26 May	Hold On	En Vogue
2 June		
9 June	The Blues	Tony, Toni, Tone!
16 June	Tomorrow (A Better You, A Better Me)	Quincy Jones Featuring Tevin Campbell
23 June	You Can't Touch This	MC Hammer
30 June	All I Do is Think of You	Troop
7 July	You Can't Deny it	Lisa Stansfield
14 July	My, My, My	Johnny Gill
21 July		
28 July	Make You Sweat	Keith Sweat

Date	Song	Artist
4 August	Can't Stop	After 7
11 August	Vision of Love	Mariah Carey
18 August		
25 August	Jerk Out	The Time
1 September	Feels Good	Tony! Toni! Toné!
8 September		
15 September	Lies	En Vogue
22 September	Crazy	The Boys
29 September	Thieves in the Temple	Prince
6 October	Giving You the Benefit	Pebbles
13 October		
20 October		
27 October	So You Like What You See	Samuelle
3 November		
10 November	Love Takes Time	Mariah Carey
17 November	B.B.D. (I Thought it Was Me)	Bel Biv DeVoe
24 November	Misunderstanding	Al B. Sure!
1 December	I'm Your Baby Tonight	Whitney Houston
8 December		
15 December	Sensitivity	Ralph Tresvant
22 December	It Never Rains (In Southern California)	Tony! Toni! Toné!
29 December		

1991

Week	Song Title	Artist
5 January	Love You Down	Freddie Jackson
12 January		
19 January	The First Time	Surface
26 January	Love Makes Things Happen	Pebbles and Babyface
2 February		
9 February	You Don't Have to Worry	En Vogue
16 February	I'll Give all My Love to You	Keith Sweat
23 February	Gonna Make You Sweat (Everybody Dance Now)	C&C Music Factory
2 March	All the Man that I Need	Whitney Houston
9 March		
16 March	Written All Over Your Face	The Rude Boys
23 March	I Like the Way (The Kissing game)	Hi-Five
30 March		
6 April	Do Me Again	Freddie Jackson
13 April	Wrap My Body Tight	Johnny Gill
20 April	Whatever You Want	Tony! Toni! Toné!
27 April		
4 May	I'm Dreamin	Christopher Williams
11 May	Call Me	Phil Perry
18 May	It Should've Been You	Teddy Pendergrass
25 May	Kissing You	Keith Washington
1 June	I Wanna Sex You Up	Color Me Badd
8 June		
15 June	Power of Love (Love Power)	Luther Vandross
22 June		
29 June	How Can I Ease the Pain	Lisa Stansfield
6 July		
13 July	Exclusivity	Damian Dame
20 July		
27 July	Baby I'm Ready	LeVert

3 August	Summertime	DJ Jazzy Jeff & The Fresh Prince
10 August	I Can't Wait Another Minute	Hi-Five
17 August	Can You Stop the Rain	Peabo Bryson
24 August		
31 August	Addictive Love	BeBe & CeCe Winans
7 September		
14 September	Let the Beat Hit Em	Lisa Lisa and Cult Jam
21 September	Don't Wanna Change the World	Phyllis Hyman
28 September	I Adore Mi Amore	Color Me badd
5 October	Running Back to You	Vanessa Williams
12 October		
19 October	Romantic	Karyn White
26 October	It's So Hard to Say Goodbye to Yesterday	Boyz II Men
2 November	Emotions	Mariah Carey
9 November	Forever My Lady	Jodeci
16 November		
23 November	Tender Kisses	Tracie Spencer
30 November	Are You Lonely For Me	The Rude Boys
7 December	I'll Take You There	BeBe & CeCe Winans
14 December	Private Line	Gerald LeVert
21 December	I Love Your Smile	Shanice
28 December		

1992

Week	Song Title	Artist
4 January	I Love Your Smile	Shanice
11 January		
18 January	Tell Me What You Want Me to Do	Tevin Campbell
25 January	Keep It Comin	Keith Sweat
1 February		
8 February	Stay	Jodeci
15 February		
22 February	Uhh Ahh	Boyz II Men
29 February	Baby Hold on to Me	Gerald LeVert with Eddie LeVert
7 March	Remember the Time	Michael Jackson
14 March		
21 March	Diamonds and Pearls	Prince and the NPG
28 March	Save the Best For Last	Vanessa Williams
4 April		
11 April		
18 April	Here I Go Again	Glenn Jones
25 April	Don't Be Afraid	Aaron Hall
2 May		
9 May	All Woman	Lisa Stansfield
16 May	My Lovin (You're Never Gonna Get it)	En Vogue
23 May		
30 May	Come and Talk to Me	Jodeci
6 June		
13 June	Honey Love	R. Kelly and Public Announcement
20 June		
27 June	In the Closet	Michael Jackson
4 July	Do It to Me	Lionel Richie
11 July	Tennessee	Arrested Development
18 July	The Best Things in Life Are Free	Luther Vandross and Janet Jackson
25 July	You Remind Me	Mary J. Blige

1 August	Giving Him Something He Can Feel	En Vogue
8 August	Baby-Baby-Baby	TLC
15 August		
22 August	End of The Road	Boyz II Men
29 August		
5 September		
12 September		
19 September	Humpin Around	Bobby Brown
26 September		
3 October	Slow Dance (Hey Mr. DJ)	R. Kelly and Public Announcement
10 October	Alone With You	Tevin Campbell
17 October	Real Love	Mary J. Blige
24 October		
31 October	Right Now	Al B. Sure!
7 November	Sweet November	Troop
14 November	Ain't Nobody Like You	Miki Howard
21 November	Games	Chuckii Booker
28 November	If I Ever Fall in Love	Shai
5 December	I Will Always Love You	Whitney Houston
12 December		
19 December		
26 December		

1993

Week	Song Title	Artist
2 January	I Will Always Love You	Whitney Houston
9 January		
16 January		
23 January		
30 January		
6 February		
13 February		
20 February	Hip Hop Hooray	Naughty by Nature
27 February	Nuthin but a G Thang	Dr. Dre
6 March		
13 March	Freak Me	Silk
20 March		
27 March		
3 April		
10 April		
17 April		
24 April		
1 May		
8 May	That's the Way Love Goes	Janet Jackson
15 May		
22 May		
29 May		
5 June	Knockin Da Boots	H-Town
12 June		
19 June		
26 June		
3 July	Weak	SWV
10 July		
17 July	Whoomp! (There it is)	Tag Team

24 July	Lately	Jodeci
31 July		
7 August	Check Yo Self	Ice Cube featuring Das EFX
14 August	Lately	Jodeci
21 August		
28 August	Right Here/Human Nature	SWV
4 September		
11 September		
18 September		
25 September		
2 October		
9 October		
16 October	Just Kickin It	Xscape
23 October		
30 October		
6 November		
13 November	Gangsta Lean	D.R.S.
20 November		
27 November		
4 December		
11 December		
18 December		
25 December	Can We Talk	Tevin Campbell

1994

Week	Song Title	Artist
1 January	Can We Talk	Tevin Campbell
8 January		
15 January	Cry for You	Jodeci
22 January		
29 January		
5 February		
12 February	Understanding	Xscape
19 February		
26 February	Bump n' Grind	R. Kelly
5 March		
12 March		
19 March		
26 March		
2 April		
9 April		
16 April		
23 April		
30 April		
7 May		
14 May		
21 May	Back and Forth	Aaliyah
28 May		
4 June		

11 June		
18 June		
25 June		
2 July		
9 July	Any Time, Any Place	Janet Jackson
16 July		
23 July		
30 July		
6 August		
13 August		
20 August		
27 August		
3 September		
10 September		
17 September	I'll Make Love to You	Boyz II Men
24 September		
1 October		
8 October		
15 October		
22 October		
29 October		
5 November	I Wanna Be Down	Brandy
12 November		
19 November		
26 November	Practice What You Preach	Barry White
3 December		
10 December		
17 December		
24 December	Creep	TLC
31 December		

1995

Week	Song Title	Artist
7 January	Creep	TLC
14 January		
21 January		
28 January		
4 February		
11 February	Baby	Brandy
18 February		
25 February		
4 March		
11 March	Candy Rain	Soul For Real
18 March		
25 March		
1 April	This is How We Do It.	Montell Jordan
8 April		
15 April		
22 April		
29 April		
6 May		
13 May		
20 May	I'll Be There For You /You're All I Need to Get By	Method Man feat Mary j. Blige
27 May		
3 June		
10 June	Don't Take it Personal (Just One of Dem Days)	Monica
17 June		
24 June	One More Chance /Stay With Me	The Notorious B.I.G.
1 July		
8 July		
15 July		
22 July		
29 July		
5 August		

12 August	One More Chance /Stay With Me	The Notorious B.I.G.
19 August		
26 August	Boombastic / In The Summertime	Shaggy
2 September	You Are Not Alone	Michael Jackson
9 September		
16 September		
23 September		
30 September	Fantasy	Mariah Carey
7 October		
14 October		
21 October		
28 October		
4 November		
11 November	Who Can I Run To	Xscape
18 November	You Remind Me of Something	R. Kelly
25 November	Exhale (Shoop Shoop)	Whitney Houston
2 December		
9 December		
16 December		
23 December		
30 December		

1996

Week	Song Title	Artist
6 January	Exhale (Shoop, Shoop)	Whitney Houston
13 January		
20 January	Before You Walk Out my Life/ "Like this and Like That"	Monica
27 January		
3 February	Not Gon' Cry	Mary J. Blige
10 February		
17 February		
24 February		
2 March		
9 March	Down Low (Nobody Has to Know)	R. Kelly feat. Ronald Isley
16 March		
23 March		
30 March		
6 April		
13 April		
20 April		
27 April	You're the One	SWV
4 May	Always be My Baby	Mariah Carey
11 May	Tha Crossroads	Bone Thugs N Harmony
18 May		
25 May		
1 June		
8 June		
15 June		
22 June		
29 June	You're Makin Me High	Toni Braxton
6 July	How Do U Want It / California Love	2PAC feat. K-CI & JoJo, Dr. Dre and Roger Troutman
13 July		
20 July		
27 July	You're Makin Me High	Toni Braxton

3 August	I Can't Sleep Baby (If I)	R. Kelly
10 August		
17 August	Twisted	Keith Sweat
24 August		
31 August	Hit Me Off	New Edition
7 September		
14 September		
21 September	Twisted	Keith Sweat
28 September	If Your Girl Only Knew	Aaliyah
5 October		
12 October	Last Night	Az Yet
19 October	No Diggity	Blackstreet feat. Dr. Dre and Queen Pen
26 October		
2 November		
9 November		
16 November	Pony	Ginuwine
23 November		
30 November	Nobody	Keith Sweat feat. Athena Cage
7 December		
14 December		
21 December	I Believe I Can Fly	R. Kelly
28 December		

1997

Week	Song Title	Artist
4 January	I Believe I Can Fly	R. Kelly
11 January		
18 January		
25 January	Don't Let Go (Love)	En Vogue
1 February	I Believe I Can Fly	R. Kelly
8 February	On & On	Erykah Badu
15 February		
22 February	In My Bed	Dru Hill
1 March		
8 March	Can't Nobody Hold Me Down	Puff Daddy feat. Mase
15 March		
22 March		
29 March		
5 April		
12 April		
19 April	In My Bed	Dru Hill
26 April	Hypnotize	The Notorious B.I.G.
3 May		
10 May		
17 May	G.H.E.T.T.O.U.T.	Changing Faces
24 May		
31 May		
7 June		
14 June	I'll Be Missing You	Puff Daddy and the Family
21 June		
28 June		
5 July		
12 July		
19 July		
26 July		
2 August		

9 August	Never Make A Promise	Dru Hill
16 August		
23 August		
30 August		
6 September	You Make Me Wanna	Usher
13 September		
20 September		
27 September		
4 October		
11 October		
18 October		
25 October		
1 November		
8 November		
15 November		
22 November	My Body	LSG
29 November		
6 December		
13 December		
20 December		
27 December	A Song for Mama	Boyz II Men

1998

Week	Song Title	Artist
3 January	A Song for Mama	Boyz II Men
10 January	My Body	LSG
17 January		
24 January	Nice & Slow	Usher
31 January		
7 February		
14 February		
21 February		
28 February		
7 March		
14 March		
21 March	No, No, No	Destiny's Child
28 March	Let's Ride	Montell Jordan feat. Master P. and Silkk the Shocker
4 April	All My Life	K-Ci & JoJo
11 April		
18 April	Lets Ride	Montell Jordan feat. Master P. and Silkk the Shocker
25 April		
2 May	Too Close	Next
9 May		
16 May		
23 May	I Get Lonely	Janet Jackson feat. Blackstreet
30 May	The Boy is Mine	Brandy and Monica
6 June		
13 June		
20 June		
27 June		
4 July		
11 July		
18 July		
25 July		

1 August		
8 August		
15 August	Friend of Mine	Kelly Price
22 August		
29 August		
5 September		
12 September		
19 September		
26 September	The First Night	Monica
3 October		
10 October		
17 October		
24 October	How Deep is Your Love	Dru Hill feat. Redman
31 October		
7 November		
14 November		
21 November		
28 November		
5 December	Nobody's Supposed to Be Here	Deborah Cox
12 December		
19 December		
26 December		

1999

Week	Song Title	Artist
2 January	Nobody's Supposed to Be Here	Deborah Cox
9 January		
16 January		
23 January		
30 January		
6 February		
13 February	Heartbreak Hotel	Whitney Houston
20 February		
27 February		
6 March		
13 March		
20 March		
27 March		
3 April	What's It Gonna Be	Busta Rhymes feat. Janet Jackson
10 April	No Scrubs	TLC
17 April		
24 April		
1 May		
8 May		
15 May	Fortunate	Maxwell
22 May		
29 May		
5 June		
12 June		
19 June		
26 June		
3 July		

Date	Song	Artist
10 July	Bills, Bills, Bills	Destiny's Child
17 July		
24 July		
31 July		
7 August		
14 August		
21 August		
28 August		
4 September		
11 September	Never Gonna Let You Go	Faith Evans
18 September	Spend My Life With You	Eric Benet feat. Tamia
25 September		
2 October	We Can't Be Friends	Deborah Cox feat. R.L.
9 October	Heartbreaker	Mariah Carey feat. Jay-Z
16 October		
23 October	We Can't Be Friends	Deborah Cox feat. R.L.
30 October	Satisfy You	Puff Daddy feat. R. Kelly
6 November		
13 November	U Know What's Up	Donell Jones feat. Lisa "Left Eye" Lopes
20 November		
27 November		
4 December		
11 December		
18 December		
25 December		

Top 10 Charting R&B Artists of the Decade

Artists	Number 1's	Top 10's
R. Kelly	8	17
Mariah Carey	7	22
Janet Jackson	6	8
Keith Sweat	6	14
Whitney Houston	5	14
Boyz II Men	5	12
Jodeci	5	10
Mary J. Blige	4	11
Tony! Toni! Tone!	4	8
Monica	4	7
Michael Jackson	3	14
Brandy	3	11
TLC	3	10
Teddy Riley (Includes Guy and Blackstreet)	3	9
Gerald LeVert	3	9
SWV	3	9
Xscape	3	9
Luther Vandross	2	9
Usher	2	5
Vanessa Williams	2	4
Aaliyah	2	4
Toni Braxton	1	9
Kenneth "Babyface" Edmonds	0	10

R&B Songs That Spent the Most Weeks at Number One

1. Nobody's Supposed to Be Here
Artist: Deborah Cox
Album: One Wish
Number of Weeks: 14
Dates: November 7, 1998 – February 6, 1999

2. Bump n' Grind
Artist: R. Kelly
Album: 12 Play
Number of Weeks: 11
Dates: February 26 – May 14, 1994

3. I Will Always Love You
Artist: Whitney Houston
Album: The Bodyguard Movie Soundtrack
Number of Weeks: 11
Dates: December 5, 1992 – February 13, 1993

4. You Make Me Wanna
Artist: Usher
Album: My Way
Number of Weeks: 11
Dates: September 6 – November 15, 1997

5. Anytime, Any Place
Artist: Janet Jackson
Album: Janet
Number of Weeks: 10
Dates: June 11 – August 13 1994

6. I'll Make Love to You
Artist: Boyz II Men
Album: II
Number of Weeks: 9
Dates: August 20 – October 15 1994

7. Bills, Bills, Bills,
Artist: Destiny's Child
Album: The Writings on The Wall
Number of Weeks: 9
Dates: July 10 – September 4, 1999

8. Song: Creep
Artist: TLC
Album: CrazySexyCool
Number of Weeks: 9
Dates: December 10, 1994 - February 4, 1995

9. Freak Me
Artist: Silk
Album: Lose Control
Number of Weeks: 8
Dates: March 13 – May 1, 1993

9. The Boy is Mine
Artist: Brandy and Monica
Album: The Boy is Mine
Number of Weeks: 8
Dates: June 6 – July 25, 1998

9. You Know What's Up
Artist: Donnell Jones
Album: Where I Wanna Be
Number of Weeks: 8
Dates: November 13, 1999 - January 1, 2000

9. I'll Be Missing You
Artist: Puff Daddy and the Family
Album: No Way Out
Number of Weeks: 8
Dates: June 14 – August 2, 1997

9. Fortunate
Artist: Maxwell
Album: Life Movie Soundtrack
Number of Weeks: 8
Dates: May 15 – July 3, 1999

The Notorious B.I.G.'s One More Chance Stay With Me, was a rap song that held the number one spot on the R&B chart for 9 Weeks from June 24 – August 19, 1995.

Top 10 Best Selling R&B Albums of the Decade

1. CrazySexyCool

Artist: TLC
Sales: 12 Million
Release Date: November 15, 1994
Label: Arista

Album Track List:
1. Intro-lude
2. Creep
3. Kick Your Game
4. Diggin on You
5. Case Of The Fake People
6. CrazySexyCool (Interlude)
7. Red Light Special
8. Waterfalls
9. Intermission-lude
10. Let's Do It Again
11. If I Was Your Girlfriend
12. Sexy (Interlude)
13. Take Our Time
14. Can I Get A Witness (Interlude)
15. Switch
16. Sumthin' Wicked This Way Comes

2. Daydream

Artist: Mariah Carey
Sales: 11 Million
Release Date: October 3, 1995
Label: Columbia

Album Track List:
1. Fantasy
2. Underneath The Stars
3. One Sweet Day
4. Open Arms
5. Always Be My Baby
6. I Am Free
7. When I Saw You
8. Long Ago
9. Melt Away
10. Forever
11. Daydream Interlude (Fantasy Sweet Dub Mix)
12. Looking In

The following albums tied for third place:

3. The Miseducation of Lauryn Hill

Artist: Lauryn Hill
Sales: 10 Million
Release Date: August 25, 1998
Label: Ruffhouse Records / Columbia

Album Track List:
1. Intro
2. Lost Ones
3. Ex-Factor
4. To Zion
5. Doo Wop (That Thing)
6. Superstar
7. Final Hour
8. When It Hurts So Bad
9. I Used To Love Him
10. Forgive Them Father
11. Every Ghetto, Every City
12. Nothing Even Matters
13. Everything Is Everything
14. The Miseducation Of Lauryn Hill
15. Can't Take My Eyes Off Of You
16. Tell Him

3. Music Box

Artist: Mariah Carey
Sales: 10 Million
Release Date: August 31, 1993
Label: Columbia

Album Track List:
1. Dreamlover
2. Hero
3. Anytime You Need A Friend
4. Music Box
5. Now That I Know
6. Never Forget You
7. Without You
8. Just To Hold You Once Again
9. I've Been Thinking About You
10. All I've Ever Wanted

The following albums tied for fourth place:

4. Mariah Carey

Artist: Mariah Carey
Sales: 9 Million
Release Date: June 12, 1990
Label: Columbia

Album Track List:
1. Vision Of Love
2. There's Got To Be A Way
3. I Don't Wanna Cry
4. Someday
5. Vanishing
6. All In Your Mind
7. Alone In Love
8. You Need Me
9. Sent From Up Above
10. Prisoner
11. Love Takes Time

4. Cooleyhighharmony

Artist: Boyz II Men
Sales: 9 Million
Release Date: April 30, 1991
Label: Motown

Album Track List:
1. Thank You
2. All Around The World
3. U Know
4. Vibin'
5. I Sit Away
6. Jezzebel
7. Khalil (Interlude)
8. Trying Times
9. I'll Make Love To You
10. On Bended Knee
11. 50 Candles
12. Water Runs Dry
13. Yesterday

The following albums tied for fifth place:

5. Secrets

Artist: Toni Braxton
Sales: 8 Million
Release Date: July 18, 1996
Label: LaFace / Arista

Album Track List:
1. Come On Over Here
2. You're Makin' Me High
3. There's No Me Without You
4. Un-Break My Heart
5. Talking in His Sleep
6. How Could an Angel Break My Heart
7. Find Me a Man"
8. Let It Flow"
9. Why Should I Care
10. I Don't Want To
11. I Love Me Some Him
12. In the Late of Night" (includes hidden track "Toni's Secrets" at 5:19)

5. The Writings on The Wall

Artist: Destiny's Child
Sales: 8 Million
Release Date: July 27, 1999
Label: Columbia

Album Track List:
1. Intro (The Writing's On The Wall)
2. So Good
3. Bills, Bills, Bills
4. Confessions
5. Bug A Boo
6. Temptation
7. Now That She's Gone
8. Where'd You Go
9. Hey Ladies
10. If You Leave
11. Jumpin, Jumpin
12. Say My Name
13. She Can't Love You
14. Stay
15. Sweet Sixteen
16. Outro (Amazing Grace...Dedicated To Andretta Tillman)

The following albums tied for sixth place:

6. Dangerous

Artist: Michael Jackson
Sales: 8 Million
Release Date: November 26, 1991
Label: Epic

Album Track List:
1. Jam
2. Why You Wanna Trip on Me
3. In the Closet
4. She Drives Me Wild
5. Remember the Time
6. Can't Let Her Get Away
7. Heal the World
8. Black or White
9. Who Is It
10. Give In to Me
11. Will You Be There
12. Keep the Faith
13. Gone Too Soon
14. Dangerous

6. R

Artist: R Kelly
Sales: 8 Million
Release Date: November 10, 1998
Label: Jive

Album Track List:
1. Home Alone (featuring Keith Murray)
2. Spendin' Money
3. If I'm With You
4. Half on a Baby
5. When a Woman's Fed Up
6. Get Up on a Room
7. One Man
8. We Ride (featuring Cam'Ron, Noreaga, Vegas Cats, and Jay-Z)
9. The Opera
10. The Interview
11. Only the Loot Can Make Me Happy" (featuring Tone of Poke & Tone)
12. Don't Put Me Out
13. Suicide
14. Etcetera
15. If I Could Turn Back the Hands of Time
16. What I Feel/Issues" Kelly

17. I Believe I Can Fly (international release)

-Disc two-

1. The Chase
2. V.I.P
3. Did You Ever Think (featuring Tone)
4. Dollar Bill (featuring Foxy Brown)
5. Reality
6. 2nd Kelly
7. Ghetto Queen (featuring Crucial Conflict)
8. Down Low Double Life
9. Looking For Love
10. Dancing with a Rich Man
11. I'm Your Angel (duet with Céline Dion)
12. Money Makes the World Go Round (featuring Nas)
13. I Believe I Can Fly (U.S. Release)/Gotham City (international release)
14. Did You Ever Think (Remix) (re-release) (featuring Nas)
15. Gotham City (re-release)

* This is a list of the best-selling albums in the United States based on Recording Industry Association of America (RIAA) certification and Nielsen SoundScan sales tracking. The criteria are that the album must have been published (including self-publishing by the artist), and the album must have achieved at least a diamond certification from the RIAA. The albums released prior to March 1991 should be included with their certified units only, as their Nielsen SoundScan sales are not complete.

* Information is current as of 1 April 2023.

Song Index
List includes only songs that are profiled.

4 Seasons of Loneliness, 57, 63
abc-123, 194
A Rose is Still A Rose, 85
A Thin Line Between Love and Hate 50, 163
Age Ain't Nothing but a Number, 129, 179
All Cried Out, 165
All the Things (Your Man Won't Do), 191
Always Be My Baby, 109-110, 231, 247
Anything, (Old School Party Mix), 117
Anytime, 198
Are You Still Down, 125-126
Ascension, (Don't Ever wonder), 133-134
At Your Best (You Are Love), 98, 160
Baby-Baby-Baby, 93, 225
Baby Hold on to Me, 194, 223
Baby I'm for Real, 154
Baby I'm for real (Natural High), 154
Baby I'm Ready, 194, 222
Believe in Love, 81-82
Betcha by Golly Wow, 164
Body and Soul, 83-84
Boombastic (Sting/Shaggy Mix), 70-71, 231
Breakdown, 126-127
Breakin' My Heart (Pretty Brown Eyes), 46-47
Bring it All to Me, 204
Brown Sugar, 160, 180
Can You Get Wit It, 52
Can't You See, 120
Candy Rain, 53, 230
Caught Out There, 148
Creep, 60, 93, 95-96, 229-230, 243, 247
Cruisin, 160
Cry For You, 59, 63, 228
Cupid, 121, 189
Do it to Me, 79, 224
Dolly My Baby (Bad Boy Extended Remix), 69
Don't Let Go (Love), 197-198, 234
Don't Take It Personal (Just one of dem Days), 181, 230
Dreaming of You, 212
End of the Road, 55-56, 63, 93, 158, 225
Everything, 167
Ex Factor, 138, 248
Eye Hate U, 84
Fantasy (Bad Boy Fantasy), 107-108, 126, 231, 247
Flex, 67-68
Forever My Lady, 59, 63, 223

Freak Like Me, 14, 97
Freek'n You (Mr. Dalvin's Freek Mix), 119
Full of Smoke, 189
Games, 26, 225
Gangsta Lean, 171-172, 227
Get it Together, 196-197
Ghetto Jam, 124, 145
Giving Him Something He Can Feel, 156, 225
Got Til It's Gone, 102
Happily Ever After, 204-205
Hey Lover, 214-215
Hey Mr. DJ, 49
Hopeless, 136
I Belong to You (Every Time I See Your Face), 144, 196
I Gotta Be, 122, 123
I Like The Way (The Kissing Game), 37, 45, 222
I Love Your Smile, 25, 223-224
I Miss My Homies, 174
I Miss You, 172
I Wanna Be Down (The Human Rhythm Hip Hop Mix), 118, 229
I Wanna Sex You Up, 29, 38-39, 222
I Will Always Love You, 40, 47, 154-155, 225-226, 243
Iesha, 35-36
If, 101-102
If I Ever Fall in Love, 47, 147, 225
If I was Your Girlfriend, 159-160, 247
If were a Bell, 76, 77
If That's Your Boyfriend (He Wasn't Last Night), 140-141
If You Think You're Lonely Now, 159
I'll Be Missing You, 173, 234, 244
I'll Be There, 146, 155-156
I'll Be There For You/ You're All I Need to Get By (Puff Daddy Mix), 213-214, 230
I'm Every Woman, 157
In My Bed, 181, 234
It Ain't Over Til It's Over, 23
It's So Hard to Say Goodbye to Yesterday, 153, 172, 223
Just Kickin It, 92, 94, 108, 227
Killing Me Softly, 14, 124, 162-163
Killing Me Softly With His Song, 162-163
Kissing You, 22, 83, 120, 222
Knockin Da Boots, 50, 226
Knocks Me Off My Feet, 163, 206
Lately, 63, 157-158, 227

(Lay Your Head on My) Pillow, 62-63, 179
Let's Chill, 36-38
Let's Ride, 119, 127, 202, 236
Love Don't Live Here Anymore, 161
Love Makes Things Happen, 19, 222
Love Should'a Brought You Home, 48, 83, 98
Love You 4 Life, 60
Make You Sweat, 194, 220
Makeda, 137
Motown Philly, 39, 63, 153
Mr. Loverman, 67, 71
Murder She Wrote, 68
My body, 28, 192, 235-236
My Boo, 92, 147
My Lovin (You're Never Gonna Get It), 39, 90, 224
My, My, My, 28, 220
Nice & Slow, 122, 199, 236
No Diggity, 190-191, 233
No Ordinary Love, 80
No, No, No, Pt. 2, 123-125, 145, 236
No Scrubs, 93, 205-206, 238
Nobody, 194, 233
Nobody's Supposed to be Here, 119, 202, 237-238, 243
Nothing Compares 2 You, 211
On Bended Knee, 56-57, 63, 249
One in A Million, 98-99
One Sweet Day, 106-107, 155, 247
Only You, 121, 189
Outside Your Door, 140-141, 198
Poison, 29-30, 35, 38, 220
Pony, 187, 233
Practice What You Preach, 83, 229
Pushin Inside of You, 203
Rain, 95, 174, 181-182
Remember the Time, 78-79, 224, 251
Rump Shaker, 40, 190
Rush, Rush, 24-25
Save the Best for Last, 89, 224
Scream, 102
Sensitivity, 30, 221
Sexy MF, 41
Shhh, 50-51
Slow Jam, 166
So Alone, 171
Somebody Loves You Baby (You Know Who It is), 80, 81

Something He Can Feel, 225
Soon As I Get Home, 14, 96-97
Soul Searchin' (I Wanna Know if it's Mine), 141
Sweet Lady, 201
Sweet Thing, 158
Tell Me, 144, 146
Tender Kisses, 20-21, 223
That's The Way Love Goes, 101, 226
The Beautiful Ones, 166
The Boy is Mine, 199-200, 236, 244
The First Night, 200-201, 237
The Secret Garden (The Seduction Suite), 75-76, 83, 220
The Rain (Supa Dupa Fly), 195
Thin Line Between Love and Hate, 50, 163
Thinkin Bout It, 194
This is How We Do It, 97, 119, 202, 230
Thong Song, 188, 207
Too Close, 182-183, 236
Twisted, 194, 233
Tyrone, 135
Un-break My Heart, 98, 250
Unforgettable, 77-78
Vision of Love, 25, 106, 109, 221, 249
Weak, 95-96, 117, 226
When You Believe, 109
Where I Wanna Be, 206
Why Me Baby, 194
With You, 21
Worker Man, 70
Yearning for Your Love, 153
You, 148
You Are Everything, 167
You Remind Me, 91, 224

Artist Index

112, 121-122, 165, 189
702, 196-197
118th Street Productions, 49
A Tribe Called Quest, 53, 162-163
Aaliyah, 52, 61, 85, 88, 98-99, 124, 160, 179, 195, 200, 228, 233, 241
Abdul, Paula, 19, 24-25
Abrams, Bryan, 38
Adu, Sade, 80
Afanasieff, Walter, 106, 144, 155-156, 165
After 7, 28, 125, 154, 220-221
Al B. Sure!, 40, 51-52, 58-59, 61, 75-76, 96, 157-158, 203, 220-221, 225
Alexander, Prince Charles, 161
Allamby, Darrell, 192, 194
Allen, Jeffrey, 46
Allure, 165
Andrews, Mark (See Sisqó)
Another Bad Creation (ABC), 35-36
Anthony, Allen, 189
Anthony, C. J., 26
Anthony, Larry, "Jazz", 188
Anthony, Paul, 165
Ashford and Simpson, 157, 213
Ashford, Nick, 157, 213
Austin, Dallas, 35-36, 39, 52, 85, 95-96, 121-122, 153, 181, 199
Austin, Johntá, 201
B-Fine, 165
B. Jon, 125-126
Baby Gee, 165
Babyface, 19, 24, 27-28, 48, 51, 55, 57, 92-93, 190, 126, 146, 166, 188-189, 206, 220, 222, 241
Badu, Erykah, 133, 135, 234
Bahr, Abdullah, 49
Baillergeau, Gerald, 196
Baker, Anita, 48, 21-22, 83-84,
Baker, Jarvis, 25
Baker, Willie James, 181
Barber, Samuel, 173
Barias, Ivan, 133
Barnes, Brandon, 198
Battle, Lavonn, 194
Battlecat, 145
Beard, Nidra, 204
Beatles, The, 57, 199-200, 207
Beavers, Jackey 101
Beckham, Steve, 84

Bedeau, Curt, 165
Belew, Adrian, 107-108
Belkhir, Mounir, 137
Bell Biv DeVoe (BBD), 29-30, 35, 38, 55-56
Bell, Ricky, 27, 29, 55
Bell, Thom, 164, 167
Belle, Bernard, 34, 36-37, 45, 78
Bennett, Mikey, 67
Beside, 38
Betha, Mason,
Betts, André, 141
Bilal, 133
Bishop, Teddy, 127
Bivins, Michael, 27, 29, 35, 39, 55, 122, 196-197
Biz Markie, 91
Blackstreet, 38, 190-191, 233, 236, 241
Blaque, 204
Blige, Mary J., 35, 69, 88, 91, 112-113, 146, 158, 161, 167, 213-214, 224-225, 230, 232, 241
Bloodstone, 154
Blow, Kurtis, 35, 92, 182
Bobbitt, Charles, 101
Bone Thugs-n-Harmony, 13, 126-127, 232
Bone, Krayzie, 98, 126-127
Bone, Wish, 126
Bonner, Everton, 68
Boogie Down Productions, 85
Booker, Chuckii, 26, 83, 225
Bootsy's Rubber Band, 97
Bow-Legged Lou, 165
Boyz II Men, 196, 203, 207, 214-215, 223-225, 229, 235-236, 241, 243, 249
Brand Nubian, 49
Brandy, 118, 182, 199-200, 229-230, 236, 241, 244
Braxton, Toni, 48, 83, 98, 125, 146, 232, 241, 250
Briggs, Kevin "She'kspere", 205
Bright, Garfield A., 47
Bristol, John, 101
Browder, Lincoln, 192
Brown, Bobby, 27, 29-30, 40, 52, 199, 225
Brown, Darryl, 146
Brown, J. B., 171
Brown, James, 40, 69, 90, 101, 120, 167, 171, 181
Brown, Mary, 123
Brown, Raphael "Tweety", 182, 188
Brown, Terry "T-Low", 182,
Brumley, Albert, 173
Bryant, Don, 195

256

Buckmaster, Paul, 161
Burke, Kareem, 189
Burrell, Bishop, 50
Burruss, Kandi, 94, 122-123, 205
Cage, Athena, 194, 233
Calderon, Mark, 38-39
Calloway, Reggie, 81, 166
Calloway, Vincent, 81
Cameron, G. C., 153
Campbell, Tevin, 50-51, 157-158, 164, 220, 224-225
Carey, Mariah, 25, 92, 100, 105-110, 112-113, 120, 126-127,144, 146, 155-156, 165-166, 221, 223, 231-232, 239, 241, 247-249
Carter, Alita, 97
Case, (Case Woodward) 127, 204-205
Casey, Brandon, 122-123
Casey, Brian, 199, 122-123
Casey, Harry Wayne, 121
Cauthen, Gregory, 172
Chaka Demus & Pliers, 68
Champion, Jason, 171
Chapman, Romell "RoRo", 35, 36
Characters, The, 201
Chew, Rico, Lorenzo "Zo", 203
Child, Desmond, 207
Childs, Amelia, 196
Chili, 19, 93, 205
Christión, 189-190
Chubb Rock, 39
Clark, Roderick "Pooh", 45
Clinton, George, 87, 181
Coffey, Terry, 22
Cole, Nat King, 77-78
Cole, Natalie, 77-78
Collins, Lyn, 39
Collins, William "Bootsy", 14, 97
Color Me Badd, 29, 38-39, 125, 222-223
Combs, Sean, 14, 20, 52-53, 69, 85, 91, 96-97, 107-108, 120-121, 126, 159, 173, 192, 199, 202, 213-214, 234, 239,
Common, 133
Conner, Keven "Dino", 50
Conner, Solomon "Shazam", 50
Cooke, Paul, 80
Cooper, Gary, 97
Cottle, Tameka "Tiny", 94, 122, 205, 206
Cox, Deborah, 119, 201-202, 237-239, 243
Crawford, Anthony "Shep", 202

Creed, Linda, 164, 167
Crouch, Keith, 118
Currier, Ted, 21
Curry, Eugene, 80
D. J. Rogers, 121
D'Angelo, 133, 135, 160, 180
Dalyrimple, Andre Lamont "Dre", 53
Dalyrimple, Brian Augustus "Bri", 53
Dalyrimple, Christopher Sherman "Choc", 53
Dalyrimple, Jason, Oliver "Jase", 53
Daniels, LaShawn, 199
Dash, Damon, 189-190
Davidson, Aqil, 40
Davis, Hal, 155
Davis, Vidal, 133
DeBarge, El, 75-76
Debussy, Claude, 25
DeGrate, Dalvin, (See Mr. Dalvin)
DeGrate, Donald, (See DeVanté Swing)
Denman, Paul, 80
Des, 203
Des'ree, 102
Destiny's Child, 52, 123-125, 145, 201, 205, 236, 239, 243, 250
DeVanté Swing, 50, 52, 58-61, 99, 119, 157, 166, 195
DeVoe, Shamari, 204
DeVoe, Ronnie, 27, 29, 55
DeWayne, Sidney, 166
Diana Ross & the Supremes, 101
Diddy, (See Sean Combs)
Diggs, Robert, 213
Dillon, Clifton, 67, 70
Dirty Rotten Scoundrels (D.R.S.), 171-172, 227
DJ Demp, 147
Domino, 124, 145
Dorn, Joel, 162
Doug E. Fresh, 36, 38
Dr. Dre, 13, 145, 190-191, 198, 226, 232-233
Dr. Freeze, 29, 38-39
Dru Hill, 166, 188, 207, 234-235, 237
Dunbar, Sly, 68
Duncan, Tabitha, 194
Dupri, Jermaine, 52, 85, 92-94, 99, 108-109, 122-123, 125, 147, 192, 199-200
Early, Dave, 80
Easley, Toriano, 45
Eastman, Barry, 83
Edmonds, Kenneth, (See Babyface)

Edwin Nicholas, 83, 171, 194, 197
Elizondo, René, 102
Elliott, Melissa "Missy", 40, 61, 98-99, 121, 195, 197
Ellis, Terry, 90, 198
En Vogue, 90, 198
EPMD, 35
Ethirdge, Marqueeze, 197
EV3, 197-198
Evans, Faith, 14, 52, 85, 96, 97, 121, 161, 173, 202, 239
Farrar, Charles, 201
Farris, Dionne, 136
Faussart, Célia, 137
Faussart, Hélène, 137
Ferguson, Bob, 154
Finch, Richard, 121
Flack, Roberta, 162-163
Floetry, 133
Ford Jr., Robert, 182
Foster, David, 77, 98, 154-155
Foster, Denzil, 62, 90, 156
Fox, Charles, 162-163
Franklin, Aretha, 85, 112, 156, 202
Franklin, Farrah, 125
Franklyn, Chevelle, 67
Frantz, Chris, 107-108
Freedom, 117
Fugees, The, 14, 124, 138, 162-163
Full Force, 165
Funk, Inc., 39
Fuqua, Harvey, 101
Fusari, Rob, 123
Fyffe, Ty, 40
G-Smooth, 203
Gaines, Calvin, 123
Gaither, Todd, 173
Galdston, Phil, 89
Gamble, Cheryl "Coko" 94-95, 117, 122
Gamson, David, 141
Gap Band, The, 153
Garrett, Siedah, 75
Garrett, Stephen "Static Major", 61, 187
Gay, Marc, 47
Gaye, Marvin, 70-71, 82, 99, 134, 154, 213
Ghost Town DJ's, 92, 147
Ghostface Killah, 119-120
Gill, Johnny, 19, 27-30, 192, 220, 222
Gimbel, Norman, 162-163
Ginuwine, 61, 187, 233

Golde, Frank, 212
Gordon, Allen, "Allstar" 117
Gordon, Irving, 77-78
Gordon, Marc, 194
Gordy-Gaye, Anna, 154
Gordy, Berry 76, 155-156
Green, James "Woody Rock", 188
Gregory, Miles, 161
Grey, Zane, 49
Griffin, Richard, 159
Grinstead LeMisha, 196-197
Grinstead, Irish, 196-197
Grinstead, Orish, 196-197
Groove Theory, 144, 146
Guy, 36-38, 40, 78, 94, 153, 172, 190, 191, 241
H-Town, 50, 163, 226
Haggins, Carvin, 133
Hailey, JoJo, 58, 159
Hailey, K-Ci, 58, 159
Hale, Andrew, 80
Hall, Aaron, 36-38, 172, 190-191, 224
Hall, Dave "Jam", 91, 107,
Hancock, Herbie, 69, 137
Hanes, Eugene, 97
Hannibal, Chauncey, 190
Hargrove, Roy, 133
Harris, Andre, 133
Harris, Keith "K.C.", 40
Harris, Livio, 97
Heavy D., 53, 58, 69, 190
Henderson, Chris, 204
Hennings, Arnold, 189
Henson, Darren, 133
Herbert, Vincent, 99, 123, 154
Herron, Cindy, 90, 198
Hi-Five, 37, 45, 222-223
Hill, Lauryn, 85, 136, 138-139, 162, 248
Hill, Loren, 97
Hitman Howie Tee, 38
Hollins, Anton, 40
Hollister, Dave, 190
Honey Drippers, The, 67, 101
Hooper, Nellee, 211
Houston, Whitney, 20, 22, 25, 40, 47, 82, 88, 100, 109-110, 112, 154-155, 157, 189, 201, 221-222, 225-226, 231-232, 238, 241, 243
Howard, Adina, 14, 97-98
Howell, Joseph, 120
Huggar, Robert "R.L.", 182-183, 239

Hugo, Chad, 148-149
Hunt, Van, 136
Hurt, Norman, 135
Hutch, Willie, 155
Ingram, James, 75-76, 220
Irby, Treston, 45
Isley Brothers, The, 89, 98, 160, 189
J. Stevie, 61, 121, 126-127, 173
Jackson 5, The, 92, 146, 153, 155
Jackson, Chris, 171
Jackson, Darryl, 50
Jackson, Janet, 24, 26, 88, 100-103, 200, 220, 224, 226, 229, 236, 238, 241, 243
Jackson, Johnny, 125
Jackson, Michael, 34, 38, 70, 75, 78-79, 102, 107, 125, 155, 199-200, 207, 214, 224, 231, 241, 251,
Jackson, Randy, 136
Jackson, Sylvester, 25
Jagged Edge, 122-123, 199, 205
Jam, Jimmy, 27, 34, 29-30, 46, 56-57, 83, 100-104, 167
James, Rick, 76, 146, 178, 180
Japser, Chris, 160
Jay-Z, 121, 160, 189, 239, 251
Jean, Wyclef, 123-124, 138
Jenkins, Marsha, 22
Jerkins, Fred, 199
Jerkins, Rodney, 99, 199
Joe, 191-192, 207
Johnson, Jellybean, 27, 46, 104
Johnson, Tamara "Taj", 94-95
Jones, Daron, 121, 189
Jones, Donell, 52, 163, 196-197, 206, 239, 244
Jones, Kipper, 118
Jones, Maxine, 90, 197-198
Jones, Quincy, 22, 51, 75-76, 83, 162, 181, 220
Jordan, Montell, 97, 119, 127, 202, 230, 236
K-Ci & JoJo, 51, 58, 126, 157-159, 232, 236
KayGee, 49, 99, 182
Keith, Michael, 121, 189
Kelis, 148-149
Kelley, Tim, 207
Kelly, R., 45, 98, 129, 134, 160, 179, 191, 204, 224-225, 228, 231-234, 239, 241,
Kelly, Tony, 70
Khan, Chaka, 46, 140, 157-158, 211, 220
Kinchen, Ricky, 46
King, Floyd, 70
Knowles, Beyoncé, 123-125, 160, 205, 212

Knowles, Ian, 171
Kool and the Gang, 38, 97
Kool G. Rap & DJ Polo, 29
Kravitz, Lenny, 23
Kweli, Talib, 133
L.E.S., 204
LaBelle, Patti, 80-82, 155, 202
Lafayette Afro Rock Band, 40, 101
Larrieux, Amel, 146
Lawrence, Billy, 204
Lawrence, Rhett, 206
Ledford, Mark, 161
Les Nubians, 137
LeVert (Group), 192-194, 222
LeVert, Gerald, 26, 83, 171, 192-194, 197, 223-224, 241
Levine, Stewart, 79
Lewis, Keri, 46
Lewis, Terry, 27-28, 30, 34, 46, 56-57, 83, 100-102, 104, 167
Lieberman, Lori, 162-163
Lil Jon, 147
Lind, Jon, 89
Lindo, Hopeton, 67
Lipscomb, Belinda, 166
Lisa Lisa & Cult Jam, 165, 223
Lisa Lisa & Cult Jam with Full Force, 165
Little, Levi, 190
Livingston, Robert, 70
LL Cool J, 13, 120, 181, 192, 194, 214-215
Long, Pamela, 120
Lopes, Lisa "Left Eye", 93, 96, 204-205, 239
Lord, Peter, 24
Love Unlimited Orchestra, The 83, 123
Lubin, LaMarr "Deuce", 171
Luckett, LeToya, 123-125
Lyons, Leanne "Lelee", 94, 181-182
M, Tony, 41
Mad Cobra, 67-68
Mahone, Carlton, 147
Maiden, Tony, 158
Manzel, 40
Marden, Arif, 157
Margulies, Ben, 106
Marie, Teena, 76-77
Martin, Andrea, 197
Martin, Carl "Groove", 47
Martin, Ricky, 165, 207
Mary Jane Girls, The 76, 97, 146, 214

Mass Order, 97
Massenburg, Kedar, 135
Master P., 125, 127, 174, 202-203, 236
Matias, Ivan, 197
Matthewman, Stuart, 80, 134
Maxwell, 133-134, 136, 238, 244
Mayfield, Curtis, 156
MC Lyte, 118, 192
McCaine, Elliott, 194
McCary, Michael, 39, 55
McCormick, Charles, 154
McElroy, Thomas, 62, 90, 156
McGill, Delaney, 171
McIntyre, Owen, 53
McKnight, Brian, 198
McLeod, Marilyn, 200
Members, Jackie, 163
Men at Large, 171
Merritt, Victor, 196
Method Man, 117, 120, 213-214, 230
Middleton, Herb, 120
Middleton, Mark, 190
Midnight Star, 166
Miller, Bernard, "Bernie" 195
Miller, Denzil, 182
Miller, Percy, (See Master P.)
Miller, Vyshonn, (See Silkk tha Shocker)
Milteer, Eric, 91
Mitchell, Brandon "B-Doggs", 37, 40
Mitchell, Joni, 102
Mo B. Dick, 174
Monica, 58, 199-200, 230, 232, 236-237, 241, 244
Moody Blues feat. The London Festival Orchestra, 162
Moore, J. B., 182
Morgan, Brian Alexander, 94-95, 117, 174, 181-182
Morris, Nathan, 39, 54-56, 107
Morris, Richard, 154
Morris, Wanyá, 39, 55-56
Mos Def, 133
Moten, Patrick, 159
Mr. Dalvin, 58, 95, 119-120
Mtume, James, 159
Murdock, Shirley, 95, 163
Murray, Ray, 20, 197
Myers, Dwight, 53
Myrick, Nashiem, 121
Naughty By Nature, 49, 182, 226
Ndegeocello, Meshell, 140-141, 198
Neal, Russell, 45

Nettlesbey, Jon, 22
Neufville, Renée, 49
Next, 182, 236
Norman, Kyle, 122
Norris, Jean, 49
Notorious B.I.G, The, 13-14, 69, 97, 120-121, 173, 213-214, 230-231, 234, 244
Nowels, Rick, 83-84
O' Connor, Sinead, 211
O'Dell, Homer, 46
O'Jays, The, 174, 178
Ol' Dirty Bastard (ODB), 107-108, 117, 126, 148
Organized Noize, 20, 122, 197
Originals, The, 154
Palladino, Pino, 133
Papa San, 69
Parker, Quinnes, 121, 189
Parton, Dolly, 154-155
Patra, 70
Pebbles, 19-20, 93, 221-222
Peebles, Ann, 195
Pela, Mike, 80
Pelzer, Keith, 133
Pendergrass, Teddy, 55, 81-82, 222
Perren, Freddie, 153
Persuaders, The, 50, 163
Phife Dawg, 53
Pierce, Oji, 119
Pimp C, 174
Pliers, 68
Poindexter, Richard, 163
Poindexter, Robert, 163
Police, The, 173
Powell, Jesse, 148
Prince, 41, 50-51, 79, 136, 159-160, 164, 166, 211, 221
Prince and the New Power Generation, 41
Prince and the Revolution, 166
Prince Markie Dee, 91, 158
Public Enemy, 35, 101, 181
Puffy / Puff Daddy, (See Sean Combs)
Puff Daddy & the Family, 173, 234, 244
Pugh, Demetrius "Red" 35
Pugh, Marliss "Mark" 35
Q-Tip, 102, 133
Queen Latifah, 49, 118
Queen Pen, 190, 191, 233
Raekwon, 19-120
Ranks, Shabba, 67, 71

Raynor, Kima, 120
Reed, Natina, 204
Reeder, Raymond, 21
Reid Antonio "L.A.", 19-20, 27-28, 48, 51-52, 55, 93, 96, 206
Richie, Lionel, 79, 224
Ridenhour, Carlton, 181
Riley, Markell, 40
Riley, Teddy, 27, 34, 36-38, 40, 45, 61, 78, 153, 190, 191, 194, 241
Riley, Timothy, 62
Roberson, Antoinette, 192, 194
Roberson, LaTavia, 123-125
Robertson, Keith, 81
Robinson, Bob, 207
Robinson, Dawn, 90, 197-198
Robinson, Smokey, 23, 160
Robinson, Terri, 53, 120
Roland, Carl, 148
Rome, 144, 196
Rooney, Cory, 91, 107-108, 158, 165-166, 204,
Rose Royce, 161, 189
Ross, Diana, 78, 101, 200
Rowland, Kelly, 123-125
Ruby, Violet, 204
Ruffin, Tamir "Nokio", 134
Rufus, 157-158
Rufus feat. Chaka Khan, 158
Rushen, Patrice, 91
RZA, 120, 213-214
Saadiq, Raphael, 62, 120
Sade, 70, 80, 101, 134
Sadler, Eric, 181
Sanders, Marcus, 45
Savage, Tamara, 200-201
Sawyer, Pam, 200
Scandrick, Marvin, 121, 189
Schwartz, Stephen, 109
Scott, Jill, 133
Scott, LaTocha, 94
Scott, Oliver, 153
Scott, Tamika, 94
Scott, Terry, 194
Scott, Vivian, 70
Seacer, Levi Jr., 41
Seal, Manuel, 52, 94, 108, 122, 199
Selena, 212
Sellers, Chris, 35
Shaggy, 70-71, 231

Shaheed Muhammad, Ali, 53, 180
Shai, 47, 147, 225
Shakur, Tupac (2Pac), 102, 117, 125-126, 191, 232
Shalamar, 204
Shanice, 25, 223-224
Shelby, William, 204
Shelton, David, 35
Shelton, Rodney, 22
Sherrod, Matt, 20
Sherrod, Paul, 20
Shipley, Ellen, 83-84
Shocklee, Hank, 29, 101, 181
Shur, Itaal, 133-134
Shy Shy, 165
Sigler, Bunny, 80-81
Silkk the Shocker, 127, 174, 203, 236
Sills, Courtney, 189
Simmons, Daryl, 28, 48, 55, 93, 99, 154, 188
Simmons, Derrick, 181
Simpson, Valerie, 157, 213
Sir Spence, 20
Sisqó, 166, 188, 207
Ski, Kenni, 189-190
Brown, Sleepy, 20, 197
Slick Rick, 38, 95, 119, 213
Sly and Robbie, 68
Sly and the Family Stone, 97
Smith Clifford, (See Method Man)
Smith, Vernon Jeffrey, 24
Snow, Tom, 212
Sons of Funk, 203
Soul for Real, 53, 230
Soulchild, Musiq, 133
South, Mark, 120
Sparks, Trevor, 69
Spencer, Kevin, 204
Spencer, Tracie, 20-21, 25, 212, 223
Spikes Kim, 97
Spinners, The, 55, 153, 164
Spivey, Kiesha, 120
Spyderman, 38
Stacy, Ralph, 188
Stanley, Steven, 107
Starks, John, 90, 101, 120
Stewart, William "Skylz", 190
Sting, 173
Sting International, 70-71
Stockman, Shawn, 39, 55-56
Stonestreet, Joseph, 190

Straite, Elliott, 29, 38
Street, Greg, 147
Stuart, Hamish, 53
Stylistics, The, 62, 104, 167
Sully, Sandra, 159
Super Cat, 69
Sweat, Keith, 36-37, 39-40, 52, 55-56, 189, 192-194, 220, 222, 224, 233, 241
SWV, 88, 94-95, 117, 174, 179, 181-182, 226-227, 232, 241
Sylvers, Leon, 204
Tarplin, Marv, 160
Taylor, Troy, 201
Tejeda, Japhe, 199
Temperton, Rod, 75, 214-215
Terrell, Tammi, 213
Terry, Rodney, 147
Terry, Tony, 21-22
Tex, Joe, 69
Thomas, Keith, 89
Thomas, Rozonda (See Chili)
Thompson, Brian, 67
Thompson, Chucky, 14, 20, 96-97, 159
Thompson, Joshua, 191
Thompson, Tony, 45
Thornton, Kevin, 38
Timbaland, 61, 98-99, 187, 195
Titelman, Russ, 158
TLC, 19-20, 60, 88, 92-96, 159, 178, 201, 204-206, 225, 229, 230, 238, 241, 243, 247
Tolliver, Dave, 171
Tom Scott and the L.A. Express, 79
Tom Tom Club, 107-108
Tony! Toni! Toné!, 62-63, 90, 179, 221-222, 241
Total, 120-121
Trackmasters, 53, 214-215
Tresvant, Ralph, 27, 29-30, 25, 221
Tribe Called Quest, A, 53, 162-163
Troutman, Roger, 163, 232
Turner, E. Jay, 171
Tyrese, 201
U God, 117
Ushay, Pierre, 50
Usher (Usher Raymond), 51-52, 92, 98, 108, 122, 124, 166, 199, 206-207, 235-236, 241, 243
Valentine, Marc, 97
Van Horssen, Linda, 204
Van Rensalier, Darnell, 47
Vick, Richard, 190

Villarreal, Tiffany, 196-197
Waddell, Lawrence, 46
Wade, Rico, 20, 122, 197
Walden, Narada Michael, 25, 51, 85, 106, 157
Waldman, Wendy, 89
Wallace Christopher, (See Notorious B.I.G., The)
Ware, Leon, 98
Warren Diane, 49, 134
Washington, Keith, 22, 83, 222
Watkins, Tionne "T-Boz", 19, 60, 93-96, 160, 205
Watson, Bo, 48, 166
Watters, Sam, 38
Way, Dave, 45
Wesley, Fred, 90, 101, 120
West, Bob, 155
West, Kyle, 206
Weymouth, Tina, 107-108
White, Barry, 26, 75-76, 83, 123, 158, 220, 229
Whitfield, Norman, 161, 163
Withers, Bill, 53, 190
Whittington, Darin, 163
Whole 9, The, 171
Wiggins, D'wayne, 62
Williams, Brandi, 204
Williams Eric, 190
Williams, Jesse "3rd Eye", 69
Williams, Kameelah, 196-197
Williams, Michelle, 125
Williams, Pharrell, 40, 148-149, 197
Williams, Stokley, 46
Williams, Vanessa, 19, 89 121, 223-224, 241
Williams, Virgo, 147
Willis, Lloyd, 68
Wilson, Bryce, 146
Wilson, Ronnie, 153
Wingo, Richard, 122
Witcher, Adrian "G.A.", 35
Wonder, Stevie, 26, 79, 145, 157, 163-164, 206
Wooten, Bobby, 194
Wreckx-n-Effect, 37, 40, 190
Wright, Betty, 38
Wu-Tang Clan, 108, 117, 120, 126, 213
Wycoff, Michael, 49
Wynn, David, 40
Xscape, 92, 94, 108-109, 122, 205, 227-228, 231, 241
Yarian, Christine, 153
Yo-Yo, 118
Zapp, 50, 159
Zhané, 49